Redeeming La Raza

Redeeming La Raza

Transborder Modernity, Race, Respectability, and Rights

GABRIELA GONZÁLEZ

OXFORD
UNIVERSITY PRESS

OXFORD
UNIVERSITY PRESS

Oxford University Press is a department of the University of Oxford. It furthers
the University's objective of excellence in research, scholarship, and education
by publishing worldwide. Oxford is a registered trade mark of Oxford University
Press in the UK and certain other countries.

Published in the United States of America by Oxford University Press
198 Madison Avenue, New York, NY 10016, United States of America.

Library of Congress Cataloging-in-Publication Data
Names: González, Gabriela, author.
Title: Redeeming La Raza : transborder modernity, race, respectability, and rights /
Gabriela González.
Description: New York, NY : Oxford University Press, [2018] |
Includes bibliographical references and index.
Identifiers: LCCN 2017056469 (print) | LCCN 2018017172 (ebook) |
ISBN 9780199914159 (Updf) | ISBN 9780190902155 (Epub) |
ISBN 9780190909628 (paperback) | ISBN 9780199914142 (hardcover : alk. paper)
Subjects: LCSH: Mexican Americans—Texas—Politics and government—20th century. |
Mexican Americans—Political activity—Texas. | Mexican Americans—Texas—Biography. |
Mexicans—Texas—History—20th century. | Transnationalism—Political aspects—
Texas—History—20th century. | Texas, South—Politics and government—20th century. |
Mexican-American Border Region—Politics and government—20th century.
Classification: LCC F395.M5 (ebook) | LCC F395.M5 G665 2018 (print) |
DDC 323.1168/720764—dc23
LC record available at https://lccn.loc.gov/2017056469

Parts of this book have been adapted from "Carolina Munguía and Emma Tenayuca: The Politics of
Benevolence and Radical Reform" in *Frontiers: A Journal of Women's Studies*, Vol. 24, No. 2/3, 2003,
pp. 200–229, courtesy of the University of Nebraska Press, and "Jovita Idar: The Ideological Origins of a
Transnational Advocate for La Raza," in *Texas Women: Their Histories, Their Lives* (2015), edited by Elizabeth
Hayes Turner, Stephanie Cole, and Rebecca Sharpless, courtesy of University of Georgia Press.

I dedicate this book to my parents,
Jorge G. and María B. González,
and to my husband and daughter,
Roger and Isabella Landeros,
with much LOVE.

CONTENTS

ACKNOWLEDGMENTS

I begin by thanking the civil and human rights activists I write about in this book and their family members who granted me oral history interviews. At the beginning of the semester I sometimes ask my UTSA students to look around and recognize the great diversity represented in our classroom. Then I encourage them to pay attention to the men and women in history who worked to make diverse classrooms like ours possible. The genesis of this book started with my desire to pay attention to transborder activists who shared a vision for a just and equitable society and pursued it by using their privileges to take on the challenges they faced.

This project, or at least part of it, started while I was a master's student at the University of Texas at San Antonio. I thank fellow graduate students and friends, Joe Belk, Dave Hansen and Sandy Rubinstein Peterson for their kindness and moral support during those early days when I was fumbling through the process of learning how to become a historian. In classes taught by Antonio Calabria, Gilberto Hinojosa, David Johnson, Juan Mora-Torres, Cynthia Orozco, Linda Pritchard, Jack Reynolds, Jim Schneider and Linda Schott I dove into local, state, national, and global histories, relishing each opportunity to place my research interests within broader contexts. In the mid-1990s, I was not yet using such terms as transborder and transnational, yet my awareness of the historical phenomena that these concepts describe grew alongside my research agenda. An internship at the Institute of Texan Cultures, organizing the Spanish colonial history files of then UT Austin professor, Antonia Castañeda, further shaped my intellectual development, introducing me to Chicana history. A class titled "Hispanics in the United States" taught by UTSA Visiting Professor Cynthia Orozco introduced me to Latina/o history. The ideas for this study germinated at the intersection of that internship with Antonia, Cynthia's course, and an independent study focused on the theme of women's voluntary associations supervised by Linda Schott. My thanks to Linda for introducing me to

comparative women's history and for supporting my decision to pursue a project focused on the life and work of Carolina Malpica de Munguía; to Cynthia
for her comparative Latinas/os history course instruction and for introducing
me to the Munguía Family papers and the LULAC archives at UT Austin; and
to Antonia for inspiring me to interrogate power dynamics and study the ways
in which naturalizing inequities breeds and sustains injustice. My thanks also to
Antonia for introducing me to the human and civil rights work of San Antonio's
Esperanza Peace and Justice Center led by Graciela Sánchez, which continues
in the tradition of consciousness-raising, questioning of power, and grassroots
activism.

Besides my internship, I also had the privilege of working as a research assistant for Professor Jack Reynolds in his Camino Real project and as a graduate assistant for the Center for the Study of Women and Gender directed by Professor
Linda Schott which was housed in the Dean's office, where I got to interact with
Associate Dean Linda Pritchard. I am grateful for the guidance I received from
these individuals who mentored me and encouraged me to pursue a PhD.

At Stanford University, my good fortune continued thanks to the dedicated
mentoring I received from my primary advisors, Professors Albert Camarillo
and Estelle Freedman. Al and Estelle brought a wealth of expertise and experience into their teaching and cultivated a sense of intellectual community in the
classroom and beyond through university centers and institutes whose programming enhanced my understanding of issues of race, class, gender, and sexuality.
From Professor George Frederickson, I learned about the role that ideologies
play in shaping political philosophies and practices. During my time at Stanford,
Professor Richard White joined the faculty. A couple of conversations with him
about my work helped me to properly identify it as transborder and transnational
history. Three teaching assistantships helped me develop my teaching skills and
added to my understandings of related historiographies. I am grateful to Al and
George who co-taught a comparative course on race and ethnicity in the United
States. Among other things, from this experience I learned that racism and ethnocentrism in this country developed alongside democratic principles enshrined
in founding documents. In my second TAship, I worked with Professor David
Kennedy in his course on twentieth century US history. One of the things
I picked up from his lectures was the importance of the 1930s and 1940s be-
cause of the Great Depression and World War II and more fundamentally, the
transformative nature of these events in American life and culture. Finally, the
Introduction to Asian American History course I TAed for Professor Gordan
Chang helped me to reflect upon the diverse experiences within communities.
In the section I led, many of my students identified as Asian American but our
discussions often revealed differing levels of perceived as well as unexamined
privilege and power dynamics based on phenotype, class, gender, immigrant or

citizenship status, and so forth. These were social relations I had casually noticed within ethnic Mexican communities, but something about playing the role of mediating teaching assistant, raised my level of consciousness about the internal dialogues that occur within ethnic and pan-ethnic communities.

This book has benefited from a vast secondary literature revealing multiple historiographies with plenty of intellectual cross-pollination. Rather than attempting to list all the scholars whose work this book draws insights from and risk forgetting someone, I will direct the interested reader to the notes and bibliography. Other influences have been the many scholars with whom I have served on conference panels and roundtables over the years. My thanks to conference participants who provided questions and comments on my work.

At various critical points in my career, Professor Vicki Ruíz has offered valuable advice about my work. I join the impressive list of scholars who have benefitted much from her committed mentoring and pioneering scholarship and who see her as a role model. Others who at various times have offered me advice about my career, read my work, or in some other way assisted me include: Norma E. Cantú, Stephanie Cole, Deena González, David G. Gutiérrez, Elizabeth Hayes Turner, Raquel Márquez, Marie "Keta" Miranda, Paula Moya, Cynthia Orozco, Emma Pérez, Harriett Romo, Ricardo Romo, Rodolfo Rosales, Sonia Saldívar-Hull, Stephen Pitti, George J. Sánchez, Rebecca Sharpless, Andrés Tijerina, Ruthe Winegarten, Elliot Young, and Emilio Zamora.

My Stanford cohort enriched my grad student experiences in significant ways. The diverse cultural and geographic backgrounds of Noemí García Reyes, Mónica Perales, Shana Bernstein, Shawn Gerth, Joe Crespino, Paul Herman, and my own underscored the concept of "unity in diversity" for me, because despite our differences, we rooted for each other and enjoyed each other's company. Special thanks to Mónica, Shana, Joe, and Paul for reading sections of my dissertation and offering excellent feedback. Other wonderful friends and colleagues who made my time at Stanford enjoyable and memorable include: Magdalena Barrera, Matthew Booker, Michelle Campos, Alicia Chávez, Marisela Chávez, Roberta Chávez, Jennifer Chin, Raúl Coronado, Rachel Jean-Baptiste, Benjamin Lawrence, Dawn Mabalon, Martha Mabie Gardner, Shelley Lee, Carol Pal, Gina Marie Pitti, Stephen Pitti, Amy Robinson, Lise Sedrez, Cecilia Tsu, and Kim Warren. I am so proud of my Stanford friends for their many wonderful contributions in their respective fields. Finally, a very special thank you to Professor Richard Roberts and two members of the Department of History staff who kept the graduate students sane, Monica Wheeler and the late Gertrude Pacheco.

My work colleagues at the UTSA Department of History have also provided me with a sense of community and inspiration and several with valuable feedback on my work. My thanks to department chair Kirsten Gardner for her brilliant leadership and unwavering support and encouragement. Kirsten, you are integrity personified. Before Kirsten, other supportive chairs included Wing Chung Ng, Jim Schneider, Jack Reynolds, and Gregg Michel. My thanks to them and to Dean Daniel Gelo for believing in the significance of my work as a teacher and scholar. Elizabeth Escobedo and I started at UTSA at the same time and became fast friends. Though she no longer works at UTSA, she remains a dear friend, and I am very proud of all she has accomplished. At the UTSA Department of History I have enjoyed the friendship and collegiality of amazing women faculty. My heartfelt thanks to Sistorians Catherine Clinton, Kirsten Gardner, Rhonda Gonzales, LaGuana Gray, Kolleen Guy, Anne Hardgrove, Catherine Komisaruk, and Catherine Nolan-Ferrell. My fellow Sistorians, know that I greatly admire your work as teachers, scholars, and engaged university citizens. Félix Almaráz, Brian Davies, Jerry González, Patrick Kelly, Andrew Konove, Gregg Michel, Wing Chung Ng, Jack Reynolds, and Omar Valerio-Jiménez have been terrific colleagues whose work I also appreciate. I am grateful for conversations and advice received from John Carr-Shanahan, Andria Crosson, Jennifer Dilley, Dave Hansen, Lesli Hicks, Dwight Henderson, Jodi Peterson, the late Patricia Thompson, and Elaine Turney.

A special thanks to all my students and advisees throughout the years. Countless classroom and office hour discussions, plus assorted faculty/student projects on many topics, including the ones addressed in this book, have enriched my teaching and research in immeasurable ways. Some of these students are currently pursuing Master's and doctoral degrees with specializations in Chicana/o history and allied fields, while others have completed their education in these areas and are teaching in colleges and universities. This is gratifying because they are pursuing their dreams and because issues of representation matter in the classroom setting as in the rest of society. I am proud of the Latina scholars currently in the pipeline or practicing in the profession, among them Terri Castillo, Jessica Ceeko, Sandra Garza, Philis Barragan Goetz, Corina González Stout, Delilah Hernández, Nydia Martínez, Sylvia Mendoza, Laura Narváez, Patricia Portales, Lori Rodríguez, Micaela Valadez, and Vanessa Valadez.

During my time at UTSA, I have had the privilege of working with research assistants Nydia Martínez, Sandra García, Sandra Wagoner, Efraín Torres, Amber Walker and Kuba Abdul; reader/grader Gabrielle Zepeda; teaching assistants Michael Ely, Erica Valle, and Jared Gaytán; and Department of History staff members past and present, Sherrie McDonald, Cheryl Tuttle, Andrea Trease, James Vagtborg, Marcia Perales, Roschelle Kelly, Judith Quiroz, and Carrie Klein. Funding from a post-doctoral Ford Foundation fellowship, a UTSA faculty development leave, and departmental travel funds have made it possible for me to visit archives and present my work at conferences.

This book could not have been written without the work of archivists and librarians at The Dolph Briscoe Center for American History, University of

Texas, Austin; UTSA's Institute of Texan Cultures; the Webb County Heritage Foundation; Archivo General de la Nación, Mexico, D.F.; Mary and Jeff Bell Library, Texas A&M, Corpus Christi, Texas; the Stanford University Libraries; Berkeley Library, University of California; The Laredo Public Library; Blagg-Huey Library, the Woman's Collection, Texas Woman's University, Denton, Texas; M.D. Anderson Library, University of Houston; and the National Archives in College Park, Maryland. I am especially grateful to Dr. Michael Hironymous and Margo Gutiérrez at the Nettie Lee Benson Latin American Library, University of Texas, Austin, Texas and Shari Salisbury and Dr. Agnieszka Czeblakow at the UTSA John Peace Library, San Antonio, Texas.

Susan Ferber, OUP Executive Editor, has encouraged me from the earliest days when I met her while still a doctoral student at Stanford. Vicki Ruíz gave a brilliant talk on *From Out of the Shadows* and advised me to meet Susan and get her business card. This is an example of what I mean by Vicki being there for me during critical points in my career. Susan, too, has been a strong supporter. The first manuscript I sent to Oxford came back from reviewers with a revise and re-submit. Susan was the first person to encourage me to go for it and has helped me to navigate through a process that for first-time book authors can be daunting. She also provided excellent editorial guidance that helped me to clarify ideas and writing style while thinking deeper about the implications of my work.

At Oxford University Press, I have also had the pleasure of working with my project manager, Maya Bringe, who has been so kind and helpful, providing me with the guidance and structure I needed. The countless doings and happenings that add up to a service-oriented professional career and a full family life bring fulfillment and happiness, but they can also compete for a writer's time and energy so having press-related deadlines and a sense of accountability to an editor is a beautiful thing. My other good fortune is working with the great copy editor, Patterson Lamb, and indexer, John Grennan. Thank you for your wonderful work.

I am also grateful to the reviewers for their generous feedback. Some of the most valuable commentary about my work and advice on how to sharpen my arguments and other such issues came from two sets of blind reviewers. Not only is this book a different book because it went through a process of multiple revisions, but I feel like a different person for having gone through it all. And in the same way I felt a deep sense of joy and gratitude once my daughter was born after a 30-hour labor, I can now happily release this book after years of gestation.

Finally, I am grateful to my family, the source of so many blessings in my life. My loving parents, Jorge G. and María B., served as my first teachers and mentors. She taught me never to give up, and he taught me how to read. They provided me with a strong foundation and always expressed faith in me. I am fortunate to still have my mami with me on earth and to have a papi angel in heaven watching over me. My siblings, Graziela, Jorge Jr., Ira, Malcolm, and Aléxiz were the original BFFs (best friends forever) in my life. Through the ups and downs of life, love and friendship remain. It is gratifying to see my siblings happy, and I thank their life partners, past and present, for bringing joy into their lives and blessing to us all. Thanks especially to Araceli, Hassan, David, and Denise.

When I married Roger, I inherited a beautiful kinship with the Landeros Family. My thanks to in-laws, Rogelio Sr. and Fidela S. Landeros for their kindness and generous spirits. My marriage brought more wonderful siblings into my life with sisters-in-law Leticia and Elisa and brother-in-law Robert. Their life partners, Jaime, Jerry, and Cristina have added more blessings to our family. Between the two of us, Roger and I have seventeen nephews and nieces, one great niece, and of these young folks, we have baptized five and confirmed one. Luis, Lisa, Araceli, Albert, Alejandra, Isaac, Cheyenne, Emilio, Alex, Iván, Layla, Jaimito, Robbie, Lea, Germán, Cristián, Diego, and Aria, thank you for your smiles and laughter, for your hopes and dreams, and for being uniquely you.

I thank my grandparents, aunts, uncles, cousins, and friends for their caring support and best wishes, especially Bernita, Conchita, Miguel, Chela, José, Raymundo, Alicia, Elvira, Lourdes, Lupita, Maricela, Claudia, Elvia, Paty, Minerva, Hugo, Marissa, Laura Elvira, Hugo Eduardo, Alma, Bruno, Alonso, Jaime, Tony, Luis, Cindy, Caitlin, Lauren, Luke, Laura, Glen, Norman, Amanda, and my entire St. Augustine High School graduating class and high school teachers, Raquel Garza, Lupita Jiménez, Diana Garza, and Peter González. We recently celebrated a reunion. Go Knights!!

To my husband Roger and our daughter Isabella, I say, I love the two of you to the moon and back. Roger, eres mi media naranja. You are my soulmate, and I admire your strength of character, integrity, and kind-hearted nature. We met when we were teenagers and from the first day, my heart told me you were the one. All these years later, you're still the one. Isabella, you are our biggest blessing, proof of God's grace in our lives. When I was pregnant with you, I made plans to teach you so many things which I have, but in all candor, I believe I have learned as much from you as you've learned from me. And for all my mama bear instincts and habits, one big smile from you or a hug makes me feel so nurtured, supported, and loved that perhaps you've already mastered the mama bear way.

It is with great pleasure that I dedicate this book to the family of my birth and the family of my creation. Our bonds are deep and meaningful and our entwined lives have taught me the most important lesson of all. The answer is always LOVE.

NOTE ON USAGE

In its usage within the United States, the appellations "Mexican-origin" and "ethnic Mexican" refer to people of Mexican descent, whether they are native-born citizens, naturalized citizens, legal residents, or undocumented residents. The term "fronterizo" emphasizes the borderlands experience more than national identity. "Mexican immigrant" will be used when making references to those involved in the migratory experience from Mexico. These terms are used throughout the book.

In Part I, "méxico-tejano," on rare occasion spelled "méxico-texano," appears. Spanish language newspapers in Texas often used this term during the first couple of decades of the twentieth century to refer to the Mexican-origin community in Texas. "Mexico" in the appellation highlighted the Mexicanist identity and nationalism common in the community during this period. Transborder activists often referred to themselves and others they represented as "mexicanos" (Mexicans), regardless of citizenship status, as a form of ethnic kinship and political solidarity. Anglo-Texans did not make distinctions between US-born and Mexico-born people, often referring to all people of Mexican descent as "Mexican" or pejoratively as "Meskin." Occasionally, the term "Tejano" is used in this book to refer to Texas-born Mexicans. In Part II, the appellation "Mexican American" appears, reflecting the emphasis on American nationalism starting in the 1920s but especially during the 1930s and 1940s. In a few instances, specifically in Chapter 6, where LULAC (League of United Latin American Citizens) is discussed, the term "Latin American" is used in the context in which activists used it such as to describe the Spanish-Speaking Parent Teacher Association, at times called the Latin American PTA.

Transborder activists used the term "la raza" (literal translation—the race) as a shorthand name for the Mexican-origin community. Early twentieth-century political activists sought to foster ethnic pride and unity across the axes of gender, class, and national differences, and so the use of this appellation conveyed Mexican cultural nationalism. In this vein, it resembles the term méxico-tejano, but la raza has a broader reach. It can be used and was sometimes used by transborder activists to describe all Spanish-speaking people or all people connected to the mestizaje experience that created Latin America and their collective struggles. The appellation la raza will appear occasionally in this study within the contexts in which these activists used it. Interestingly, in the 1930s and 1940s activists also used the term la raza from time to time to refer to Mexican-origin people, but for them it did not carry the same political currency. For Mexican American activists, la raza served more as a cultural identifier than a political one, whether they used it in reference to people of Mexican descent or to the larger family of Spanish-speaking people throughout the western hemisphere or the world.

The term "gente decente" that translates to "decent people" was commonly used among the middle and upper classes in Mexico as well as among middle-class Tejano communities to distinguish those deemed to be "respectable" because they lived in compliance with a set of bourgeois values from those who did not subscribe to this lifestyle or the ideological assumptions undergirding it. The term could carry both class and race undertones, but despite this, some within the lower classes adopted gente decente identities to the extent that they strove to climb the socioeconomic ladder or that they associated gente decente with notions of goodness and living an exemplary life.

"Anglo-American," "Anglo-Texan," "European American," or "whites" is used throughout this study to refer to people socially constructed as white, both those who are Texas born and those migrating to the state later in life. When a reference is needed to denote migrants from Europe, the term "European immigrant" is used.

Redeeming La Raza

Introduction

Redeeming La Raza in the World of Two Flags Entwined

> Our society is comprised of women of Mexican-origin and birth. . . . It is dedicated to educational goals among the less fortunate sisters of our community who live in a state of real intellectual, moral and economic abandonment.
>
> —Carolina Malpica de Munguía to the Governor of Querétaro, Querétaro, Mexico, March 26, 1939

In 1939, Carolina Malpica de Munguía wrote to the governor of Querétaro and other Mexican governors asking them to send representative handicrafts from their states to display at an art exhibition.[1] She organized this event to promote Mexican culture among impoverished Mexican-origin Westside residents, especially the women, in San Antonio, Texas. Uplifting Mexican women formed the core of Malpica de Munguiá's community activism. On June 12, 1938, "influenced by the social and cultural redemption labors so successfully sponsored by the Consulate General of Mexico," she formed a female voluntary association to help lower-middle-class and working-class Mexican-origin women in San Antonio.[2]

Under the slogan "Todo Por la Patria y el Hogar" ("All for country and home"), Malpica de Munguía founded the Círculo Social Femenino, México (Female Social Circle, Mexico). Later renamed Círculo Cultural "Isabel, la Católica" (Cultural Circle, "Isabella, the Catholic"), this organization engaged in charitable projects, such as collecting donations for individuals and families in need; participated in cultural events such as the Fiestas Patrias (Mexican holiday celebrations); helped the Mexican consulate, the Mexican Library Association, and the Mexican clinic; procured legal aid services and medical services for people in need of these; organized English-language and sewing courses; and carried out myriad other activities that instilled a sense of Mexican cultural nationalism in Mexican-origin people as they navigated everyday life in American society.[3]

Ultimately, Círculo Cultural was a vehicle for female benevolence and for restoring the culture of *la patria* (Mexico) in the face of growing Americanization and the dilution of Mexican identity. It promoted a common ethnic identity to unify Mexicans across class lines as they struggled against racial discrimination and devastating poverty. But redemption was a political project that went further than American and Mexican nationalisms, for what Malpica de Munguía sought for Mexican-origin women and their families was their successful integration into modern life.

When this Mexican-born, educated, middle-class woman surveyed Westside San Antonio, she saw it in a state of economic and cultural decline. Her response was to bring together other women to operate the Círculo "to procure the moral and intellectual improvement of 'women of modest means' so as to benefit the community."[4] Women's self-improvement, they believed, would translate into community betterment. In this way, the Círculo recognized women's central role in confronting changes brought on by the forces of modernization.

Proud of her heritage, Malpica de Munguía retained her Mexican citizenship while working to advance Mexican cultural nationalism in her adopted country and helping Mexican-origin people adjust to life in the United States. She envisioned her role as creating social and cultural bridges between the two nations. She hoped to instill in Mexicans and Mexican Americans a sense of ethnic pride and unity and to demonstrate to Euro-Americans the value of a community that they increasingly denigrated as racially inferior. She intervened, subtly and not so subtly, using a discourse of domesticity that thinly veiled the gradual empowerment of women in the public sector as they challenged and changed the male-dominated political cultures of modern societies.[5]

The hybridized politics of Malpica de Munguía and other transborder activists emerged from a commitment to a struggle for rights within the racialized and conflicted bi-national spaces of modern Texas, the United States, and Mexico. Their activism needs to be understood as part of the nineteenth- and early twentieth-century processes of modernization in both countries, which were marked by national government support for economic development, increasingly strong civic political cultures, and a Victorian cultural ethos that over time blended into an increasingly modernist outlook among the developing middle class. Malpica de Munguía experienced this modern middle-class reality, but when she stepped into her role as community activist, she also dealt with the after-effects of economic modernization on a less privileged population.

The Westside men, women, and children mired in poverty who concerned Malpica de Munguía represented a mix of multi-generational Tejano and Mexican immigrant families employed in established and developing industries such as agribusiness, railroad work, light manufacturing, and an assortment of service jobs. Most of these jobs paid low wages and offered few prospects for advancement. And yet, these and similar types of jobs animated the modern economic engines that saw a vast transformation of the American West from a conquered land with abundant resources to an industrializing region.[6]

Industrialization in the American Southwest, as in the Northeast, created the modern social environment defined by the development of markets, mass production, and commodification that increasingly took production out of the confines of the household. This story of economic development is a transborder one, connecting the US Southwest and Mexico, but the broad parameters are global. Invariably, becoming a modern society involves political, social, cultural, and economic changes connected to industrialization, urbanization, secularization, and bureaucratization. While modernization tends to be associated with Western Europe and the United States, in reality, it happened and continues to occur in diverse parts of the globe and at a varied pace.[7] Critical to modernization are capital, resources (natural and technological), and labor power.

The United States, like any nation seeking development, has historically sought these major elements. An aggressive economic expansionism created the impetus for the ideological construct of Manifest Destiny even though democratic ideals served as inspiration and justification for the spread of American dominion across the continent. Ultimately, Manifest Destiny facilitated the quest for capital-generating enterprises, resources, and labor power because it allowed Americans to pursue self-interests and corporate interests in the name of cherished political principles. So great has been the lure of profits that the very health of democracy has been entwined with economic progress, for a nation of plenty can better safeguard the rights and privileges of its citizenry. But for all the magnificence and glory of American expansionism across the continent, the costs have been extraordinary. The weightiest burdens have been carried by those historically excluded from the American body politic, making redress all the more challenging. This has created a history of conflict often romanticized or mythologized, but nevertheless real and ever present, silently informing social roles and relations to the present day.

In south Texas that historical conflict came by way of the Texas Revolt (1835–36) and the US-Mexican War (1846–48) and created such an impact that by the first half of the twentieth century, people inhabited a US-Mexico border area shaped by an antagonistic relationship between neighboring nations and between Anglos and Mexicans. Mexican-origin borderlands people, *fronterizos*, experienced life as a conquered people long after the Treaty of Guadalupe-Hidalgo in 1848 had established their rights as citizens of the United States. For their part, Anglo-Americans in the region generally defined Mexicans, whether native or foreign born, as a problem, not a people worthy of rights.[8]

The labor power needs of a growing American regional economy in the newly acquired territories determined the role of Mexicans incorporated into the United States. They picked crops for the agribusiness sector, laid tracks for railroads, worked mines for precious metals, and did many other dirty, potentially dangerous, and often low-paying jobs. Modernization forces in Texas and elsewhere thrust a majority of Mexicans into a proletariat class—the less fortunate sisters (and brothers) that Carolina Munguía found to be in a "state of real intellectual, moral and economic abandonment."[9] In the early years of this economic development project, a diverse workforce fed the labor needs of this massive engine of growth. Then, as immigration restrictions on Europeans and Asians created labor shortages, North American companies actively recruited Mexicans by offering them free rail transport and wage advances. But why were increasing numbers of people in Mexico accepting these jobs and migrating north?[10]

Mexico, too, became enmeshed in modernization during the last half of the nineteenth century. By the eve of the Mexican Revolution in 1910, foreign investors and Mexican elites owned much of Mexico, and their investment projects created serious socioeconomic dislocations. Liberal land laws, for example, encouraged development through privatization and the concentration of land in only a few hands. This destroyed communal land systems that had allowed peasants to maintain self-sufficiency. Thrown off the land, Mexico's most vulnerable found themselves reduced to being day laborers. No longer in control of what they produced, these workers had but one commodity to offer: their inexpensive and much needed labor. Although many rural Mexicans migrated to their nation's growing urban centers, the greatest magnet proved to be the United States, a country long accustomed to importing cheap labor.[11]

Mexican-origin people experienced the transborder dynamic as a paradox. The modern world emerging in the United States and Mexico disconnected them from agricultural traditions and thrust them on a foreign land that had once been theirs. The work of their hands contributed significantly to the transmutation of the land's resources into wealth for an American society that despised them, seeing their presence as a burden and the two cultures as irreconcilable. Yet economic realities in both nations meant that Mexicans would continue to migrate north and many would settle permanently in the United States. There they moved into *barrios*, poverty-stricken ethnic enclaves largely untouched by the advancements of modern life.[12]

Like the inhabitants of other borderlands with competing nationalisms and cultures, fronterizos along the US-Mexico border had to address issues of identity and community within broader contexts of modernity and nation-building. In this process, a middle class consisting of Mexican immigrants and Mexican Americans played a pivotal role, seeking to modernize *la raza* through transborder activism focused on the attainment of rights.[13]

This book focuses attention on those who questioned and disagreed with the dominant society's designation of Mexicans as an inferior people. Transborder activists opposed race-based discrimination and sought to "save" la raza by challenging their marginality in the United States. The quest for rights itself represented a modernist intervention in a racist society. However, their efforts at redemption were not limited to societal transformations. They also invested much energy into effecting individual and communal changes among Mexican-origin people. Activists such as Malpica de Munguía expressed faith in the tenets of modern society, believing that the best hope for the underprivileged lay in their adaptation to the best aspects of modernity. By lifting them out of their "state of intellectual, moral, and economic abandonment," activists believed they could redeem la raza.

This study examines the paradoxical nature of the transborder human rights project that activists engaged in during the first half of the twentieth century. It looks at how these activists challenged modern social hierarchies that consigned them to second-class citizenship. And it asks what made their struggles for freedom modern. Using Malpica de Munguía as a starting point, it presents other cases of transborder activism that demonstrate how the politics of respectability and the politics of radicalism operated, often at odds but sometimes in complementary ways.

Redeeming La Raza examines the gendered and class-conscious political activism of Mexican-origin people in Texas from 1900 to 1950. In particular, it questions the inter-generational agency of Mexicans and Mexican Americans who subscribed to particular race-ethnic, class, and gender ideologies as they encountered barriers and obstacles in a society that often treated Mexicans as a nonwhite minority. How did these Mexican-origin activists respond to the severe poverty, discrimination, and violence they witnessed? How did the geographic and cultural borderlands informing their lives shape their responses? And how did concepts of race, ethnicity, class, gender, and nation influence the strategies they chose?

Middle-class transborder activists sought to redeem the Mexican masses from body politic exclusions in part by encouraging them to become identified with the United States. Redeeming la raza was as much about saving them from traditional modes of thought and practices that were perceived as hindrances to progress as it was about saving them from race and class-based forms of discrimination that were part and parcel of modernity. At the center of this link between modernity and discriminatory practices based on social constructions lay the economic imperative for the abundant and inexpensive labor power that the modernization process required. Labeling groups of people as inferior helped to rationalize their economic exploitation in a developing modern nation-state that also professed to be a democratic society founded upon principles of political egalitarianism.

Thus, transborder activists worked within highly racialized environments and used a gendered class politics as they sought to deny white supremacists their excuses for depriving Mexican-origin people of their human and civil rights. Redeeming la raza was about discrediting the "Mexican problem" narrative or racial scripts that informed fear-based exclusionary movements whose prominent and loud voices included nativists calling for immigration restriction, eugenicists clamoring for racial purity, social scientists providing the intellectual justifications politicians needed to institutionalize racism, white supremacists building an extensive Jim Crow southern society, and working-class ethnics claiming whiteness and adopting racist attitudes toward groups in even more precarious positions than their own.[14]

Mexican activist communities used all the resources at their disposal to respond to external conditions and effect social change. Thus, this is also a story about more privileged Mexican-origin people encouraging less privileged raza to modernize and meet a standard of acceptable society. A strategy of gaining rights by attaining respectability undergirded the human and civil rights efforts of most of the transborder activists featured in this study. This approach presupposed that there was something inherently wrong with the aggrieved party and that in order to attain rights, they had to meet a certain cultural standard. What was supposed to be the Enlightenment's highest ideal, "inalienable or natural rights," became "conditional rights" based on the laws and/or customs of a particular government or cultural group—in this case the governments of the United States and Mexico and the modern middle classes and other elites of both nations, who collectively strove for their respective nation's progress. However, in examining the Magonista movement and the labor activism of Emma Tenayuca, this book acknowledges the alternative vision of other activists who sought to redeem or save la raza, not through respectability but through a radical politics of transformation. In the case of the early twentieth-century Magonistas, change could only come through revolution. By the 1930s, Tenayuca's quest for social justice relied on militant organizing designed to make the promises of New Deal liberalism meaningful for Mexican Americans.

Redeeming La Raza posits that there were significant continuities between the lives of many Mexican migrants to the United States and their descendants. Modernity, in the form of industrialization, urbanization, concentration of power, and the bureaucratization of society, touched many of their lives prior to their immigrating. Even when this was not the case, their migration was connected to transnational economic forces holding the United States and Mexico in an asymmetric relationship. Both were modern nation-states defined by a capitalist economic engine that bound the weaker nation to the dominant one and by social stratifications organized around race, ethnicity, class, gender, and ultimately citizenship.[15]

In Mexico, however, class offered social mobility within the racial order, at least for some. Nineteenth-century Mexico had the distinction of having experienced Vicente Guerrero, a mulatto; Benito Juárez, an Indian; and Porfirio Díaz, a *mestizo*, as presidents. Many transborder activists, therefore, saw education and class mobility as mechanisms to combat racial discrimination. Class in both countries was related not only to an individual's connection to the modes of production and consumption but also to understandings of gender, race, and respectability.

The modernist centerpiece of transborder activism was the concept of progress, which on the social level translated into self-improvement and community uplift. Privileged with educational opportunities that had allowed them to "overcome" racism, these activists taught other ethnic Mexicans, many of whom participated in working-class life and culture, to place their faith in the redemptive powers of personal transformation, which aligned with the ideal of the modern individualistic society. The success of middle-class Mexicans cast serious doubt on the idea that Mexicans were an inferior race, incapable of modernizing.[16]

The modern ideals and perspectives of the middle class did not appeal to everyone. Within the Mexican-origin community in Texas, the vast majority existed as a proletariat class, subjected to the worst socioeconomic byproducts of modernization. In time, educational attainment, military service, and access to higher-paying, postwar industrial jobs created opportunities for upward mobility. Thus, working-class people who aspired to a higher socioeconomic status could potentially achieve this goal for themselves or their children. For those who did, a middle-class status seemingly allowed them to divorce themselves from their humble roots. Thus, as the social and cultural worlds of the upwardly mobile changed, they developed an awareness of themselves as distinct from their working-class cousins who, in turn, nurtured their own class consciousness in reaction to a developing Tejano middle class as well as in response to their subordinate positionings within the worlds of work in a capitalist society. While racism most forcefully impinged upon the lives of the lower class, it occasionally affected the middle class. This meant that at least some middle-class Tejanos would remain politically united with their less fortunate brethren, if not always ideologically aligned.[17]

Once they secured employment as clerks, business owners, service providers, and in other "white collar" jobs, Tejanos expressed their modern outlook by becoming politically active to secure human and civil rights. Unlike their working-class counterparts, who retained strong ethnic identifications and connections, the middle class more readily assimilated, in part because the move was a lateral

one from Mexican to American nationalism. In other words, prior to assimilation, this middling group had engaged Mexican nationalist discourses through
transborder familial ties, business exchanges, and the Spanish-language media.
The ideas they adopted resembled American national discourses because both
were rooted in modernity.[18]

In addition to status climbing among Tejanos, it is important to examine the
Mexican immigrant middle class whom historian Richard A. García calls *los ricos*
(the rich ones). Their class ideology was just as potent as that of native Tejano
elites, yet it was not necessarily a direct product of Americanization. Modernity
binds middle-class people across nationality and geography; *gente decente* (lit-
erally, decent or respectable people) in Mexico had much in common with
middle-class people elsewhere, including the rising Tejano middle class. Many
of the transborder activists featured in this study, whether Tejano or Mexican,
identified as gente decente. They saw in the politics and culture of respectability
the best prospects for economic elevation and the best hope to combat "the
Mexican Problem."

An increasingly modern Mexican mainstream culture adopted a gente decente
mindset that would have been familiar to the American middle class as well as the
upwardly mobile working class in both nations. Although most gente decente had
economic structural advantages, historian William French has shown that some
workers, especially skilled ones, subscribed to middle-class ideals and adopted
the cultural norms propagated by elites and reformers seeking to "uplift" and
"modernize" the working classes. Sobriety, a strong work ethic, respect for authority, and patriotism figured prominently among those cultural norms.[19]

Whether middle-class transborder activists called themselves Mexicans or
Americans, these cosmopolitan individuals had much in common with middle-
class Americans. Although Mexican American merchants and professionals
catered to a much less prosperous Mexican clientele and could not always cultivate a more lucrative Anglo clientele due to racial discrimination and segregation, they shared with Anglos a fluency in the culture and language of
modernity.[20] On an everyday level this meant that the Mexican-origin middle
class could cultivate cultural and political influences and use them to promote
a social uplift agenda connected to their struggles for rights. Carolina Munguía,
for example, shared a culture of modernity with both Mexicans in Mexico
and Anglo-Americans in the United States and used her influence to develop
relationships and secure resources for working-class people from both societies.
For example, as a leader in the Spanish-Speaking PTA, she established important connections with Mexican-origin mothers, Anglo-American teachers, and
Anglo school administrators.[21]

The Mexican upper class in Texas had always possessed a modernist orientation. In early nineteenth-century San Antonio, elites such as José Francisco

Ruíz, José Antonio Navarro, and Juan Seguín became political brokers between Mexicans and Anglos as well as serving as economic and cultural leaders. Their belief that Anglo-American settlement in Texas, with its connections to the global cotton trade, would lead to the region's economic development served as their primary impetus for promoting a liberal immigration policy.[22]

After Mexico lost its far north to the United States, some elite Tejanos, such as Juan Cortina, poured their material resources and energy into militant resistance movements. These insurgent movements faced violent suppression and, while making heroes out of their leaders within Mexican borderlands communities, they also escalated tensions between Anglos and Mexicans.[23] By the early twentieth century, elites no longer favored such tactics and instead turned to other means of addressing the racial discrimination and poverty plaguing Tejanos and Mexican immigrants. A final uprising, known as the Plan de San Diego, took place in 1915, led by Carrancistas, the followers of Mexican revolutionary Venustiano Carranza, and Tejano anarchists Aniceto Pizaña and Luis de la Rosa. Carranza used the Plan de San Diego to manipulate US-Mexico relations, but promoters of the plan saw it as a means of liberating oppressed peoples from Anglo-American domination. The plan called upon Mexicans to join forces with blacks, Indians, and Japanese people to kill all white males over the age of sixteen and to reconquer Mexico's lost territories. A number of raids in 1915 and 1916 were connected to the plan, resulting in twenty-one Anglo deaths. However, the Anglo counterinsurgency in response to these raids led to the deaths of hundreds, perhaps thousands, of Mexicans, mostly innocent people not party to the raids.[24]

While the Plan de San Diego's violent suppression has been seen as a catalyst for a peaceful civil rights movement among Mexican Americans, this book posits that by 1915 transborder activists had already created nonviolent organizations and networks designed to address the problems Mexican-origin people faced in Texas. While the activists who came before the Order of Sons of America and the pro-assimilationist League of United Latin American Citizens (LULAC) did not systematically promote Americanization as part of their agenda, they also did not mount a campaign against it. Instead, they advocated a form of Mexican nationalism connected to the creation of the modern Mexican nation-state. Most important for their local needs, a Mexicanist identity served to unify Mexican-origin people into a movement concerned about the rising levels of anti-Mexican sentiment and racist violence. In the aftermath of the Plan de San Diego, some of these activists might have been inspired to turn from Mexican to American forms of nationalism. However, rationales for political activism during the early twentieth century may have been inspired by myriad influences in addition to the violence surrounding the plan—for example, the impact of World War I mobilization efforts on ethnic Mexicans and a transnational progressive movement.[25]

Gente decente transborder activists shared with European American counterparts both an affinity for modern capitalist culture and a penchant for reform as a means of divesting society of modernity's most offensive elements. For European American progressives these offensive elements of modernity included political fraud, vice, and ill manners assumed to be especially rampant among the working class; corrupt business practices; and dangerous monopolies. Transborder activists shared many of these concerns, but the issue that generated the greatest interest and reform spirit was racism, precisely because it consigned Mexican-origin people to a subordinate position in Texas. With few exceptions, white progressives either ignored racism in the United States or made matters worse by promoting nativism, eugenics, disfranchisement of nonwhites, and segregation.[26]

While the historiography on white progressives is extensive, when the lens is focused on Mexican-origin activists, what appears is a struggle against racial discrimination that took shape even as these reformers struggled with their own race and class constructions, produced by exposure to Jaime Crow in Texas and a Spanish colonial legacy.[27] Like their middle-class counterparts in the United States and Mexico, these border progressives enjoyed privileges, such as education, connections, and access to resources, as well as a developing class consciousness. This awareness reminded them of the divide between their elite cultural community and the Mexican masses, a chasm they hoped to bridge through fervent calls for ethnic unity. While they subscribed to a belief in the power of individual transformation, the call for cultural redemption represented a communal exercise in social uplift and collective resistance to oppression.

Redeeming La Raza covers a critical half-century that marked the modernization of the American Southwest and Mexico. Racist constructions of Mexicans as inferior served to justify their proletarianization and political disfranchisement. Gente decente transborder activists responded by challenging negative images of Mexicans and calling for an end to racist injustices. In so doing, they contributed to the US-Mexican borderlands human rights movement.

Part I focuses on the first three decades of the century when activists pursued their modernist vision on Mexican nationalist terms. This section explores how Mexico's liberal nationalist politics, the Mexican Revolution, and the Mexican diaspora shaped borderlands or fronterizo politics in Texas. Early fronterizo human rights efforts relied heavily upon a classical liberal philosophy that held the political and economic rights of the individual as sacrosanct. Activists believed that in both Mexico and the United States, authorities made a mockery of individual rights for Mexican-origin people, thereby generating a need for reform movements. Transborder activism in this period reflected a concern with how Mexicans residing in both nation-states would negotiate changes wrought by modernization and claim rights amid social and institutional projects invested in the dehumanizing exploitation of Mexicans.

Chapter 1 argues that middle-class méxico-tejano liberals used the political strategies of social change, cultural redemption, and social stability in their efforts to address the specific needs of Mexicans in the state, especially the struggle against racial discrimination. The two major divisions within liberal nationalist politics in Mexico—the liberal Masonic community upholding moderate to conservative perspectives and the anarcho-syndicalist movement of Ricardo Flores Magón, known as Magonismo, representing the more radical strains of the Mexican Revolution—were re-created along the US-Mexican border, the subject of Chapter 2. Chapter 3 explores the ways in which fronterizos participated in the Mexican Revolution, highlighting the activist career of Leonor Villegas de Magnón, who used a maternal vision to carve out a public space for herself and other women revolutionaries.

Part II examines activists who began to frame their political agendas in American terms yet continued to use modernist and transnationalist perspectives and approaches to advance their political agendas. The activists of this era found inspiration in New Deal liberalism and benefited from the deracialization of the concept of citizenship taking place in the United States during and after World War II.

The establishment of the League of United Latin American Citizens in 1929 was a crowning moment for Tejanos. Some of its founding members had served during World War I and, influenced by this experience, had developed ethnic American identities and political strategies. Even as this shift in borderlands politics took shape, transnational views and understandings continued to influence community activism. Chapter 4 explores how Mexican political exiles Rómulo and Carolina Munguía used a variety of strategies to improve the lives of Mexican-origin people in San Antonio and foster harmonious relations between the United States and Mexico.

While the Munguías were born in Mexico, activists also emerged from among native-born Tejanos. San Antonio labor leader Emma Tenayuca, born and raised in the United States, recognized the plight of Mexican-origin workers in the United States as connected to that of workers in Latin America through an exploitative capitalist system and sought justice for Texas workers through labor organizing and New Deal liberalism, the subject of Chapter 5. Chapter 6 argues that LULAC used the Good Neighbor Policy, Franklin Delano Roosevelt's non-interventionist foreign policy in Latin America, and the patriotic rhetoric of World War II to advance its civil rights agenda, reminding Americans that the fight to save democracy abroad could not be divorced from the struggle to secure democracy at home.

By 1950 LULAC was well on its way to dismantling the various structures that had segregated Mexican-origin people. While 1900 to 1911 marks the beginning of the méxico-tejano organized human rights effort, the late forties and early fifties mark the advancement of a human and civil rights agenda that still motivates transborder activists.

Transborder activism reflected a fluency in Mexican and American nationalisms born of a significant comfort level with modernity. For the middle-class Mexican-origin men and women invested in social progress, violations of liberal principles in Porfirian Mexico and the denial of la raza's civil and sometimes human rights in Texas represented affronts to the egalitarian ideals enshrined in modern political concepts of liberty and natural rights inspired by the Enlightenment. Possessing educational and socioeconomic privileges, these activists crafted a strategy of cultural redemption designed not just to address the injustices la raza faced regularly but to disprove racist theories of Mexican inferiority used to justify their subjugation. In this way, gente decente sought to redeem la raza in the world of two flags entwined.

PART I

MODERNIZING MEXICO AND THE BORDERLANDS, 1900–1929

Social Change, Cultural Redemption, and Social Stability

The Political Strategies of Gente Decente Reform

It appears that the Mexican race is condemned to be the Jewish race of
the American continent and to an eternal pilgrimage, first from North
to South and now from South to North.
—*La Cronica*, November 12, 1910

This joyless dictum introduced an article entitled "Barbarismos" in the Spanish
language newspaper published by Nicasio Idar in Laredo, Texas.[1] The article
discussed the recent arrest of twenty-year-old Antonio Rodríguez by sheriff's
deputies in Rocksprings. The guilt or innocence of Rodríguez, charged with
the murder of Mrs. Lem Henderson, an Anglo-American woman on a ranch
near town, will never be known. While he was imprisoned, a mob of Anglo-
Americans stormed the jailhouse, kidnapped him, and burned him alive.[2]

This incident was one of many instances of violence directed at Mexicans
during the early twentieth century. *La Crónica* denounced the savage behavior
of the vigilantes and the inaction of local officials, while highlighting the international implications of the Rocksprings case. On November 9, residents of
Mexico City took to the streets, protesting Anglo-American aggression against
Mexicans in Texas.[3] US newspapers reported that demonstrators stomped on
the American flag, attacked Americans on the streets, and vandalized their
property. Only military force, the papers claimed, could subdue the crowds.
According to one report, American lives had been lost in Mexico City, but *La
Crónica* charged these newspapers with exaggeration and stated that Americans
abroad had suffered no injuries or deaths.[4] The article did not condone the tactic
of mass demonstration, but it did applaud Mexicans in Mexico for protesting the
unfair treatment of Mexicans in Texas. *La Crónica* exhorted the demonstrators

to put pressure on the Mexican government to deploy its diplomatic capital in an effort to bring the Rocksprings criminals to justice.[5]

Nicasio Idar and his family continued to use newspapers to monitor anti-Mexican sentiment and to protest racial discrimination and violence. In addition, the Idars assisted Mexicans through fraternal orders, ladies' auxiliaries, and civic clubs. In 1911, the Idar family's organizational efforts culminated in El Primer Congreso Mexicanista (hereafter referred to as the First Mexicanist Congress). The brainchild of Clemente Idar, Nicasio's eldest son, the First Mexicanist Congress invited Mexicans throughout Texas to attend a weeklong conference in Laredo. A circular promoting the congress announced its main objectives: to seek mutual protection and ensure respect and justice, to study the most effective way to procure instruction for méxico-tejano youth, and to advocate the improvement and well-being of la raza.[6]

This chapter examines the First Mexicanist Congress and its offshoot, La Liga Femenil Mexicanista (hereafter referred to as the League of Mexican Women), as organizations that reflected a sophisticated and gendered transborder political culture that developed in response to racism and poverty facing both diasporic and indigenous Mexican communities. This political culture borrowed ideas across borders, picking and choosing which elements of the dominant culture to adopt and what parts of native culture to retain.[7]

Laredo's history differs from that of other Texas towns because of an accommodation between Mexican elites and Anglo newcomers who intermarried, Mexicanized to some extent, and collaborated in the governance of the community.[8] Thus, in this city, an "Anglos versus Mexican" dichotomy does not describe the city's social dynamic. While the Idars and other gente decente supported some labor activism, they also subscribed to a modernist value system not always compatible with the prerogatives of workers.[9] This chapter highlights the liberal capitalist ideas undergirding the lives and public work of transborder activists and asks: What privileges did gente decente enjoy that other méxico-tejano families did not? How did such privileges influence their work and the positions they took in public life?[10]

Within the middle-class sector of méxico-tejano society, at least three political strategies of reform informed a gendered transborder political culture: the struggle for social change, advocacy for cultural redemption, and the search for social stability. In the first approach, advocates for social change called for a transformation in race relations, mainly an end to racial discrimination. Within Mexican-origin communities, social change reformers often supported unionization efforts in Texas and Mexico. A second approach called for cultural redemption, organized around a philosophy of moral, cultural, and material uplift that developed into the political strategy of respectability.[11] This strategy, similar to that used by African American reformers in industrializing America, involved the positive portrayal of Mexican-origin people in an effort to combat discriminatory notions that defined Mexicans outside the rubric of citizenship.[12]

Third, social stability reformers, while advocating social change at the state level and amicable relations between Anglos and Mexicans, were less willing than other reformers to accept major transformations within Tejano society and in Mexico. During the Mexican Revolution, these reformers called for an end to political corruption but often criticized the more radical demands for social and economic justice. In Laredo, social stability reformers at times supported unionization as a means of protecting capitalism from itself, as they feared that unheeded calls of the workers for social justice might lead to revolution and anarchy. But their support for unionization had its limits; these reformers strongly opposed the socialistic sympathies of some unions, seeing them as a direct threat to social stability.

Individuals and groups sometimes combined elements of these discourses. For example, Nicasio Idar sought social change in the form of an end to racial discrimination, as indicated by his newspaper monitoring anti-Mexican sentiment and his participation in a civil rights conference. Idar also believed in cultural redemption as a strategy. *La Crónica* existed to uplift the Mexican people in Texas by promoting ideas about progress and moral and intellectual development. Occasionally the quest for social stability also influenced Nicasio Idar, as when he broke with Ricardo Flores Magón whom he had embraced when the Magonistas first reached Laredo as exiles from the Porfiriato. By 1911, Flores Magón, who had begun his political and philosophical movement toward anarchism, no longer supported the liberal Francisco Madero. Such a radical turn on the part of Flores Magón and his followers did not inspire confidence in the more conservative Nicasio Idar who believed the liberal revolution of Francisco Madero offered more social stability than the utopian Magonista vision. He went so far as to call Ricardo and Enrique Flores Magón "traitors."[13]

Nicasio Idar's "search for order" meshed well with his identity as a middle-class transborder activist.[14] He, along with his family, shared a cultural identity based on privileges such as education, "mental work" occupations, and business associations and friendships with other influential Laredoans, be they economic elites or cultural leaders.

Although both men and women used all three political reform strategies, women tended to gravitate toward social change and cultural redemption while men dominated the social stability strategy. Furthermore, men and women engaged in activism informed by their understandings of gender roles and either adherence to or disavowal of social conventions. Even as women worked alongside men in struggles against racial discrimination, some offered a critique of gender inequities within these civil rights projects.[15]

Male and female activists consumed the dominant culture's modernist ideologies and systems, but in the process, they developed a political agenda to end some of the more exploitative elements embedded within them. Transborder activists tailored the discourses of liberal capitalism to address the issues of political disenfranchisement, economic exploitation, and social discrimination.

An analysis of constructions of class and gender by middle-class ethnic Mexicans in the border town of Laredo, Texas, during the early part of the twentieth century revealed a positivist worldview that sought human perfectibility through moral, intellectual, and material progress. Middle-class méxico-tejanos found in the ideas of scientific progress a blueprint for society.[16] They also adhered to an ideal of female domesticity and male breadwinners. Thus, for middle-class families seeking a place in the modernizing world, husbands competed and earned the family's living in the public sector and wives maintained the family home and raised their children.[17]

Laredo sat far from the centers of power, but its elites conversed fluently in the mainstream language of capitalism and modernity. History and geography also ensured Laredo's place as a site of significant transborder activism. Established in 1755 on the Rio Bravo (Rio Grande) River by Captain Tomás Sánchez de la Barrera y Garza, Laredo formed a part of the Nuevo Santander settlements of Spanish colonizer José de Escandón. Early Laredo's economy consisted of goat, sheep, and cattle raising and its population slowly climbed from eighty-five inhabitants in 1757 to 2,043 by 1870. Politically, in less than a century, Laredo experienced dramatic changes in sovereignty beginning with Mexico's independence from Spain in 1821. The successful Texas Revolt from Mexico in 1836 led to the creation of the Texas Republic. Laredo, part of the area known as the Nueces Strip due to its location between the Nueces and Rio Grande rivers, was claimed by both Texas and Mexico. Residents of Laredo allied with Mexico; however, feeling that they had been neglected by that nation's central government, in 1838 this community and the surrounding region revolted and by 1840 insurgents declared their independence as the Republic of the Rio Grande, designating Laredo as the capital. The Mexican army crushed the revolt. The US defeat of Mexico in 1848 meant that Laredo would become part of Texas, which by then had been annexed to the United States.[18]

The American Civil War brought greater commercial opportunities to the border. With the Union blockade of the southern coast, cotton had to be transported through Brownsville, Texas, and then sent to European markets via Mexican ports. Fear that Union troops might destroy cotton bales should Brownsville be captured led to the redirection of cotton from Brownsville to Laredo. However, this trade, while significant, is not what made Laredo a modern town.[19]

The economically dynamic border community of Laredo underwent a significant industrial and social transformation with the coming of the railroad in the 1880s and the in-migration of Anglos and Mexicans. In 1881, Laredo's main newspaper, the *Laredo Times*, was established, the Texas Mexican Railroad from Corpus Christi arrived, and the International and Great Northern Railroad reached Laredo from San Antonio. The Mexican National railway linked Nuevo Laredo to Mexico City by 1887. This transportation network secured Laredo's claim of being the gateway to Mexico and brought economic growth. Among the industries that thrived thanks to the railroads were coal mining and onion farming. Overall, a shift away from ranching and toward commercial agriculture, industrial manufacturing, and wholesale merchandising fueled economic development. This, in turn, attracted people to the area, and Laredo's population mushroomed from 3,811 in 1880 to 13,429 in 1900.[20]

Politics in Laredo during this period reflected competition between a new elite consisting of a commercial class (the Botas) and an older elite (the Guaraches). After a violent confrontation connected to the contested city election of 1886, the two factions came together as the Independent Club, a Democratic Party machine. In the new century, Laredo emerged as a hotbed for the Mexican Revolution of 1910. Instability in Mexico meant that Laredo would serve as a refuge for the many Mexican citizens seeking peace and stability. Oil and gas finds in south Texas during the first couple of decades of the twentieth century further enticed people to move to the region. By 1920, Laredo had 22,710 inhabitants and by 1940 almost 40,000 people called Laredo home.[21]

The Idars: A Family and Their Struggles for Social Change

The Idars figured prominently among Laredo's newcomer families. One individual symbolizes the family's extensive activism on behalf of Mexican people in the United States and Mexico. Nicasio Idar was born in Port Isabel, Texas, and met Jovita Vivero, from San Luis Potosi, Mexico, on the border. They married and had nine children. Of humble origins and largely self-educated, Nicasio possessed tremendous drive and energy. After marriage, he found profitable employment in the railroad yards of Nuevo Leon, Mexico. Jovita and the children remained in their fifteen-room home in Laredo. Nicasio worked as a yardmaster for twenty years and organized workers in the city of Acambaro. According to his son, Aquilino, Nicasio formed the first union of railroad workers in Mexico, La Orden Suprema de Empleados Ferrocarrileros Mexicanos (Supreme Order of Mexican Railroad Workers) in 1890.[22] In time, the Idar family gained enough financial stability to allow Nicasio to leave railroad work altogether.

In Laredo, the enterprising Nicasio began working for and later became publisher of *La Crónica*. The newspaper's motto was, "We work for the progress and the industrial, moral, and intellectual development of the Mexican inhabitants of Texas," and it reported on lynchings, segregation, and any other forms of human and civil rights violations.[23] Often its news reporting displayed a muck-raking style, reflecting deep concerns about various injustices, key among these, inequities in education.

School segregation flourished during the period from 1920 to 1942, though its origins can be traced to the turn of the century.[24] In 1910 and 1911, Clemente Idar wrote a series of articles in *La Crónica*, pointing out that it was unfair for méxico-tejanos to have to pay school taxes while being excluded from full participation in the educational system. Idar encouraged the Mexican consul in Laredo to investigate, but he only examined the largely méxico-tejano populated counties of Webb, Starr, and Zapata where school segregation was not a problem. Nonetheless, Idar continued writing about school segregation, arguing that such discrimination violated the Treaty of Guadalupe-Hidalgo. Many méxico-tejanos wrote letters to *La Crónica* revealing the extent of such segregation.[25]

Disappointed by the lack of concern displayed by the Texas state government and the inability of the Mexican government to protect Mexicans abroad, Clemente Idar's journalistic crusade taught him that the only people who could effectively help méxico-tejanos were the méxico-tejanos themselves. The harsh realities of poverty, discrimination, and violence directed against Mexican-origin people inspired Clemente to develop the idea of the First Mexicanist Congress. This congress explored many important issues but, ultimately, its objective was to unify all ethnic Mexicans in Texas. Without a unified community, the cause would not move forward.

The Idar family played a pivotal role in the construction of la raza as a cultural and political tool designed to unite all Mexican-origin people in Texas regardless of citizenship. As the main initiators of the First Mexicanist Congress, a vehicle for the propagation of social change and cultural redemption discourse, the Idar family embodied many of the characteristics of méxico-tejano middle-class reformers. Like many residents of south Texas, they experienced life as fronterizos, residents of the geographic and cultural borderlands between nation-states.

Legacies of conquest and the cheap labor needs of a developing agribusiness economy made its fronterizo inhabitants particularly vulnerable to economic exploitation. *La Crónica* reported with indignation the economic imbalances in the state of Texas and described how Mexicans were relegated to menial, low-paying jobs in agriculture and domestic service. The newspaper also became a mouthpiece for méxico-tejano civic organizations, among these, Mutualistas, mutual aid societies providing some economic assistance and benefits to their members. Nicasio belonged to many local groups.

Historians have examined these local voluntary associations for their integral role in Mexican organizational life in the United States.[26] Focusing on mexicano mutual aid societies in Texas between the 1880s and 1920s, Emilio Zamora found a political culture based on an ethic of mutuality comprised of three elements: fraternalism, reciprocity, and altruism. Given the many prejudices and discriminatory practices they faced, what Mexicans needed most was to build a sense of community, an essential "cultural frame of reference for Mexicans in public life." For Zamora, this cultural frame of reference is decidedly mexicano and primarily working class. The Mexican-origin community in actuality represented more than one constituency. This makes the ethic of mutuality all the more vital for méxico-tejano politics, for it was needed to foster a sense of ethnic pride and unity meant to transcend the boundaries of class, and, to some extent, gender.[27]

Public life among Mexicans in Texas was imbued with strong mutualist and nationalistic values as expressed in Spanish-language newspaper articles and the speeches delivered at El Primer Congreso Mexicanista. It can be tempting to interpret mutualistas and other elements of Laredo's transborder political culture as evidence that Mexican organized life in this border community was centered on working-class values and that class divides among Mexicans, if they existed, were insignificant. A closer look at the Idars and gente decente political languages of reform illustrates the variegated nature of borderlands politics at the turn of the twentieth century.

The three eldest Idar children, Clemente, Jovita, and Eduardo, became prominent in public life through journalism. They wrote articles for *La Crónica* until 1914, when the newspaper ceased operations. Clemente and Jovita wrote from Laredo, while Eduardo served as a correspondent from Brownsville. At various points, Jovita and Eduardo either worked for or started other newspapers, such as the Spanish-language newspaper in Laredo entitled *Evolución*, which enjoyed a wide readership in Texas, Mexico, Cuba, and other Latin American countries.[28] Brother and sister teamed up to report on the Mexican Revolution and World War I.[29]

Unionism ran deep in the Idar family. For Clemente Idar, it became his life's vocation. As a young man, he worked for *Collier's Magazine* and quickly earned a reputation as a talented salesman. While traveling in south Texas, American Federation of Labor (AFL) president Samuel Gompers heard about him.[30] The AFL had recently come under attack from its Mexican counterpart, La Confederación Regional Obrera Mexicana (CROM or the Regional Confederation of Mexican Workers), which charged the AFL with discrimination against Mexicans in the United States. Furthermore, Gompers hoped to secure Mexican president Venustiano Carranza's support for the Allied cause during World War I.[31] In 1918, Gompers hired Clemente Idar to organize

Mexican-origin workers. Clemente established AFL locals in Laredo and in 1919 continued his efforts in San Antonio. Although Idar organized unions throughout Texas and in Mexico, he focused his efforts on Laredo, the San Antonio area, and Corpus Christi.[32]

Wherever he went, Clemente Idar took note of the conditions under which Mexican workers labored. In his capacity as an AFL organizer, he wrote a letter from Martindale, Texas, a tiny community northeast of San Antonio, to Mexican president Álvaro Obregón in 1921 expressing great indignation: "In the course of two tours [of the cotton rich central Texas region], I have gathered impressions I will never be able to forget in reference to the suffering, the tyranny, and the state of semi-slavery in which Mexicans who engaged in agricultural labor live." Calling the state "Barbaric Texas," he pleaded with the Mexican president to launch an investigation. Ultimately the letter was intended to inform Obregón that a good number of Mexicans wished to return to Mexico, either as repatriates or as colonists. The Mexican government had designated certain areas for Mexicans living north of the political boundary who wished to settle in Mexico as colonists. Clemente was confident that an investigation would vindicate the workers and bolster their claim for assistance from the Mexican government in their plans to return to Mexico.[33]

In one of the letter's last paragraphs, Clemente referenced American petroleum capitalists in Mexico who sought to interfere with the Mexican government and change its constitutional law. He then made a link between American attempts to dominate Mexico and the mistreatment of Mexicans in the United States, clearly understanding the transnational nature of the asymmetrical power relationship between Americans and Mexicans.[34]

Clemente Idar's work reflected his personal background as a member of a transnational family and the increasingly transnational nature of workers' unions. For one thing, he called for Mexican immigrants to be included in American unions. At a time when even US-born Mexicans faced tremendous discrimination, this position seemed radical. Clemente understood that workers' rights transcended political borders. He emerged as a player in the international workers' arena, serving as a mediator between the AFL and the CROM and as a translator at activities of the Congress of the Pan American Federation of Labor. During the administration of Mexican president Plutarco Calles (1924–28), he accepted an invitation to organize workers in Mexico for a year.[35]

The plight of the Mexican-origin worker needed to be addressed not only through labor organizing but through civil rights as well. Both Clemente and Eduardo Idar were active in the formation of the League of United Latin American Citizens (LULAC), founded in 1929. Clemente wrote the constitution of the Sons of America, one of the three organizations from which LULAC formed. Eduardo co-authored the LULAC Constitution and the LULAC Code.

On some issues, such as women's rights, Clemente in particular held a progressive position. However, on the matter of whether LULAC should be opened to Mexican nationals living in Texas, both Idar brothers favored exclusion.[36] The latter position represented a generational departure from the Mexican nationalist politics of the First Mexicanist Congress, in which their own family had played a critical leadership role, to the advocacy of American citizenship advanced by LULAC.

How can Clemente Idar's radical position to include Mexican immigrants in American labor unions be reconciled with his conservative position to exclude non-US citizens from LULAC? Political expediency in terms of LULAC and globalization in terms of labor unions offers the best set of explanations. The initial phase of LULAC's development as a voluntary association revolved around the issue of agency within the American political structure that limited formal participation to a citizenry narrowly defined on the basis of birth and naturalization. Thus, if LULAC hoped to create reforms within this system, it needed to underscore its own claims to legitimate participation by placing US-born Mexicans at the forefront of the struggle for civil rights. On the other hand, workers operated in a global economy where corporations crossed borders as easily as workers migrated across political boundaries in search of economic opportunities. Multinational corporations attracted an international workforce as witnessed by the global mass migrations of the nineteenth century. Within this context, labor organizers such as Clemente Idar envisioned a broader definition of citizenship based on the economic rights of transnational workers.

While Clemente and Eduardo struggled for the rights of Mexican-origin people in Texas, their younger brother Federico became a champion of labor in Mexico. Born in Mexico while his mother visited her family, Federico spent much time with his relatives in Monterrey. During the Mexican Revolution, Federico and his older sisters Jovita and Elvira joined Leonor Villegas de Magnón's Cruz Blanca (White Cross), a medical organization that traveled with the forces of revolutionary leader Venustiano Carranza.[37]

After the revolution, Federico Idar started working for the railroad in Mexico. He helped organize La Union de Conductores Maquinistas Carroteros y Fogoneros (The Conductors, Locomotive Engineers, Draymen, and Firemen's Union). As the general secretary for all the railroad brotherhoods in Mexico, he traveled extensively throughout Mexico and Central and South America, organizing railroad workers in countries such as Guatemala, Panama, and Honduras.[38] His popularity among the workers led to his election as a Mexican state senator from the state of Nuevo Leon. In 1939, while preparing to deliver a report before the Mexican congress on the Camisas Doradas (Gold Shirts), a fascist group he had been investigating, he was assassinated.[39]

Figure 1.1 La Crónica publisher Nicasio Idar and his sons, Clemente and Eduardo.
084-0589, General Photograph Collection, University of Texas at San Antonio, Special
Collections—Institute of Texan Cultures. Courtesy of A. Ike Idar.

Like her brothers, Jovita learned to harness and focus her energies and talents
at an early age. According to her niece, Nicasio took great pride in his daughter's
intelligence and delighted in her strong will. Besides sending her to the Laredo
Seminary (later Holding Institute), a school known for its excellence in English
language instruction, Nicasio had educated her at the Domínguez Institute.
There, a specialist in foreign languages, Professor Simón G. Domínguez,
taught and mentored Jovita. Jovita's mother, with whom she shared her name,
also showed her young daughter much love and appreciation. The world that
nurtured the Idar children was a far cry from the world of racial discrimination,
poverty, and violence that they would devote their lives to changing. Their world

included books, music, church, family, vacations in Mexico, and, above all, the guidance of kind and community-oriented parents.[40]

In the course of their activism, members of the Idar family faced considerable dangers during an era of revolution and diplomatic tensions. Clemente's life was threatened at least twice, and Federico's assassination appeared to be politically motivated. Jovita Idar faced grave danger as well. In 1914, Mexican revolutionary Manuel García Vigil wrote an editorial piece for a Laredo newspaper, *El Progreso*, criticizing the Woodrow Wilson administration's military intervention in Veracruz.[41] In retaliation, the Texas Rangers set out to destroy the office and printing presses of *El Progreso*. Jovita was on the newspaper's staff at the time, and the intrepid writer stood before the Rangers in defiance, daring them to knock her down. The Rangers backed down, but they returned early the next morning to destroy the building and equipment and arrest the workers.[42] According to Aquilino Idar, the Texas Rangers found Manuel García Vigil, beat him severely, put him in jail, and later tried to lynch him. Nicasio Idar, the justice of the peace at the time, contacted a friend, District Judge John F. Mullally, who ordered the release and hospitalization of García Vigil.[43]

Jovita Idar trained as a teacher and was gifted with excellent teaching skills and instincts. She also became the publisher of a weekly bilingual educational

Figure 1.2 Journalist and human rights advocate Jovita Idar at *El Progreso* newspaper print shop, 1914. 084-0592, General Photograph Collection, University of Texas at San Antonio, Special Collections—Institute of Texan Cultures. Courtesy of A. Ike Idar.

magazine, *El Estudiante* (The Student), and devoted much of her energy to political journalism and civil rights activism.[44] She played an active role in the Mexicanist Congress as an organizer and president of the League of Mexican Women.[45]

After her marriage to Bartolo Juárez in 1917, the couple moved to San Antonio where both joined the Democratic Party. Jovita Idar Juárez served as a precinct judge for many years. Few Mexicans served as election officials during the 1920s and 1930s, so for a Mexican American woman to serve as precinct judge was extremely rare.[46] Her commitment to activism superseded her husband's, who seemed content to stand back and offer moral support. As she had done in Laredo, Jovita opened a school in San Antonio. She also worked as an interpreter for Spanish-speaking patients in a county hospital and brushed up on her Italian by writing articles for *La Voce de la Pattria*, a San Antonio Italian language newspaper.[47]

Always a devout Methodist, she became active in La Trinidad Methodist Church. She served as conference president of the United Methodist Women and co-edited *El Heraldo Christiano* (The Christian Herald), an organ of the Rio Grande Conference of the Methodist Church.[48] Her views on women and gender reflected a nineteenth-century concept of maternal Christian authority. In an article for *El Heraldo Christiano*, Jovita reminded her female readers about their special responsibility as women and as Christian mothers. The home, the church, and the state all formed an important part of universal education, but she argued that the education a child received at home from the mother represented the most important factor.[49]

In addition to providing them with economic resources and superb bilingual education, Nicasio Idar further solidified his children's destinies by actively mentoring them. He devoted much time to the education and edification of each of his nine children.[50] Son Aquilino remembered.

> Out in the yard, my father used to sit right there and all of us, seven brothers and two sisters, used to form a circle around him. And he would talk to us about Mexicans, about Mexican Americans; how to fight for the Mexican people; what to do for the Mexican people. How to think. Don't let anybody tell you how to think because you are a free thing. You are standing on the face of the earth on your own two feet. So, you use your brain to work your way up from any situation. He said you don't depend on anybody to tell you that you're going to heaven, to paradise, or this and that. You're gonna stay here until you die, and you're gonna fight your way out.[51]

Nicasio Idar taught his children the dual message of mutualism (helping other Mexicans) and free thought that informed his own activism. His ideas dovetailed with contemporary broader positivist ideas popular in Mexico. Nicasio, like Mexican positivists, turned away from metaphysical speculations and explanations of society, strongly believing that the logic and reason of free-thinking people better served the goal of social progress. Unlike positivists of the Porfiriato leadership variety, however, Nicasio's social progress agenda included the cultural edification of all Mexicans, not just elites or *criollos* (persons of Spanish descent born in Spanish America). He and other cultural redemption reformers believed that the underprivileged masses could be educated, elevated, and redeemed through a political culture grounded in an ethic of mutuality. His strong commitment to these principles led to his involvement in several social and fraternal méxico-tejano organizations in Laredo. He helped found the Gran Concilio de la Orden Caballeros de Honor (hereafter, the Order of the Knights of Honor) and the Sociedad "Hijos de Juárez" (hereafter, Sons of Juárez Society). Both organizations followed Masonic rituals and attracted a following among middle-class and working-class méxico-tejanos.[52]

The Idars belonged to the gente decente sector of society. They possessed educational privileges and some of the economic privileges enjoyed by the middle class. They also adopted a value system that inspired them to believe in and to seek social progress and human perfectibility through moral, intellectual, and material uplift. Thus, their activism cannot be solely explained by their firm commitment to social change reform. At the heart of their activism lay a strong desire to effect social change through cultural transformations or the cultural redemption of Mexican-origin people, particularly the underprivileged. Cultural redemption reform, manifested in fraternal orders and mutual aid societies, prepared the way for the First Mexicanist Congress and its campaign for social change.

Cultural Redemption Reformers

Fraternal orders and mutual aid societies are examples of cultural redemption reform organizations that preceded the First Mexicanist Congress. Looking closely at the Order of the Knights of Honor sheds some light on méxico-tejano fraternal orders and mutual aid societies, precursors to later civil rights organizations. Founded in 1910, this fraternal order boasted a healthy membership in communities such as Brownsville (280 members), Laredo (90 members), and Corpus Christi (80 members). Smaller south Texas communities such as Beeville and Victoria also participated, and the organization became transborder when a branch opened in Monterrey, Nuevo Leon, Mexico. In Laredo, Nicasio Idar served as lodge secretary.

The foundational principles and objectives of this organization aligned with Nicasio's social and political views. In fact, *La Crónica* published an article on behalf of the fraternal order that communicated its objectives and strategies. The article began by lamenting the "laziness of Mexicans in Texas regarding the matter of associations."[53] According to the anonymous author, who might have been Nicasio himself, "their [méxico-tejano] aspirations need to be more elevated and not only focus on the formation of mutual aid societies that more than anything else develop beggary and awaken hatreds and ambitions."[54] Instead, the author called for organizations with a longer range of vision that, while providing the usual benefits of associational life, would contribute toward a change in ideas, intellectual progress, and a culture of understanding. Ultimately, organizers of the Congress believed that improving the intellectual culture of la raza and attaining respectability provided a productive means for elevating la raza.[55]

The article then critiqued the divisions among méxico-tejanos, particularly the selfish shortsightedness of the comfortable class for their lack of loyalty to the group and their lack of respect for Mexicans of modest means.

> It is not possible . . . to attain respectability, trust, and protection within the American nation, if we ourselves do not have this with our co-nationals; if we believe that the Mexicans are unworthy of our association with them, of us joining their associations, we should not expect that the Americans would gladly receive us in theirs. If we do not have trust in the men of our own race how can we expect other races to have trust in us?[56]

The author stated that the "American race" was united, and the "Mexican race" would do well to follow this example. Their divisiveness and its attendant animosity, according to the author, made Mexicans appear a degenerate and contemptible people to the Americans.

The alternative, presented in the article, was to be a man of honor, un caballero de honor. Who was this gentleman? He was a Mexican, and as the article explained, "to be Mexican means to be loyal, noble, generous, magnanimous, honorable, patriotic, virile, because these qualities are in our blood, they are innate, they are the inheritance of our race."[57] When enough men of honor united, they could achieve lofty objectives.

> That is why the Order of the Knights of Honor was founded, an association that has as its object to elevate the current condition of the Mexican who resides in the United States, by means of fraternal bonds; but by practical, generous, ample means, helping each other mutually, as brothers, all the members of the order, for the goal of attaining respectability, NOT BY BRUTAL FORCE nor by violating the rights of others, but by intellectual, moral, and pecuniary superiority.[58]

The discourses of cultural redemption and reform pervaded fraternal life and mutualism. Respectability would be the crowning achievement of these efforts, and no one would dare to deny rights to a noble and dignified people.

These objectives represented the template of middle-class méxico-tejano organizational life during the early twentieth century. Less than a year later, in September 1911, the Order of the Knights of Honor scheduled their convention to coincide with the First Mexicanist Congress. The Congress produced the Gran Liga Mexicanista de Benficencia y Protección (Great Mexican League for Beneficence and Protection) and the Mexicanist Woman's League, whose main concerns included civil rights, cultural retention, and education.[59]

Organizers of the Congress relied on an extensive social network to gain wide coverage for this conference. Nicasio Idar was an active Freemason, and his family contacted lodge members throughout the state, particularly in Brownsville, Corpus Christi, and Laredo. They also relied on the impressive system of mutual aid societies throughout the state. For months they published articles in *La Crónica* calling together the various lodges and special guests. They also invited journalists and all Mexican consulate officials. Where there were no organizations, the Idars urged Mexicans to set up associations so that they could send a delegate to the conference.[60]

During this period, méxico-tejanos adhered to an arrangement whereby men and women socialized and organized along gender lines.[61] The world of Masonic lodges, for example, was male dominated. *La Crónica* separately reached out to women. On September 14, 1911, a brief advertisement addressed to Mexican women from both Laredo, Texas, and Nuevo Laredo, Mexico, appeared on its front page.

> The Mexicanist Congress is honored to respectfully invite the beautiful sex from these sister cities, to its meetings, with the security that they will always find in them something noble and great to learn, and they will not find the most minimal act or word that might injure their susceptibility.[62]

Though owned by Nicasio, *La Crónica* operated as a family business. Daughter Jovita and sons Clemente and Eduardo played critical roles, writing and editing articles for the weekly. As an active participant, Jovita might have written the special invitation to women published by *La Crónica*, but it is unlikely that she had herself in mind when she wrote about their vulnerability.[63] Nevertheless, an invitation for women to attend a political function needed to be worded carefully for several reasons. First, politics was seen as a male domain and, as such, it was associated with potential vice and corruption as well as potentially offensive language and behaviors. The author of this invitation tried to assure the "respectable ladies" that not only would their presence be appreciated, but also that their sensibilities would not be damaged. Second, the author spoke of the convention meetings as an educational venue for women. Women were understood to be under the tutelage of men and, therefore, their participation would not disrupt notions of a political natural order whereby men were seen as more politically experienced and astute than women.

The author wrote in the gendered language of a bourgeois society, yet the paternalistic tone must be balanced with the inherently radical meaning of inviting women to participate at a time when gender conventions relegated women, particularly middle- and upper-class women, to the home and other private spaces. Thus, the invitation's text contains two competing discourses: one reinforced a gendered construction of women as "the weaker sex" in need of protection, and the other advanced a feminist discourse of inclusiveness encouraging women to step into the public arena alongside men in order to participate in the defense of la raza.

Having issued these invitations, the Mexicanist Congress opened to great anticipation and excitement. In honor of the Mexican Independence holiday and to take advantage of the cheaper train rates during this time of celebration, organizers decided to hold the conference during the week of September 14–22, 1911, in the heart of downtown Laredo. Thus the mood seemed particularly festive and patriotic, though the matters at hand were serious. The list of attendees included two delegates from each of the twenty-four Order of the Knights of Honor lodges, representatives from other Masonic lodges, mutual aid societies, *agrupaciones protectoras* (protective groups), social groups such as El Club Internacional de Laredo (the International Club of Laredo), delegations from Mexico, the press, a small number of women, and other guests.[64]

Shortly after Nicasio Idar's welcoming address, the convention elected an executive board.[65] Following this parliamentary procedure, the Congreso's work began with a series of formal *discursos*, discourses or speeches, delivered in high oratorical style. Throughout the week, attendees listened to various speakers and participated in *conferencias*, or workshops. Children also participated, singing patriotic songs and reciting patriotic poems.[66]

The Reinforcement of a Mexicanist Identity

Because social change could not be effected without solidarity, the reformers who sought an end to racial discrimination focused on cultural and political unification among Mexicans in Texas. An examination of the speeches delivered during the week of the Congress reveals a strong sense of love and patriotism for the Mexican nation among participants. The country was constantly referred to as *la patria*, which translates as fatherland, though there is evidence that Congresistas (Congress participants) thought of Mexico as female. Severo E. Peña, a representative from Nuevo Laredo, declared,

> To say *Patria* (motherland) is to say love and to feel the kiss of our mother, the caresses of our children, the light from the soul of the woman who tells you I love you. She is that mother who when suffering calls us to liberate her from the infamy of the outrages of foreigners and traitors; don't think that because you live far from this motherland, she will forget you and deny you someday. No, never, for which reason, you should always be grateful, you should always remember your nationality, that the blood that runs in your veins is the same blood of Hidalgo, the same blood of Juárez, it is Mexican blood.[67]

Peña equated Mexican motherland with the Mexican woman and the family, presumably those relationships most prized by Mexican men. Like the conventional long-suffering Mexican mother, the Mexican motherland had known sorrow. Here Severo Peña made references to the invaders of Mexican territory: the Spanish, the Americans, and the French. Despite this history and regardless of how far her children lived from her, Mexico remained the ever-vigilant mother who would never deny her progeny. Indeed, Mexican consular officials were ever watchful of the conditions of Mexicans in the United States during the twentieth century. Even during the nineteenth century, the Mexican government made it clear it would not forget its citizens across the border and demonstrated this by sponsoring repatriation and colonization programs in northern Mexico.[68]

The construction of la raza as a Mexican ethnicity involved a creation myth featuring a pantheon of national heroes. The Cuahtémocs, Hidalgos, Juárezes, and Maderos were transformed into almost superhuman liberators and definers of *lo mexicano* (all that is Mexican). Politically speaking, such social projections of heroes from the past worked well, inspiring Congresistas to throw off the yoke of oppression and dare to be free as their ancestors had.

But freedom—in this case, freedom from discrimination—required far more than inspiration. The second element of the Mexicanist identity was collectivity. If Anglos failed to distinguish between US-born Mexicans and Mexican nationals, treating both poorly, were not all Mexicans in Texas in the same predicament? Regardless of citizenship, many ethnic Mexicans, whether border residents or living in the interior parts of Texas, identified with at least the broad outline of a common culture and certainly a common social situation. In fact, the social in some ways preceded the cultural. As historian David Gutiérrez has argued, the new international boundary created in 1848 and the American racial hierarchy imposed on it left the Mexicans already living there feeling like outcasts. Gutiérrez suggested that, "In these difficult circumstances, the very idea of *lo mexicano* of 'being Mexican,' consequently became significant in ways that it had not been before the North American invasion."[69]

The Mexicanist identity, as portrayed at the First Mexicanist Congress, reflected the transnational nature of people's lived experience. As far as Congresistas were concerned, a Mexican remained a Mexican no matter what part of the world he or she called home. Severo E. Peña made the point passionately, "And don't think that because we cross the river, because we live in this land that once belonged to us, or because we enroll . . . in registries that la raza will be lost. . . . We are Mexicans here and in any other part of the world."[70] Clearly, efforts to promote the imagined community of la raza led to the development of a strong nationalist consciousness. In Texas, transborder activists promoted this mentality as a unifying base critical in the struggle for human and civil rights.

Uplifting and Redeeming the Mexican Masses

A number of issues received considerable attention at the Mexican Congress, including school segregation, economic exploitation, the denigration of the Spanish language and culture, lynchings, and segregation in public facilities.[71] At the base of this mistreatment, as some Congresistas understood it, was a lack of respect for Mexicans on the part of Anglo-Texans. Since they knew that their Mexican compatriots represented a hardworking sector of society, they must have had even more difficulty comprehending how Mexicans could be treated so poorly. A speaker who introduced himself as *un Mexicano* expressed this sense of frustration and indignation by comparing Mexicans to Anglos: "with frequency they [Mexicans] are treated with a shameful contempt by the Americans, treating them like a degenerate or uncultured race. The fact that Americans in Mexico are seen as sons of heaven, like privileged beings does not serve as a preventive for such unjust treatment [of Mexicans in Texas]."[72] Congresistas seemed keenly aware of the unequal relations between Anglos and Mexicans in Texas as well as the asymmetrical geopolitical relationship between the United States and Mexico. This sense of being under another's thumb inspired much talk of uplifting the masses. Though the intention behind the rhetoric was often a genuine desire to eradicate human suffering brought on by poverty and racial discrimination, the political strategy of uplift carried class implications. The same speaker, "un Mexicano," proclaimed:

> This very condition [oppression] is suffered by méxico-texanos in the regions where La Raza has not known how to raise itself above the rest, for it is just to confess that there are many, very many méxico-texanos (among them you and many in Laredo, Texas) who have known how to

attain an honored place. Making a judicious study, you find that north of San Antonio is where our poor brothers suffer most and where it is difficult to find a blood Mexican occupying a post as judge or alderman, or even a police job or work as a clerk in a public office.[73]

The anonymous author of this speech saw many of Laredo's méxico-tejanos as exceptional people, having known how to raise themselves above the rest. In reality, these elites seldom had to do much self-uplift since the influence of well-to-do Mexicans in this community remained strong even after the arrival of European immigrants in the latter part of the nineteenth century. Native-born Anglos and European immigrants who settled in Laredo tended to adopt the Spanish language and elements of Spanish-Mexican culture. Intermarriages between Spanish Mexicans and Anglo-Americans often solidified developing trade and economic relationships among Laredo and Nuevo Laredo's elite classes.[74]

Much less common were intermarriages between newcomer Anglos or Europeans and working-class ethnic Mexicans. However, through annual Diez y Seis de Septiembre and George Washington's birthday celebrations involving parades and much fanfare, civic leaders sought to integrate all sectors of Laredo society. A reporter for *Leslie's Weekly Illustrated* who visited the city during the 1910 Washington's birthday celebration seemed shocked that "the Mexicans appeared to be as enthusiastic in celebrating the great American statesman's birth as were the native Americans."[75]

Ties across class were far more precarious than the ties across ethnicity among elites. Rather than obscuring class conflict, the celebration of Washington could be interpreted as reinforcing hierarchies since it placed elites at the center of community life, while the masses served as mere spectators who watched as the wealthy donned expensive colonial dresses at a parade. The lavish attire would also be worn at an elegant ball reserved for the city's upper class.

Beyond obscuring Laredo's unique social structure, the strategy of uplift also promoted a vision of social progress shared by many members of the gente decente. Francisco J. Fernández, for example, spoke of the Mexicanist Congress as a "formidable lever that will impel the Mexican people residing on foreign soil, by means of moral, intellectual, and material education to level itself to the height of prominent men in this country." Congresistas dreamed of the day when more Mexicans would hold prominent positions in commerce, industry, agriculture, and politics.[76]

Although Congresistas acknowledged the unfair nature of Anglo-Mexican relations and denounced discriminatory practices, they assigned specific responsibilities to Mexicans. Mexicans needed to perfect themselves as much as possible, particularly along moral and intellectual lines. The elevation of the Mexican element in Texas became one of the prime objectives of the méxico-tejano middle class. Regardless of income, all Mexicans were called upon to behave like "decent people." Only by uniting as gente decente could they hope to raise themselves from the lowest rungs of society. The First Mexicanist Congress served as a vehicle for this "lifting as we climb" strategy. This task seemed so critical and formidable to one Congresista that he declared that "the undertaking is monumental . . . . [Y]ou propose, to save, redeem, and emancipate by means of union, education and culture a virile people like the Mexicans who have lived under the iron rule of the foreigner due to their ineptitude."[77]

Their modernist discourse of social progress focused on the efforts of the individual and the community even as they fashioned a postmodern critique of the structural barriers erected against Mexicans in Texas and Mexico. They used the discourse of individual and community responsibility as a tool in the fight to eradicate pernicious stereotypes. At a time when anti-Mexican sentiment was on the rise and virulent stereotypes abounded, the strategy of respectability defied racist conventions by daring to place Mexicans on equal moral and cultural ground with Anglos.[78]

Congresistas used the strategy of redemption and salvation to describe not only their compatriots in Texas who needed help but also to underscore how their project of unification served their beloved patria. Indeed, helping a Mexican brother amounted to paying homage to this motherland. Gregorio E. González, a delegate from Nuevo Laredo, spoke of the great Independence Day celebrations in Mexico designed to honor the nation and praised Mexicans in Texas for their equally or perhaps more compelling tribute to the motherland.

> Its absent sons, those whom the vicissitudes of life have obligated to look for bread outside the motherland, meet today in a single place as a single son to watch out for the well-being of their brothers, to look for the means to make less sorrowful the exile, to protect their lives and interest where there is a lack of support from the laws, customs, and their uses.[79]

On some level, if the Mexican motherland was seen as mother, and the Mexican masses in Texas were seen as brothers, it follows that the honorable role for the educated méxico-tejano was to assume the responsibilities of a protective son and brother. In fact, several speakers spoke of defending Mexico from foreigners and demanding justice in Texas courts on behalf of all Mexicans. The concept of the male protector was deeply ingrained in the méxico-tejano psyche.

Perhaps the clearest example of the importance assigned to this protector role can be seen in fraternal life among méxico-tejanos. Congresistas belonged to one or more mutual aid societies and fraternal orders. Professor Simón G. Domínguez spoke on behalf of the Respectable Society Sons of Juárez, a prominent Masonic fraternal order in Laredo. During his introduction, Professor Domínguez compared his lodge to the Mexicanist Congress stating that both groups sought the same goal: the unification of la raza. Once united, the Congress could attend to the business of uplifting and protecting. Domínguez explained the matter clearly: "The congress will have as its object the moral and intellectual perfection of La Raza, being in addition a center of protection for the same, in order to attain the respectability and well-being that we are deserving of."[80]

With such a strong influence from the mutual aid and fraternal orders communities, it is not surprising that one of the products of the First Mexicanist Congress was the founding of La Gran Liga Mexicanista de Beneficencia y Protección (The Great Mexicanist League for Beneficence and Protection). In its constitution, the League made its aims explicit.

> Its object will be to develop the principles of morality, culture, instruction, fraternity between its co-associates; to protect them when they are unjustly processed and sentenced, when acts in conflict with the laws of the country are committed against them; to create a policy fund for the relatives of dead members and guard so that the Mexican children not be excluded from the schools where the Saxon children attend.[81]

Figure 1.3 Jovita Idar at an inauguration with members of the Union of Stone Masons and Bricklayers (Union Local de Albaniles), circa 1915. On the platform are (l. to r.) Jovita Idar, Professor Simón Domínguez, and his daughter. 084-0599, General Photograph Collection, University of Texas at San Antonio, Special Collections— Institute of Texan Cultures. Courtesy of A. Ike Idar.

The set of objectives for this organization showcased their gente decente values: their developing human and civil rights sensibilities and strategies; their fundamental principle of mutuality; and underlying all, their acceptance of their role as protectors of others. These others included women, children, and those discriminated against, such as *el elemento obrero*, the workingmen's element.

Obeying the Impulses of their Hearts and Protesting from the Pedestal

The conference program offers some clues about the participation and role of women at the First Mexicanist Congress. For example, Lisandro Peña, after thanking the organizers of the Congress and proclaiming with great satisfaction the conference motto, "Todo por La Raza y para La Raza" (All by the Mexican people and for the Mexican people), appraised his surroundings with deep satisfaction: "The profusion of light and the exquisite good taste of the adornments in this hall, the various musical numbers, and above all the compact and select feminine element, contributed to the complete success of these meetings of the First Mexican Congress of Texas."[82] Not missing a beat, Francisco J. Fernández delighted in his own tribute to the ladies, addressing them as "you particularly, enchanting ladies, who with your beautiful presence you have come to beautify and enhance whatever flower vase of odoriferous and fragrant flowers there be in these conferences."[83]

The enchanting ladies, however, were there to do far more than beautify and enhance the décor. Soledad de la Peña, one of the two women speakers at the Congress, linked the education of women to the struggle for civil rights.

> Your task has been arduous . . . humble gladiators of the rights of the méxico-tejano . . . but you will no longer be alone in the fight, for there remain thousands of hearts in this populace that will second you. . . . I, like you, believe that the best means to achieve this is to educate the woman, instruct her, encourage her while respecting her.[84]

In exchange for education, women would "struggle for the well-being of the Mexican people on foreign soil . . . be strong . . . [and] surrender the sword and the flag to them [with these words]: return my son, with it [the flag] or with it wrapped around you."[85] The patriotic rhetoric depicted here is similar to the nationalistic discourse of "republican motherhood" of Revolutionary-era American politics that elevated mothers as primary caregivers for their role in transmitting cultural values and providing children's first civic lessons.[86] Similar, in early twentieth-century south Texas, it was up to the mother to "educate [the children] so that they may never feel ashamed of saying that they are Mexicans."[87]

Expressions of republican motherhood were not delivered solely for the benefit of the men. Some women also believed this role had the potential of expanding the private domestic world into the public realm through politicized motherhood. During a meeting of the League of Mexican Women, which organized soon after the Mexicanist Congress, teacher María Rentería delivered a speech on Mexican heroines Leona Vicario and Rafaela Lopez. *La Crónica* published her presentation, probably through the auspices of Jovita Idar, who served as president of the League. In this speech Rentería argued that throughout Mexican history women played active roles and had been just as patriotic as the men. Studying history, one would find "beautiful examples of mothers who sacrificed themselves for the sake of their children, of wives who faced a thousand dangers in order to save their husbands and aggrandize the nation." In Rentería's estimation, Mexican women had repeatedly proven themselves. Men might have sacrificed their lives on the battlefields, but some women did that too. Furthermore, women served as nurses, messengers, financial benefactors, and above all, as inspiration. As Rentería put it, women inspired men "with their resignation and faith, for these are one of the principal weapons of the woman."[88]

Rentería's words go to the heart of Mexicana consciousness, which emanates from the gaps in power structures. While the feminism that took shape in Mexico between 1870 and 1940 bore certain similarities to North American and European feminism, such as the desire to reform gender inequalities, it represented an indigenous creation with roots in *Marianismo*, the cult of feminine superiority named after the Virgin Mary. Like the North American concept of the "cult of true womanhood," Marianismo esteemed women for possessing qualities as such purity, piety, submissiveness, and domesticity. This distinct female culture formed the bedrock upon which women's associational life developed.[89] In María Rentería's case, the documents do not reveal whether she used the term "feminism" to describe herself or whether she identified ideologically with all of its precepts.

Women had clearly responded to the demands made during each of the Mexican nation's important moments, but the work of women also extended into the future through their children. Toward the end of the conference, *La Crónica* reported activist Leonor Villegas de Magnón's comments on women as shapers of the next generation.

> "The hand that rocks the cradle is the one which governs the world."
> The intelligence, know-how, and riches that the small citizens whom
> God has entrusted to us . . . will provide for the nation later depends

on us. With how much longing we should guard the moral and physical education of so precious a cargo![90]

It seemed only logical to educate women, but Villegas de Magnón took this one step further. While education and the acquisition of skills made women better mothers, this preparation also served the direct interests of women. Villegas de Magnón took issue with the custom of keeping women from this knowledge. She declared, "And regarding the feminine sex, the self-love of our people that prevents women from learning to work is false. If in our youth we were taught all manner of labors as a luxury, as an adornment, we would avoid bitter suffering later on."[91] Leonor Villegas de Magnón understood that while many men provided for their wives and children, there would always be some men who abused, neglected, or abandoned their families.

Whether the male participants of the Mexicanist Congress thought about the issues raised in Villegas de Magnón's feminist critique remains a mystery, but examining the words that men used in support of women can shed some light on their understanding of gender and politics. Education for women outside the bounds of motherhood inspired little enthusiasm from some men. During the course of the conference an unidentified participant asked: "Is the education of the woman of our race indispensable so that she may occupy a distinguished social position only or also to mold the tender intelligence of her children; forming for them a character that will serve them as a base throughout life?" Professor Simón G. Domínguez provided a telling response on behalf of the Masonic Society Sons of Juárez: "What is absolutely necessary is to educate the woman of the race so that she may mold the tender intelligence of her children; and this very deed will make her occupy the most distinguished social position."[92]

Among this body of educated, liberal-minded community activists, informed motherhood stood as the highest aspiration for Mexican and méxico-tejana women. Women such as Soledad de la Peña, María Rentería, and Leonor Villegas de Magnón and men such as Simón G. Domínguez all spoke of the importance of educating mothers, underscoring the relationship between women, the family, and the state. And yet, the mere fact that these women participated in such a public forum allowed for the possibility of developing a feminist consciousness from which to critique male privilege, such as Leonor Villegas de Magnón's demand that women be educated so as to avoid dependence on potentially abusive or neglectful partners.

When not using her skills and knowledge to shape the young minds and raise the healthy bodies of her children, a patriotic Mexican woman might direct her energies toward the protection of someone else's children. Single women were encouraged to fill such roles. Miss Hortencia Moncayo stood before the

Mexicanist Congress on behalf of León Cárdenas Martínez, a fifteen-year-old boy convicted of murder and sentenced to death who was believed to be innocent by méxico-tejanos. When Laredo's Sociedad de Obreros "Igualdad y Progreso" (Workmen's Society "Equality and Progress") sent the governor of Texas a petition signed by the most prominent citizens of the community, they bought the condemned boy more time. Hortencia Moncayo pleaded with Congresistas to lend their support to the worthy cause by making contributions to the Martínez defense fund.[93]

In response to contributions she collected, the Agrupación Protectora Mexicana (Mexican Protective Group) honored Moncayo with an acknowledgment of gratitude and presented her with the organization's seal. The statement from the president and secretary emphasized women's special roles as protectors of children.

> Yesterday's telegrams from the Associated Press have informed us of your very noble and patriotic conduct, having presented yourself before the respectable Mexicanist Congress of this cultured city of Laredo, and exposed that related to the new trial that the courts have conceded the boy León Cárdenas Martínez, Jr., presumed responsible for homicide. These noble acts, kind Miss, can only originate from the Mexican woman; of those women who have never failed in their sacred duties, on behalf of the descendants of Doña Josefa Ortiz de Domínguez, la Corregidora de Querétaro and of Doña Leona Vicario.[94]

Women could be educated, and they could speak in public as long as they fulfilled their sacred duties as primary caregivers for their families and the broader family of la raza.

Sacred duties to family and community thus gave women a special license in méxico-tejano political culture. Soledad de la Peña began her speech to the Congress by explaining her participation. "Obeying the impulses of my heart, I have dared to occupy this rostrum so that from it I might emit my humble concept regarding the works that this high body has proposed to carry into effect."[95] Was Soledad de la Peña simply "obeying the impulses of her heart" or did she say this because that type of introduction was expected of women orators? Her words reveal the nuanced political strategy of a Mexican woman committed to fighting racial discrimination, but doing so within the structures of patriarchy. Her words might have been an effort to justify her public speaking while soothing potentially threatened male egos. By admitting that as a woman she could not but obey the impulses of her heart, she potentially made it easier for the men to overlook her boldness.

Interpreted differently, perhaps Soledad de la Peña not only obeyed the impulses of her heart but also had enough confidence in her emotions to express them freely. In other words, her presence before a large male-dominated audience at a conference, her call for women's education to foster civic motherhood, and her public expressions of Mexican nationalism revealed the spirit of a hearty patriot. It is possible that she, like most of the highly enthusiastic speakers at the conference, experienced strong patriotic stirrings from the heart, although unlike the male orators, she admitted that she had succumbed to them. Ultimately, because her message fell within the bounds of a woman's sacred duties, most male listeners probably approved of her presence and her message.

Protesting from the pedestal—that is, speaking from the authority of respectable Mexican womanhood—at times involved self-deprecation. Before delivering a rousing speech, Hortencia Moncayo began with a few humble words that camouflaged a powerful and radical message made even more inspirational and compelling because a woman said them.

> I have the honor to speak before this illustrious auditorium, representing the school "La Purísima," to which I belong and because this meeting is about nothing less than a noble and high goal; the union of the Mexican people on foreign soil. Therefore, I beg that you might excuse whatever faults I might incur on account of my sex and the lack of extensive knowledge about this transcendent matter, but I do it hoping that all in whom runs the blood of Cúauhtémoc unite as one and be respected by any foreigner who wants to treat them as beasts of burden, for the Mexicans have always been free and sovereign, and they have shed their blood for liberty and in the name of the beloved country that witnessed our birth.[96]

As caballeros de honor, honorable men who pledged to protect Mexican women and children and la raza as a whole, they probably took Hortencia Moncayo's words to heart. Given the political status of Mexicans in Texas and the prevalence of the concept of gente decente, both respectable manhood and respectable womanhood involved some forms of self-sacrifice for the greater good—for family, for community, for la raza. Thus, the gendered discourses of respectability and cultural redemption worked in tandem with the larger project of uniting all Mexicans in a struggle against racial oppression. In this space, women practiced a "feminism-in-nationalism," to borrow the phrase from historian Emma Pérez. While seemingly repeating and reinforcing patriarchal discourses, the female participants came to inhabit a male-dominated space and expanded the domestic sphere by participating in its politicization.[97]

The League of Mexican Women and the Politics of Benevolence

Women participated in largely male-dominated forums such as the Mexicanist Congress, but they also organized as women in order to address other cultural redemption issues. Their projects often involved attempts to provide cultural and moral uplift for others. Organized in 1911 and presided over by Jovita Idar, the League of Mexican Women developed during the First Mexicanist Congress. The women of the League framed their political participation in terms of benevolence or the alleviation of social ills through charitable projects. Benevolence allowed civic-minded gente decente women to transform their moral imperatives into a plan of action.[98] Two months after the creation of this group, members consisting of "numerous and very respectable young ladies of Laredo" began their charitable work in earnest. The League committed itself to providing free education to two destitute children. School teachers María Rentería and Berta Cantú each offered the services of their respective *escuelitas* (little schools). The League also decided to buy the children new clothes and school supplies.[99]

As educators, several of whom operated their own schools, League members prioritized the education of youth, but widespread poverty also commanded their attention. As an article in *La Crónica* put it (probably written by Jovita Idar):

> One of the ends for which this society shall labor will also be to pro-
> vide some help to the poor of Laredo. Some have been visited who find
> themselves in the most complete misery and abandonment, for whom
> clothes have been provided by some of the young women and food by
> the respectable Señora Doña Tomasita de Mendoza.[100]

Besides informing the community about their activities, the purpose of the article was to advertise a benefit for the League at the Solorzano Theater. The author justified the League's need to raise funds by stating that the organization did "not count on pecuniary elements for its members all belonged to the noble working class."[101]

In reality, working-class lives differed considerably from those of the educators. Oral histories of Laredo residents in the early twentieth century reveal the extent of the poverty in the Azteca neighborhood.[102] Elena Medellín de Ramírez, for example, remembered how challenging it was for her father, a blacksmith, to provide for their family of eight children. The family survived on a regular diet of coffee and flour tortillas.[103] Various members of the family had to work in order to "get by," picking cotton during the Great Depression. Reynaldo García recalled that while their father operated an herb stand at the *mercado* (town market), the children needed to work. Reynaldo got his first wage-earning job at the age ten or eleven, working at a bakery, and running errands as early as four or five in the morning. He quit school in order to accommodate his work life. After their father's death, his sister worked at the Singer Sewing Machine factory to earn money for groceries, and Reynaldo earned the rent money by working at the smelter. [104] Because many working-class children and young adults needed to work, education represented a luxury.

The concept of gente decente encompassed a broad range of people from wealthy merchants, to low-salaried teachers, to skilled workers, and perhaps even the very poor, provided they met middle-class moral standards. However, for a group of professionally trained teachers to identify themselves as members of the working class seems like a stretch unless it was political symbolism. In part, the connection with the poor signified women's identification with another group perceived as somehow weak and in need of protection. Furthermore, at a time when the expansion of capital across south Texas made workers particularly vulnerable and labor unions began to make inroads, many méxico-tejanos from the middling ranks did, in fact, align themselves with workers and unions. Various members of the Idar family, including Nicasio, Clemente, and Federico, participated in labor activism, even though they enjoyed certain privileges beyond the reach of most Mexican workers during the early twentieth century. Besides being a political or charitable organization, the League created a social and cultural space for its educated membership. For one thing, they enjoyed access to the media through their president, Jovita Idar. The group held their meetings in private homes, among these the Idar family home. They sponsored literary readings and musical and theatrical productions, which generated funds for their charitable projects. [105] The group possessed a marked sense of gente decente identity that associated respectable Mexican womanhood with certain values and aspirations.

> This association, that actively works for the general advancement of its co-associates, that holds studying and learning sessions, sessions where culture is acquired and talent is developed without orgies and unhealthy ambitions, that dedicates itself to the realization of noble and generous ends does not count on pecuniary elements. [106]

Embedded in the text is the message that regardless of financial means, people could still be educated, cultured, accomplished, moral, noble, and generous. The image of this group of "working-class" women educators exuding respectability and honor had its own political implication, for it meant that despite unequal economic relations, the working poor were going to be measured against the same moral and cultural standards claimed by the more privileged sectors of society, standards believed to hold the key to better treatment for Mexicans in Texas.

What is apparent is that members of the League of Mexican Women sought to identify with those who existed in society's margins and to improve the lives of the poor to the greatest extent possible given their own constraints.

The strategy of cultural redemption is an important element of the transborder political culture that at times seemed like social control, but in reality attempted to bring about social transformation by challenging negative stereotypes used to justify the exploitation of Mexican people. The women of the League worked from the margins as méxico-tejana and Mexicana women but also carried their message beyond the margins into certain elite spaces their privileges afforded them. They facilitated transborder activists' claims to the political agency needed in the project of empowering their community.

Social Stability Reformers and the "Threat of the Mexican Masses"

The developing méxico-tejano middle class was caught between their allegiance to the capitalist-driven culture of progress and their humanitarian sympathies for the working poor. This led to a complex political strategy of mediation as they struggled to embrace diverse groups under the rubric of gente decente. After all, reconciling class rifts facilitated the greater goal of unification or becoming la raza. But in this project of reconciliation, social change and cultural reformers were more likely to enact a civil rights agenda than social stability reformers whose strategies and goals revolved around containing real and perceived threats from below.

Socially, and to some extent politically, these reformers showed support for the working class. An analysis of newspaper articles, however, reveals how the social stability reformers came to define la raza in terms that favored two of the major prerogatives of capitalistic society, order and progress. Furthermore, they expected the men and women of la raza to adhere to nineteenth-century bourgeois social ethics of the male breadwinner and female domesticity. While other middle-class reformers also valued traditional gender roles, social stability reformers seemed more threatened by women's participation in public arenas, and they believed that the welfare of families and communities was at stake.

El Democrata Fronterizo, a Spanish-language newspaper owned by middle-class Mexican immigrant Justo Cárdenas, in particular, pursued the political strategy of order and progress. It devoted some of its columns to the threat of the disobedient masses and ways to avoid anarchy. Gente decente writers such as Italian American Luis Bruni, a member of one of Laredo's most economically and politically powerful families, wrote articles exhorting his social class to institute reforms lest the masses revolt and destroy "civilized society."[107] Bruni admonished,

> Bourgeoisie, millionaires, owners of trusts, think about it well; the proletarian cause is your cause; the misery of the poor is your misery. What we want is not communalism, nor anarchism, nor the division of property, nor the extermination of capital; what we want is the extermination of misery, in other words, a prudent economy by means of an increase in wealth through production ... that the product of capital be united to work and distributed proportionately amongst all, with love, equality, and justice.[108]

Ignoring the needs of the poor, according to Bruni, would lead to anarchism, for the masses were becoming cognizant of the unfairness embedded in a social structure where the few dominated the many.[109] Bruni might have paid dearly for his seemingly bold positions, for his wealthy father, Antonio M. Bruni, disinherited him.[110] But if his father had read the newspaper articles closely, he would have noticed that his son was not seeking an end to capitalism, but rather to save capitalism from the "threatening masses" by reaching some type of accommodation with them.

While Luis Bruni focused on broad economic and sociological concerns, others developed behavior-based critiques. Educator and Freemason Simón G. Domínguez expressed a strong aversion to what he considered the vices of the "proletariat class." Domínguez helped to organize a party for the Sociedad Mutualista Sons of Juárez and was concerned that some of the guests might bring alcoholic beverages, which might upset fathers of young women in attendance. In a letter to Nicasio Idar, Domínguez summed up his views:

> The proletarian class, without literature, without teachers, without moral education, without culture, without centers of recreation or instruction, dedicated completely to the hardest and most vulgar tasks, does not find in their misery any recreation other than the one provided by the vilest of vices: drunkenness.[111]

The fear of the masses and social disruption formed a part of the baggage brought by gente decente Mexican immigrants, particularly from the industrializing centers of northern Mexico. Driven by such fears, the middle-class people of Chihuahua, William French argues, tried to impose their work ethic and value system onto miners. In Mexico, permanent workers often subscribed to middle-class values because they aspired to join their middle-class ranks, while temporary or transient workers resisted this imposition.[112]

Elliot G. Young argues that many workers in Laredo also adopted or internalized gente decente values. These workers tended to join mutual aid societies and fraternal orders. "Worker organizations" often mirrored the value system of the middle class because many leaders reflected this background. Mary Ann Clawson has made a similar argument for Anglo-American fraternal orders that sought to transcend class differences by emphasizing their race and gender solidarity as white men. Both Young and Clawson acknowledge that the strategy can work both ways. That is, while fraternal orders can be used by the middle-class leadership to exert forms of social control, or at least social influence, on the working-class membership, workers can use the voluntary associations as a means of getting ahead as individuals and perhaps even as a class.[113]

But not all workers joined fraternal orders. Many, in fact, joined the ranks of the Federal Labor Union (FLU), an affiliate of the American Federation of Labor. The FLU focused primarily on railroad workers but also accepted workers from other industries, including the unskilled. Initially, social stability reformers such as publisher Justo Cárdenas and Luis Bruni showed support for the union. But when the FLU went on strike against the Mexican National Railway in 1906–07, and as the union began to gravitate toward socialism and workers grew bolder in asserting their rights, they lost the support of *El Demócrata Fronterizo*.[114]

A fierce battle of words ensued between *El Demócrata Fronterizo* and *El Defensor del Obrero* (The Defender of the Worker), an organ of the Federal Labor Union (FLU). The position of *El Demócrata Fronterizo* seemed to be pro-labor as long as labor operated within a pro-capitalist framework. *El Defensor del Obrero*, however, spoke of organizing against capital; of demands not requests; of the rights of workers, not the harmony of the classes; and ultimately of socialism. In response or reaction, *El Demócrata Fronterizo* derided such claims as utopian. One article stated, "The socialist system, we must admit, was not made for our planet. In the natural human condition the absorption of the individual by the state does not fit and has never fitted."[115] In another article, the newspaper criticized and portrayed FLU leaders as parasites who lived at the workers' expense. The writer attacked union leaders for making the workers believe that "day laborers without cultivation, real machines, are above artisans, above industrialists, above commercial merchants, above engineers, above attorneys, above those who think, study and work." While others devoted themselves "night and day to the study of great projects," the article continued, "the common laborer, the machine man, slept soundly without a care." The writer then encouraged *El Defensor del Obrero* "to moralize the working classes, awakening in them legitimate aspirations to progress, and not to take advantage of their ignorance and evil passions in order to launch them toward socialism."[116]

Just as social stability reformers' support for workers' rights hinged on a set of conditions, so too did their support for women's rights. The emancipation of women made sense to these reformers as long as men emancipated them and as long as these freedoms flourished within the context of the family circle. In an article addressed to working-class men, *El Demócrata Fronterizo*'s premier social critic, Luis Bruni, pleaded with men to protect their women and to stop treating them as slaves. Bruni believed that as natural protectors of women, men had often taken advantage of women. He wrote in 1906:

> In those remote centuries, the only end of the primitive beings was the hunt and war, and the natural physical weakness of the woman, certainly, could not follow the reign of the man. . . . [T]he woman needed necessarily to invoke the protection of man. But whoever asks for protection, receives conditions, and it is here that woman is humiliated, subjected to man; it is here that man, proud, arrogant, becomes oppressor; it is here, in sum, the primordial origin of the moral disequilibrium of two human beings, equally loved by God.[117]

The same Luis Bruni who saw the injustice of unequal relationships between the sexes by 1911 found himself writing about the "dangers of women's individualism." Bruni criticized suffragists in industrialized countries such as the United States and France, lamenting how modern civilization had "taken control over the hearts of women." Echoing Theodore Roosevelt, he spoke of "race suicide" as the "sad fruit" of the high levels of liberty claimed by the modern woman. He opposed the United States' anti-immigration policies as shortsighted, for he believed that immigrants rejuvenated the nation with the values of "morality, respect for the husband, intense love for the children, and the sanctity of the domestic home." [118] Ultimately, Bruni believed that these should be the ideals of wives and mothers; and to the extent that American women deviated from these roles, the United States moved closer to its own demise.

Luis Bruni did not limit his critique to suffragists. He also disparaged female benevolent societies. Rather than seeing benevolence as an extension of women's roles as caregivers into a broader public realm, as social change reformers understood it, Bruni saw the work of women's associations as a threat to the family and the "natural" social order. He wrote that

> when woman, invaded by the passion of her individualism loses track of her duties as wife and mother . . . that is where the danger begins! . . . [S]he drapes herself with the mantle of affected philanthropy and charity which she pretends to spread in the world of suffering, [this] is an easy recourse to hide her sins. . . . The high and noble ideal of the family is disappearing in society, and with it, unfortunately, are

disappearing one by one the sentiments of morality, of love, and of abnegation.[119]

Bruni never mentioned particular associations or women by name, but the activities of middle-class women in Laredo might have precipitated Bruni's attacks. Gente decente women participated in a variety of voluntary associations, from church societies to the League of Mexican Women. The 1911 general directory of the city of Laredo records several female-based associations, including the Ladies Society, Hijas de María (Daughters of Mary), Ladies of Macabees, and the Woman's Missionary Society. In addition, both Catholic and Protestant churches listed various prayer meetings, rosary and benediction sessions, and other religious services in which women participated and may have played leadership roles.[120] Second, at least some gente decente women expressed sympathies for the Magonistas revolutionary movement. A few, such as Sara Estela Ramírez, joined the ranks of the Partido Liberal Mexicano (PLM) or the Mexican Liberal Party.[121] A few years after Bruni wrote his articles, his sister Adela became involved in La Cruz Blanca, the medical brigade started by Leonor Villegas de Magnón.[122] The women who volunteered their services during the Mexican Revolution more than likely had some previous experience in volunteer work.

To Luis Bruni, volunteer work represented a major threat to social stability because it took women outside the home and gave them an opportunity to explore their "individualism." By contrast, social change and cultural redemption reformers such as members of the Idar family welcomed and encouraged the presence of women in volunteerist politics. While they adhered to the same nineteenth-century Mexican and American gender roles of female domesticity and male dominion as did the social stability types, social change reformers supported the idea that women's sacred duties as wives and mothers could and should be expanded beyond the home into the community for the greater service of la raza. The resultant gendered political culture, while restrictive in many ways, also presented women with opportunities to express themselves in public platforms such as that of the First Mexicanist Congress.

A further contrast can be made between the discourses of reform. Social stability reformers who sought to integrate workers into their grand scheme of progress and order failed to understand the extent of workers' frustration with the capitalist system in Laredo. These reformers tended to support Mexican dictator Porfirio Díaz for bringing peace and order to Mexico, although some of them criticized Díaz for his political abuses. Nevertheless, they agreed that what Mexico needed was political reform, not social revolution. Thus, they were highly critical of Ricardo Flores Magón and his Magonista anarcho-syndicalist movement.

Social change reformers seemed to understand that some social and economic transformations needed to occur if social justice was to be achieved. The Magonistas initially found support in Laredo from *La Crónica*. However, as the Magonistas turned to a socialist, and later an anarchist, agenda, they lost the support of Laredo's middle-class reform community and lost some of their members, such as Sara Estela Ramírez, who joined a more moderate faction of the movement. Nevertheless, *La Crónica's* critiques of the Magonistas came years after *El Democrata Fronterizo*'s attack on the revolutionary movement. This is not surprising given that the writers of *El Democrata Fronterizo* had displayed a more conservative approach than those who wrote for *La Crónica* and saw the Magonistas as a threat to social stability long before this group made its anarchist intentions known. Indeed, *El Democrata Fronterizo* was more likely to communicate in the language of social stability while *La Crónica* often expressed calls for social change. This distinction is significant, for not all members of the gente decente adhered to the same political philosophy and sets of strategies, even though they might have shared certain privileges and formed part of the same cultural community. The social and cultural reformers described here created a variety of political discourses within the gente decente.

Finally, the strategy of cultural redemption, a strategy often pursued by women reformers, was predicated on the notion that in a racist world that relied on negative imagery of Mexicans to justify inequalities, a culture of respectability based on material, moral, and intellectual uplift would help Mexicans transcend the miseries marring their lives. Cultural reformers and social change reformers were often the same people. For example, the Idar family utilized both strategies. Some social stability reformers may have incorporated the strategy of cultural redemption as well, but their motive was different from that of the social change reformers. When a social stability reformer spoke the language of uplift, the intent was not so much so that the oppressed Mexicans would enjoy more freedoms and justice, but that the masses, once properly moralized and cultivated, would not pose a threat to the order and progress of civilization.

Within the context of the transborder political culture, social stability reformers, while also seeking solutions for social problems, did so from a decidedly conservative platform. Economic imbalances, they felt, could lead to revolutions that would disrupt and even destroy liberal capitalist structures. Their attempts to harmonize the different elements of society served the purpose of preserving that world, not transforming it on the level envisioned by social change and cultural redemption activists who both engaged the gendered discourses of liberal capitalism and challenged them.

The violence that gave rise to the first large-scale, organized civil rights effort on the part of Mexican-origin people in the United States exemplifies the neo-colonial relationship between the United States and Mexico and between Anglos and Mexicans in Texas. Mexicans living in the United States at the end of the US-Mexico War (1848) became citizens through the Treaty of Guadalupe-Hidalgo, but they were not treated as such.

These asymmetrical power relationships compelled méxico-tejanos to organize and advocate for human rights. In the interstices of the American and Mexican worlds, fronterizo or borderlands people were able to imagine ways to address issues of racial discrimination, political disenfranchisement, and economic exploitation that framed their lives. As they engaged in this process, they developed a transborder political culture distinct from the mainstream politics of the United States and Mexico and yet in conversation with each and borrowing from both. To the extent that méxico-texanos engaged in broader global discourses, their political culture was also transnational.

The strategies of social change, cultural redemption, and social stability represented various perspectives informing fronterizo political culture and at its center stood the idea of a unified community working for a common cause. The political agency of fronterizos was built on a foundation of strong ethnic identification and calls for unity. Uniting Mexican people in Texas required transcending class and gender differences. But constructions of class and gender tended to be reinforced rather than eliminated, and so calls for unity came to rely on another social construction that sought to encompass Mexicans wherever they might reside—the concept of la raza. People who embraced a raza identity did not constitute a sovereign nation, for in Mexico the criollos governed them and in the United States they represented a conquered people. Despite this, they understood themselves to be a part of a community bound together by cultural associations yet diffused enough to require people to "imagine" themselves as part of a larger whole.[123]

Concepts of la raza had existed throughout Latin America, constructed within histories of Spanish conquest, *mestizaje*, and both European and American imperialism. These legacies of conflict, negotiation, and contestation informed the creation of la raza in Texas. The primary focus here has been on how méxico-tejanos constructed la raza in relation to their unique struggle in the United States, living, to borrow from Juan Seguín, as "foreigners in their native land" and yet remaining connected in various ways to la raza in Mexico.[124]

For Mexicans in Texas, their connections to the motherland and to each other grew stronger as racist treatment politicized them, solidifying their sense of belonging to la raza.[125] In time the social construction of ethnic identity in south Texas, like gender roles and class hierarchies, took on a naturalized character. Far more than a political strategy, this identity developed as an essence in the minds and hearts of a people becoming la raza and could galvanize communities.[126]

Within this highly nationalistic transborder political culture, discourses of gender found an audience eager to integrate women into the broader struggles for rights. México-tejana women worked alongside men in the campaign against racism and yet raised awareness about gender issues. In the process, they politicized domesticity, linking it to the human rights struggle of their "imagined community."

Gente decente transborder activists had enough awareness of their privileges as literate, middle-class people to use these advantages in the service of a social justice struggle for the broader community of la raza. Furthermore, despite their connection and identification with liberal capitalist precepts, their lives as borderlands people facing the particular challenge of de facto Jaime Crow structures also engendered in them the development of a competing identification as an oppressed group, ready for political activism.

Beyond the fact that participants had mixed ancestral ethno-racial backgrounds, they also existed in a transcultural liminal space. In her incisive analysis of mestiza consciousness, cultural theorist Sonia Saldívar-Hull underscores the multiplicity, ambiguity, and even contradiction interplayed at the crossroads of two disparate societies.[127] Precisely in such a dynamic space could the New Mestiza[o] oppositional consciousness thrive and formulate the attitudes, beliefs, values, and strategies needed to tackle the distinct problems facing Mexicans in Texas. The transborder political culture had taken root and herein men and women combined their understandings of marginality and privilege to make demands on Anglo-dominated society. Their voices heralded the birth of a modern Mexican-American human and civil rights movement ready to confront modern racism.

Masons, Magonistas, and Maternalists

Liberal, Anarchist, and Maternal Feminist Thought within a Local/Global Nexus

> Capital, authority, clergy: Herein lie the somber trinity that makes of this beautiful earth a paradise for those who have monopolized in their claws . . . the product . . . of generations of workers, and a hell for those who . . . work . . . leaving in this manner a humanity divided into two social classes with diametrically opposed interests: the capitalist class and the working class.[1]
> —*Regeneración*, Los Angeles, California, September 23, 1911

Despite the differences in political approach among the gente decente reformers, the greater contrast was between these liberals and the Magonistas who took liberal reform to the radical extreme of anarcho-syndicalism. This chapter examines this contrast between liberals, many of whom were Freemasons, and the Magonistas. Flores Magón and his Magonismo followers denounced abuses on both sides of the border long before others did, and their analysis of what was wrong was more far-reaching than the liberals'. While liberals engaged in Mexico's revolutionary struggle aimed to expand the political voice of the people, Magonistas sought economic and social transformations. Magonistas were concerned with the plight of workers and demanded a dismantling of the exploitative power structures, not merely an expansion of political rights. Yet, despite their contrasting views of how best to promote the common good, liberals and Magonistas shared similar attitudes toward women, adhering to a maternal feminist vision.[2]

While Magonismo theoretically supported feminist ideals, in practice the movement tended to subsume the plight of women within that of the workers generally. To the extent that they romanticized women's traditional roles, Magonistas resembled the middle-class liberals they critiqued heavily. Both the liberal Freemasons and the Magonistas favored a maternalist vision of women that many experienced as female domesticity. However, maternalism implied a

sense of female authority on matters pertaining to the home, family, and community. In other words, as mothers, women could claim authority over an expanded domestic realm with political infiltrations into an otherwise forbidden
public world. For all the romanticizations of women as idealized wives and
mothers in Mexico and its borderlands with the United States, women lived and
worked, experiencing struggles but also achieving some effective outcomes for
themselves as women and for their families and communities. These women understood the language of maternalism and used it to create pockets of support
or even widespread alliances for their causes. Like liberal activist women Jovita
Idar and Leonor Villegas de Magnón, Magonista women carved out spaces for
themselves in the world of male-dominated politics. This chapter also discusses
the agency of Magonista women operating within the parameters of a nationalist
struggle for liberation led by men who saw the contributions of the "fairer sex" to
the revolution within a maternalist framework.

The voluntary associations of Freemasons, Magonistas, and maternal
feminists reveal the fluid dynamics of transborder political culture, illustrating
the creative and varied responses to shared problems. Transborder activists engaged with ideas and practices at the local, state, national, and transnational
levels. Their political strategies to the problems of racism and poverty were informed by constructs of gender, class, and race-ethnicity, and by ideas of citizenship and nation.

Also examined is the inherently transnational nature of both Freemasonry,
with its liberal capitalist operating framework, and Magonismo, with its anarcho-
syndicalist "workers of the world unite" paradigm. By 1910, the Catholic Church
faced a fierce competitor for the loyalties of ethnic Mexicans—in particular,
women. The liberal Masonic community had developed a highly gendered
critique of the church. This chapter demonstrates how both Mexican liberalism, represented by the anticlericalism of an active Masonic community, and
Magonismo, represented by the Partido Liberal Mexicano (PLM), influenced
activism in south Texas, contributing significantly to the creation of a transborder political culture. That two of Mexico's most powerful ideological and
political camps re-created themselves in communities such as Laredo and San
Antonio underscores how easily south Texas activists adapted some of these
ideas. The heated debates between liberals and clergy in Mexico could be just as
intense when transplanted in the borderlands where the Idars used *La Crónica* to
expound on the virtues of liberalism and Freemasonry while heavily critiquing
the Catholic Church.

The origins of Masonry lie in seventeenth- and eighteenth-century liberalism. With chapters throughout the world, Freemasonry adheres to a philosophy of service to humanity, which has enmeshed the fraternal voluntary
association into many realms of public life. It is not surprising that many of

the political leaders of the United States, Mexico, and other nations have been Freemasons. In Mexico, Freemasons had long played significant roles in various reformist campaigns, including the struggle for Mexico's independence from Spain, the nineteenth-century War of Reform, and the Mexican Revolution. The US-Mexico borderlands served as yet another political stage for this secret society. Freemasons belonging to oppressed minority groups have used their Masonic philosophical tenets and organizational skills and networks to address social inequities. In the border community of Laredo, méxico-tejano Masons participated in the incipient struggle for human and civil rights.

Figure 2.1 Nicasio Idar was a thirty-third degree mason. Here he is wearing Freemasonry regalia. Nettie Lee Benson Latin American Collection, University of Texas Libraries, University of Texas at Austin.

By 1881, Laredo had Masonic Lodge #547, an American lodge that served the English-speaking community and those who identified with the United States, especially Laredo's Anglos. For Spanish speakers and those who, regardless of citizenship, nurtured a sense of Mexican cultural nationalism, the town boasted the Grand Mexican Masonic Lodge of Texas, the Order of the Knights of Honor, No. 14 Masonic Lodge, which had formed by the early twentieth century, and a Mexican lodge named in honor of Mexican president Benito Juárez that had formed by 1923.[3] The purpose of these fraternal orders as well as local area mutual aid societies was to achieve unity among la raza. They provided material assistance to members in need or to their families, such as widow and orphan benefits. For some organizations, unity allowed members to go beyond benevolence, stepping into the world of political activism and struggles for reform. This was the case for the Order of the Knights of Honor under whose auspices the First Mexicanist Congress was convened in 1911.[4]

Like Mexican and méxico-tejano Freemasonry, Magonismo started out with a reformist agenda. Both Freemasonry and Magonismo had roots in nineteenth-century Mexican liberal struggles for reform and both would play a role in the Mexican Revolution. By the fall of 1911, Mexico's revolution was well under way. Once a liberal reformer, Porfirio Díaz had turned into a much-denounced dictator. Indeed, his thirty-five-year reign became associated with the oppression of many sectors of Mexican society. Díaz had resigned in May and sailed for Europe, leaving a vacuum soon filled by another Freemason, the moderate rebel Francisco Madero.

Ostensibly, Díaz's removal from power and Madero's ascendancy was promising. However, to the leaders of the radical anarcho-syndicalist party, the Mexican Liberal Party led by Flores Magón, the political reforms of Madero's administration did little to counteract looming threats. Magonistas believed that antireelectionism and freedom of the press represented mere band-aids in a society marked by class conflict, autocratic rulers, and a powerful Catholic Church. Other discontented Mexicans saw in Madero's ascendancy further postponement of their ultimate goals. The Zapatista Movement in central and southern Mexico focused on land redistribution and peasant rights and gave no support to leaders whose interests conflicted with their own.[5] Amid this political climate, the astute Don Porfirio, preparing to leave for Europe, turned to his military escort and said: "Madero has unleashed a tiger. Now let's see if he can control it."[6]

The tiger that Madero had unleashed violently ravaged Mexico for ten years. Not until the early 1920s did Mexico stabilize in the aftermath of the revolution, although peace proved elusive as the Cristero War pitting the Catholic Church against the state broke out in the late 1920s. While Madero is credited with unleashing the revolution, the Magonistas served as *sembradores*, cultivators of the seeds of rebellion. By the late 1890s, the political activities of those who had banded together as members of the PLM led to their persecution and eventual exile to the United States. Particularly in the American Southwest, the PLM renewed its revolutionary ideology and launched the earliest organized attacks on the Porfiriato (the over-thirty-years rule of Mexican dictator Porfirio Díaz from 1876 to 1880 and from 1880 to 1911). It also established coalitions with American leftist groups including the International Workers of the World (IWW) and outspoken anarchists such as Emma Goldman.[7] What started as a critique of conditions in Mexico ultimately turned into an analysis of world systems judged to be unfair and oppressive to the majority of the world's population.

As a transborder movement for social change, Magonismo influenced méxico-tejano political culture, inspiring Mexicans in the United States, particularly the working class, to demand labor rights. Furthermore, Magonista leaders developed a political analysis that tied the local racial caste system in Texas to the struggle between workers and capital in the western hemisphere and beyond. They sought to inspire méxico-tejanos to see the connections between class and race and to demand fundamental rights that were the birthright of all men and women.[8]

Mexico for Mexicans!

Before they focused on racism in Texas, Magonista efforts centered on a revolution to claim Mexico for Mexicans. That project began with the rise to power of Don Porfirio Díaz. On 21 November 1876, a triumphant General Porfirio Díaz entered Mexico City having led a successful revolt against Sebastián Lerdo de Tejada, successor to Benito Juárez, the Mexican liberal president who had led the cause against the French and their conservative Mexican allies and who worked to consolidate the nation. Thus began El Porfiriato, or the reign of Don Porfirio Díaz.[9]

Porfiriato leaders represented a conservative faction within the Mexican liberal tradition. Conservative liberals believed in the sanctity of private property, social progress, and economic development, but they did not place personal freedoms at the center of the liberal nation. In fact, they strove to create a regime governed by "scientific politics" whereby the central government, guided by a powerful executive and scientifically trained advisors, determined the destiny of the nation-state by placing order and progress above individual liberties. In part, liberal conservatives (or Mexican positivists) believed that such centralization would be necessary until the Mexican masses were prepared to assume the responsibilities of full citizenship.[10]

The Mexican people did, in fact, understand the responsibilities of citizenship quite well as they practiced a form of grassroots democracy. Before the executive office under Díaz amassed so much power, Mexican democracy had primarily been expressed at the local municipal level where people participated in politics in impressive numbers. These were direct elections unlike state- and national-level elections in which "representatives" of the people chose leaders.[11]

The official explanation for indirect elections was that they safeguarded these offices from undue influences stemming from local interests. Ultimately, the representatives of the people or electors switched their allegiance from the people to powerful authorities that sought to control electoral outcomes. Lacking advocates, nonelite Mexicans suffered limits put on their political participation and representation after 1887. President Benito Juárez's liberal revolution of the mid-nineteenth century had narrowed the gap between the government and the governed, but the Díaz regime abrogated the social and political contract embedded in the Constitution of 1857.

The people pulled back from state and national politics to their communities and worked to hold on to as much political autonomy as possible; however, this municipal retreat only increased the power of the oligarchy in state government. Leaders in higher office showed even less regard for the people. Government spending on public services decreased, rule became even more authoritarian, and rigged elections were commonplace. Even local-level politics succumbed to corruption as the jefe politico (district chief), once an elected servant of the people, became an appointee of the governor. Jefes politicos devolved into Porfirian political bosses. The so-called constitutional reforms of 1887 made reelection of officials legal, so corrupt politicians could remain in office longer. Even before that, the National Guard, which had served as an organized citizen network, had been disbanded. The remaining armed forces were put under federal jurisdiction. By 1907 this degeneration of political democracy gave rise to opposition movements stemming from various constituencies, among them workers, middle-class social clubs, liberal constitutionalists, progressives, social Catholics, Protestants, and anarcho-syndicalist organizations.[12]

Prior to these mass mobilization efforts, the Porfirian regime had succeeded in creating a semblance of political stability. Its "scientific politics" had achieved favorable conditions for investment. Porfirio Díaz made it his primary goal to modernize Mexico, earning it a respectful place among the family of nations. The country's history of devastating wars and coup d'états, as well as the rise of banditry, justified a policy promoting law and order. Díaz astutely co-opted many of the bandits into a rural police force known as the rurales, which he used to suppress peasant revolts and to intimidate those who disagreed with his policies.[13]

Once he secured some measure of internal stability, Díaz opened up Mexico for massive foreign investment from the United States and Europe. By 1902, American investment in Mexico stood at $500 million, growing to $1.5

billion by 1910. William Randolph Hearst claimed vast cattle ranches, the Guggenheims and their American Smelting and Refining Company set up ore smelters, William Doheny owned the Mexican Petroleum Company, and the Waters Pierce Company (linked to Standard Oil) controlled the petroleum-rich Mexican Gulf Coast.[14] This investment capital transformed Mexico into a nation linked by 14,000 kilometers of railroad track with fast developing urban centers.[15]

Economic changes also affected many Mexican families as foreign investment in Mexican mines, petroleum, minerals, and agriculture attracted people from southern Mexican states to the more industrial northern states and more centrally located industrial areas such as Mexico City, Puebla, and Veracruz. These new jobs promised a liberal labor contracting system, monetized salaries, and a free labor market based on supply and demand as opposed to debt peonage. The newly constructed railroads facilitated long distance travel, and people soon established migration chains, which in a generation or two would extend across the border.[16]

Seemingly on the rise, Mexico enjoyed increased government investments in education and public hygiene. Liberals paid special attention to schools because they saw them as drivers of secular social change. But the rate of social change also depended on the economy, and Mexico faced steep economic challenges. Between 1870 and 1913, the international economy took off as free trade, the free expression of ideas, and the movement of capital across borders became common practices. When Mexico experienced a drop in purchasing power, its dependence on international market activity became apparent. No longer able to modernize its productive sector, its export business suffered. Essential imported machinery and supplies cost significantly more. While other nations converted to the gold standard, Mexico continued to rely on globally devalued silver, which discouraged direct foreign investment. Even Mexican capitalists plowed their profits into opportunities abroad rather than investing in Mexico. Ultimately, Mexico's economy did not expand on a par with the tremendous growth of a new international economic, financial, and trading system.[17]

The negative consequences of Mexico's modernization project can also be discerned at the social level. The Porfiriato era witnessed a growing rift between the rich and the poor. While a few elites enjoyed unprecedented personal wealth and a cosmopolitan lifestyle, the vast majority of Mexicans endured severe poverty, and a small middle class lived precariously close to poverty.[18] The oppression suffered by Mexicans at the hands of their own rulers went hand in hand with the unfair practices of American companies in Mexico. American capitalists operating in Mexico quickly established the custom of paying American employees in Mexico more than resident Mexicans for the same work. In addition, Mexicans endured dangerous working conditions and long working days. Women and children were especially vulnerable to exploitation. Eager to please the Americans, Díaz allowed such practices to flourish. The 1906 strike at the Cananea Mining Company in Sonora broke out over this dual-wage system and other hated policies.[19]

The dire conditions of the poor during the Porfiriato, as well as Díaz's denial of political and human rights for the Mexican people, led to the development of an opposition movement centered on the San Luis Potosí "Ponciano Arriaga" Liberal Club, established in 1900. The intellectuals who founded this club advocated the three "goals of nineteenth century liberalism: democracy, anticlericalism, and free enterprise."[20] An early leader of the Liberal Club or Precursor Movement was engineer Camilo Arriaga, a member of a displaced elite family. Other prominent leaders included the Flores Magón brothers—Ricardo, a law student, and Jesús, a lawyer, men of humble origins whose *mestizo* parents had been involved in the liberal reform movement of Benito Juárez. The brothers had participated in student demonstrations and began to value journalism's role in educating and propagandizing the masses. Ricardo worked for the anti-Díaz newspaper, *El Democrata*.

In 1900, the brothers embarked upon the daring venture of publishing a radical newspaper, *Regeneración* (Regeneration), a political organ dedicated to liberating Mexico from the clutches of dictatorship. In the newspaper's early days, Ricardo Flores Magón, who abandoned law school for journalism and organizing, operated as a liberal seeking reform in Mexico. These reforms included the rejuvenation of the liberal Constitution of 1857; a return to the anticlerical official policy of the Juarista government; and limits on foreign economic expansionism in Mexico.[21]

Although the United States no longer openly expressed desires to acquire more Mexican territory outright, American capitalist interests already owned a significant portion of Mexico's resources, and they treated Mexican workers on both sides of the border shamefully. Economic interests became one of the pillars of American foreign policy early on, as American capitalists began to connect their ability to survive with their ability to develop foreign markets for their surplus production.

The other major pillar of foreign policy was a sense of cultural superiority and a missionary zeal to dominate other societies for purposes of converting them to "the American way of life." Exporting American culture also created a desire in foreign societies for US goods and services. In the case of Mexico, both the economic and cultural aspects of American foreign policy proved detrimental as the former led to the transfer of resources from Mexican to American hands, and the latter gave Americans in Mexico license to inculcate American values for the purpose of "civilizing" a nation. Only in this way could the so-called Mexican Problem be resolved.[22]

Mexican intellectuals and activists at the time—the Flores Magón brothers, chief among them—critiqued the role of the American empire in Mexico. Along with many members of the middle class and displaced Mexican elites, they rallied around the cry "Mexico for Mexicans!"

Two Visions for a Mexico for Mexicans

Many agreed that Mexico should be for Mexicans, but radicals and liberals disagreed on which approach to take to accomplish the goal. Early on, the radically inclined Magonista movement took a strong anti–Catholic Church position. Its first leader, Camilo Arriaga, issued a manifesto on August 30, 1900, calling for the creation of Liberal Clubs and for a national convention to be held at San Luis Potosi in February 1901 to denounce resurgent clericalism. The renewed strength of the Catholic Church, despite the anticlerical 1857 Constitution and Reform Laws, represented the conciliatory strategy of the Porfiriato toward the clergy and its willingness to compromise long-standing liberal principles for its purposes of consolidation.[23]

Díaz's plan to integrate the church into his regime worked so well that even church officials acknowledged the special relationship. In a June 1900 speech before the General Assembly of International Congress of Catholic Agencies, Bishop José María Ignacio Montes de Oca y Obregón stated, "Under the benevolent leadership of President Díaz and with the support of Mexico's women, the Church in Mexico had achieved 'the prosperity it enjoys today.'" This alliance served as a clear indication to liberals that clerical, economic, and political elites had regained control of Mexico, making a mockery of the Reform Laws. It also motivated the unification of Mexican classical liberals at the San Luis Potosí conference to contain clericalism and to effect the application of the Reform Laws through legal channels.[24]

Ricardo Flores Magón and his brother Enrique enthusiastically awaited the liberal conference, hoping to turn priest-baiting liberals into anti-Díaz militants. Fifteen Masonic lodges attended and the San Luis Potosí conference was dominated by anticlerical speeches. Yet Flores Magón's statement that the "Díaz administration is a den of thieves!" turned out to be the political high point of the gathering. A month later, Arriaga issued a manifesto that went beyond anticlericalism, attacking the "dominating dictatorship," the "semi-official press," and the "personalist, undemocratic, and inappropriately named *Científico* Party." The liberals called for the establishment of a national party and the replacement of Díaz with a "generous, able, and progressive man."[25]

Under the auspices of the "Ponciano Arriaga" Liberal Club, liberals began to move toward the left, calling not only for restraints on the Catholic Church but also for a strong critique of the Díaz government. The transition from anticlericalism to anti-Díaz militancy was completed by November 1901 when liberals Camilo Arriaga and José María Facha issued a manifesto that addressed the need for agrarian reform, revealed the Díaz regime's exploitation of the Yaqui Indians, and attacked foreigner capitalists, "the privileged classes," and the Díaz dictatorship.[26]

The radicalization of the liberal group was in part facilitated by the government's ruthless suppression of political opposition. Suppression, in turn, led to divisions within the sector of liberal discontent. Upper-class moderate liberals, as well as strongly anticlerical Protestants and Masons, left the movement. Nevertheless, far more people joined the liberals and by 1901 some 150 Liberal Clubs operated openly, while many more met clandestinely.[27]

Through its newspaper, *Regeneración*, the reformist liberal cause gained exposure not only in Mexico but also in the American Southwest. An avid reader of *Regeneración* and a devoted supporter of the anti-Díaz movement, Mexico-born Laredo resident Sara Estela Ramírez offered her services to the cause despite her poverty, illness, and hostility to Magonismo by some sectors of her community. Ramírez worked as a Spanish teacher at the Laredo Seminary, a Methodist missionary–operated school for boys and girls, and may have been recruited by a local mutual aid society, as was the custom in those days. Many Texas schools discriminated against Mexican schoolchildren, and so Tejano leaders often recruited young educators in Mexico to teach at schools focusing on Mexican-origin children. Aware of the transborder struggles of Mexicans, Ramírez searched for solutions through activism. In a letter to Ricardo Flores Magón, she explained, "I am resolved to spend the little energies of my life in favor of liberalism, in spite of the mean insults . . . in spite of everything. We shall form the club without any doubt, besides it is necessary to prepare the terrain."[28] Ramírez's commitment soon earned her a respected position within the movement. She served as the Laredo representative of the "Ponciano Arriaga" Liberal Club based in Mexico and struggled to create a liberal club in the border city.[29]

Following in the liberal political tradition popular in Mexico as well as among progressives in the United States, Ramírez believed in the evolution of a more egalitarian society, and her critiques of the Díaz regime and attraction to the PLM stemmed from this political orientation. In addition to her work as a teacher and as a spokesperson for the reformist liberal cause, Ramírez composed poetry and published, beginning in June 1901, two newspapers—*La Corregidora* and *Aurora*. *La Corregidora* propagated liberal ideas very much aligned with early Magonista thought.[30]

Ramírez corresponded regularly with Ricardo Flores Magón between 1900 and 1904, often expressing her political views and the challenges she faced because of them. In 1901, for example, she mentioned the difficulty of initiating a liberal club in Laredo. A September 1903 letter found Ramírez calling for more newspapers "to awaken the public spirit . . . to educate the people and awaken their energy." She also wrote about her family's opposition to her activism and her personal turmoil.

> I was subjected by impotence and contrarieties. A tenacious position of some of the members of my family caused me to suffer much. . . . I didn't know what to do or how to reappear in the grandiose struggle; everything has passed now, finally, and I have returned to caress the beautiful liberty that smiles at me and relentlessly points out to me the despot who obstructs her from shining in our heaven.[31]

The lack of a critical mass of liberal supporters in Laredo illustrates the tremendous odds facing the anti-Díaz movement at this early stage. As a *sembradora*, or cultivator of the seeds of political change, Ramírez experienced many of the same insecurities and vagaries defining the lives of other activists. In December 1903, she faced dire straits: "Our lack of resources is complete and I don't know when we will find the solution."[32] In her subsequent letter, she expressed utter despair: "If I tell you that my days are black and continue to be black," she wrote, "I will tire you, although my blacknesses have become, as Juanita says, proverbial."[33]

Beyond poverty, the anti-Díaz movement faced persecution. While Ramírez was safe in Laredo, she worried constantly about her colleagues and friends in Mexico. Besides Ricardo Flores Magón, Ramírez also corresponded with Camilo Arriaga. To Flores Magón, she wrote, "Arriaga wrote yesterday with the alarming news, that assassins abound and our associates are in danger." When she learned about the imprisonment of fellow women activists Juana Belén Gutiérrez de Mendoza and Elisa Acuña y Rosseti, she expressed sorrow: "My black hours increase, my beloved Ricardo, with the sad situation we are all in. I think about my dear imprisoned, ill sisters, and my heart hurts not to be able to help them."[34]

Operating an anti-Díaz campaign in Mexico caused the Flores Magón brothers and other participants to be subjected to harassment, arrest, and violence, which they occasionally tried to escape north of the border. On January 4, 1904, their group arrived in Laredo. Sara Estela Ramírez welcomed them warmly, as did other liberal méxico-tejanos. In February, the "Ponciano Arriaga" Liberal Club met at Ramírez's home to discuss plans for a revolution, the reestablishment of *Regeneración*, and the founding of a new political party. Those present included both Mexicans and méxico-tejanos, both men and women, among them Ricardo and Enrique Flores Magón, Camilo Arriaga, Santiago de la Hoz, Paulino Martínez, Santiago de la Vega, Elisa Acuña y Rossetti, and Juana Gutiérrez de Mendoza.[35]

Over the course of the meeting, the ideological and political differences between the two major leaders became evident, as did the personal nature of a leadership struggle. A moderate faction coalesced around Camilo Arriaga, while the
more radical faction pledged their support for Ricardo Flores Magón. Ramírez
tried to find a middle ground, but to no avail. The group split, and she moved to
San Antonio in 1904 with members of the more moderate faction.[36] In her last
known letter to Ricardo Flores Magón, a disillusioned Ramírez wrote,

> I believed that there was union and true fraternity in our
> group. . . . I believed we could triumph, keep misery away from our-
> selves and be true redeemers, apostles of an idea; but it was not that
> way. . . . I was mistaken in my beliefs and today I don't know what to
> say about what I believe or hope for. . . . Each of those disenchantments
> leaves me a sorrowful impression on my soul.[37]

Although Ramírez did not directly blame either man for the schism, she eventually felt a greater affinity with the liberal reform agenda of Arriaga and was
unwilling to move in a the more radical direction. Still, she hoped that Flores
Magón might accept her decision without rancor: "I don't believe that my decision, absolutely spontaneous, will make me deserving of your enmity."[38]
Nonetheless, the break in their correspondence indicates that Flores Magón
may have felt embittered and betrayed. When Ramírez died at age twenty-nine
in 1910, fellow journalist Clemente N. Idar pointed out at her funeral that "she
found herself abandoned by her friends and struggled with this rejection."[39]

Moderates were not the only ones who moved to San Antonio. The Flores
Magón brothers also made their move in 1904 and reestablished *Regeneración*
there. San Antonio, being farther from the border, offered more protection to all
political factions exiled from Mexico before and during the Mexican Revolution.
Still, for the radicals, even San Antonio proved an unstable haven. So, to avoid
further persecution in Texas, they moved in 1905 to St. Louis, Missouri, where
they founded the Mexican Liberal Party. Flores Magón moved from liberal reform to a vague form of socialism, and by 1908, the Magonistas would embrace
anarcho-communism. By then the Magonistas had moved their operation to Los
Angeles, having been persecuted and arrested in St. Louis.[40]

In Laredo, the popularity of the Magonistas waned as they moved toward socialism. *El Democrata Fronterizo* of Laredo developed a critique of the Magonista
movement. In an article in 1907, for example, Jacobo Ayala Villarreal ridiculed
the Magonistas for their intra-group conflicts, stating that rather than focus
on which Magonista would get what post upon overthrowing Díaz, the group
would do best to concentrate on overthrowing the regime first.[41] By 1911, *La
Crónica* condemned the Magonistas as "socialist swindlers who with the money

of thousands of reckless but honest workers gave themselves the grand life."[42] According to *La Crónica*, if the socialist utopia became a reality, it would lead to the loss of more Mexican land to Americans, making the Flores Magones traitors. Given that Nicasio Idar, publisher of *La Crónica*, was also involved in the real estate market, it is not surprising that he and his associates found the Magonista shift to socialism and anarcho-communism both contrary to classical liberal principles and threatening to their business interests.[43]

The critiques of the Magonista movement also broadened to include critiques of American leftist movements that were sympathetic to and assisted the Magonistas. In one instance, *La Crónica* strongly condemned American socialist John Kenneth Turner's book, *Barbarous Mexico*, for grossly misrepresenting Mexico. A friend of Ricardo Flores Magón and his Mexican Liberal Party, Turner had traveled to Mexico between 1908 and 1910 to collect materials for his book with the assistance of Lázaro Gutiérrez de Lara, a PLM socialist. *Barbarous Mexico* reflected the shared belief of the American left and the PLM that the Mexican people suffered tremendous oppressions, particularly the peasantry and the workers. Besides reporting on the widespread poverty and exploitation of many Mexican workers, Turner exposed Díaz as a repressive dictator ruling over an unwilling people who maintained his power through intimidation and violence. For years, Díaz had received much praise for bringing order and modernization to Mexico, and Turner's book caused an uproar for exposing the less savory aspects of Mexico's development.[44] Although liberals, too, were critical of the dictatorship, many took offense with Turner's portrayal of Mexico as a backward country. *La Crónica* presented a strong Mexican nationalist critique of Turner's analysis, painting the well-intentioned socialist as an interloping Yankee doing far more harm than good to the legitimate reform movement in Mexico.[45]

While cognizant of the many ills of Porfirian authoritarianism and concerned about economic policies that hurt Mexico's working classes, the Idar family was not prepared for the anarcho-syndicalist revolution heralded by the Magonistas. Freemasonry represented a type of modernity that the Idars found congenial to their value system as interlocutors within the broader universe of bourgeois culture. Federico Idar, like his family members in Laredo and San Antonio, belonged to a Freemason lodge in Monterrey, Nuevo Leon, Mexico. His papers reveal much about his philosophy. These articles are unsigned. Idar may have been the author or perhaps these were speeches delivered by fellow Masons at their lodge meetings. In either case, the fact that Idar kept these documents and his family later donated them to a university archive says something about the importance the Idar family attached to the ideals represented in these papers.

The Nuevo Leonesa Freemason Lodge motto—"Potent work and immaculate life"—conveys much about the purposes of the fraternity. In terms of the immaculate life, a February 1931 essay demonstrates the need for self-discovery as a stepping-stone toward self-actualization. "The Masons in the lodge, as a first condition to be useful, should discover who we are. We should find ourselves, go toward the spirit using intelligence and from this point reach the soul to get from it all that is of value." At the center of such exercises lay a strong commitment to fraternity, local and national communities, and the world. Leading an immaculate life at heart was about preparing oneself for the potent works of service that each Mason was called to manifest.[46]

The tenets of Freemasonry were formed in Britain, and wherever subjects of the Empire went, they either formed or joined an existing lodge in an effort to facilitate their transplantation into a foreign society. Masonic lodges provided members with emotional, social, intellectual, and material resources to help them adapt to life in the colony. At the heart of their intracultural core value system lay three principles. The first principle was a universal brotherhood adopted by the fraternity in an effort to heal religion-based divisions. They accomplished this by admitting members of different faith traditions. The only requirement was a belief in God or a supreme deity sometimes referred to as the "Great Architect." Second, Freemasons adhered to the principle of tolerance, also connected with their desire to achieve a universal brotherhood. Finally, they preached and practiced benevolence. Masons were supposed to assist other Masons in need and if a Mason died, his widow and orphans were supposed to be able to count on the brothers to assist in any way possible. Additionally, lodges participated in charitable projects of benefit to nonmembers or the community at large.[47]

It seems ironic that men of color in Texas and Mexico eagerly adopted a tool for empire. And yet, Mexican and Tejano Freemasons used the imperial discourse to advance an agenda for human and civil rights. Although Mexico was not a part of the British Empire, its politics, nonetheless, navigated between two imperialistic strains, the legacies of three centuries of Spanish colonial dominance and a neo-colonial relationship with the United States. México-tejanos communicated with Americans in the modernist language of Masonic brotherhood, sharing with them the privileged linkages to the Enlightenment, philosophical ties that included a harsh critique of authoritative institutions such as the Catholic Church.

The negative opinion that many méxico-tejanos of the middle class held of the Magonista movement by 1910 makes it unlikely that Magonismo influenced *La Crónica's* strong anticlerical positions. While Magonismo inspired many méxico-tejano workers and activists, middle-class méxico-tejanos, though often sympathetic to Magonista calls for social justice, did not embrace the anarcho-communist vision that Ricardo Flores Magón and his followers struggled to achieve. The anti-Catholic articles in the pages of *La Crónica* reveal two far stronger influences: traditional Mexican liberalism and Freemasonry.[48]

Many of these méxico-tejano liberals who arrived in south Texas during the 1880s from the northern states of Mexico were well versed in Mexico's history and revered that nation's champion of republican ideals and liberal reform, Benito Juárez. Like their counterparts in Mexico, méxico-tejano liberals desired a constitutional government and representative democracy focused on protecting the natural rights and political liberties of citizens. In this framework, capitalism served as a means of maximizing economic utility. Transnational liberals tended to steer clear of hard-line ideology, making room for the possibility of broader government participation, especially as a means of regulating capitalism when abuses threatened the greater social and economic good. [49]

In the United States, republicanism, Protestantism, and capitalism grew alongside each other, more or less peacefully, under the broad ideological framework of classical liberalism, whereas in Mexico, Protestants have always represented a religious minority. With the vast majority of Mexicans practicing Catholicism, the Catholic Church and those supportive of the clergy were able to survive the ascendancy of liberalism during the nineteenth century. The battle against the church and its conservative defenders made Mexican liberalism unique in its, at times, single-minded focus on an anticlerical agenda. Thus, it made sense that the first political opposition conference held in San Luis Potosí critiqued Díaz first and foremost for allowing the church to regain some of its past glory and power. Only later, with the influence of radically minded activists such as Ricardo Flores Magón, did liberals channel their reformist energies toward some of the other abuses of the Porfiriato.

With such a strong anticlerical liberal heritage, it was not surprising that middle-class méxico-tejanos in Laredo took issue with the policies and practices of the Catholic Church. A second influence also helps to explain their staunch positions. Many Mexican and méxico-tejano liberals belonged to fraternal orders. The history of Freemasonry in Mexico dates to the birth of Mexican liberalism and the nation itself. Many Mexican revolutionaries, including the "Father of Mexican Independence," Catholic priest Miguel Hidalgo, were Freemasons. So too were Benito Juárez and Porfirio Díaz, as was Francisco Madero, leader of the liberal cause.[50]

Madero's connection to liberal Masonry, as well as his background as a *norteño* with familial and business connections in northern Mexico and Texas, made him a particularly appealing revolutionary leader to the middle-class fronterizo community.[51] Alarmed by Díaz's abuses in Mexico, they also hoped for post-revolution political stability and free enterprise in the motherland since they remained culturally and economically tied to it.

Like their brothers in northern Mexico, fronterizo liberal Freemasons sought to get rid of a despised tyrant and to bring about political reforms with enough economic programs to change an abusive capitalist system. Significantly, they associated the Catholic Church with the nation's "backwardness" and saw it as complicit in the historical abuses of Mexico's conservative rulers, including Díaz. Hence, much of their energy focused on anticlerical campaigns. For their part, church leaders in Mexico and throughout the world condemned and often excommunicated men who became Freemasons, arguing that the secretive nature of Masonic societies made them suspect, dangerous, and anti-Catholic.

La Crónica's Anticlerical Crusade

Liberalism and Masonry joined to produce a méxico-tejano-gendered critique of the Catholic Church. These liberal Masons expressed their displeasure that Catholic priests often invaded the sacred space of the family and thus exercised "unnatural" influence over wives and mothers. At the heart of *La Crónica's* critique of the Catholic Church lay the classical liberal idea of "separation of church and state." The Constitution of 1857 as well as the Reform Laws sought to eliminate special corporate privileges granted to the Catholic Church. As an anonymous *La Crónica* writer pointed out in 1910,

> Fifty-three years ago, Mexico, the nation of Juárez, Ocampo y Lerdo de Tejada, proclaimed the most free, most liberal and wisest constitution; placing upon it as an ineludible base, the principle of "separation of church and state!" How many intrigues and treasons, how many vexations and degradations did the corrupt Mexican clergy commit in order to obstruct the liberty of the nation![52]

The author reminded readers that patriotic Mexicans stood up against the clergy, an invading French army, and those who betrayed the nation to defeat the "black bird that extended its sickening wings over the territory and conscience of the Mexican nation."[53]

La Crónica condemned religious fanaticism and blamed it for Mexico's high illiteracy rate. Reprinting a story about 30 million Mexican Catholics celebrating the December 12 feast day of La Virgen de Guadalupe, of whom a significant number were Indian, a *La Crónica* writer disdainfully editorialized,

> Our readers will judge these conditions deficient in culture and civilization in which the overwhelming majority of the inhabitants of the Mexican Republic find themselves .... [E]ighty three percent are illiterates who vegetate like pariahs, unconscious of their existence

and ignorant of their rights and duties as citizens of a Republic that proclaims to figure in the vanguard of the most cultured and powerful nations on earth.[54]

The writer blamed the caretakers of the basilica of La Virgen de Guadalupe and the church in general for keeping the people in a state of ignorance in order to exploit them. Going so far as to call the basilica a "gold mine" for its owners, the writer accused the church of enriching itself while the Indian and the nation atrophied. According to this writer, a nation's truest treasure was the intellectual development of its people, a process the church in Mexico undermined.[55]

La Crónica frequently reprinted articles upholding science as the "mother of civilization, cultured and refined," while denigrating religion as "degradable, acrimonious, oppressive, and inhuman."[56] It often compared Masonry and Roman Catholicism. In one such article, J. Peña Barrera argued that the fruits of "Romanism" had been "fanaticism, errors, superstitions, infamies, immoralities, exploitations, hypocrisies, inquisitions, poisonings, wars, crusades, adulteries, persecutions, sarcasms, tortures." When it came to Masonry, Peña Barrera opined that its fruits were "healthy, sweet, and useful to humanity, the nation, society, the home, to freedom of conscience and thought, truths, greatness, morality, union, harmony, progress, perfectionism, Constitution, reforms, liberty . . . democracy, republicanism, liberal institutions, and justice." Romanism had produced cruel inquisition leaders such as Torquemada, Barrera noted, while Masonry counted on republicans such as Washington, Hidalgo, and Juárez among its most illustrious members.[57] Nonetheless, most Mexicans in Mexico and Texas related to the Catholic Church in some capacity, if not always as devout followers, at least as nominal Catholics. Thus, *La Crónica* defended itself from its detractors by pointing out how Catholic leaders failed to practice what they preached.

The debates between *La Crónica* and *La Revista Católica* of New Mexico best illustrate the antagonistic relationship between Masonic liberals and the Catholic Church. The main subjects of these debates tended to be the role of women within the church and society and the role that the priesthood played in the community. Masons believed that the priests exercised too much influence over the female laity and, by extension, their families. The struggle over the minds and hearts of women was a vicious one because both liberals and the church understood that women functioned as the transmitters of cultural values to future generations. Thus, it was critical for both liberal Freemasons and conservative clergymen to compete for women's loyalty, if their particular worldview was to prevail. The Jesuit priests in charge of *La Revista* challenged the writers of *La Crónica* to justify their position that men should be the sole owners of a woman's secrets, her consciousness, and even her soul, to which *La Crónica* responded:

> Woman belongs to man in her entirety and should not have secrets from him; in the sacred sanctuary of her conscience only her husband should penetrate; and no other intruder should violate it; the woman belongs to her husband as her husband belongs to her only. It is the most sacred pact that can be celebrated between two human beings ... and if you, abdicating your sacred right to be men in every sense of the word, do not know what it is to be husband and father of a family, how do you pretend to be masters of the conscience and secrets of woman and to direct her in the sublime mission of wife and mother?[58]

While this philosophy held the promise of equal opportunity for all, its development in modernizing societies still reflected a patriarchal ethos whereby husbands could exercise supremacy over wives. In addition, republicanism accommodated, rather than challenged, patriarchy, at least initially. Liberal méxico-tejanos carried a vision of the idealized republic in their minds and worked to recreate it in society. In this world, husbands served their country as soldiers and patriotic citizens while their wives supported the nation by sustaining the household and family, fulfilling the sacred mandate of raising civic-minded children.[59]

The author also referred to biblical passages for evidence of God's intent that man and woman become one and form a home.[60] According to the author, men and women belonged to a "natural order," which priests violated when they decided not to exercise their God-given right to be husbands and fathers. Furthermore, in competing with husbands for their wives' attention, priests violated property rights, for in the "natural order" women belonged to men.

México-tejano liberals seemed preoccupied with the significant influence that Catholic priests had on many families through the agency of women. As long as his wife remained devoted to priests, a man, no matter how liberated from church dogma, might experience the dominance of the church in his own household.[61] The main enemy appeared to be the confessional, where a priest received free access to the social life of families and women confessed their intimate secrets and longings.[62] To have their male authority within the family violated by the exchange of personal and familial information from their wives to priest confessors represented a serious threat. Ultimately, what méxico-tejanos feared most was not the physical corruption of the women in their households but the struggle over the hearts and minds of women. As a *La Crónica* writer stated plainly, "We do not want the woman to stop believing in whatever God strikes her fancy .... [W]e only want to destroy the idols of the woman's heart and have her turn her face once again to her God so that she can adore him with more intelligence, freely, not for pay."[63]

How women actually weighed in on the debate between liberalism and clericalism is difficult to assess because some authors of anticlerical articles chose to remain anonymous. Jovita Idar and Sara Estela Ramírez regularly contributed articles to *La Crónica* so it is possible they might have written anticlerical pieces. Since Ramírez was a member of the Mexican Liberal Party and Idar belonged to the Methodist Church, these two women who did not have significant ties to the Catholic Church might have been in a position to critique it. One anticlerical article signed simply "Una Cristiana," which may have been written by a woman, echoed anticlerical diatribes but called for maternal authority.

> The confessional scares me, and I advise mothers to teach their daughters to confess their guilts and faults to God, or to confess them to their mothers instead of confessing them before the lattice of the confessional, to the ear of a man who has no right to listen to the conscience of youth, and who is susceptible to feel all of the human passions precisely because he is human and celibate. The mother loves her daughters with heartfelt, immense, pure, and incomparable love, and she is the legitimate confessor of the family and the legitimate counselor of the home.[64]

While the writer intended to de-legitimize the role of the priests in family life, these words also convey the liberal position that many méxico-tejano Masons held regarding women. Though a traditional role based on a "naturalized order," the role of the wife and mother was also invested with powers believed to be the exclusive domain of women. Indeed, many middle-class women within the méxico-tejano community expanded their nurturing roles into the public arena. Their male counterparts often accepted maternalist political strategies that took women outside the home, but they simultaneously celebrated women's traditional roles as caregivers and nurturers.

Individual freedom to worship without the intercession of popes and priests became a central issue for liberal Mexicans in Mexico and Texas. Questioning institutions that stood in the way of freedom, such as Catholic Church, represented a first step in questioning all institutions that limited the political liberties and rights of a nation's citizenry. Liberal gente decente méxico-tejanos, though great admirers of American republican institutions on an abstract level, also formulated a critique of the racial and class discrimination permeating these institutions. Some méxico-tejanos only critiqued racial discrimination, leaving their class privilege uninterrogated. On the subject of Mexican politics, the record is mixed for liberal méxico-tejanos, with some taking on proactive left-of-center positions, others remaining loyal to the established government, and still others opting for moderate reforms. The left-of-center position of the Magonistas and the méxico-tejano liberal agenda that set the stage for fronterizo politics coexisted within transborder political culture. Both reimagined their particular local concerns for the plight of Mexican-origin people as part of a broader international struggle for labor and civil rights, reiterating that la raza existed as a transborder people.

Magonismo and the Quest for Justice in Texas and Beyond

Ricardo Flores Magón, like the liberals, had also challenged the authority of the Catholic Church as one of the three most dominant institutions in Mexico. But even before he crossed over into the United States, Flores Magón's energy centered on an economic system, capitalism, and the state power that protected it. His experiences in the United States inspired him to cast a much wider net than the struggle for Mexico's working classes. Flores Magón sought to understand the plight of Mexican workers toiling abroad under the system of global capitalism. Soon Magonistas analyzed the discrimination they witnessed in the United States as well as the persecution they experienced both as Mexicans and as labor and revolutionary organizers.

The Magonistas were also part of the international anarchist movement that spanned from the 1840s, when French writer Pierre-Joseph Proudhon began to advocate his ideas of individualist freedom, the rejection of government and nonworking proprietors, economic equality, and free association, to 1939, when the Spanish Republic and anarchists were defeated by fascist Francisco Franco. Like anarchists elsewhere, the Magonistas sought to dismantle what they saw as the oppressive capitalist system and the complicitous state. While Proudhon and other anarchists emphasized the sovereignty of the individual, the PLM focused on the sovereignty of the people. Proudhon appreciated the concept of mutual aid, and Flores Magón probably agreed with him, delighting in seeing Mexicans and the southwestern US Mexican-origin people join together to help members of their community. The view that people could come together in cooperation and govern themselves without institutions that would interfere with the people's rights and liberties represented the utopian dream of a group heavily persecuted but idealistic enough to envision a transnational movement of the downtrodden against those who profited from their labor.[65]

Although Flores Magón used Mexican nationalism to build his movement and galvanize people against a common enemy, he succeeded in transcending nationalism on a couple of levels. First, he worked well with American leftists and was highly aware of the radical ideas of his era from across the globe. Second, because he stretched "nationalism" to be more inclusive, he could organize among borderlands Mexican-origin people and help them seek redress from racism and economic inequities.[66]

Flores Magón and his compatriots stayed in Texas for only a year, but their impact on radical ethnic Mexican politics cannot be underestimated. In the central Texas cotton belt between 1912 and 1916, as historian Emilio Zamora shows, Mexican workers involved with the Texas Socialist Party and the Land League often traced their ideological roots to Magonismo and some participated in PLM organizational drives and attacks on the Mexican government of Porfirio Díaz.[67]

In Laredo, socialism thrived briefly in 1906 within the ranks of the Federal Labor Union (FLU), a group that led a strike against the Mexican National Railway Company. This union organized workers throughout the industry, ignoring craft-based distinctions. The FLU used its main organ, *El Defensor del Obrero*, to publish responses to attacks levied upon it by the middle-class newspaper, *El Democrata Fronterizo*. While *El Democrata Fronterizo* called for harmony among the classes, the reformation of capitalism, and patience and self-edification among the workers, *El Defensor del Obrero* took on a militant socialist position, demanding for their rights as workers.[68]

It is unclear whether the proletariat consciousness expressed in *El Defensor del Obrero* owed a direct debt to Ricardo Flores Magón and his associates. The presence of PLM sympathizers in Laredo, however, is certainly evident. In a letter from October 1905, Ricardo Flores Magón, then living in St. Louis, wrote to Laredoans Crescencio and Francisco Villarreal Márquez asking for advice on how to smuggle 8,000 copies of *Regeneración* across the international border. In this same letter, he implored the Villarreal Márquez brothers to be patient, for only through careful planning and implementation might the revolution succeed.[69] Several months later, Flores Magón wrote to the Villarreal Márquez brothers to congratulate them for their "noble enthusiasm" for the cause and to agree with them that a peaceful revolution represented an unrealistic hope. They also reiterated that revolution required patience and judiciousness. Only through superb organization and the intelligent marshaling of resources, he argued, could they ever hope to present a formidable challenge not just to the Díaz government but to the entire corrupt structure that allowed tyrants to thrive. Flores Magón critiqued the bourgeois political revolution, particularly its principal leader, Francisco Madero, and called for a social revolution that truly represented the interests of the people. He further warned the Villarreal Márquez brothers about those who possessed too many ties to the establishment to appreciate the liberal vision, including his former ally, Camilo Arriaga.[70]

Ricardo Flores Magón's liberal vision of society had gravitated toward a socialist (and later anarchist) agenda. Seeing the working classes in Texas, Mexico, and throughout the world as hopelessly tied to an abusive capitalist system, Flores Magón and his followers came to believe that only by completely remaking society could workers have a chance at true emancipation. An analysis of the PLM's newspaper, *Regeneración*, and other writings provides insight into how the Magonistas understood their cause through the multiple lenses of Texas's racial hierachy, Mexico's revolutionary struggle, and the antagonisms between classical liberal and socialist/anarchist visions of society.

Early Magonista letters dated between 1904 and 1906 often emphasized two key themes: liberalism and nationalism. In a 1905 letter addressed to Señor Don José María Valenzuela, Magonista professor Librado Rivera and Antonio L. Villarreal wrote that "the people" sought popular sovereignty and would achieve it with the press as their guide. "The flame of patriotism burns in millions of hearts from whose influence will the young Mexican nation emerge more beautiful, richer, and more handsome . . . . [W]e are attracted by the . . . ideal of humanity. Progress!"[71]

Liberal hallmarks such as freedom of the press, rule by popular sovereignty, and concepts of justice and liberty are all present in Magonista writings, as are treatises about Mexican nationalism and patriotism. During these early years, the Magonistas often hid any anarchist tendencies, presenting a liberal reform program to the public. In 1905, for example, the PLM closed its organizational statement with the words "Reform, Liberty, and Justice."[72]

By the time of the Mexican Revolution, the Flores Magón brothers and their followers had either undergone an ideological transformation or no longer hid their true political ideas and intentions. In an article published in *Regeneración* on April 3, 1911, the Magonistas clearly distinguished themselves from bourgeois reformers, though they still called themselves liberals. They wrote that Madero's Antireelection Party sought "to found . . . a bourgeois republic like the United States." This goal made it natural for left-leaning liberals to organize the PLM as an oppositional party. Magonistas believed that the Antireelection Party considered the PLM a threat to "the survival of the bourgeois republic that guarantees to the politicians, the job-seekers, the rich, all of the ambitious, to those who wish to live at the expense of the suffering and slavery of the proletariat."[73] According to the Magonistas, agitation and revolution were the only ways to resolve social inequities in Mexico. They asked for three things from the workers everywhere in the world: "world protest against the intervention of the powerful in Mexican affairs, workers' consciousness and determination to propagate the doctrines of social emancipation . . . , and money, money and more money for the fomentation of the social revolution in Mexico."[74]

Díaz served merely as a figurehead for the larger enemy, worldwide cap-italism and the bourgeois sociopolitical structure that protected it. Only by expropriating and redistributing the land and by handing the means of pro-duction to the workers could true emancipation and redemption be attained. However, wresting power from Mexican landlords would not solve all of the problems because Americans claimed so much of Mexico's land and resources. In a sharp analysis, Ricardo Flores Magón argued that the imperialist politics of the North American giant not only created antagonisms between the United States and Latin America but also served to "divide and conquer" the different races living in the hemisphere.

Not the North American people, but the greediness of the great North American millionaires; that country's plutocracy's thirst for gold has been the origin of this sentiment that makes the fraternity among the citizens who popu-late this continent difficult and slow, for while those who have emancipated our-selves from the principles of race work to create fraternal bonds among all men, the millionaires, the great negotiators, the bandits of finance, try with their acts to divide the nations, to open chasms among the diverse races and the diverse nationalities, so in that way, they secure their empire: "divide and conquer," said Machiavelli.[75]

Flores Magón went on to list the outrages committed by American capitalists upon citizens of Colombia, Venezuela, and other nations whose only crime was living on rich lands that tempted the greed of "Wall St. vampires." These "vampires," according to Flores Magón, supported and sustained tyrants such as Díaz in Mexico and Manuel Estrada Cabrera in Guatemala precisely because such dictators gave them free rein over foreign lands, resources, and peoples. Thus, according to Flores Magón's Marxist politics, the workers of the world needed to rise up as "one man" to challenge global capitalism.[76]

Flores Magón's analysis easily shifted from the global to the local. Having spent time in the United States, he noticed the harsh treatment received by Mexicans there, particularly in Texas. In an article condemning the horrific lynching of Antonio Rodríguez in Rock Springs, Texas, Flores Magón wrote in 1910:

All know with what disdain the Mexican race is generally treated, all know that in Texas, Mexicans are treated in a manner worse than Blacks. In the hotels, restaurants, and other public establishments in Texas, Mexicans are not admitted. The official schools close their doors to the children of our race. Semi-savage North Americans use Mexicans as target practice. . . . In the so-called courts of justice, Mexicans are generally judged without any formality whatsoever and they are sentenced for hanging or to suffer tremendous sentences, without there being evidence, without the smallest suspicion that they might have committed the crime for which they are made to suffer.[77]

These degradations were as detestable as the degradations suffered by Mexicans in Mexico at the hands of rich North American investors who considered Mexico "a conquered nation" and fair game for them. The racial divide promoted by capital made fraternity and love between the two races all the more difficult. Thus, the Magonistas' political trajectory shifted from a struggle for liberal reform in Mexico, to a campaign against Díaz, to a global battle against capital that underscored the relationship between the propagation of capital and the creation of racialized caste systems.

In making a connection between racism and capitalism, Flores Magón saw how lower-class Mexicans paid the heavy price of modernity while the more privileged class in Mexico and foreign investors accrued the benefits. In an article defending a group of PLM revolutionaries who were falsely accused of killing Sheriff Candelario Ortiz and arrested by Texas Rangers as they made their way to Mexico, he angrily lashed out against the authorities for selectively arresting revolutionaries based on their class and politics. "Our comrades were at a great distance from where the body of the minion of the law was found. Nevertheless, upon them they are trying to place responsibility for a dog of capital for the simple reason that our brothers imprisoned in Texas are poor and rebels."[78]

This article, in addition to condemning North American authorities for detaining PLM revolutionaries, sought to raise the consciousness of méxico-tejanos in hopes that they might lend moral and financial support to the cause of freeing the revolutionaries. Flores Magón reminded them of their own plight as second-class citizens in Texas.

> Who among you has not received an outrage in this country, for the only reason of being a Mexican? Who among you has not heard of the crimes committed against persons of our race? Don't you know that in the Southern part of this nation Mexicans are not permitted to sit in restaurants next to a North American? Have you not entered a barbershop where you have been told, after being looked over from head to toe, "Here we do not serve Mexicans?" Don't you know that the U.S. prisons are full of Mexicans? And have you even counted the number of Mexicans hanged in this country or who have perished burned by brutal multitudes of White people?[79]

Flores Magón went on to make a plea for contributions toward the legal defense of the fourteen imprisoned PLM rebels and called for a day-long strike in protest. If these measures did not bring about the desired results, he declared, the only remaining option would be to rise up against injustice using the barricade and dynamite.[80] To Flores Magón, the PLM struggle to free Mexico from tyranny and the méxico-tejano struggle for human rights were related and could require anarchist solutions across the national border.

Flores Magón blamed the lack of global worker solidarity on capitalism, which created national and racial divides between the working classes. The links he drew between global capitalism and the creation of racial nationalist divides are instructive but also limited. For one, his analysis focused on elites, solely blaming wealthy capitalists for the race-based divisions found within the working classes. He failed to recognize that workers who identified with the dominant "white" racial group also benefited from racial hierarchies.[81]

Under special circumstances, Mexicans benefited from the social construction of whiteness when white landowners chose them instead of white tenants and sharecroppers who refused to work for the lower wages paid to Mexicans. As these lower-class European Americans lost ground on the agricultural ladder, some Mexicans gained economically and socially since farmers came to see them as more reliable and, thus, desirable workers. Racist socialist labor leader Thomas Hickey also praised Mexicans for possessing the courage to join labor movements more readily than their European American counterparts. Still, Mexicans were being admired for their willingness to be exploited, on the one hand, and to risk their livelihoods and lives, on the other.[82]

A second critique of Magon's analysis of the absence of transnational worker solidarity is that it fails to account for worker identification with bourgeois values. In Mexico, as in the United States, some workers rebelled against their middle- and upper-class employers, but many others accepted the status quo and even planned for their own social and economic mobility by adopting a middle-class value system. For example, permanent mine workers in the Mexican state of Chihuahua often adopted middle-class values with the hope of someday climbing out of poverty.[83] Just because a group might be materially representative of a working class does not mean that this group identifies with a working-class ethos on a psychological or ideological level.

During the early years of the twentieth century it might have seemed realistic for an idealist such as Ricardo Flores Magón to imagine a world where Mexican workers could find working-class allies in other nations, including the United States. What is significant about the Magonista analysis is not so much the connection between class and race that it tried to draw but rather the local/ global nexus sustaining these relationships. Flores Magón understood that the local conditions of fronterizos in Texas and the Mexican proletariat in Mexico were part of transnational phenomena. Having experienced marginalization within two societies enmeshed in these developing economic structures and willing to use their privileges as educated men and women connected by the

PLM transnational network to help those exploited by capitalism, Magonistas represented the more radical side of the transborder political culture.

Women's Emancipation from Capitalist Exploitation within a Natural Order

The Magonista Marxist analysis went beyond race and class. In an essay addressed to Mexican women, Ricardo Flores Magón formulated a gender analysis that placed women on par with men in terms of the degree of suffering they sustained under a brutal capitalist system.

> Compañeras [female comrades], do not fear the revolution. You constitute one-half of the human species and what affects humanity affects you as an integral part of it. If men are slaves, you are too. Bondage does not recognize sex; the infamy that degrades men equally degrades you. You cannot escape the shame of oppression. The same forces that conquer men strangle you.[84]

In reality, it was far more challenging for women than for men to survive under capitalism. "Because you are a woman you are paid less than men, and made to work harder. You must suffer the impertinence of foreman or proprietor; and if you are attractive, the bosses will make advances."[85] Thus, women were both equally oppressed as workers and particularly vulnerable as women workers.

What Flores Magón failed to acknowledge was that patriarchy, not capitalism, had been the longest and most enduring oppressive ideology for women. Indeed, the radical group never achieved its lofty goals for women because it could not imagine them outside a traditional "natural order."[86] When Flores Magón exhorted women to do their part for the revolution, it consisted of supporting men.

> Your duty is to help man; to be there to encourage him when he vacillates; to stand by his side when he suffers; to lighten his sorrow; to laugh and to sing with him when victory smiles. You don't understand politics? This is not a question of politics; this is a matter of life or death. Man's bondage is yours and perhaps yours is more sorrowful, more sinister, and more infamous.[87]

In calling for the propagation of traditional gender roles, Magonistas further contributed to the oppression of women—an oppression that went far beyond class exploitation. In this sense, the Magonista gender analysis proved as limiting as their race analysis.[88]

Magonistas went so far as to decry feminism as an affront to the "natural order" of the sexes. In a *Regeneración* article, Práxedis Guerrero denounced feminism as "the fundamental antagonism to women's emancipation." To him:

> there is nothing attractive about a masculine female who is divorced from her sweet mission as a woman; there is nothing desirable about a woman who prefers to be manly instead of womanly. . . . Equality between the sexes will not make men out of women; instead it will enforce equal opportunities without disturbing the natural order between the sexes. Women and men must both fight for this kind of rational equality because without it there will only be tyranny and misery.[89]

In this natural order, women's primary function consisted of nurturing and serving their husbands and family at home. Within the context of the revolution, this meant encouraging their male relatives to fight to protect that home. Ironically, it was the revolution that took many Magonista women into the public arena.

Among the group of Magonista women who helped to define what the revolution meant for them were the outspoken women journalists who wrote articles in Mexico, Texas, and California, including the Villarreal sisters and Paula Carmona de Flores Magón. Margarita Ortega and her daughter Rosaura Gortari were two daring women soldiers who smuggled supplies from California into Baja California, Mexico. Gortari died during an escape. Huerta's army captured her mother who was tortured and killed.[90] Some women such as Josefa Fierro smuggled weapons across the same border. This mother ingeniously hid rifles under baby carriage bedding before placing her infant daughter Josefina on top. Resilient women such as María Talavera and Juana Gutéirrez de Mendoza survived imprisonment. And feminists who challenged the unequal treatment of women included Sara Estela Ramírez, Elisa Acuña y Rosetti, and Blanca de Moncaleano.[91] As the revolution progressed, more and more women joined men in the battlefields as camp followers, messengers, spies, and soldiers, but it was the journalists who left writings that offer a glimpse into how they understood their economic and political condition as Mexicans and as women.

As precursors to the Mexican Revolution, alongside men, women expressed liberal ideas that became radical expressions of discontent during the authoritative regime of Porfirio Díaz. On the matter of economic conditions in Mexico, the Director of *El Obrero: Periódico Independiente* (The Worker: Independent Newspaper), Andrea Villareal encouraged PLM supporters, stating:

> We must aspire for the economic improvement of the masses. We want Mexico to stand out as an educated people among the nations of the

civilized world. This must be the goal in the fight against the present
dictatorship. We struggle on behalf of civilization and the moral and
material progress of the Mexican proletariat.[92]

Engaging in the struggle for Mexico's progress underscored the liberal dream
of the nineteenth century that many felt Díaz had violated. Critics of the government tended to be passionate but sometimes expressions of political unrest
reached a fervent intensity born of persecution sanctioned by a corrupt set of
laws. On her time in prison, Juana Belén Gutiérrez de Mendoza, an activist imprisoned multiple times, reflected:

> Prison, with its cruel realities, informed me of my distance from reality.
> I no longer believed that the downfall, death, or any sort of suppression
> of the President of the Republic was sufficient to resolve all problems.
> That the multitude of human beings, tortured in the name of the law, all
> at once changed my criteria; that immense pain . . . would not be cured
> with democratic bandages. . . . It would have been impossible to end all
> that with a simple and exact application of the law, especially given that
> it was precisely the application of that odious instrument which had
> transformed humanity to a monster.[93]

Her male counterparts in the PLM's *Regeneración* shared Gutiérrez de Mendoza's
criticisms of the Díaz regime and at first praised her work with *Vésper: Justicia
y Libertad*! (Evening Star: Justice and Liberty), an anti-Díaz newspaper she
founded, characterizing the newspaper as virile with "the columns of our
esteemed colleague being so nourished by advanced ideas."[94] Gutiérrez de
Mendoza allied herself to the Mexican Revolution's precursor movement early
on, joining the Club Liberal Camilo Arriaga (Camilo Arriaga Liberal Club). At
the group's 1901 Congress in San Luis Potosí, she served as First Committee
Member, working on the group's manifesto, which was heavily anticlerical.[95]

Women such as Gutiérrez de Mendoza and teacher and political activist Elisa
Acuña y Rosete joined in mixed-sex liberal clubs but also founded all-female organizations such as Las Hijas de Cuauhtémoc (the Daughters of Cuauhtémoc).
The many projects that these women were involved in would have an impact in
Mexico and to some extent the borderlands area since several of them found in
Laredo and other US cities a temporary haven from persecution. Feminist in
their perspectives and modes of activism, these organizations, as well as women-
created newspapers plus the female networks that sustained them, provided
fertile ground for the development of not just political attacks directed at the
dictatorship but also critiques of Magonismo for failing to satisfactorily address
gender issues, principally women's rights, and for creating alliances with the

American left that did not necessarily reflect needs in Mexico. Indeed, when the PLM exiled community split in Laredo between the factions of Ricardo Flores Magón and Camilo Arriaga, Sara Estela Ramírez was joined by Juana Gutiérrez de Mendoza and Elisa Acuña y Rosete in siding with Arriaga.[96]

Ultimately, Gutiérrez de Mendoza returned to Mexico, but her relationship with Flores Magón never mended. She attacked the Flores Magón brothers, stating that they had lost their legitimacy. Gutiérrez de Mendoza criticized Magonismo's association with North American labor unions and their socialist affiliation, accused them of trying to introduce Yankee Protestantism in Mexico, and believed that they had mishandled Club Ponciano Arriaga funds because they charged admission at conferences. Gutiérrez de Mendoza also used the pen to address Magonismo articles that maligned her.[97]

Rather than attacking her political or ideological ideas, Ricardo Flores Magón sought to discredit the widowed Gutiérrez de Mendoza with aggressive personal attacks, accusing her of having a lesbian relationship with Elisa Acuña y Rosete. In turn-of-the-century Mexico, women's morality determined their treatment in society and their public legitimacy if they had active lives outside the home. Morality for women was tied to sexuality and was often policed by men. Thus, by impugning her reputation, Ricardo Flores Magón sought to neutralize Gutiérrez de Mendoza's political voice and her right to participate in public debates. On a broader level, Flores Magón did not believe that women should have an official political voice. He was against female suffrage, arguing that capitalism and not a denial of political rights represented the true enemy of women.[98]

Women journalists addressed this sexism shared by many men on the left. Blanca de Moncaleano, the editor and director of *Pluma Roja* (Red Pen), encouraged male readers to "allow women to educate themselves and to think on her own." To the men involved in the liberation movement who were not conscious of how they were suppressing women, she directed her harshest critiques. "Consumed by their supposed superiority, conceited in their ignorance, men believe they can achieve the goal of human emancipation without the help of women. Men are the real thieves of women's natural rights." No wonder her newspaper's motto was "Before me, the star of my ideal. Behind me, men, I do not look back."[99]

Leftist men struggled against the abuses of capitalism but leftist women struggled against capitalism and patriarchy. While agreeing with the men about the need to struggle against the oppression of workers around the world and promote revolution, women did so on their own terms and sometimes, as in the cases of Sara Estela Ramírez, Juana Gutiérrez de Mendoza, and Elisa Acuña y Rosete, that meant leaving the PLM altogether to join another group of political activists. In a sense, PLM women had two agendas. On the one hand, along with their brothers, they crossed the socially constructed boundaries of class,

race, and nation. On the other hand, their contributions to the revolutionary
movement took shape within a gender-crossing context.

Fronterizos living on the border between the United States and Mexico during
the first two decades of the twentieth century were exposed to passionate liberal, radical, and maternal feminist ideas found in the printed pages of Spanish-
language newspapers published as close to home as Laredo and San Antonio,
as well as more distant Los Angeles and Mexico City. Articles published in
La Crónica, El Democrata Fronterizo, Vésper, Regeneración, and many other
newspapers permeated and shaped fronterizo political culture, connecting
local conditions in Texas with the global processes leading up to the Mexican
Revolution.

Mexican liberalism and Mexican radicalism both started out as elements of a
reformist agenda designed to curb the abuses of the Porfiriato. But while Mexican
liberals, many of them associated with Freemasonry, sought to reform the capitalist system, safeguard the political freedoms guaranteed by the Constitution
of 1857, and eradicate the Catholic Church's influence in state affairs and social
life, Mexican radicals sought to steer the developing revolutionary movement
down a Marxist path that promised global worker solidarity, the redistribution
of wealth, and the elimination of capital's preponderance in working-class life.
To that end, they sought not only to overthrow Porfirio Díaz but also to destroy
what they considered to be a highly corrupt system. Magonistas often critiqued
the liberal reformers, accusing them of seeking to perpetuate the bourgeois
corrupt system from which they derived ample benefits. The liberal Masons
attacked Magonistas, accusing them of being freeloaders who lived off the naïve
working class. Ultimately Ricardo Flores Magón and the PLM's most radical
contribution to Mexican-American political culture was not the nationalistic
nature but rather the global scope of their enterprise.[100]

Even though the Magonistas spoke theoretically about women's equality to
men, they would have agreed with middle-class liberals that women's highest
role was that of wife and mother. To that end, any activity performed by women
outside the home needed to follow a maternalist agenda. When women ventured
outside the home, they were to perform "motherly" acts for the community at
large, caring for the less fortunate and elevating the standards of decency in the
public sector. Precisely because of females' value to the family and the nation-
state, liberals jealously guarded their claim on women from their primary competitor for their attentions—the Catholic Church. In the radical vision, women
also cared for their husbands and children at home. Any work performed outside the home needed to advance the revolutionary cause. Women served as
inspiration, motivating their male relatives to fight, and, as workhorses for the
revolution, devoting much time and energy to the revolutionary family.

Although women often seemed to fulfill the vision men held of them, subtle and not so subtle forms of feminism manifested themselves in the transborder political culture. Both Masons and Magonistas ultimately represented marginalized elements within the dominant Texas and American political structures. As people of Mexican origin advocating on behalf of other Mexican people, they used whatever privileges they had, such as education, material resources, and networks, to take on societal problems of poverty, discrimination, and violence. Although they would not achieve many of their goals, the fundamental objectives of unifying Mexicans, instilling them with pride in their culture, and politicizing and at times galvanizing them into action were achieved. Thus, even as they competed for the hearts, minds, and souls of Mexicans in Texas, both labored to transform the lives of people for the better. As this struggle continued, they would pass the torch to a later generation of transborder activists.

3

Crossing Borders to Rebirth the Nation

Leonor Villegas de Magnón and the Mexican Revolution

Leonor Villegas de Magnón was ready to serve Mexico's revolutionary family but as a liberal reformer rather than as an anarchist. An upper-class wife, she had written articles in support of Francisco Madero and the cause for political reform, but she soon had an opportunity to take her participation into a new realm when the revolution arrived in the border area of Laredo, Texas, and Nuevo Laredo, Mexico.

Gunshots coming from the direction of Nuevo Laredo in the early hours of March 17, 1913, prompted Leonor Villegas de Magnón in Laredo to dress quickly and make frantic telephone calls to friends and family on both sides of the Rio Grande River. Indeed, revolutionary General Jesús Carranza, brother to Venustiano Carranza, the leader of the Constitutionalist rebel forces, had attacked a small garrison in Nuevo Laredo. The *Federales* (federal government troops) were outnumbered, but a group of civilians assisted them until reinforcements arrived. In Laredo, Villegas de Magnón grew frustrated, unable to reach people by telephone. She wrote a note for her children: "When you get up, go to your uncle's house. Wait for me there. I'll be back soon." She then stepped outside her home and stopped a large car driven by a chauffeur. The driver obeyed her orders to take her to the offices of *El Progreso*, a liberal newspaper operated by friends. Once there, she painted a big red cross on a piece of paper and affixed it to the car's windshield. She convinced her friend, Jovita Idar, a writer for *El Progreso*, that they ought to go across the river to help the wounded. Before long, Villegas de Magnón had convinced four other young women to join her. When they stopped at a local pharmacy to pick up supplies, the owner, Don Flavio Vargas, handed Villegas de Magnón a basket of first-aid supplies and a towel-wrapped bundle concealing a bottle of whiskey. As the car approached the bridge over the Rio Grande to Mexico, the gutsy Villegas de

Magnón ordered the chauffeur to drive across. When he refused, she pushed the whiskey bottle's long neck hard against the chauffeur's back, simulating a gun, and he proceeded across the border.[1]

The women spent the next few days picking up wounded men from both factions off the streets of Nuevo Laredo, saving many lives. The rebel forces of Jesús Carranza lost the battle largely because of misinformation. Thinking that the federal forces had arrived to fortify the city, they retreated prematurely. The wounded Carrancista (or rebel) soldiers were held captive. Soon it became known that these soldiers were being mistreated and that the Mexican Red Cross was a partisan organization, working on the side of government forces. Upon learning of the mistreatment of rebel soldiers at the federal hospital, Villegas de Magnón, with the aid of nurses and servants, carried out a rescue mission. In the middle of the night, forty wounded men were ferried across the river to her home, which became a makeshift hospital. At this point, Leonor Villegas de Magnón, shocked and angered by the Red Cross's partisanship, organized the White Cross in Laredo, Texas. While the White Cross had impartially aided all the wounded in the battlefield, it soon declared its sympathies for the Carrancista or Constitutionalist cause and would later follow the Carranza army throughout Mexico. For the moment, however, Villegas de Magnón's declaration in favor of the rebel forces meant that she and her nurse corps could only cross into Nuevo Laredo under penalty of death.[2]

The life and work of Leonor Villegas de Magnón exemplify the transnational political roles some women as fronterizas played during the Mexican Revolution. Transborder activists saw in the revolution the opportunity to stretch the boundaries of nation and, for women, opportunities to expand traditional constructions of gender.[3]

A product of the US-Mexican borderlands and the Mexican bourgeois, as well as a graduate of Anglo-American Catholic schools in Texas and the US Northeast, Villegas de Magnón carved out a role for herself and for other women interested in actively participating in the Mexican Revolution. Educated, with access to books and newspapers, and often related to professional men with social, familial, commercial, and perhaps even political ties to their counterparts in Mexico, these women considered political events in Mexico of critical importance. Understood as an act of patriotism in the service of the nation, women's active participation could be defended and even strongly supported. Villegas de Magnón traveled extensively without her husband and children, supervised large numbers of men and women, administered resources, and consulted with Mexican revolutionary leaders. She even placed herself in the middle of heated battles. As adults, her children expressed admiration for their mother's heroic deeds.

Villegas de Magnón's maternalism was part of feminist consciousness that informed some of the political practices within the transborder political culture.

She promoted her bold ideas in ways her male associates, including the rebel Venustiano Carranza, may have found nonthreatening. She understood that in order for women to gain something, men had to be willing to give up something. She believed that both men and women, not just women, were responsible for improving conditions in society for everyone.

Villegas de Magnón took a pragmatic approach to politics, using her considerable class and educational privileges to carve out a space for herself and other fronterizos. Maternalism provided her with an opportunity to apply her ideas and labors far beyond the home, just as it had given women across ethnic groups access to public places and a voice in political circles deemed otherwise off-limits to their sex at a time when they were not even allowed to vote.[4] Leonor Villegas de Magnón defined her incredible revolutionary activities in helping other patriots rebirth the nation as an extension of her duties as a patriotic Mexican mother. And yet, as head of a national medical brigade, she stepped beyond the bounds of domesticity. While at times she gave voice to the language of maternalism, at other times both her words and actions displayed her strong feminist sensibilities.

While maternalism gave Villegas de Magnón's work in the public sector legitimacy, she also claimed a political genealogy with nineteenth-century Mexican liberalist roots. An outspoken liberal reformer, she was as comfortable discussing partisan politics as bandaging the bodies of fallen men. Like many of her middle-class fronterizo contemporaries, Villegas de Magnón subscribed to liberal principles stemming from the Mexican reform period (1858–1872) and the Mexican Constitution of 1857. She hoped for the rebirth of a liberal democracy in Mexico and followed Francisco Madero and Venustiano Carranza in the struggle for political reform. Her political vision and that of other Mexican liberals was revolutionary in that it called for the eradication of the Porfiriato; however, to the extent that the revolutionaries who came to power remained committed to a liberal capitalist democracy, the tenor of the Mexican Revolution was more reformist than revolutionary.[5]

The Mexican Revolution would take Villegas de Magnón from Laredo to northern Mexico, all the way to Mexico City, and back to the border in 1914. When her background as a transnational activist and her contributions to the Mexican Revolution are examined, what emerges is a portrait of a woman effectively using whatever strategies she could to participate in male-dominated spaces.

Two Flags Entwined

Leonor Villegas de Magnón's transnational identity was shaped from the time of her birth. The second of four children of wealthy Spanish-born merchant

Joaquín Villegas and his wife Valeriana Rubio de Villegas, Leonor was born in the border city of Nuevo Laredo, Tamaulipas, Mexico on June 12, 1876. Her brother Leopoldo was born the previous year in Corpus Christi, Texas, and after Leonor came Lorenzo (born in Cuatro Ciénegas, Mexico) and Lina (born in San Antonio, Texas). Since two of her children were born under the American flag and two under the Mexican flag, Valeriana once declared, "I shall wrap the flags together and they will be like one."[6]

The concept of two flags entwined defined every aspect of Leonor's life and family background. Her father, a descendant of nobility who gave up his rights of primogeniture, had set out from Carandia, Santander, Spain, in the 1860s, first settling in Cuba and then migrating to Texas, where he made his fortune in ranching, mining, and export-import industries. Villegas built his wealth in fine imported goods and produce raised at the Hacienda San Francisco, his ranch outside Nuevo Laredo. His enterprises connected the United States to Mexico, Cuba, other places in Latin America, and Spain. The Villegas family lived in opulent homes in both Nuevo Laredo and Laredo. Villegas operated a mercantile store on the American side and held interests in Mexican mines, in the iron foundry in Monterrey, and in the smelters of Torreón. Leonor's mother, Valeriana, grew up in the bilingual and bicultural border areas of Brownsville, Texas, and Matamoros, Tamaulipas. Despite their mother's early death, the Villegas children inherited a fronterizo or borderlands identity.

The remarriage of Leonor's father changed the course of the Villegas children's lives. The new Señora de Villegas, Eloísa, convinced Joaquín to send his children to boarding schools. Leonor lived in the Ursuline Convent in San Antonio from 1882 to 1885, followed by four years at the Academy of the Holy Cross in Austin. From 1889 to 1895, she attended the Academy Mt. St. Ursula in Bedford Park, New York City, where she graduated with honors and a teacher's diploma.[7]

Eloísa felt that a young lady's education was not complete without a trip to Europe so she convinced Joaquín to take Leonor and her sister Lina traveling in France and Spain for six months. They visited the Paris Exposition in 1900, witnessed the crowning of Alfonso XIII, mixed socially with the well-to-do, and got to know their father's relatives in Spain. Unlike his sisters, Leopoldo was encouraged to pursue a practical profession and graduated from New York Law School. Once back in Laredo, he participated in male civic organizations, joined his father's businesses, and began his political career, eventually becoming mayor of Laredo and city court judge.

Leonor returned to Laredo after her European grand tour. On January 10, 1901, at the age of twenty-five, she married Adolfo Magnón, a native Laredoan. Magnón's paternal grandfather had served as a colonel in Benito Juárez's army, which succeeded in ousting the French from Mexico. In addition to his strong familial ties to Mexico, Magnón also worked as an agent for the train and steamship lines in Mexico City. The newlyweds set up their home in the Mexican capital, where their three children, Adolfo Jr., Joaquín (Joe), and Leonor were born.[8]

Leonor enjoyed a lavish lifestyle and access to high society in the capital but also felt compelled to address the poverty of the masses. By 1910, she became attracted to the political movement of Francisco Madero, a wealthy *hacendado* from northern Mexico whose speeches against the aging dictator Porfirio Díaz captivated the imaginations of those eager for political change in Mexico. In 1909, after Díaz announced that Mexico was ready for democracy, Madero wrote *La sucesión presidencial en 1910*, a mild critique of the Díaz regime, which launched him into the national spotlight. As the Anti-Reelectionist Party's presidential candidate in 1910, he ran on a platform of effective suffrage and non-reelection of Díaz and future holders of the presidency. To ensure his victory, Díaz ordered Madero's imprisonment. In the meantime, Madero sympathizers such as Leonor Villegas de Magnón expressed their commitment to his democratic cause. Villegas de Magnón picked up her pen, explaining, "I shall write fiery articles. I'll send them to my friend Nicasio Idar, editor of *La Crónica*, in Laredo. We will ignite the flames of love and friendship for Madero." After his release from prison, Madero exiled himself in San Antonio, Texas, where he plotted Díaz's overthrow.[9]

Unfortunately, Villegas de Magnón's activism against the Díaz regime led to the confiscation of the Villegas family holdings in Mexico. This news devastated her father. On August 10, 1910, Villegas de Magnón received a telegram summoning her to Laredo, where her father was gravely ill. She arrived barely in time to ask for his forgiveness for the trouble her articles caused him. Joaquín Villegas admired his courageous and rebellious daughter who since youth had displayed independence of thought and action. To his remaining son, Leopoldo, Joaquín Villegas left the keys to his safe, store, and house. One half of Villegas wealth went to his widow and the rest to his children, with Leopoldo serving as trustee. For Leonor Villegas de Magnón, sharing in her father's fortune, in addition to receiving the support of her brother Leopoldo and his family, allowed her to be active on a considerable scale, contributing time and energy as well as financial resources to the cause.[10]

Hotbed of the Mexican Revolution

Adolfo Magnón had become involved in the growing revolutionary movement in Mexico City and could not leave the country. Leonor and the children remained in Laredo, which she considered a hotbed of the emerging Mexican Revolution. From there she continued to write pro-Madero articles for local newspapers. In late May 1911, Díaz stepped down from power, and in October Madero gained the support of Francisco Villa's northern rebels and was elected president.[11] Leonor Villegas de Magnón believed this portended Mexico as being on the path toward democracy. In an article in *La Cronica* dated September 7, 1911, she extolled Francisco Madero's virtues as a leader, revealing much about her own political beliefs. "We no longer need the machete and rifle to learn the duties of citizenship," she wrote. "Madero treats us like rational beings, as is required of a civilized nation." It was Madero she had in mind when she wrote, "The idea of loyalty and respect for government taught through reason and guided by conscience will help us comply with our duties as good citizens, since these ideas should be completely determined by reason."[12]

Reason alone would not suffice to govern justly. What made Madero distinct, according to Villegas de Magnón, was his democratic spirit. "He leaves ample room for all. We can all follow our particular political ideology without fear of reprisal." But making room for all did not mean compromising sacred liberal principles, such as the separation of church and state. "Religious beliefs," argued Villegas de Magnón, "when intermingled in the affairs of state prevent progress for humanity." Here it is evident that her liberal convictions were far stronger than her many years of Catholic education.[13]

Responding to charges that Madero had reached an accommodation with the ousted dictator's followers, she assured readers, "It is monstrous, false, and impossible to believe that our great hero should have made secret compromises with any party or sect." In addition to religion, the military had been the other great pillar of the previous conservative regimes in Mexico. Villegas de Magnón expressed her concern about them: "We also need in our country, the military establishment, the armies, but not so they attack their countrymen. We do not want them to intimidate their own brothers, but rather we want protection from the foreign enemy." Addressing the ongoing armed rebellions and banditry, Villegas de Magnón declared, "A leader cannot be held responsible for chaos and intrigues created by the enemy, and if the cause is a good one, it will triumph."[14]

Fronterizos offered ample support to Madero. He had blood ties to Laredo's Farías, Vidaurri, Ortiz, and de la Garza families. In 1912, *El Progreso*, a Spanish-language, pro-Madero newspaper was founded in Laredo. Leopoldo Villegas financed it, and two of Leonor's friends, Santiago Paz and Osvaldo Sánchez, served as editors. Enjoying wide circulation throughout South Texas, *El Progreso* covered the Mexican Revolution and served as a forum for Mexican writers.

More than ideas passed freely across the border. The conflict in Mexico led to periodic evacuations of Mexicans from villages and towns at or near the border into towns such as Laredo.[15] To help local leaders deal with this problem, Villegas de Magnón founded a civic organization called the Union, Progress, and Charity (UPC). UPC soon attracted about one hundred members, many of them Madero sympathizers, who worked to raise money for needy exiles from Mexico.[16]

A strong anti-Madero faction led by exiled Mexican general Bernardo Reyes also worked from the safety of Laredo and San Antonio to depose the president. Reyes had served as military commander under Díaz, and his supporters believed he should have been his natural successor. After Díaz's resignation, Reyes mounted a campaign for the presidency but withdrew from the race when he realized that the odds favored Madero. Upset but determined to be Mexico's leader, Reyes exiled himself in south Texas and began to conspire against Madero. He chose Laredo as a principal invasion point, plotting with both San Antonio and Laredo residents. In San Antonio, his key ally was Francisco A. Chapa, a druggist, journalist, and prominent figure in Texas politics. In Laredo, he worked closely with Webb County sheriff Amador Sánchez, a local political leader and direct descendant of the city's founder.

Another major Reyista co-conspirator in Laredo was Antonio Magnón, Leonor Villegas de Magnón's brother-in-law. Villegas de Magnón lived across from the jail that Sheriff Sánchez used as headquarters for his Reyista political activities. There, Reyistas such as Sánchez; Magnón; Rodolfo Reyes, a prominent lawyer and son of General Reyes; Marshall Hicks, Reyes's legal advisor; and General Gerónimo Treviño plotted to destroy the Madero presidency. At one point, much to her consternation, the Reyistas used Villegas de Magnón's own house as temporary headquarters.[17]

The Reyes conspiracy ended in utter failure. On November 18, 1911, the American consul in Nuevo Laredo, Alonzo B. Garrett, reported to the US secretary of state that Reyes and Sánchez were arrested on charges of violating neutrality laws. Forty-five rifles and 20,000 cartridges were confiscated from the conspirators. The next day, the State Department learned that General Reyes had been indicted by a federal grand jury.[18] Reyes jumped bail and returned to Mexico where he declared a revolt. Unable to raise an army, he was captured in February 1912 and spent a year imprisoned. Back in Texas, Reyistas Francisco Chapa and Amador Sánchez were found guilty in a federal court in Brownsville, fined $1,500, and released. Antonio Magnón also paid fines. President Taft pardoned Sánchez and Chapa before leaving office. Thereafter, Sánchez continued his anti-Madero activities discreetly.[19]

These transnational activities involved many political and military leaders of the Mexican Revolution and their followers. Given the repression and violence in Mexico during those years, the United States represented a relatively safe place to plot their rebellions. Other advantages included accessibility of arms, which were smuggled across the border, and sympathizers and recruits gathered from among the méxico-tejano population. The Flores Magón brothers, Ricardo and Enrique, were the first to utilize these transnational advantages in the service of building their movement. The US Department of Justice and Department of State were aware of much of this clandestine activity and worked to stop the violation of the nation's neutrality laws. Nonetheless, people, ideas, arms, and supplies continued to make their way across the border.[20]

The squashing of the Reyes conspiracy marked an example of the US government successfully enforcing its neutrality laws. However, Madero's enemies not only plotted against him from north of the border but also tirelessly schemed in Mexico City and waited for their opportunity. Their plan began to evolve as an embattled Madero administration struggled against a critical American Embassy and uprisings from disgruntled revolutionaries and counter-revolutionaries. US ambassador to Mexico, Henry Lane Wilson, saw Madero's presidency as a threat to US economic interests in Mexico and other spheres of influence. He did not believe the country was ready for democracy and thought that Madero's leadership would only lead to further rebellions and general instability, challenging Americans' ability to do business in Mexico. He wanted a return to *Porfirismo*, with its rigid control of the Mexican populace and accommodating attitude toward American investors. Among his enemies in Mexico, Madero faced challenges from revolutionaries such as Emiliano Zapata and former Maderista, Pascual Orozco, both unhappy with how the revolution had turned out; there was also pressure from counter-revolutionaries, such as Félix Díaz, nephew of Porfirio Díaz.[21]

Dissatisfaction with Madero soon turned into outright rebellion. The US ambassador demanded that Madero guarantee the safety of Americans in Mexico, further adding to Madero's long list of concerns. In February 1912, anti-Maderistas occupied Ciudad Juárez, across the border from El Paso, Texas. The following month, Orozco revolted against the president. By April, Álvaro Obregón proclaimed his opposition to Madero. The followers of Zapata also had a history of opposing the Maderista government. For Ambassador Wilson, these revolts served as further evidence that Madero's regime was weak. Ironically, by February 1913, Madero's government was on its way to establishing political stability in Mexico, so his enemies needed to make their move quickly. On February 9, part of the army initiated a coup d'état, which succeeded in the release of Félix Díaz and Bernardo Reyes from prison. The Decena Trágica (Tragic Ten Days), an insurrection in Mexico City, had commenced.

The American ambassador called for Madero's resignation as a means of securing peace and protecting American lives and business interests in Mexico. He convinced the Spanish minister to inform Madero that his resignation was the best means of attaining peace. Madero cabled President Taft protesting this threat of American intervention. Taft assured him that no such threat had been issued. Indeed, the whole affair was part of the political machinations of Ambassador Wilson; the British, Spanish, and German ministers; and the anti-Madero forces.[22] Madero remained firm in his resolve to remain president.

Regrettably, his appointment of General Victoriano Huerta as commander-in-chief of government military forces led to his demise. Even as he pretended to be fighting the insurrectionists, Huerta cut a deal with these counter-revolutionaries and betrayed both Madero and Vice President José María Pino Suárez by having them arrested. On February 22, 1913, Huerta had them executed on the way to the Federal District penitentiary. Huerta was named interim president, but in reality, he functioned as a military dictator.[23]

On the border, on February 15, in the midst of the Decena Trágica, pro-Huerta forces led by army and police authorities captured Nuevo Laredo without firing a single shot. General Andrés Garza Galán, a one-time Reyista conspirator, emerged as military chief of the city. The pro-Huerta forces imprisoned local officials and had the local garrison troops declare allegiance to them.[24] A few days later, the news of Madero's death was greeted with protests across the river in Laredo. Maderistas joined the ranks of the Porfiristas already exiled there. The voices of three anti-Huerta writers seemed particularly compelling. Manuel García Vigil, who later became the governor of Oaxaca; José Ugarte, who later served as Mexico's minister to South America; and Carlos Samper, who controlled the Mexican associated press all wrote articles for *El Progreso*. All three were Villegas de Magnón's friends and demanded a government based on the principles of liberty, justice, and equality. In her memoir, *The Rebel*, Villegas de Magnón wrote that "loyalists in Laredo banded against Huerta, rallying around the prominent figure of Melquíadas García."[25] What these protesters and others needed was a new standard-bearer of the Maderista call for political reform. They soon found their advocate in Venustiano Carranza, the governor of the northern state of Coahuila, a strong critic of Huerta's regime, and Madero's former minister of war.

Carranza's followers, known alternately as Carrancistas or Constitucionalistas because of their emphasis on a return to constitutional legality, established Saltillo, the capital of Coahuila, as their headquarters. From his Hacienda de Guadalupe near Saltillo on March 25, 1913, Carranza issued his Plan de Guadalupe, signed by over 150 anti-Huertistas or anti-Federalists, since Huerta controlled Mexico's federal army. The plan declared Huerta's coup unconstitutional. It also declared civil war and named Carranza the first chief of the Constitutionalist movement. What followed was a series of successful military campaigns over fifteen months to remove Huerta from power, in which Laredoans played pivotal roles.[26]

The Mexican National White Cross: A Borderlands Creation

When the revolution arrived at the border, both Mexican-origin and Anglo-American women from south Texas to southern California mobilized through social service organizations to meet the demands of incoming war refugees. Villegas de Magnón's Union, Progress, and Charity organization sought to meet the needs of refugees in Laredo, while in San Antonio, the Women's Board of Missions of the Methodist Episcopal Church South created the Wesley Community home to assist 6,000 to 8,000 Mexican refugees in an eight-block section of South Laredo Street.[27] Women's voluntary associations also proved invaluable. The Mexican consulate could not meet the increasing demand for services of ever-growing Mexican immigrant communities, and so a female-dominated social service branch of women volunteers called the Cruz Azul (Blue Cross) set out on missions to help the sick and the poor. Headquartered in San Antonio, it had branches in fifty-two Texas communities, including Laredo.[28]

In addition, female partisans on the border became involved in other capacities, the best known being the women of the Magonismo movement.[29] Teresa and Andrea Villarreal founded the radical publication *La Mujer Moderna* (The Modern Woman) in San Antonio, and in El Paso, Isidra T. De Cárdenas published *Voz de la Mujer* (The Woman's Voice). Also, in El Paso, the Daughters of Chuahtémoc was affiliated with the Liberal Party.[30] Through the medical brigade Leonor Villegas de Magnón established, she promoted benevolent, humanitarian aid to combatants, but she was undeniably a partisan who aggressively supported Carranza through her work and by choosing to follow and assist Carranza's Constitutionalist army.

The Constitutionalist army took a two-prong approach to wresting control from the Federalists throughout the northern Mexican states. Venustiano Carranza led troops to the northwestern state of Sonora while leaving his brother Jesús, along with Laredo native Pablo González and Luis Caballero, in charge of the northeastern states. By focusing on this region, the Carrancistas hoped to gain control of the border areas and thereby control the movement of arms. Huerta quickly reinforced the Federalist position in these areas.

On March 17, 1913, General Jesús Carranza's forces, with a woman leading the charge, attacked a small garrison in Nuevo Laredo. They were, however, repulsed by the Federalists and a group of civilians. The woman and many others perished. Federal soldiers often executed the wounded rebel soldiers in the streets. On the outskirts of the city, many lay dead, but Leonor Villegas de Magnón and her friends helped some of the wounded survive. At the Mexican hospital, five Laredo doctors assisted Villegas de Magnón's nurses.[31] In Laredo prominent citizens and businesses contributed to relief funds for clothes, medicines, and food for the Mexican hospital.

Villegas de Magnón's well-known political positions drew many partisans to her cause. One was a young woman named María de Jesús González, a school-teacher and telegraph operator from Monterrey. González, a supporter of Carranza, had traveled to the border to meet Villegas de Magnón and to inform her that several women in Mexico, among them Marie Bringas de Carturegli (an aristocrat from Sonora and the wife of a prominent doctor), Trinidad Blanco (a telegraph operator and her sister), an unnamed teacher from Coahuila, Juanita Mancha, and the Blackaller sisters (also teachers from Monterrey), had all joined the Constitutionalist revolution and would soon be in the Laredo area to assist her with the wounded.

After González had rested, Villegas de Magnón sent her off to the nearest Constitutionalist camp with messages for General Lucio Blanco and General Pablo González. When these women returned to their home communities, they continued both to work as nurses and to perform tasks as propagandists and messengers. The Blackaller sisters ended up working in a hospital in Monclova, Coahuila, and as volunteer nurses in Piedras Negras, Coahuila, and Matamoros, Tamaulipas. Villegas de Magnón played a role in organizing them; for example, she asked Marie de Carturegli to serve as the president of the Constitutional White Cross in Sonora.[32]

María de Jesús González might have alerted the Constitutionalists that she and other telegraphers had intercepted a message from the Federal commander in Matamoros requesting reinforcements. The intercepted message may have caused a delay and thus created an opportunity for the Constitutionalist army to attack the vulnerable Federalist border town. General González by then had given up on a counterattack on the heavily fortified Nuevo Laredo so he joined forces with General Jesús Carranza to attack Matamoros, across from Brownsville. This strategy proved successful and reinvigorated the Carrancistas, who set about planning their next attack on Nuevo Laredo. Meantime, María de Jesús González continued to travel along the border delivering messages to Constitutionalist leaders. Her next mission was to board a train in Laredo with assistance from Villegas de Magnón and one of her major assistants, Laredo teacher María Villarreal, who had many former pupils and friends working in the railroad. María de Jesús González, an eighteen-year-old woman, traveled to El Paso, Texas, and crossed the border to Ciudad Juárez, where she met with the First Chief Venustiano Carranza to inform him of the work of the White Cross.[33]

Soon the Carrancista cause would call upon its faithful followers on the border, but in the aftermath of the 1913 battle, Villegas de Magnón settled down to a quiet life as a kindergarten teacher for the children of some of Laredo's most prominent families. While her sister-in-law watched over her three children, Villegas de Magnón worked to set up Laredo's first kindergarten in a hall made available to her by her brother. She opened this school not long after her return from Mexico in 1910 and became popular for her active and imaginative role in her pupils' educational development. In one instance, she had them dress up in historical costumes of the United States and Mexico and hired a professional to photograph them.[34] According to Maria del Carmen Guardiola Offer, one of her young pupils at the time, Mrs. Magnón was a kind and devoted teacher who treated all of her students fairly. Even after many decades, this former student recalled with wonder how Mrs. Magnón could be so kind to the children of Federals such as herself. Although her father, Colonel Gustavo Guardiola Aguirre, was charged with defending the Federalist position in Nuevo Laredo and later ascended to the rank of general, this did not influence Mrs. Magnón, who as her student put it, "was a Carrancista but with the children of Federals she turned a blind eye. She was so good and kind."[35]

Other volunteer nurses also resumed their normal lives. María Villarreal, for example, had once taught at the Laredo Seminary (Holding Institute), a Methodist school, but due to her mother's ill health she opened a private school at home. It was one of the first schools in Texas that specialized in bilingual education. Villarreal also taught advanced methods in math.[36]

The everyday lives to which Villegas de Magnón and Villarreal had returned soon ended. On January 1, 1914, the Carrancistas, under the command of General Pablo González, attacked Nuevo Laredo once more. They were repulsed three times in a battle that proved to be one of the most violent clashes in northern Mexico. There were reports of up to 300 dead and many more wounded on the first day.[37] By January 4, General González retired downriver after 600 of his soldiers were killed and another 600 wounded. There they awaited reinforcements to initiate a second attack.[38]

Mexican citizens again sought refuge on the American side, but this time they were held back because the bridge was closed after the United States placed an embargo on the crossings. United States consul Alonzo Garrett wired Washington about the crisis and succeeded in getting the bridge reopened so Nuevo Laredo could be evacuated.[39] On the American side, Villegas de Magnón instructed her servant Pancho to navigate his skiff downriver until he found Carrancista General Lucio Blanco's men. Blanco controlled Matamoros and had men posted along the river. Pancho was to deliver the message that federal reinforcements had arrived in Nuevo Laredo from Monterrey. Once the wounded started arriving at her home, Villegas de Magnón sprang into action, calling upon volunteer nurses María Villarreal, Bessie Moore, and Lily Long to help her care for them. The kindergarten hall was turned into a makeshift hospital and the living room of Villegas de Magnón's home became an operating room. Villegas de Magnón's brother Leopoldo offered an additional building across the street and the Sons of Juárez fraternal order donated their hall. Within twenty-four hours these three emergency hospitals began to receive wounded Carrancista soldiers, housing up to one hundred by nightfall.[40]

Overnight, US troop reinforcements arrived from Lampasas, Texas, and took positions along the riverbanks to prevent shooting from breaking out. The people of Laredo, many of whom were sympathetic to the Constitutionalist cause, did what they could to assist Villegas de Magnón. Some brought bed linens and mattresses, food, and medicines. American and Mexican doctors worked together. Outside, citizens picked up wounded soldiers brought to the riverbanks and took them to Villegas de Magnón's home in their cars and buggies. One hundred fifty wounded men were cared for/nursed in the three makeshift hospitals while others stayed in private homes. Carrancista commanders made frequent trips of inspection to these hospitals.

Villegas de Magnón had everybody around her working for the cause. She entrusted two young women waiting to meet her with a mission to pick up three wounded soldiers at the Orfila ranch about sixty miles downriver. Later, she learned that these young women were, in fact, Venustiano Carranza's nieces. Although embarrassed, she concluded that everybody had a role to play in the service of his or her country.[41]

Although she and her family resided in the United States, Mexico was the country that Villegas de Magnón and the members of the White Cross, Mexican-origin and Anglo American alike, pledged to assist in this moment of national crisis. But while her memoir speaks to her personal motivations for joining the revolutionary cause, less is known about the people who joined the White Cross, though some information about their identities can be drawn from an analysis of census records.

Who Participated in the White Cross?

Why would residents of Laredo, Texas, among them US citizens, join a revolutionary movement in a foreign nation? It seems understandable that they would volunteer their services during the Battle of Nuevo Laredo since this was Laredo's sister community and strong social and economic ties linked the border towns, but this does not account for their joining a traveling medical brigade. The members of the White Cross brigade expressed their commitment to Mexico's revolutionary movement, specifically Carranza's cause, through their willingness to volunteer their services beyond the Laredo area to west Texas and into Mexico, many of them going as far as Mexico City.

Leonor Villegas de Magnón's memoir mentions the names of at least eighty-one people from the border region of south Texas and northern Mexico affiliated in some capacity with the White Cross at various times. Though most probably were native to the Laredo-Nuevo Laredo area, some might have been from the surrounding countryside or border towns up- and downriver.[42] According to Villegas de Magnón, there were three distinct types of participation in the White Cross. Of the eighty-one border area participants, eighteen were doctors (most from the United States but a few from the Mexican side).

She also refers to eleven benefactors whose participation consisted of donating money, medical supplies, or clothing and food for wounded soldiers. The vast majority contributed any number of services. Some worked as nurses, others handled administrative tasks, some were railroad workers who used their skills to help transport the medical brigade across northern Mexico, still others focused on creating and disseminating Carrancista propaganda materials, and a small fraction engaged in occasional spying missions.

Despite the limitations of the census, much information can be gleaned from identifying thirty-three individuals who appeared in the 1910 records. The Idar family proved to be committed participants in the White Cross. Sisters Jovita and Elvira served as volunteer nurses. Jovita traveled with the brigade from Monterrey, Nuevo Leon, to Mexico City and she later served as secretary. Besides her nursing services, Elvira also served as vice president of the first brigade, assembled after the 1913 battle of Nuevo Laredo, and she worked as director of hospitals of the second brigade assembled after the 1914 battle. Jovita and Elvira's eldest brother, Clemente, served as White Cross secretary, a position that Jovita would later hold. Clemente Idar advised Leonor Villegas de Magnón to request that Venustiano Carranza nationalize the White Cross, a move that was approved in due time. Clemente's brother Federico traveled with the White Cross throughout Mexico and, like his siblings, served as staff secretary.[43]

Out of the thirty-three White Cross participants listed in the 1910 census, four were doctors, eleven were material benefactors, and eighteen served as rank-and-file members, whether working as nurses or in some other capacity.[44] While women cared for the wounded or performed administrative and other lower jobs, most of the men served as financial supporters and doctors, with a few male participants working alongside women as members of the medical brigade. Photographs of the White Cross bear out this gendered division of labor.[45]

Information about occupations reveals much about gender as well. In the census, twelve members, eleven of them post-school-age females, reported "none" for their trade or profession. The one male who reported "none" for this question was fourteen years old in 1910 and still attending school. Of this group only one was categorized as "wife," the others were categorized as "daughters" who lived with parents and siblings. However, these adult-age daughters often worked as assistant housekeepers, helping their mothers run the household, and other sources reveal that some of these women were very much involved in family businesses. Although Jovita and Elvira Idar listed "none" for trade or profession, both worked for their family's newspaper *La Crónica*. Besides journalism, Jovita trained as a teacher. Her sister kept the family financial books. Dr. Lowry's wife also appears to have no profession, and yet she worked as a dance teacher, possibly at home.[46] In sum, the census does not provide an accurate picture of the economic contributions made by women to their households.

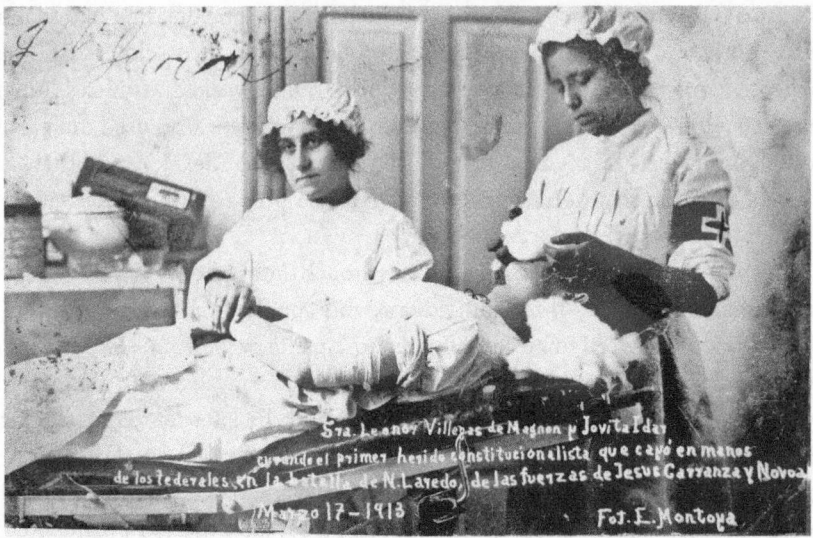

Figure 3.1 Leonor Villegas de Magnón (left) and Jovita Idar (right) nursing the wounded during the Mexican Revolution, circa 1914. 084-0597, General Photograph Collection, University of Texas at San Antonio, Special Collections—Institute of Texan Cultures. Courtesy of A. Ike Idar.

While male children often appear as "clerks" or "cashiers" for family enterprises, female family members' roles in running both households and businesses are erased. Also, an analysis of the "relation to head of household" census category reveals that White Cross benefactors and doctors held the primary role within the patriarchal family structure. It also indicates that the medical brigade's rank-and-file members tended to be in subordinate positions within the family.

Age also differentiated members from benefactors and doctors. Members were younger than the supporters and doctors, so it is not surprising that the majority of the members appear as single in the 1910 census. By contrast, most of the benefactors and all of the doctors were married. Most of the members were women and most of them were single, which is logical since those without children were more likely to volunteer. While only three members reported having children, nine benefactors and the four doctors reported offspring.

The benefactors and doctors appear to have been better off financially than the members. Male members reported occupations as common laborer and a printer. By contrast, the benefactors' occupations included small business ownership, ranching, banking, politics, and the mercantile trade. The four doctors had established their medical practices. Further, the benefactors and doctors appear as "employers" or working on their "own account," while the members often appear as "workers" or this space was left blank on the census. While individual members might have been low-wage earners or non-wage employees who worked for family enterprises, an analysis of their fathers' occupations reveals a more complex picture of subordinate positioning within privileged families. In fact, some of these young female volunteers were the daughters of the town's successful ranchers, merchants, and politicians. Adela Bruni was a young volunteer whose father, Antonio Bruni, was a rancher, banker, and politician—at one point, considered to be the wealthiest man in Webb County.[47]

Attesting to the transnational nature of the organization, half of the members were born in Mexico and the rest in Texas. Slightly more than a third (36 percent) of the benefactors were born in Mexico; the others hailed from Europe and the United States. Three of the doctors were US born and one was Canadian. Based on parents' birthplace, familial association with Mexico seemed stronger among the members than among the benefactors. In answer to the question of whether the person was able to speak English, or if not, what language did the person speak, 61 percent of the members spoke English and the rest spoke Spanish. Eighty-two percent of the benefactors spoke English, with the two remaining designated as Spanish speaking. All four doctors spoke English.

As a sign of their privilege, all participants in the White Cross reported that they could read and write. Over one half either owned a home or lived with their parents who owned a home. Almost 82 percent of the benefactors and 75 percent of the doctors reported home ownership. In sum, White Cross members, benefactors, and doctors all were from middle- to upper-class families. While the organization had both US-born and foreign-born participants, English was the dominant language among the majority of White Cross participants.

Advocating for Fronterizos

Although some White Cross members came from comfortable circumstances with fairly well-to-do parents, they were far from being rich in their own right, and at times they might have struggled. Villegas de Magnón asked Carranza for some type of recompense for members of the White Cross. In a letter dated May 22, 1914, she stated:

> I permit myself to manifest to you that since all of its (the White Cross') members are poor persons who in loyalty have been affiliated to the saintly cause of constitutionalism which you lead with dignity, I wish they'd be compensated according to their abilities with some benefit for the cause and for themselves.[48]

For example, she asked that the Laredo railroad men who operated Carranza's train to Mexico City be rewarded. For her secretary, Mrs. Long, she requested that her husband who worked as an architectural engineer be given a contract and a recommendation. For her nurses, both married and single, she asked that the revolutionary cause support them, either in the hospital in Laredo, the customs house, or the blood hospitals in Monterrey. She also asked Carranza to look upon the self-sacrificing Dr. de la Garza with special favor. As for herself, she seemed to require no particular reward except for "the satisfaction of having fulfilled my duty as a patriot."[49]

The word "poor" as used by Villegas de Magnón was disingenuous in a border community where the truly "poor" struggled daily to earn enough money to eat and did not enjoy the privileges that members of the White Cross did. But her use of the term is significant since she advocated the right of borderlands people to be compensated by Carranza for their contributions to *la revolución*.[50] Villegas de Magnón was aware of this legacy of neglect of fronterizos by both the United States and Mexico, and she sought a just reward for border people who had contributed so much to the Mexican Revolution.[51]

International Law versus Transnational Reality

Leonor Villegas de Magnón's engagement with the transborder political culture placed her in a delicate situation with the American state. During the Mexican Revolution, US soldiers were stationed along the border in case the conflict spilled over onto American soil and threatened US lives and property. These soldiers were prohibited from interfering in conflicts beyond American borders in which the United States was not officially involved, as this would violate neutrality laws. Inevitably, the conflict in Mexico did spill over into south Texas on numerous occasions. By examining two such instances—the incident at the Marfa refugee camp and the detainment of Mexican soldiers at Fort McIntosh in Laredo—the transnational nature of the US-Mexican border comes into sharper focus. Above and beyond a nation's sovereign laws and international agreements, individuals transcended geographic borders in the name of self-preservation.

The first of these two instances concerned refugees and wounded soldiers. After Francisco "Pancho" Villa's rebel forces, led by General Ortega, defeated the Federal army at the Battle of Ojinaga in late 1913, Huertista General Salvador Mercado's 3,000 remaining Federal soldiers and civilians, including women and children, escaped across the border to Presidio, Texas. United States soldiers led the refugees on a forced march north to Marfa. They were then sent to refugee camps, where they remained, enclosed by barbed wire, for the duration of the conflict.[52]

The second incident occurred in the aftermath of the Nuevo Laredo battle of 1914. US officials faced a similar problem when Carrancista soldiers were brought to the White Cross hospitals in Laredo. Under the care of nurses and both American and Mexican doctors, these wounded men made steady progress and many recovered. The issue at hand, however, was what to do with them after recovery, since they could not travel freely on American soil. When Huerta officials discovered that Carrancistas were so well treated by Laredoans, they issued protests to US officials, reminding them that Federal soldiers seeking refuge in Presidio had received no such courtesies and, in fact, were being held in refugee camps in Marfa. In response, US soldiers, ready to arrest any Carrancista who attempted to walk away, surrounded White Cross hospitals. Leaving was precisely what the recovered soldiers needed to do, for their commander had sent word that all soldiers able to stand needed to report back to their posts.[53]

Leonor Villegas de Magnón had two powerful reasons for getting involved in this conflict. First, she knew that the American soldiers would turn the men over to the Federales in Nuevo Laredo once they had recuperated, after which they would be either imprisoned or executed in Mexico. Second, she was committed to the Carrancista cause. She knew that the rebel army needed survivors to fight other battles. Villegas de Magnón planned and executed some risky schemes to spirit away as many soldiers as possible. She took advantage of the fact that to the Anglo-American soldiers stationed outside the hospital, all Mexicans, whether native Laredoans or Mexican soldiers, looked alike. When the milkman came to deliver cans of milk, she had him trade clothes with a soldier, who then walked away unmolested. She got caught, but the reprimand she received did not stop her from carrying out her next ploy. When some Carrancista soldiers died, she reported a higher number of dead and had live men transported in sheets and coffins. Once when an American soldier opened a coffin and asked why the dead man was wearing shoes, the ingenious Villegas de Magnón convinced him that it was a Spanish custom. The White Cross also enlisted the help of a doctor who lived across the street from the hospital. Some of the patients were taken from the hospital to the doctor's office for treatment. The numbers of those who returned to the hospital began to decline until the captain realized what was going on and objected. In time only thirty-three men remained at the hospital.

It is possible that Villegas de Magnón did more than help the soldiers evade the US sentries posted at hospital doors. According to her son, Joe Magnón, "She took them out [of the hospital] and took them to San Ignacio [thirty miles downriver from Laredo] where she crossed them back to Mexico." In order to prevent any more disappearing acts by Carrancista soldiers, US soldiers arrived one day with moving vans and took them all to Fort McIntosh. When Villegas de Magnón pleaded with them not to take the men, the captain responded, "We would like to leave them here, Señora, but they don't seem to want to stay. They disappear."[54]

White Cross nurses regularly visited the soldiers and brought them their mail and clean clothes. Villegas de Magnón hired a lawyer, family friend Otto Weffing, to lobby Governor Oscar B. Colquitt of Texas on behalf of the Carrancista soldiers held in custody, but this strategy failed. She also wrote letters to Washington, DC, arguing that while the Federal soldiers held in Marfa had crossed the border with arms, the Carrancista soldiers in Laredo had been brought over unconscious and wounded. She further argued that by imprisoning them, rules of hospitality had been violated.[55] Senator Morris Sheppard of Texas wrote on behalf of Villegas de Magnón and her cause to the War Department, which sent the matter to the State Department. Secretary of State William Jennings Bryan sided with Villegas de Magnón.[56] On April 3, 1914, the thirty-three interned Mexican soldiers were released from Fort McIntosh.[57]

The significance of these events lies in the ability of a Mexican-origin woman to negotiate with representatives of the American state. Her class, education, and networks provided her with the ability to engage state and federal government officials on a sensitive international matter. Villegas de Magnón crossed geopolitical boundaries as she actively participated in war battles. She expressed maternalist and humanist sensibilities as she cared for wounded soldiers and sought to protect them by saving them from the Federales. By doing this, she provided Carranza's rebel army with yet more soldiers to fight for the cause. In the course of saving their lives, Villegas de Magnón found herself in the middle of an international event, caring for battle-beaten Mexican rebel soldiers and negotiating for their lives with American male public officials at all levels of governance.

All the Way to Mexico City

While Leonor Villegas de Magnón awaited the outcome of her efforts on behalf of the Carrancista soldiers held at Fort McIntosh, she received word from the Constitutionalists in Matamoros that the White Cross was needed in the El Paso/Ciudad Juárez area. In Ciudad Juárez she would meet the leader of the Constitutionalist army, First Chief Venustiano Carranza. She quickly made arrangements. She left Elvira Idar and María Villarreal in charge of the hospital in Laredo. She also selected the brigade members who were to accompany her to El Paso and into Mexico. Twenty-six White Cross staff people prepared for the journey, among them volunteer nurses and several men with expertise in running a railroad train and doing propaganda work. Also joining the party were sisters; three married couples; two mothers with their daughters; Mrs. Lily Honeycutt Long, wife of a Laredo doctor and Villegas de Magnón's personal secretary, friend, and companion; the secretary and treasurer of the White Cross;

and a staff photographer. Villegas de Magnón left her three children in the care of her brother and sister-in-law.[58]

On April 5, 1914, the Constitutional White Cross arrived at the El Paso station, and the next day, Villegas de Magnón and Lily Long were escorted to Ciudad Juárez where they met with Venustiano Carranza. The original Laredo White Cross unit moved with the Constitutionalist army, establishing brigades and branches in every city they traveled through. On June 8, Carranza appointed Leonor Villegas de Magnón head of the National White Cross. Lily Long was reassigned to another Carrancista battalion, and Jovita Idar replaced her as Villegas de Magnón's secretary.[59]

In her memoir, Villegas de Magnón recounts the journey from the Chihuahua border area to Mexico City, following the Carrancista Fourth Battalion. She witnessed the falling out between Pancho Villa and Venustiano Carranza, the conflict between revolutionaries and the old guard, desecrated churches and "palatial haciendas turned into stables," and many horrific battles that paved the way for an eventual Carrancista triumph. Villegas de Magnón met many revolutionaries, including the real-life Adelita of folk song fame and Coronela Carmen de la Llave, also known as La Marietta. Through it all, Villegas de Magnón remained steadfast and loyal to the cause. Even as the Federalist army burned her family's home and many other buildings in Nuevo Laredo after another Carrancista attack, she remained focused on helping Carranza's revolution succeed all the way to Mexico City.[60]

Return Home

Despite the political volatility that continued to plague Mexico, the White Cross's goal of remaining with the Constitutionalist army until Carranza assumed power at the capital was achieved. Villegas de Magnón was battle weary and pleased by the thought of returning to her family in Laredo. The next day, the White Cross Brigade marched with Carranza's army into Mexico City. The first chief duly recognized its great contributions. On August 16, Leonor Villegas de Magnón, eager to see her children, resigned. Other members of the White Cross from the Laredo area followed suit. All pledged to return should an emergency warrant their services. She returned to the border with her nurses and a heavy heart for leaving behind the national public health projects she had hoped to carry out on behalf of the Mexican people.[61]

In early October 1914, she was still engaged in Mexican revolutionary activity as trouble resurfaced. The revolutionaries were turning on each other and new fighting had broken out. Leonor Villegas de Magnón was instructed to take over the military hospital in Nuevo Laredo. The trouble started when the animosity between Villa and Carranza escalated to such a degree that Obregón, a Carrancista general, forced Villa out of Mexico City. Villa returned to his native Chihuahua, where he beheaded the brothers of Carrancista general Maclovio Herrera. Stationed in Nuevo Laredo, General Herrera focused on exacting revenge on Villa, while rumors circulated that Villa might attack the city. The border braced for another battle.[62]

The White Cross assembled once more to reopen the war-ravaged hospital. Many from Laredo made generous donations. Villegas de Magnón donated 2,000 pesos. American doctors were ready to render assistance. The night before the battle, Villegas de Magnón received a visitor. White Cross secretary Federico Idar told her that a false report was spreading around town that General Herrera would "let stray bullets go over to the American side." As a result, Fort McIntosh soldiers were put on high alert and prepared to shoot back. Villegas de Magnón and Idar crossed over to the Mexican side to warn General Herrera that his troops must be as far away from the border as possible, preferably meeting the enemy in the hills of Tamaulipas, where there would be no chance of engaging with US troops. Herrera heeded their warning and the battle took place in the outskirts of Nuevo Laredo, thus averting a major international crisis. Villegas de Magnón later learned that General Herrera's soldiers accidentally killed him on April 17, 1915.[63]

Nuevo Laredo was not only General Herrera's final battle but also Villegas de Magnón's. While in the United States in April 1920, Leonor Villegas de Magnón received a letter from Carranza informing her that his own generals had turned against him. She returned to the border immediately and awaited further news. The following month President Venustiano Carranza was ambushed and killed, and one of his generals, Álvaro Obregón, came to power. There was no more work to be done in Mexico City for the Carrancistas, so the Magnón family returned to Laredo.[64]

Although Leonor Villegas de Magnón resumed her teaching career in Laredo, she returned to Mexico later in life. In addition to sacrificing much of her time and energy for the White Cross and the Mexican Revolution, she spent large sums of money, possibly her entire inheritance, on her White Cross work. A woman who had been born into great privilege, she remained a wage-earning person throughout most of her life.

In 1941, she became a member of Mexico's National Defense Auxiliary Women Volunteers. The following year she worked for the National Statistics Ministry in Mexico City. While there, she received numerous honors for her earlier humanitarian work. She was also involved in the International Women's Club. Between 1945 and 1947 she worked on her own parcel of land through Rancherías Camargo, Tamaulipas. Furthermore, she sought veteran status for the nurses of the White Cross, seeing their work as "an act of 'social justice.'"

During the early 1950s, Villegas de Magnón tried to publish her memoir but was turned down by several publishing houses. Published posthumously by her daughter, *The Rebel* drew attention not only to Villegas de Magnón's labors but also those of many women and men from the border that she feared would otherwise be forgotten.[65]

Maternal Feminism and the Act of Rebirthing the Nation

Whether they intended to help their sister city during its time of crisis or to help depose the usurper Huerta, the men and women who participated in the White Cross did so with an awareness that they were assisting in the process of rebirthing the Mexican nation. These fronterizos, though safe on the American side, were willing to invest their time, energy, money, and perhaps even their lives in a transborder mission of mercy on behalf of Mexican revolutionaries struggling to bring about political and social reform.

The participation of male fronterizos in these enterprises is not surprising. After all, the Mexican revolutionaries themselves often sent envoys to Texas and other border states in an effort to muster all types of support, from securing funds and weapons to recruiting men to join their precursor movements. More compelling is the extensive participation of middle-class women from the border area who hailed from privileged gente decente backgrounds and risked their safety for a distant cause. These women often worked as teachers and in other professions, which made them aware of the social, economic, and political structures in Mexican society that needed to be reformed. While working-class women involved in the revolution often worked as *soldaderas* (camp followers and combatants), the middle-class women served as spies, propagandists, and couriers.[66] Villegas de Magnón and her followers also engaged in such activities, but their main contribution was the work of the White Cross.

In a way, it was their privilege that best positioned the members of the White Cross to gain awareness of the significant events of the age. What Americans living in the interior of the United States saw as a foreign revolution was far more significant to fronterizos. For the fronterizos who stood to lose from the demise of the Porfiriato, the Mexican civil war represented an outrage led by uncivilized men, but to reform-minded fronterizos, such as those who joined the White Cross, la revolución was nothing short of the noble struggle of patriotic men and women to re-create the nation.

Although most of the women in the White Cross were single, they had to put certain filial responsibilities on hold during their missions of mercy. A few of the women were wives and mothers. Villegas de Magnón's situation was particularly

complex because she was raising her three small children alone while her husband lived away from the family, but her brother and sister-in-law cared for
the children while she was busy with White Cross matters. Given societal
norms, one might wonder how the Laredo community responded to mothers'
decisions to leave their children in the custody of relatives or friends while they
participated in the revolution. One student, when asked whether Mrs. Magnón
was in any way criticized for her work with the White Cross, replied, "I don't
think so. I never heard of that. If they did I never heard it. What I do know is that
people admired her."[67]

Leonor Villegas de Magnón's memoir makes no mention of any negative
attention although she does discuss how her political work brought financial
challenges to her father, whose Mexican properties were under attack once his
daughter entered public life. Also, in the letter asking Carranza to reward White
Cross members she stated she did her work gladly but "against the will of my
own family," which may have meant political disagreements with her husband.[68]

The Mexican government certainly honored Villegas de Magnón's services.
As president, Carranza awarded her five medals for her service to the Mexican
nation. Mexico's secretary of national defense declared her a veteran of the
Mexican Revolution. Between 1939 and 1975, Villegas de Magnón, along with
60,000 Mexican women, applied to the Ministry of Defense for veteran status
and had to provide an application and "two or more certificates from an already
recognized veteran who testified to her activities during official revolutionary
periods and described the details of her service." Only 450 were granted veteran
status with its pension benefits. The difficulty of attaining veteran status might
have been connected to Carranza's Ministry of War and Navy's decision in 1916
to retroactively decommission women who had attained military rank during
the armed phase of the Mexican Revolution. Women were also prohibited from
rejoining the army and were expelled from the military, which meant a loss of
pensions and the status accorded to members of the military family.[69]

Leonor Villegas de Magnón herself offered some thoughts about the roles
of women in society. In an article she wrote for *La Crónica* in 1911 to express
support for the First Mexicanist Congress, particularly its efforts to invite
women, she saw it as a time of great promise and opportunity for women. She
wrote, "If we give a retrospective glance we shall see that women did not occupy
the place that today is given to us, and today, more than ever we should make
ourselves dignified of this place that is apportioned us." She went on to state that
women needed to march in the direction of progress that the nation was moving
toward.[70]

She understood that in a patriarchal world any advancement of women's
rights required the cooperation of at least some men. Carefully crafted phrases

such as "the place that today is given to us," and "this place that is apportioned us" belie the reality of mixed gender cooperation with implicit and, at times, explicit scripts of how power would be shared or negotiated.

At the center of this negotiated power was a form of maternal feminism grounded in both an awareness of the obstacles women faced and a consciousness of women as important contributors to nation-building. Women could attempt to seize this apportioned power as long as they understood that these new freedoms needed to be used for the greater good of their families and community. In other words, stepping beyond the domestic sphere might be acceptable if it meant the blessings of the harmonious household would be extended to the community at large. If women's work outside the home made the world a better place, the next generation would grow up to become patriotic citizens, which benefited the state, and responsible workers, which benefited capitalism. Thus, maternal feminism focused on the modernist project of nation-building, which made republican mothers out of Villegas de Magnón and other women trying to remake the Mexican nation. Maternal feminism also created a space for Villegas de Magnón to voice her belief that men and women are both accountable for the creation of a world free of sexism. Given the delicacy of the matter, she carefully worded her willingness to negotiate power with men.

Nowhere is this more profoundly stated than in an undated and unsigned letter Villegas de Magnón probably wrote to Venustiano Carranza. More than likely, she gave her friend Jovita Idar a draft in order to get some feedback before sending it to Carranza. In the letter, she praises the noble cause of the revolution and quickly conveys her modernist republican motherhood message.

> It is not enough that the current generation receive a parcel of land conceded by the Revolution. It is not enough that the economic situation of our working class and poor people be improved. The blessings of a republican, democratic, popular, and representative government are not enough. The free exercise of the franchise is not enough. The Revolution should get to the bottom of things, cultivating in the crib of the home new generations, healthier generations, more robust, better nourished, and better prepared to fulfill their destiny.[71]

The letter also alludes to the role of the White Cross in ensuring Mexico's glorious future through the regenerative works of its many branches and asks for Carranza's authorization and support in these endeavors. Villegas de Magnón offers specifics, discussing her vision of federations of Mexican women in each of the states in the Mexican Republic working to eradicate the "vices that may be more directly the causes of the degeneration of our species." The work of these women would contribute toward the "formation of character" and "the cultivation of the brain." Their focus would be future generations of Mexicans.[72]

Addressing a major Mexican leader from a very traditional and patriarchal background, she boldly requests his support in tying the female-operated project to the nation's future. To soften her message, Villegas de Magnón used the gendered language she imagined Carranza would appreciate.

> I ask you, sir, to forgive the humility of my efforts and the very limited reach of my intelligence before such grave problems, but I assure you that I do not fear, nor do I feel weak to fight as I am, and I only ask you grant me the privilege of carrying out my labors within a wide and complete system of organization and discipline; and I understand that later on will come many others capable of developing them in great magnitude.[73]

She continues with more self-deprecating language in an effort to drive home her message of national transcendence and the significant role women should play.

> My sex being so weak and modest and humble my work, I already feel wounded by the poisoned passions and betrayal, but I now realize that all healthy work needs to pull with it an army of enemies and unjust and cruel souls that submit to great trials of suffering the character of those who are inspired in good works for others![74]

Villegas de Magnón goes on to state that nothing will deter her, for her will is firm. She speaks of her "woman's dreams," "the impulses of her enthusiasm," "her love of *la patria*," "her love of humanity," and of "her infinite desire to give expansion to the forces of practical utility that the institution I preside over offers, and in so feeling moved, I obey the push of a law of evolution that never wants to waste forces and energies born in virtue, in good faith and in the love of good." Here she clearly connects her work and that of other women to nothing less than the evolution of society.[75]

The letter ends with praise for Carranza who, according to Villegas de Magnón, has nourished her with his clean philosophy of his life and his character. She expresses gratitude to him "with all the respect that a woman is capable of when she encounters a reformed man of the people." She also thanks him for "the glorious privilege you have conceded us, elevating our institution to the category of a robust, healthy, and well-disciplined national association." Later she thanks him and other commanders for the rations and courtesies they extended White Cross members and closes by stating that the National White

Cross will provide the republic with men and women who will conduct themselves with integrity and patriotism.[76]

Judging from these expressions of gratitude, the letter might have been written right after Carranza nationalized the White Cross.[77] What is clear is the author's efforts to negotiate some concessions for a predominantly female organization committed to the revolutionary struggle. Using the language of maternalism, Leonor Villegas de Magnón sought to carve out a space for women in the Mexican nation's new body politic. In her vision, it was not just the nation being born, but many opportunities for women in society and for the border communities invested in Mexico's future.

Leonor Villegas de Magnón would not have called herself a maternal feminist, but she was aware of the power that discourses of motherhood could have in society. In some of her writings she expressed the significant role of mothers in shaping the destiny of children and, by extension, nations. Such expressions legitimized her work in the public realm because they communicated that what she and other women were doing was for a purpose greater than themselves, a message that resonated among some of her contemporaries, including men.

The men and women of the White Cross traversed geopolitical, national, and gender and class borders in their missions of mercy. Whether or not they had children, female volunteer nurses could claim the mandate of motherhood as they nursed Mexico's wounded children back to health. Thus, while the soldiers ushered in a new era in Mexican history through violent struggle and death, the medical brigade witnessed the birth of a new nation by saving the lives of revolutionaries struck down.

The significance of Leonor Villegas de Magnón and the White Cross lies not in how many revolutionaries they saved. Rather, their work highlights the significance of fronterizos, particularly the members of the White Cross, in the Mexican Revolution. Villegas de Magnón and the transborder activists coupled their awareness of challenges facing Mexicans with their access to resources in an effort to negotiate whatever they could from dominant societies on both sides of the border.

PART II

BORDERLANDS MEXICAN AMERICANS IN MODERN TEXAS, 1930–1950

4

"Todo Por la Patria y el Hogar" (All for Country and Home)

The Transnational Lives and Work of Rómulo Munguía and Carolina Malpica de Munguía

When José Rómulo Munguía Torres was born in 1885, Porfirio Díaz had been in power for nearly ten years. Rómulo's father, Rómulo Franquilino Munguía, a government employee, made his opposition to Díaz known by supporting one of Díaz's political rivals, General Ramón Corona. For supporting Corona, the senior Munguía was arrested and sent to Mexico City's notorious Belén prison, where he died in 1893. His son was only eight years old at the time, and by the age of twelve, he had to leave school and join his older sisters in the workforce to help support the family. Munguía's life would be forever altered by the fate of his family under a repressive regime, inspiring him to join the revolutionary cause.[1]

In Puebla, sixty-six miles away from Mexico City, the widowed Patricio Malpica worried about his young daughter, Carolina, not having a female role model. To address this, he enrolled her in a private Methodist school operated by English women. At the Instituto Normal Metodista (INM or Normal Methodist Institute), Malpica was not only taught the subjects required of teachers in training but also how to "behave like a lady and all the niceties." Although she received an education that prepared her to become self-supporting, Malpica's ultimate goal was to marry and raise children. Indeed, when she married Rómulo in 1916, Malpica gave up a successful career as a teacher and administrator.[2] But her life, like Rómulo's, would be shaped by the Porfiriato and the Mexican Revolution, and while she left paid labor, she never gave up the spirit of public engagement of her formative years.

Rómulo and Carolina Munguía were guided by a belief in the power of and potential for individual and social transformations, reflecting their coming of age during an era of revolution in Mexico and Progressive-era reforms on

Figure 4.1 Rómulo Munguía as a boy with his parents. Nettie Lee Benson Latin American Collection, University of Texas Libraries, University of Texas at Austin.

both sides of the border. In their public endeavors throughout their lives, they sought to rescue Mexican-origin people from social decay and cultural and intellectual abandonment. Over the course of their fifty years of service to the San Antonio community, they nurtured a concern for the plight of *el méxico de afuera* (Mexicans in the United States), pursuing a reform agenda that underscored their keen awareness of how much sociocultural and institutional systems needed to be modified to achieve true equity in society.

Although they often worked together on projects, this husband and wife team differed in their activist styles. Both labored to improve the lives of Mexicans in San Antonio, but they often assumed gendered roles. Like many of their contemporaries, their upbringing was informed by the ideals of male breadwinning and female domesticity, which they carried into their community service work. However, they circumvented gender conventions as needed, particularly Carolina.

For the Munguías, gender was not the only fluid construct; so, too, was race. They well understood that Mexicans were the victims of racism. Even though they knew that European Americans saw them as a separate and inferior biological "race" and even though they themselves sometimes used the term "la raza" to self-identify, they used it to describe their Mexican ethnicity or nationality, not any supposed innate or genetic biological difference. Their son, Rubén Munguía, asserted that when his parents used the term they meant Mexican ethnicity, not biological "race."

While the Munguías understood and admired the social safety net offered by Progressive Era and New Deal American political culture, their own philosophy of helping those in need was forged in their country of origin and brought across the border. Because the Munguías grew up in Mexico, any attempt to understand the ideas that motivated these transnational activists must begin there.

The Impact of the Porfiriato and the Revolution

A few years after his father's death, Rómulo found employment in a printing company. By the time he was fourteen, his mother, Inés Torres y Méndez, had also died. Munguía moved to Mexico City and lived for a time with his married sister. There he apprenticed with Francisco Gutiérrez, a family friend who published *El Hijo del Ahuizote* for the Flores Magón brothers.[3]

By the 1904 presidential election, the many liberal clubs that had formed across the nation united to field an opposition candidate. The government responded swiftly by disbanding these groups and arresting leading members. Victims of the government's repression included the employees of *El Hijo del Ahuizote*; everyone there was arrested. Munguía escaped an execution sentence due to his youth. The government prohibited the Flores Magón brothers from publishing in Mexico, and so they and many of their followers exiled themselves in the United States. Munguía stayed in Mexico City, where he worked for the American Book and Printing Company.[4]

Figure 4.2 Rómulo Munguía as a young man with his older sisters. Nettie Lee Benson Latin American Collection, University of Texas Libraries, University of Texas at Austin.

Rómulo Munguía's politicization continued throughout his young adulthood. In 1907, he organized the first union of typographers, but pressured by the government, the group disbanded. A few continued to meet and penned pro-worker legislation, which they offered to General Bernardo Reyes, hoping he would adopt it in his presidential platform in 1908. Many young liberals, such as Munguía, thought Reyes the most viable candidate to unseat Díaz in the upcoming election. By this time, Munguía worked as a foreman of *El Diaro*, an influential pro-Reyes newspaper in Mexico City. Reyes did, in fact, have presidential ambitions; however, Díaz suppressed his movement and sent the popular general to Europe to keep him away from Mexico during election time. During Reyes's absence, Francisco Madero rose to prominence and eventually won the presidency.[5]

While rebellious fervor animated the lives of many, others such as Patricio Malpica in Puebla remained on the sidelines. And yet, his daughter's life took shape under the revolution's shadow, and she would give up her successful career to marry Rómulo Munguía, a revolutionary whose weapon of choice was the pen.

Most women in Mexico could not choose to give up paid labor upon marriage. Working-class families depended on the labor of wives and even children to survive. This worried middle-class reformers who tended to associate female wage labor with the disintegration of the family. To them, the middle-class ideal of female domesticity carried within it the keys to social order and progress.[6] Thus, reformers (many of whom worked for the Porfiriato) sought to restructure the working-class family along the lines of a middle-class model in order to safeguard the family and stabilize society.[7]

Through the educational system, the Porfiriato, and later the revolutionary state, elites sought to teach Mexican students, especially working-class and rural children, bourgeois values. The Methodist Institute of Puebla (formally the Normal Methodist Institute), where Carolina Malpica received her education, formed part of this state-mandated educational project. Celebrating the school's seventy-fifth anniversary, G. Báez-Camargo explained:

> Emerging at a time when public education, despite the generous efforts of Gabino Barreda, Justo Sierra and Ezequiel Chávez, had barely begun to consolidate itself, and despite their reform fervor barely reaching the hamlets and farmhouses of the rural Mexico, the INM from its humble origins, began to send year after year its apostolic generations of teachers to labor, not only in modest classrooms in urban primary schools, but also in the bare rooms of the rural schools.[8]

The service provided by the Methodist Institute in training schoolteachers was considered a service to the nation-state, in their efforts to integrate the poor and

Figure 4.3 Carolina Munguía's 1911 graduation from Instituto Normal Metodista in Puebla. She obtained a teaching certificate and would go on to do graduate work in English. Photo courtesy of Mrs. Elvira Cisneros.

rural, predominantly indigenous, communities. At the center of these educational issues was a debate over values.

Certain values, it was believed, facilitated the creation of the well-organized family unit, a unit able to reproduce a healthy and obedient workforce on a minimal income. In this configuration, the private family received sanction, while the value of community was downplayed through a critique of the public life of working-class people.[9] This public life was considered dangerous, for according to reformers, it "generated immorality, lack of discipline, and political consciousness and action."[10]

The continued development of the public school system during the Porfiriato heralded the government's commitment to economic modernization, for the educational system was "highly explicit in its intent to create an efficient and pliable modern labor force to meet the needs of private capital accumulation."[11] Unlike some Mexican leaders who saw the degraded status of the lower classes as a result of biology, Secretary of Education Justo Sierra believed that the working class and even the peasantry could participate in the development of a modern Mexico if their social and cultural deficiencies were rectified by education.[12] As architect of the public school system, Sierra saw capital, the state, and the family as needing to work together for economic development. Capital created jobs, the state institutionalized structures, which supported capital, and the family reproduced labor and transmitted values.[13]

Figure 4.4 Carolina Munguía honored by the Methodist Institute for her life achievement. Nettie Lee Benson Latin American Collection, University of Texas Libraries, University of Texas at Austin.

Because women were considered the primary transmitters of cultural values, the state encouraged both male and female education. Through schooling, the state would have an opportunity to replace traditional attitudes toward women with "scientific" values. Porfiriato liberals found women to be overly devoted to the Catholic Church, and they feared this religiosity would interfere with the creation of the modern family and society. This modern society rooted itself in bourgeois values, such as thrift, punctuality, obedience to authority, sobriety, love of work, discipline, and patriotism.[14]

Generally, education for women was designed to teach them middle-class values. Elementary school curricula focused on home economics, and higher learning rarely trained women in anything other than teaching and secretarial work. Industrial schools for girls reinforced gender roles with courses in cooking, sewing, hat making, decorating, and artificial flower making. The objective was not only to prepare them for marriage but also to equip them with the attitude and skills required to create an efficient and moral household. Addressing the female students of Escuela Miguel Lerdo de Tejada, Sierra articulated the state's purpose clearly: "'You are called to form souls, to sustain the soul of your husband; for this reason, we educate you .... [W]e [men and women] form a single personality called to continue the perpetual creation of the Patria [nation-state].'"[15]

At her private Protestant school, Carolina Malpica received the best education available to women in Mexico at that time. She was trained as a professional teacher and had experience in administration, yet her education was intended to instill in her middle-class female values. Malpica was an accomplished pianist, and she sewed, embroidered, gardened, and carried out domestic tasks expertly.[16] She was raised with an awareness of women's distinct roles and with an understanding that motherhood placed women in the position of transmitter of cultural values.

Besides raising children with proper cultural values, women were to function as guardians of society's moral fabric. It was understood that the unsavory elements of capitalism, such as brutal competition, often compromised a man's principles and wore him down psychologically. Under such circumstances, a man's home was truly his refuge from capital's excesses, and it was the woman who maintained his haven.[17]

Attempts by government and middle-class reformers to restructure the working-class family using a middle-class mold were only partially successful because working-class women could not afford to stay home. Rather than attacking the social, political, and economic roots of female wage earning, these reformers blamed the individual. For them, personal transformation was the key to restoring the family. Night classes and work schools were established for working-class adults of both sexes. There they were taught industrial skills and received instruction on civilized behavior. Primary school lessons were intended to overcome "the material and moral deficiencies of the home." At school, the children were critiqued for what they ate, what they wore, and how they lived.[18]

Carolina Malpica taught at the elementary school level for a number of years. No record of her lesson plans remains, but she likely propagated middle-class ideologies in her classroom, given her education in a Protestant middle-class school. One can surmise that her pedagogical approaches reflected the Porfiriato's acculturation project, for although she earned her teaching certificate in 1911, when the regime was being challenged, the educational system created under Díaz remained fairly intact.

After she finished her teacher training, Malpica completed post-secondary work in English. Soon after, she began to serve as the principal of a Methodist school in Orizaba, Veracruz, which closed after the outbreak of the Mexican Revolution. Malpica's work as a fourth and fifth grade teacher in her own school in Puebla was also interrupted by political unrest. Malpica subsequently landed a job as the city's primary school inspector or supervisor.[19] Because of the scarcity of qualified teachers in Mexico, Malpica's employment seemed ensured so long as she remained single.[20]

Malpica met Rómulo Munguía while he organized the Conciertos Cívico-Populares (Popular Civic Concerts) in Puebla. At the time, she was a teacher at the local orphanage and Rómulo was in charge of the Office of Revolutionary Propaganda in Constitutionalist-controlled Puebla.[21] By then, he was a committed revolutionary. Through his journalism, Munguía expressed many of his beliefs, especially on labor. He argued, for example, that women workers needed to be organized, for disunity among the working class led to their exploitation, since women were often used as scab labor. He also supported organizing out of a sense of fair play, as he stated in an article titled "Adelante, Compañeras" (Onward, female comrades).[22]

> It was natural for such a thing to occur [the organization of women workers]. It should not be surprising nor should the actions of our female comrades be judged as a phenomenon. On the contrary, it should be seen as the social evolution of women and as an innate and necessary thing, as restitution of the liberties and rights that for centuries have been denied them by cruel egotism.[23]

Munguía's main purpose was to push the Constitutionalist agenda. In Constitutionalist-held areas, Munguía was able to take ideology a step further by actually helping to organize workers, an activity in which he had considerable experience. In 1911, he had joined La Cámara Nacional del Trabajo (The National Chamber of Work), an organization of men and women committed to organizing all workers regardless of trade or affiliation. Its motto had been "Todo por la Patria y el Hogar" (All for the Country and the Home), a motto that Carolina adopted years later. La Cámara organized for the moral and material improvement of the suffering Mexican worker in all manifestations of life; mutual assistance in all necessary cases; faithful compliance with their duties as workers toward the nation, society, and self; and the growth of the association and defense of national industry. These were the goals Munguía would continue to fight for, eventually becoming president of the organization.

To improve workers' lives, La Cámara advocated regulating working hours, paying compensation for job-related accidents or illness, offering wages high enough to ensure a minimum standard of living, and passing laws protecting women and child laborers. Munguía favored La Cámara's agenda. His brief stay in New York City where he learned the operation and maintenance of linotype also inspired him. He recommended offering an educational program between the United States and Mexico so workers could train and eventually return to Mexico as skilled craftsmen to teach others their newly acquired skills. In so doing, they could promote their nation's industrial development and ensure the ability of others to make a decent living. Finally, Munguía's ideological agenda included a reconceptualization of the role of government. Whereas the Porfiriato had violently suppressed labor organizing, the new government envisioned by Munguía would serve as an impartial mediator between labor and management. Furthermore, the government would protect Mexicans and their jobs from foreign encroachment. He especially wanted the Mexicanization of key jobs.

Even though La Cámara was highly politicized in terms of its labor prerogatives, the leadership of this organization forbade both religious and political discussions for fear of creating rifts within the membership. Only the labor agenda was examined. The group was able to offer the membership social security benefits, a national bank, agricultural cooperatives, and its own newspaper, *El Obrero* (The Worker). The ultimate goal for La Cámara was worker self-sufficiency. During this period, the last years of the Porfiriato, La Cámara protested the imprisonment of strikers and spoke out against foreign capital.[24]

Munguía had supported the ascendancy of Madero to power in 1911, but his presidency turned out to be weak on achieving gains for labor. Despite strikes, the legislation that resulted from settlements was rarely enforced. Labor came to rely too much on the government, and the government could not or would not do enough for workers. Nevertheless, Munguía worked within the Madero administration. In February 1913, when Madero and his vice president José María Pino Suárez were assassinated, La Cámara was disbanded. In the aftermath of Francisco Madero's betrayal by Victoriano Huerta, the governor of Coahuila, Venustiano Carranza, emerged as the leader of a short-lived alliance of the anti-Huertista forces. During the struggle to remove the anti-labor Huerta from power, Rómulo joined the Constitutionalist army and served as an "information officer" heavily involved in propaganda activities, such as setting up pro-Carranza newspapers.[25]

The Malpica family disapproved of Rómulo Munguía, Carolina's choice for a marriage partner, according to Rubén Munguía, the couple's second son. Munguía was of humble origins, but more important, he was a labor activist and, even worse, a revolutionary. Revealing her strong personality, Carolina married Rómulo in spite of her family's misgivings.[26]

Despite their different backgrounds, Rómulo and Carolina shared a common outlook. Both favored reforms and participated in the Conciertos Cívico-Populares (Popular Civic Concerts) organized by Rómulo with the blessing of his boss, Constitutionalist military governor of Puebla, Luis G. Cervantes. They were part of a community effort in which teachers, students, journalists, and workers produced social and cultural programming. Besides providing free entertainment, these concerts also operated as a vehicle to transmit the opinions of the day or the Constitutionalist message. These programs featured the Puebla state orchestra and local artists and performers. Patriotic speeches on topics such as labor and agrarian reform, the role of the church in the new Mexico, and the pros and cons of strikes formed a part of the program as well.[27]

During these years, Rómulo Munguía continued his labor organizing. He did so on multiple levels, through the publication of *Nueva Patria* (New Nation), giving politicized speeches at the concerts, organizing yarn and textile workers and graphic artists, and establishing the Oficina Técnica del Trabajo (Technical Office of Employment) and La Junta de Vigilancia de Patrones y Trabajadores (The Committee for Vigilance of Bosses and Workers). These organizations tried to safeguard workers' rights by calling for the enforcement of legislation meant to protect workers and honor collective bargaining. He did not support strikes, however, believing that workers were not financially stable enough or united enough to be successful. He also did not support any type of violence in strike activities.

Ultimately, Munguía advocated education as the best avenue for workers to transcend their limited circumstances. He envisioned three major literacy and educational programs projects: la Academia del Obrero (the Worker's Academy) to educate workers for a better life; Proyecto de Ley para el establecimiento de las Escuelas Técnicas Industriales en el Estado de Puebla (the Legislative project for the establishment of industrial technical schools in the state of Puebla), which would function as a trade school to teach workers needed skills and allow them to earn a respectable place in society; and El Proyecto para la Reorganización de los Cursos en la Escuela de Artes y Oficios del Estado (the Project for the reorganization of courses in the State School of Arts and Crafts), which would ensure that the children at the orphanage would have opportunities to improve their lives. This project was basically a proposal to reorganize the welfare institutions.[28]

Munguía's many plans evaporated when President Carranza removed the socialist governor Cervantes from office in 1916. Rómulo Munguía was able to remain director of the School of Arts and Crafts and the state orphanage. He also became involved in local politics, serving as a councilman in municipal government.

The movement President Carranza led attracted and inspired liberals such as Rómulo Munguía who worked for the petit bourgeois's vision of a modern capitalist state with enough social reforms to foster class harmony and maintain the system yet at the same time protect Mexican workers from exploitation by foreign investors. Unlike the Porfiriato, which suppressed political rights valued by the middle class, the new government fostered the development of Mexicans' (especially middle-class Mexicans') political voice.

By 1925, Munguía no longer held favor with the revolutionary government. Disillusioned, he had written articles critical of Carranza's political heirs. Although he supported labor movements that sought compromises with capital, he felt that in trying to accommodate labor, Alvaro Obregón and Plutarco Calles had veered too far to the left. As he saw it, it was an opportunistic left led by Luis Morones, the labor czar under Obregón and later Calles, who controlled the Confederación Regional Obrera Mexicana (CROM) and used his influence to line his pockets. Under Morones, the government was used to crush independent unions. Essentially, CROM and the Mexican government used each other to establish a long-lasting relationship that, according to Munguía, benefited the professional labor organizer Morones and the government but not the Mexican worker. In December 1925, Munguía, utterly disappointed by what had become of the revolutionary movement, fled to the United States, narrowly escaping arrest. His wife and children joined him four months later, after the family home and business had been sold.[29]

The Munguía Family and San Antonio's Mexican-Origin Community

The Munguías settled in San Antonio, a magnet for Mexican immigrants as well as migrants from other parts of the nation. By the 1930s, "the capital of South Texas" and "the metropolis of the Southwest" had become the place to go for business, recreation, educational pursuits, and savoring of diverse cultural influences. Since Spanish colonial times, San Antonio had served as a center for trade and commerce with a military presence, and these economic aspects characterized the city into the twentieth century.

The early twentieth century brought significant demographic changes for the city's Mexican-origin people. In 1900, for instance, residents of Mexican descent stood at 13,722, or 25.7 percent of the total population, which mushroomed to 103,000, or 46.3 percent, by 1940. Unfortunately, growing numbers did not translate into upward mobility because racism and modernization relegated Mexican-origin people, in particular the lower class, to the status of a racialized caste. They were considered by Anglo residents to be better suited for the many low-paid labor jobs created by commercial ranching and later agribusiness, industrialization, and a developing service sector. Along with African Americans, they faced racialization and segregation, except that for blacks this marginalization took the form of de jure segregation on the east side of the city while Mexicans found themselves confined to the west side by custom. Political exile Rómulo Munguía entered this neighborhood as an educated professional who, along with his wife, established their family as pillars of their adopted community.[30]

In 1926, Rómulo Munguía arrived virtually penniless in San Antonio, but he was soon hired as shop superintendent for *La Prensa* (the Press), a Spanish-language daily newspaper founded in 1913 by Mexican exile Ignacio E. Lozano. He had scant knowledge of the English language, but at forty-one years of age, he was determined to succeed. Fortunately, in the colonia, he did not really need a strong command of English. The first years in the United States were difficult for the Munguías with the onset of the Great Depression. The rest of the family had to pitch in—for example, sons Rafael, Rubén, and Guillermo sold popular magazines like the *Saturday Evening Post, Liberty,* and *Collier's* in the downtown business area. Carolina and the children also shelled pecans at home, and during the early 1930s, she hosted a half hour radio program in Spanish on KONO five days each week. Called *La Estrella,* the show featured local talent, conversation, and classical music. The Eugene Roth family owned KONO, and the Munguías paid for their show by securing ads. Through the show, Carolina sought to connect with her new Spanish-speaking San Antonio community and provide them with refined programming. Although they had been a politically persecuted family in Mexico, they held a higher socioeconomic status there than in the United States. Despite initial language barriers and financial challenges, however, the Munguías steadily progressed. Together the Munguías reared seven children and started a business.[31]

Although *La Estrella* succeeded, Rómulo Munguía faced too much competition in radio and he yearned to start a printing business. He was able to purchase the equipment and soon was serving the printing needs of a bilingual San Antonio. The print shop's success can be attributed to a number of factors, in addition to Munguía's skills. At the time, Anglo-American printers often discriminated against people of color, so not only Spanish-speaking business owners and some Anglo customers but also local Chinese grocers used Munguía Printers for their advertising needs. Second, Munguía received training via correspondence courses in Spanish from the International Correspondence School of Scranton, Pennsylvania, that focused on advertising. Third, the business was a family affair, which probably cut down on labor costs. Rafael focused on the linotype operation, Rubén became the general manager, Guillermo worked as pressman, and Rómulo Jr. and Enrique served as press feeders. Elvira answered the phones and performed odd jobs around the shop. Nevertheless, the business did have non-family employees—twenty full-time workers by 1941.[32]

Within a few years, the Munguías owned a business, a house, an automobile, and even a telephone.[33] Their home in the "respectable" neighborhood of Prospect Hill symbolized their success. A middle-class enclave, Prospect Hill, was economically and culturally a world apart from the Westside, where

Figure 4.5 Rómulo and Carolina Munguía at Munguía Printers celebrating with their employees the anniversary of the business. Nettie Lee Benson Latin American Collection, University of Texas Libraries, University of Texas at Austin.

residents lived in tenements or shacks.[34] Even though they all lived in and around the Westside, the gulf between the Mexican working class and the Mexican middle class was considerable. Unlike the majority of Mexican immigrants, the Munguía family arrived with significant personal resources. Rómulo Munguía, a self-taught intellectual and political thinker, had experience in the printing business, and Carolina's education and teaching experience prepared her to take on leadership roles within her new community.[35]

The working class suffered significantly due to discrimination, substandard education, and inadequate skills. They held the worst-paid jobs in the city and were vulnerable to layoffs during hard times.[36] The Mexican middle class

Figure 4.6 Pan-American Optimist Little League. Rómulo Munguía shared the success of his business with the community by sponsoring a youth baseball team. Nettie Lee Benson Latin American Collection, University of Texas Libraries, University of Texas at Austin.

that consisted of businessmen, professionals, and highly skilled workers had greater educational and financial resources, and they found lucrative economic opportunities in San Antonio. Even if they were discriminated against in the city's Anglo-dominated economy, they could cater to a ready-made Mexican market on the Westside.[37]

The sections of the Westside inhabited by the poorest Mexicans generated the lowest tax base, resulting in few, if any, city services. There were very few parks and playgrounds, sidewalks, front yards, paved streets, street lamps, or adequate sanitation and drainage systems.[38] Further aggravating the situation was the city's inability to respond to increased immigration from Mexico and migration from outlying rural areas. Thus, many residents lived in crowded shacks and battled an assortment of diseases.[39] While the Westside represented one of the nation's worst slums, it was also considered the Paris of the southwest urban barrios due to its extensive social cultural events.[40]

In the realm of education, working-class children enjoyed far fewer opportunities than their middle-class counterparts. The city's residential segregation meant that most of the Mexican children from working-class families were educated in the inferior Westside public school system, which had fewer schools and teachers and less funding than Anglo schools.[41] A few prosperous middle-class Mexican families sent their children to public schools beyond the Westside, and some opted to educate them in Mexico.[42] The Munguía boys attended Westside public schools, but unlike the children of the poor, their parents could afford to supplement their education.[43] Additionally, middle-class children did not have to interrupt their school year to join relatives on the migrant trail, like many of the working-class children often did.

To the Munguías, the Westside Mexican-origin community seemed in dire need of institutional change, but just as important would be the choices each family made about what to resist and what to adapt to in order to survive within the American system. Even though they were fervent Mexican cultural nationalists, the Munguías understood that adaptation, perhaps some acculturation, was in order, and yet they believed that Mexican-origin people needed to know and appreciate their cultural roots. They needed to be culturally redeemed as gente decente and gain strength from such an identity in the struggle against racial discrimination. To that end, the couple engaged in individual and joint projects designed to elevate the profile of the Mexican-origin people in their own eyes as well as those of the Anglo-American community.[44]

The Munguías reminded the San Antonio community of the great privilege of having their origin in Mexico, a country rich in cultural traditions with a proud history. Their consciousness of raza marginalization inspired them to work to empower this vulnerable sector of society and to effect social change within and outside the Mexican-origin community. Having been a teacher in revolutionary Mexico, Carolina Malpica de Munguía naturally took an interest in educational projects. She taught Spanish classes at the Wesleyan Institute (later Trinity University), engaged in literacy work, and participated in El Patronato, the group responsible for the establishment of the permanent extension school of La Universidad Autónoma de México in San Antonio.[45]

The social and educational conditions of Mexican-origin people were of greatest concern to Carolina. Despite their troubles, she believed that the less advantaged could be "socially and culturally redeemed." She attributed the debasement of the Spanish language to the fact that Mexicans born and raised in the United States were less able to access Mexican culture. Her Spanish-language radio program begun in 1932 was designed to educate listeners on subjects such as literature, music, geography, and Mexican culture.[46]

Círculo Cultural "Isabel, la Católica"

On June 12, 1938, Carolina Malpica de Munguía, "influenced by the social and cultural redemption labors so successfully sponsored by the Counsel General of Mexico," formed a female voluntary association to help lower middle-class and working-class Mexican-origin women in San Antonio.[47] Under the slogan "Todo Por la Patria y el Hogar" (All for country and home), she founded the Círculo Social Femenino, México (Female Social Circle, Mexico). Later changed to Círculo Cultural "Isabel, la Católica" (Cultural Circle, "Isabella, the Catholic"), the organization was a vehicle for cultural redemption and female benevolence. Members worked to restore the culture of la patria (México) in the city in the face of growing Americanization and the dilution of a Mexican identity. It promoted a common ethnic identity to unify Mexicans across class lines in a struggle for survival amid racial discrimination and poverty. According to its statement of principle, the society sought "to procure the moral and intellectual improvement of 'women of modest means' so as to benefit the community," which they felt to be economically and culturally deteriorating.[48] The Círculo was operated by women, for the benefit of women, a self-help ideology that recognized women's centrality to community uplift.

The members of the Círculo Cultural met twice a month on Sunday afternoons in a hall at the Mexican library. Although the names of forty-six women appear on the organization roster, an average of twenty to twenty-five attended the meetings. Malpica de Munguía, assisted by six officers, served as president of the society. Beyond conducting general housekeeping tasks and listening to self-improvement and educational speeches, the members of Círculo Cultural engaged in a number of benevolent activities. For example, they took up donations for individuals in need, supported the Fiestas Patrias (Mexican holiday celebrations), helped the Mexican consulate and the Mexican clinic, organized cultural events, and raised money for charitable projects, such as the purchase of food baskets. The Mexican Clinic had been established in 1925 through the fundraising efforts of Cruz Azul Mexicana and, under the auspices of the Mexican consulate, it assisted poor families in San Antonio and throughout Texas. Mexican-origin doctors treated an average of 200 patients a month, and their work depended on community support. Círculo Cultural saw the role of the Mexican clinic as vital to the community and sent delegates to the Cruz Azul Mexicana convention.[49]

Although there were a few lower middle-class women in Círculo Cultural, most members belonged to the working class. These women had few resources, and like most people of color during that time, they were isolated from mainstream institutions. Malpica de Munguía sought to expand their social horizons and help them adapt to a foreign and often hostile world.[50]

Malpica de Munguía sought to make life easier for club members by securing resources for them. For example, she acquired the services of two Mexican-origin lawyers so that the women could consult them on issues involving US laws and politics. She sought the services of doctors, nurses, and teachers for the benefit of the members, serving as the contact between the club and the Anglo-American community. She also informed members of educational opportunities, such as free sewing and English classes.[51]

While such cultural negotiation expanded members' social network and re-sources, cultural nationalism, or an emphasis on "all things Mexican," celebrated ethnic pride and unity and tended to obscure class differences. That Malpica de Munguía exercised cultural nationalism is evident from a form letter she sent out to Mexican governors asking them to donate a representative handicraft from their state to be used in an art exhibition.[52]

Malpica de Munguía was not so much trying to preserve Mexican culture as she was advancing a particular vision of Mexican culture. To members of the native-born working class in the Westside community, Mexican culture was reflected more in *corridos* about the "rinches malvados" (evil Rangers), for they had been here long enough to know about the violent Texas Rangers. More recent working-class arrivals might have connected with Mexican culture corridos about "Adelitas in Revolutionary Mexico." Over time Mexican and American cultures had melded into a "Tex-Mex" style in the lives of Westside residents. Yet by categorizing Westside residents as being in a "state of real in-tellectual . . . abandonment," Malpica de Munguía essentially negated their experiences and imposed her own understanding of culture on them. She prob-ably did not see it as an imposition but as an intervention designed to help a pre-dominantly rural and formally uneducated people survive in an urban, capitalist, and Anglo-dominated world. Her celebration of Mexican culture at a time when Anglo-Americans denigrated it was a subtle form of resistance.[53]

Despite the fact that Malpica de Munguía seemed to assume that all Mexican-origin women had the same cultural needs, she succeeded in attracting both Mexican and Mexican American women to the club. Ethnic pride took various forms: in addition to the Mexican art exhibit, all minutes and correspondence were written in Spanish. The society's theme song was the "Mixteca," a very pop-ular song expressing feelings of sorrow brought on by life away from Mexico. Malpica de Munguía periodically delivered talks on issues related to Mexico, and the Fiestas Patrias, Cinco de Mayo, and Dieciséis were observed religiously.[54]

The society's association with the other members of the Colonia Mexicana (Mexican-origin community) also served to foster ethnic pride. Círculo Cultural sent representatives to the Mexican clinic and la Asociación de la Biblioteca Mexicana (the Mexican Library Association), a Mexican consulate project. They also made donations toward the campaigns of young Mexican women running for queen of the Fiestas Patrias.[55] Society members made honorary members of a former consul, two lawyers, and a teacher in appreciation for past assistance and future support. The lawyers provided free legal advice and the teacher gave free art classes for the children of members and participated in the arts and crafts exhibition.[56]

Female Benevolence

The second component of Carolina Malpica de Munguía's quest for community uplift was female benevolence. She believed that clubwomen had a distinct responsibility to help others, but answering the challenge given to them as "women, wives, and Mexicans" had to be done a certain way. Carolina Malpica de Munguía's daughter, Elvira Cisneros, described her mother as the type of person who did not believe in "banging on doors" to achieve goals. Malpica de Munguía harbored hopes that Mexicans and Mexican Americans could be accepted by mainstream society, or at least that the worst elements of racism might be avoided, if only they became more "respectable." For example, her daughter remembered the importance her mother placed on self-improvement and on "being clean, courteous, and hardworking."[57] To her, acceptance did not mean assimilation but simply fair and equal treatment regardless of ethnicity.

Malpica de Munguía's concept of proper gender roles was doubtless influenced by her own upbringing. Although she observed traditional gender roles by focusing her energies on raising a family and running a household, she actively participated in the family business, took care of the payroll at times, and shelled pecans at home during a particularly financially difficult period.[58] Nonetheless, a middle-class notion of "lady-like" behavior was encoded in Círculo Cultural's bylaws. Emphasizing the need to maintain peace and preserve harmonious relations, the club had a rule expressly forbidding the general discussion of any subject that could seriously disrupt order.[59] And yet, being "lady-like" did not stop members from engaging the world outside domesticity.

Central to the idea that women bore moral responsibility for society were two measures of personal conduct: a woman's personal integrity and interpersonal relationships. To address the first, Malpica de Munguía delivered talks or invited guest speakers to discuss issues such as vice and its threat to female morality and *el honor de la mujer* (a woman's honor).[60] The club's rules were designed to foster good relations among members, and Malpica de Munguía safeguarded the club from too much divisiveness.[61] Despite one or two minor incidents, the members of Círculo Cultural worked successfully to bridge class differences, and no evidence exists that such differences undermined their ethnic unity.[62]

Aware of the vast material differences between the *gente humilde* (the poor) and the *gente comoda* (comfortable classes) to which she belonged, Munguía reasoned that the only division that counted was the one between the gente decente (the decent people—the high society of reason, manners, and culture) and the *gente corriente* (the common or crude people—the mass society of emotions, ill manners, and no culture). Immersed in these ideas that elevated maternalism as women's highest role, Munguía promoted among Mexican-origin women a middle-class ideology similar to that of many late nineteenth- and early twentieth-century Anglo-American and African American female activists that was informed by concepts of modernity and social progress. Malpica de Munguía's son, for example, described his mother's community service as an extension of the work she performed at home, nurturing and caring for others.[63]

Carolina imbibed these ideas from both a modernizing Mexican state and an educational upbringing by British Methodists. Promising to police themselves and other women as they brought the values of the traditional home into the broader community, maternalists such as Carolina Munguía were free to participate and even become leaders in all types of public arenas.

Activities were designed to foster ethnic pride and unity, but there is some evidence that class differences did cause some tensions within the club. In a letter addressed to the members the president wrote, "As to the moral life of our society, with great sincerity I tell you that I am not satisfied, for knowing each to be from different parts of the city it seems that we do not understand each other. We do not trust each other."[64] After Malpica de Munguía wrote the letter, the club continued to operate for ten months, but then the minutes ended abruptly. There is no mention in the minutes or correspondence of an impending crisis. Malpica de Munguía's son speculated that perhaps the society broke up because of World War II, as did various voluntary societies. With four sons in the service, Malpica de Munguía decided to focus her energies on the American Red Cross.[65]

The Paradox of Race in Modern Mexico

Although both Malpica de Munguía and African American women leaders were able to bridge class differences, they went about it in different ways. Malpica de Munguía organized along gender and ethnic lines, while African American women united along gender and racial lines. The Munguías and others used la raza, an ethnic identifier, as shorthand for describing Mexican-origin people in Mexico and across the globe.[66]

It is not surprising that they conceived of the term "la raza" along ethno-nationalist lines because a major cultural project of the revolutionary state was to engender a unified nationalist identity that would safeguard against the divisive racial stratifications inherited from a deeply entrenched Spanish colonial legacy. Ironically, revolutionary Mexico produced an Indigenista movement marked by racial ideologies that continued to privilege the notion of biological race. Philosopher, writer, and politician José Vasconcelos developed the concept of the "cosmic race," which promoted a theory of mestizo racial superiority based on the notion that mixed-race people inherited the best traits of Indians and Europeans.

It should be noted that Mexico's indigenous populations had no part in the development of these theories. Vasconcelos, Manuel Gamio, and other proponents of such theories mainly were mestizos with western educations. They had been raised and educated in Porfirian Mexico, influenced by social Darwinism, Spencer's evolutionism, and Comte's Positivist ideas. These imported ideas, when placed in the context of Mexico's highly stratified society, meant that in order to bring the country together as a nation, the Porfiriato took on an aggressive position of forced integration and assimilation, denigrating the cultures of Mexico's many indigenous groups. The state relied on racist theories to justify its mistreatment of those who fell outside the modern, nationalist rubric. It even attacked the communal land system, economically dislocating Indian communities. The expectation was that Indian peasants would become the urban and rural proletariat that modernization required.

The Indigenista reformers grew up witnessing the many economically motivated and racially charged abuses sustained by Indians and were sympathetic toward their plight. However, they continued to talk as if racism was a biological factor rather than a social and political construction. Furthermore, Mexico as a society continued to prize "whiteness," and dark-skinned Mexicans remained subject to discrimination.[67]

Intelligent, educated, and cultured, Malpica de Munguía knew from her own experience that having brown skin in no way determined her cognitive capacities or ability to engage in modern society. She harbored hopes that in a world free from discrimination and with the proper role models and opportunities for advancement, la raza could be elevated in every way. This notion that a just society could be shaped by environment and the creation of opportunities as opposed to ideas of social progress connected to social Darwinism, make the concept of la raza, as applied by the Munguías, subversive in Jaime Crow Texas. For them, there was no such thing as a biological "Mexican race," only a diverse nation with a substantial mestizo population and a shared Mexican nationality.

The Munguías, while avoiding racialist ideologies, were nevertheless in step with other modern social and political concepts found in both countries, such as the state's use of institutions like the school system to integrate or nationalize groups of people not easily assimilated into the nation's social and cultural fabric. As an educator in Mexico, Malpica de Munguía had been a direct participant in this process, and as a community activist in the United States, she searched for ways to help the Mexican-origin community in San Antonio adapt to the American system. This did not make her a proponent of outright assimilation. Rather, she believed that some integration and participation in national life would be necessary for the survival of Mexican-origin people. Isolation would only worsen the problems this community already faced. Like her husband, Malpica de Munguía had faith in the power of education and devoted much of her energy toward the goal of making the educational experiences of Mexican-origin children more effective and meaningful by getting Spanish-speaking mothers involved.

In Step with the PTA

Starting out with a strategy of benevolence inspired by her concern for schoolchildren and driven by a desire to help their mothers, Malpica de Munguía began volunteering in the Crockett Elementary School Spanish-Speaking PTA, which became a vehicle for reform.[68] From the 1920s through 1950s, the Spanish-Speaking PTA in Texas sought to address the needs of Spanish-speaking parents and their children. The first local groups organized as early as 1923 and gained recognition from the Texas Congress of Parents and Teachers in 1927. Spanish-Speaking PTA chapters represented the first voluntary associations of Mexican-origin women that substantially interacted with mainstream society. As immigration from Mexico increased, and after 1915 school attendance became compulsory, Texas schools saw rising numbers of Mexican-origin students in the classroom. Unfortunately, mothers who could not speak English were alienated from the regular PTA meetings, but the Spanish-Speaking PTA allowed for open communication channels between Mexican mothers and Anglo-American teachers.

In San Antonio between 1931 and 1933, the Men's Council No. 2 of LULAC organized eight Spanish-Speaking PTA chapters, including the Crockett Latin American Parent-Teacher Association with founding president Mrs. Paula Villarreal de Jones. LULAC leaders strongly encouraged women to support these PTA organizations rather than LULAC or even Ladies LULAC.[69] It is not surprising that this civil rights organization placed such a strong emphasis on the PTA since education was one of the major fronts they used to fight racial discrimination in society. More intriguing, an organization that strongly encouraged Mexican Americans in Texas to speak English actually established Spanish-Speaking PTA chapters. Ultimately, LULAC realized that unless the mothers of Mexican and Mexican American schoolchildren could engage using their own language, the essential relationship between parents and teachers would not be forged and Mexican-origin students would continue to have a dismal educational experience.

Carolina Malpica de Munguía worked tirelessly to make student life at Crockett Elementary anything but dismal. In 1910, only 10 percent of the school's students were of Mexican-origin, but by 1941, that figure had risen to

90 percent.[70] By the late 1930s, the Crockett Latin American PTA had seventy-six members.[71] It functioned through committees, such as beneficence, salubrity, finance, outreach, and program. As president of the chapter in 1938, Carolina led the group through a period of tremendous achievement all the more commendable because San Antonio's working-class Mexican population was still reeling from the effects of the Great Depression. So many children attended school hungry that the Latin American PTA opened a dining room. Many children lived in Westside hovels with poor or nonexistent sanitation, so the Latin American PTA had showers built in schools. To clothe indigent schoolchildren, they organized sewing circles. They also provided medical aid for these students. Often the members rolled up their sleeves and got to work. For example, during the lunch hour, some of the members served meals to children at the Home of Neighborly Service Center. Other times they involved members of the community, such as when they engaged Mexican American barbers to provide free haircuts for the children. Through the year, they were faithful fundraisers, gathering donations to buy the children clothes and shoes as well as Christmas baskets for their families.

Malpica de Munguía's leadership eventually expanded beyond Crockett Elementary. Between 1940 and 1941, she served as head of the Spanish-Speaking Department of the San Antonio PTA Council in District 5. In this capacity, she oversaw other Spanish-Speaking PTAs within her district, visited

Figure 4.7 Rómulo and Carolina Munguía at Christmas. Navidad del Niño Pobre (Christmas for the Poor Child). Nettie Lee Benson Latin American Collection, University of Texas Libraries, University of Texas at Austin.

seven schools, and attended executive PTA meetings. She also organized a new PTA chapter and attended the state PTA convention where she displayed the work of Spanish-speaking children. Ultimately, Carolina Malpica de Munguía believed that through the PTA, Mexican-origin parents would help promote understanding with Anglo-American society. To that end, the Crockett Latin American PTA welcomed Anglo-American teachers in its membership and made Crockett's school principal, Herman Hirsch, its honorary president. Teachers served as officers—Sara T. Lucksinger as treasurer and Clevie Bryan as director of publicity—and each committee, except for one, had at least one Anglo-American teacher. Sixteen out of the thirty teachers at Crockett Elementary belonged to the Latin American PTA, which perhaps reflected their genuine concern with the plight of Mexican-origin children or the effectiveness of Carolina Malpica de Munguía's leadership. In any case, to have seventy plus Mexican-origin women and more than half of the Anglo-American teachers working together in a Spanish-Speaking PTA at a time when Mexicans in Texas experienced de facto, if not de jure, segregation represented a remarkable accomplishment.[72]

Mexican-origin people in Texas certainly had some Anglo-American supporters, but even among allies there were cultural challenges. Mrs. T. J. Martin, an Anglo who headed the department to coordinate the Spanish-Speaking PTAs, sought to reach Mexican-origin mothers through the use of the Spanish language. She had PTA materials printed in Spanish and asked Consuelo E. Herrera, a teacher from Austin, to translate articles for the state magazine, *Texas Parent-Teacher*. In 1941, the magazine began a Spanish column entitled *El Hogar Creativo* (The Creative Home). Later it added another column titled *En Defensa de la Niñez y de la Juventud* (In Defense of Childhood and Youth). At the same time, Mrs. Martin was a strong advocate of assimilation, encouraging Spanish-speaking parents to speak English and learn about American history and government. She also called upon immigrants to become naturalized citizens. Her department published a pamphlet on citizenship written in Spanish.[73] Mrs. Martin eventually lost her position to Mexican American lawyer Manuel González because members of the Spanish-Speaking PTAs felt that they needed a leader who spoke Spanish, which she did not.[74]

Despite occasional moments of cultural disconnect, a shared gendered class ideology gave activists such as Carolina Munguía an opportunity to find common ground with the PTA. The National Council of Mothers, the organization that would grow into the National PTA, was founded in 1897 as a forum in which women could exert their rights as mothers to influence public policy in the interest of bettering the lives of children. As an organization, it did not support women's rights or the struggle for equality between the

Figure 4.8 Parent-Teacher Association for Crockett Elementary School. Carolina Munguía sits third from left. Munguía served as head of the Spanish-speaking Department, District 5 of the San Antonio PTA in 1940 and 1941. Photo courtesy of Mrs. Elvira Cisneros.

sexes. Originally, it functioned along hierarchical lines, attracting mainly elite women and then incorporating local groups throughout the country into the National Congress. Not until the 1920s and 1930s did Mexican-origin women and other nonwhite and nonelite women join the association. The National Congress of Mothers was effective in producing some impressive Progressive-era reforms, including kindergarten classes, hot lunch programs, child labor laws, mandatory immunization, a public health service, and a juvenile justice system.[75]

While American progressives searched for order in society through rationality, education, organization, bureaucracy, and professionalization, Mexican reformers also introduced reforms in public as well as private life that encouraged a greater role for government in people's everyday lives, including the educational reforms of Mexican secretary of education, Justo Sierra. By the time Malpica de Munguía arrived in the United States, her education and professional training meant that she prioritized children's welfare followed by the well-being of the family as the central unit of organization in society, which would lead to the creation of a more perfect citizenry devoted to the nation's progress. Malpica de Munguía found a home in the PTA because its belief system mirrored her own reform mentality in many important ways. In addition, like the PTA, Malpica de Munguía adhered to the notion that women, as mothers, played a key role in the processes of cultural and political edification.

That Malpica de Munguía believed in women's special role is evident in her essay, "Why We Should Belong to the Parent, Teacher Association." She wrote, "One of the biggest associations known . . . is sustained by the forceful energy, by the incomparable valor and by the faith that only inhabits the feminine heart." She praised the teacher as the other special human being "in charge of forming in that child the base . . . that foundation of a whole nation."[76]

She ended by spelling out the organization's three objectives: "Home, Community, and Country."[77] A look at the PTA creed, authored by Benjamin O. Wist, as well as some of the programming of this period, shows how closely Carolina Malpica de Munguía's ideas reflected the organization's philosophies. PTA members of the 1930s and 1940s believed that the home was the most important institution for society's welfare, that the school was "the best agency" created to cooperate with the home in the critical task of "building human char- acter," that teachers had boundless faith in the future and their service and love for the child could only be surpassed by that of the mother, that the child was the hope of tomorrow, and that the PTA was "an organization of parents and teachers created by these in the interests of their most priceless possessions, the child."[78]

The San Antonio Council Parent-Teacher Association Bulletin contains abun- dant examples of how the PTA put its philosophy of child edification, family strengthening, community betterment, and patriotic service to the nation into practice.[79] In order to promote the edification of the child, for instance, they had a "Character Education" Committee, intended to promote emotional maturity in adolescent boys and girls. It seemed to target girls in particular, emphasizing the importance of their education in "domestic management, home nursing, and child care." Given that the association believed that women were key cul- tural transmitters of values and the child's first teacher, it seemed imperative that young women develop an early mastery of all things related to the home and children.[80]

Tying the theme of women's critical role in society to the connection between child and nation became even more important during World War II. One PTA bulletin exhorted women to "educate ourselves in home and family life because the future of our great nation lies in the home rather than in politics or armies."[81] Gearing up young people, families, and the community in the service of a nation at war was nothing new to Carolina Malpica de Munguía after her experiences in her native Puebla during the Mexican Revolution. Nor was it new to transborder activists, such as Jovita Idar and Leonor Villegas de Magnón, who knew all too well the significant roles women could perform during a national crisis.

In Malpica de Munguía's rendition of the transborder political culture, women could cross over into public spaces wearing the robes of maternalism; Mexicans could survive in the United States by galvanizing around the ethnic construction of la raza selectively adapted to American society; and activists could transfer their identities, political strategies, and ideologies across national borders, tailoring them to the circumstances of their community work in the United States. At the center of all this Carolina Malpica de Munguía placed Mexican women, whom much of her work involved and was meant to benefit.

Don Rómulo and the Colonia Mexicana

Rómulo Munguía also understood and appreciated the significant role of women, in times of both peace and war. Well aware of the many contributions of women during the Mexican Revolution as fighters and as workers, Munguía also examined the role of Mexican women in the United States. Like his wife, he believed that women had a sacred mandate to manage the home and guide children along the path toward emotional maturity and responsible citizenship. In an undated essay, probably written in the late 1960s or early 1970s, Rómulo Munguía criticized the youth of the era as having lost their way and placed blame on the parents, calling on mothers to reclaim their mandate and set things right.

> I recommend that as women, lovers of the happiness of the home, of a brilliant future without obstacles for our children, desirous of the elevation of La Raza and especially as good Christian women, go preach to all and every mother that suffer the pain of not having known how to prepare the beings entrusted upon them. That they unite with you and, all united, achieve the reconquest. Ground that for now we are about to lose: the salvation of our youth.[82]

Munguía was probably not happy with the counterculture and might have objected to the separatist political strategies of the Chicano movement. He was nearing the end of a long and productive life both in Mexico and in the United States. He had struggled incessantly to end discrimination in the United States by instilling ethnic pride among Mexican-origin people and by working to bring about greater understanding and harmony between the peoples of the United States and Mexico. Like the pre-Chicano movement generations, he believed that the best way to end racism was through education, educating the victim of racism about his or her own self-worth and rights, and educating the oppressor about the benefits of cultural diversity and tolerance. An examination of his work in San Antonio illustrates this strategy of social transformation.

As Rómulo Munguía's business thrived in the late 1930s and 1940s, he hired more employees and dedicated more time to community projects, including the publication of *El Pueblo* (the People), a weekly bilingual newspaper that covered the Colonia Mexicana (the Mexican colony or Latin Quarter) on the Westside of San Antonio and issues on both sides of the border. One of the organizations he became heavily involved with was the Comisión Honorífica Mexicana (The Honored Mexican Commission), a group of community leaders that worked closely with the Mexican consul to organize Mexican citizens living abroad, address the problems they faced, and meet their needs.[83] Munguía printed *Vínculos*, the organization's bulletin, but he also traveled with the staff of the consulate office throughout the consul's jurisdiction, which included Colorado, Louisiana, New Mexico, Oklahoma, and Texas. On these trips, the consul advised emigrants of their rights and responsibilities and tried to organize them. Efraín Domínguez, a former consul, remembered that Rómulo "was committed to various charitable works and legal reforms that would benefit the community." Because of his background as a labor activist, Munguía was often asked to address issues pertaining to labor organization among Mexican workers.[84]

Munguía also participated in the Comité Patriotico Mexicano (Patriotic Mexican Committee), which mounted the annual Fiestas Patrias, the Deiz y Seis and Cinco de Mayo celebrations. Munguía served as an organizer and publicized these events in his newspapers, *El Pueblo* and *La Voz de México* (the Voice of Mexico). Through these publications, he also informed the public about Mexican heroes and carried messages from government officials in Mexico and Texas, including the Good Neighbor Commission of Texas. These special events carried the international significance of the Fiestas Patrias, while politicians' speeches and writings carried the message that Mexicans living abroad had a responsibility to help foster improved relations between the two nations. Munguía's work in San Antonio closely resembled his work in Puebla on the Popular Civic Concerts. In both places, he sought to instill a sense of patriotic duty in the citizenry through carefully crafted social and cultural programs promoted as free entertainment.[85]

As a businessman, Munguía connected with other compatriots through La Cámara Mexicana de Comercio (the Mexican Chamber of Commerce), an association of Mexican businessmen in San Antonio whose business was conducted in Spanish. Munguía served as secretary for eight terms and chronicled the activities of La Cámara throughout the 1930s and 1940s in his newspapers *Actividades* (Activities) and *La Voz de México*. Through La Cámara, Munguía became involved in literacy programs and other community projects. In the eyes of M.C. Gonzales, another community advocate,

> Mr. Rómulo Munguía, because of his firm and valuable connections
> in Mexico and his love for anything that was Mexican, placed him,
> as a member of the Chamber, in a position of bringing about closer

Figure 4.9 Consulado General de México car. Rómulo Munguía sits in the middle seat of the back row. Nettie Lee Benson Latin American Collection, University of Texas Libraries, University of Texas at Austin.

Figure 4.10 Rómulo Munguía at a Fiestas Patrias celebration. Nettie Lee Benson Latin American Collection, University of Texas Libraries, University of Texas at Austin.

contacts, both social and in a business and educational way, with prominent people in Mexico City and Puebla. His contribution and valuable efforts were felt and much appreciated, and will be for years to come.[86]

Munguía's transnational perspectives and ties served him well both in terms of raising ethnic awareness and cultural pride and in terms of helping to materially elevate the Mexican business community in San Antonio through profitable transborder economic activity.

Though Munguía never became an American citizen, he admired the orderly political process in the United States and sought to help the Mexican-origin community by supporting progressive US political leaders, such as San Antonio mayor Maury Maverick. He also supported Catholic Church efforts to improve the lives of Westside residents. In particular, he worked with Father Carmelo Tranchese, longtime pastor of Our Lady of Guadalupe, both writing for and printing *La Voz de la Parroquia* (the Voice of the Parish) for the church. *La Voz* often expressed support for labor causes, among these the Pecan Shellers' Strike of 1938. However, when it became clear that communists formed a part of the strike's leadership, the church withdrew its official support. Munguía moved on to other projects.

Amid Rómulo Munguía's many projects, two long-term ones stand out as representative of his belief system and political strategies. Concerned about the plight of Mexican immigrants and their offspring, he formed an organization designed to address their needs. Agrupación de Ciudadanos Mexicanos en el Extranjero (ACME), which was active during the 1940s, set out to meet the needs of la raza and to bring honor to Mexico and Mexicans. ACME sought to inform Mexican-origin people about their rights and responsibilities in the United States; to teach people about the history and culture of Mexico; to foster an interest in the economy, government, statistics, politics, and sociology; and to maintain an unadulterated form of the Spanish language and teach it to the next generation. Members spoke out against discrimination, but they also discouraged misbehavior on the part of Mexicans and Mexican Americans, which was beneath the dignity of la raza.[87]

The World War II years and immediate postwar era proved to be a time when cooperation replaced confrontation in US-Mexican relations. Aware of the impact of international events, some Mexicans in the United States such as Rómulo Munguía sought to improve the condition of Mexicans abroad by arguing that they best served as a bridge between the two countries and deserved more attention from the Mexican government. ACME believed that the Mexican government could and should do more to help Mexicans abroad. In 1946, at the grand assembly of the Partido de la Revolución Mexicana (PRM), Mexico's postrevolutionary dominant political party, Munguía, representing ACME, expressed support for Mexican presidential candidate Miguel Alemán Valdés. Munguía made his case for el méxico de afuera (Mexicans living abroad), stating, "We should consider that in any part of the world where a Mexican citizen resides, there Mexico is symbolized."[88] He spoke for the substantial numbers of Mexicans living in the United States who identified with Mexico culturally and spiritually. These people, Munguía pointed out, had been mistreated on both sides of the border, for neither government had attempted to educate them so as to improve their socioeconomic lot. Munguía asked the Mexican government to set up a commission to determine the number of Mexicans and Mexican Americans in the United States, to spell out their rights and responsibilities, to investigate racial and cultural discrimination as well as the legal recourses available for the victims of this discrimination, and to encourage Pan-American solidarity. He also called for more extensive training of consular corps so that they could defend Mexicans abroad. Though it is unclear whether Mexico followed ACME's extensive recommendations, by 1951, thanks to the persistence of the organization, the Mexican government began to allow Mexicans abroad to vote in national elections.[89]

ACME represented a transnational project created by an activist seeking to help those caught in a geopolitical space between the United States and Mexico. Munguía used the language of Franklin Roosevelt's Good Neighbor Policy and World War II hemispheric unity to speak out against discrimination in the United States. He also held Mexico accountable. Like Carolina, Rómulo attempted to mediate between people at the local level and the two nation-states whose policies affected their lives. Using his platform as a respected community leader of some means who was conversant in two languages and two cultures and plugged into sociopolitical networks in two nations, he brought together the dominant transnational discourses of the period and the community whose rights he struggled to secure.

El Patronato: Mexican Cultural Nationalism Struggles to Survive

As the immigrant generation began to be replaced by their children, the ideas of ACME, particularly its high interest and participation in Mexican politics, began to seem outdated and perhaps even unpatriotic. Many among the second generation turned to LULAC and the American GI Forum to help them claim their rights as US citizens.[90] As the US-born children of immigrants acculturated, their parents began to note changes in their attitudes toward Mexico. While they respected the nation as part of their family's past, many also expressed indifference toward the motherland as they focused their energies on the ongoing development of their identities as ethnic Americans.

One noticeable change involved the Spanish language. While many among the second generation could speak both English and Spanish fluently, a growing number spoke mostly English or a combination of the two and did not prioritize teaching their children the Spanish language. Texas was notorious for punishing Mexican-origin children who spoke Spanish in school, which may explain the loss of the Spanish language over time. Both Rómulo and Carolina Munguía were gravely concerned by this loss and joined forces with others to help preserve Mexican culture and the Spanish language for future generations. Rómulo took on a visible role in this endeavor.

Like his wife, Rómulo Munguía believed that a love and appreciation for Mexico and Mexican culture as well as the Spanish language might culturally and intellectually uplift the Mexican-origin community in San Antonio. Education also held the key to better relations between the United States and Mexico. These beliefs had been honed into political strategies of cultural redemption and social transformation that marked his work with the Mexican Consulate and with ACME. His next project also emphasized these themes.

In 1943, a Mexican lawyer, Manuel Pacheco Moreno, initiated a series of Spanish language extension courses in San Antonio in association with the Universidad Autónoma de México (UNAM). These courses were first taught in 1944 and continued until 1964. What was unique about these classes was that they were taught by some of the finest professors employed at this top university. The Mexican consulate in San Antonio, as well as concerned Mexican-origin members of the community such as Munguía, aided in this process. They generated support for the program and promoted the courses within the community. UNAM paid the professors' salaries and Mexico's Department of Foreign Relations covered their travel costs. In addition to Spanish language classes, lectures were offered on Mexican archaeology, art, history, and literature. A course on the international rights of Mexican citizens living in the United States also formed part of the curriculum.[91]

The course extension program faced numerous challenges. By 1952, San Antonians involved with these extension courses began to worry that lack of demand for these by assimilated second-generation Mexican Americans might lead to their extinction. A group of Mexican-origin and Anglo-American community leaders formed an association known as El Patronato de los Cursos de Extensión de UNAM (Patronage or Sponsorship for the extension courses of the UNAM) or El Patronato, for short, to preserve the program.

El Patronato sought to elevate interest in the extension courses and promote the Spanish language and culture. The Mexican government continued to support this program financially because it served as a way to dispel racial and cultural stereotypes about Mexico and Mexicans among Anglo-Americans.[92] It also hoped to maintain a harmonious relationship with the United States in

Figure 4.11 Rómulo Munguía with University of Puebla students posing by a school bus. Nettie Lee Benson Latin American Collection, University of Texas Libraries, University of Texas at Austin.

order to bring about a more equitable economic relationship in the postwar period.[93]

Rómulo Munguía served as El Patronato's first president, and under his leadership, the organization accrued much support, including from Anglo-American women. These women saw value in a bilingual San Antonio, and the organization promoted the idea that the extension courses would lead to better international understanding. Ads for the courses appeared in both English and Spanish, and tuition was set as low as $3 to attract students. The extension courses were taught at various places, mainly high schools and colleges, before the entire program was moved to Trinity University in 1965. Besides the language courses, other offerings included "Trade in the American Continent," "Pre-Columbian Cultures in Mexico and Peru," "Today's Latin America," and "Today's Mexican Novel."[94]

In 1957, El Patronato changed its name to El Patronato de la Cultura Ibero-Americana (The Patronage of Ibero-American Culture) to reflect the greater level of formality of the group and their desire to promote the culture of Mexico and other Hispanic countries. Munguía probably did not object to this change, for he had always been an advocate of Pan-Americanism. Throughout the 1960s and 1970s, the classes continued to attract students, and visiting professors always received a warm welcome in San Antonio. In 1972, a permanent resident branch of the UNAM was established in San Antonio. Housed in downtown San Antonio, it offered all of the regular classes as well as a study abroad program in Mexico.[95] The resident branch of UNAM in San Antonio has attracted many third generation Mexican Americans who were inspired to take Spanish language and culture courses, in part because of the Chicano Movement's emphasis on rediscovering and reconnecting with a cultural heritage that had previously been deemphasized amid their struggle for economic and political integration. In this way, UNAM San Antonio helped to turn into reality Rómulo and Carolina Munguía's transnational dream of a bilingual and bicultural San Antonio.[96]

At a time when the nationality "Mexican" had been reconfigured as a racial identifier in the United States, the Munguías reminded people that both "Mexican" and "la raza" denoted culture, even as these terms developed racialist connotations. In so doing, they employed the concept of la raza in a subversive manner that undermined the American racial hierarchy defining Mexican-origin people as nonwhite and therefore beyond the realm of US citizenship.

The Munguías identified as proud Mexican cultural nationalists exiled in the United States who, nevertheless, appreciated the benefits of acclimating to their new home. Rómulo and Carolina Munguía understood that some level of acculturation was needed to survive in the United States, but what they objected to and felt threatened la raza's ability to survive was the state of social decay and cultural abandonment in the Westside. They were appalled that so many people had lost touch with their culture of origin and developed a mixture of Mexican and American cultures most obviously seen in the use of "Spanglish" or "Tex-Mex" forms of communication. Ultimately, the Munguías believed that Mexican-origin people needed to foster an understanding and appreciation for their Mexican heritage before they adopted elements of the US culture so as to strengthen their identity, withstand the pressures of racial discrimination, and select only those characteristics of American culture that benefited them.

Aware of how the many stereotypes of Mexicans were used to justify social, economic, and political inequities in US society, Rómulo and Carolina Munguía made the cultural redemption of Mexicans in the United States their top priority. Far more than a superficial makeover, it represented an extension of the nation-building process they had started in revolutionary Mexico to the diasporic community in the United States.

How the Munguías went about redeeming la raza reflected their gendered socialization, with Rómulo operating as the committed crusader for social reform and Carolina Malpica de Munguía subscribing to the often-exalted concept of "motherhood" and frequently turning to charitable works to address society's problems. Maternalism helped to legitimate her activism within patriarchal society. Yet the strategy of female benevolence could, at times, subvert gendered conventions by using the realm of charity work to accomplish some structural changes as well. Such was the case with Malpica de Munguía's work with the Latin American PTA, which began as an act of benevolence to reach out to Spanish-speaking mothers who needed help and ended up as a reform effort to make the school system more responsive to the needs of these mothers and their children. At times, Malpica de Munguía's methods appeared unconventional for a woman whose identity seemed defined by traditional gender and class conventions.

The Munguías used their considerable class and educational privileges to craft strategies in line with a transborder political culture geared to promote community empowerment. Through such organizations as the Latin American PTA, Círculo Cultural "Isabel, la Católica," ACME, and El Patronato, they employed gendered strategies of cultural redemption and reform reflective of their experiences as a transnational family and expanded these to serve Mexican immigrants and Mexican Americans.

5

La Pasionaria (the Passionate One)

Emma Tenayuca and the Politics of Radical Reform

> Everyone felt we [Communists] were trying to take over the govern-
> ment. What we were trying to do was organize labor, organize the un-
> employed, so they would have their rights.
> —Emma Tenayuca, quoted in the *San Antonio*
> *Express-News*, March 6, 1988

> There should exist something greater . . . that will speak higher of us
> as women, wives, and as Mexicans—that is the betterment of our
> people . . . . [W]e might bear in mind our theme—all for country
> and home.[1]
> —Carolina Malpica de Munguía to the members of the Círculo Cultural
> "Isabel, la Católica," San Antonio, January 8, 1938

On August 25, 1939, labor leader and Texas Communist Party chair Emma Tenayuca barely escaped with her life as she and other party leaders attempted to hold their party's state convention at the San Antonio Municipal Auditorium. As a large anti-communist mob 5,000 strong prepared to storm the building, police guided party members to a secret tunnel. Everyone escaped safely, but that day marked the end of Tenayuca's public career in radical reform politics. Two days after the Municipal Auditorium riot, the ladies of the Círculo Cultural "Isabel, la Católica," led by their president, Carolina Munguía, held their bimonthly meeting at the San Antonio Latin American Center. The members of this female benevolence organization delved into a full agenda consisting of a report on securing free legal aid for the poor, sending delegates to a conference at the Mexican Library, and planning for an upcoming art exhibit sponsored by the Círculo. Tenayuca and Munguía shared a vision—to help la raza—but they chose to do so in different ways.[2]

The organizational work of Mexican-origin people in Depression-era San Antonio reflected a diversity of ideas and strategies. Responses to the challenges of racial discrimination and severe poverty in the city's Westside ran the gamut

from Munguía's maternalist and benevolent practices to Tenayuca's radical reform politics. Emma Tenayuca believed that communism could serve as a means
to "organize labor, organize the unemployed so they would have rights."[3]

Although Tenayuca married during the height of her political activism,
she did not organize her activities around the mantle of domesticity. She wed
Homer Brooks in 1937 and divorced him in April 1941; they had no children
together. As an activist, she turned to the Communist Party and organized as a
worker, not as a mother, which often placed her at odds with gender and class
conventions.

Tenayuca was a Mexican American. Like LULAC members, she found hope
in Roosevelt's New Deal as well as the Good Neighbor policy. She reminded
Americans that the Good Neighbor policy needed to begin at home to be cred-
ible abroad. By this she meant that Anglo-Americans needed to give racial
minorities equitable treatment vis-á-vis whites or risk losing the confidence of
the Latin American nations. Where she differed from LULAC was in her affiliation with the Communist Party. Tenayuca believed that working people needed
to unite regardless of citizenship in their quest for human, civil, and labor rights.
Belonging to an international organization also gave her a global perspective

Figure 5.1 Wedding portrait of Emma Tenayuca and Homer Brooks. Photo Courtesy of
ITC/*San Antonio-Express News*/ZUMA Press.

from which to analyze workers' lives across national boundaries, including Mexican workers in Mexico and Mexican workers in the United States.

Political Lessons from Home

Crossing the borders of social constructions and hierarchies began at home for Emma Tenayuca. Born on December 21, 1916, in San Antonio, Texas, she was the first daughter of eleven children born to Sam Tenayuca and Benita Hernández Zepeda. Her mother's family traced their heritage to the Spanish colonial period in Texas. Some members of her extended family ostracized her father, Sam Tenayuca, because he was, as they put it, *puro Indio* (pure Indian). Emma could have claimed the privileges of whiteness from her maternal family, but she chose to side with her father and spent her life working on behalf of people who faced exclusion at the societal and institutional levels. Thus, her formative experiences of discrimination took place within the family.[4]

As a child of the Depression era, Tenayuca first became interested in politics through the influence of her maternal grandparents, the Zepedas, who were registered voters and followed local and state politics.[5] One memorable event was the gubernatorial election of Miriam "Ma" Ferguson in 1924, who was running after her husband, Governor James "Pa" Ferguson, had been impeached for embezzling $75,000 from the University of Texas. The Zepeda clan galvanized around Ma Ferguson's campaign because, as Tenayuca put it many years later,

> Mrs. Ferguson had taken a very strong stand against the Ku Klux Klan. I have recollections of banners that read, Only White Protestant Americans. That left me out. So because Mrs. Ferguson took such a strong stand against the KKK, my parents and grandparents voted for her.[6]

The lesson she learned was that Mexican-origin people needed to support candidates who supported them or, at least, who held discriminatory forces at bay.

Emma Tenayuca also developed an early understanding of transnational politics. At age six or seven, she listened to various "soapbox" speakers from one or another faction of the Mexican Revolution on Sunday outings to the Plaza del Zacate (Milam Square) in San Antonio.[7] There she first learned about the anarcho-syndicalist Magonista movement and their newspaper, *Regeneración*. There she first saw the exiled masses lining up for low-paying jobs in faraway fields. At a young age, Tenayuca began to see the connections between exploitative systems in Mexico and the United States. Moreover, she took note of how those victimized by capitalism on both sides of the border were all dark-skinned peasants and working-class people.[8]

There were important transborder links between the labor movements in the United States and Mexico. For example, Tejanas such as María Solís Sager and Emma Tenayuca received training from El Colegio de Obreros (The Workers University) in Mexico City in the mid-1930s. Whenever a US-based strike involving a large number of Mexicans took place, a pattern of cross-border solidarity developed, with Mexico's Confederación de Trabajadores Mexicanos (CTM) lending support and advice to the Congress of Industrial Organizations (CIO). The CTM had been prodded by the Mexican Communist Party to establish a joint organization with the CIO. They had also encouraged the Communist Party in the United States to address the problems of Mexican workers in that country. The CTM applauded Mexican labor strikes in the United States, including the ones in San Antonio.[9]

Becoming an Activist

Tenayuca's introduction into the world of organized politics began in school. As she later recalled:

> During my first year in high school, I joined the Ladies LULAC auxiliary. . . . When the matter of discrimination really started to dawn on me was during the course of the Depression when I saw the poverty. . . . I attended their meetings. I noticed that their policy[,] and I followed it for awhile, was one of Americanization. . . . I delivered a talk on "I Am an American," or something like that.[10]

This association with LULAC was short-lived because Tenayuca disagreed with the group's original policy of distancing itself from Mexicans of foreign birth. Her family had been in Texas for centuries, and so Tenayuca fit with the group's Mexican American membership, but instead she criticized LULAC for failing to acknowledge that Anglo-Americans treated all Mexican-origin people as second-class citizens. "And this is what really made me rebel against the LULACs. No matter how clean you were, how well-scrubbed your neck was, if you had a name like Garcia, it was bad."[11]

For Tenayuca, Mexicans needed to unite on the basis of their ethnic identity, not divide over citizenship, class, or educational status. She enjoyed privileges of citizenship, education, and socioeconomic status that most Mexicans in America did not have. She never worked as a cigar roller, pecan sheller, or field hand, but she identified with the struggle of those who did and gave her life to these causes.

La Pasionaria 149

As a woman of color with working- and lower middle-class roots, however, she could empathize with and comprehend the plight of the poor.

Tenayuca also joined a reading group at Brackenridge High School. Like other youth groups during the 1930s, they read works by Marx and Tolstoy, kept abreast of current events, and discussed society's inequities in a student newspaper. As she put it, "All of us were affected by the Depression. We became aware that there were some aspects of the free enterprise system which were highly vulnerable."[12]

Her early organizing experiences happened almost spontaneously, even before her high school graduation. At age sixteen Tenayuca joined the second Finck Cigar strike. The first cigar strike began in August 1933 and lasted thirty days. Led by Mrs. W. H. Ernst, hundreds of female employees of the cigar company struck for a number of reasons. Employees had made numerous complaints about their ill treatment at the plant. Miss Gonzales, financial secretary for the Cigar Maker's Union in San Antonio, characterized the matter as one of unfairness.

> Before the strike a worker would hand in, say 400 cigars. Finck would say that only half of them were good; that's all the worker got credit for. If the worker asked what was the matter with the cigars, or how she could make them better, he would say, "Isn't my word good enough?" One did as he said or quit. He would give the girls material, and he always used the poorest material he could buy, and demand that they get so many cigars out of it. If they failed, they had to pay him for those they were not able to make.[13]

Other complaints included production quotas that led to speed ups, getting charged for being late to work, and being given only five minutes to use the bathroom. Further, every morning 375 workers were expected to wash their tools in ten minutes, yet the company provided only three faucets. According to Mrs. W. H. Ernst, "Finck took all the 'roll overs' [poorly rolled cigars] without paying the workers for them. These 'roll overs' are patched by the 'patchers' and are put in with the best. There is no such thing as a bad cigar."[14]

Drawing much support from the Westside, some labor unions, and a few Anglos, the first cigar strike ended when the mayor, siding with Finck, imposed a settlement on the workers. He convinced workers that Finck would increase wages and improve working conditions and rehire them if their leader, Mrs. Ernst, would not return. The union, including Mrs. Ernst, agreed to this settlement, but Finck did not follow through. Only a few strikers got their jobs back and Finck fired the most active protestors. When Mrs. Ernst initiated another strike, she and a couple of workers were arrested. The others ran off, and Finck convinced them to return to work.[15]

Three months later, workers had another grievance against Finck when he decided to stop complying with the National Recovery Administration (NRA) by cutting prices for his cigars, which would negatively affect their wages. In August 1934, a strike ensued with violent encounters between strikers and scabs. This time the mayor stayed away, and Sheriff Albert West got involved. Not only were sixty-five young women jailed, but deputies also visited the homes of strikers and threatened to deport them if they did not return to work. The strike lasted seven months and left a record of considerable police brutality as "baton-wielding sheriff's deputies" broke up the picket line and arrested many strikers.[16]

Despite the dangerous nature of this strike, women came back after their release from jail in an effort to hold the line. Brave teenaged Tenayuca joined the picket line in solidarity with the women and was arrested for her involvement.[17] Reflecting on this experience in an interview many years later, she declared, "I was picked up too. . . . My father applauded me. My mother thought I was just wasting my time. Typical Spanish reaction."[18]

According to her niece, Sharyll Soto Teneyuca, her aunt participated in the Finck Cigar strike mainly for social justice and humanitarian reasons:

> I don't think she ever set out to be an organizer or even an activist. She was compelled to do something about the human suffering she witnessed. She was aware of human injustice—even as a child she had been aware of it. Because of her deep compassion, she couldn't ignore it. It happened that she was a gifted speaker and organizer and could mobilize workers. She was able to communicate to people that by working together, they could change their condition.[19]

Sheriff West made a comment about using his new boots to kick the Finck Cigar strikers—all women. Then, a prominent San Antonio leader casually commented on how easy it was to break a strike by calling the immigration authorities. Indeed, immigration officials often got involved, although some of the strikers were born in the United States. Tenayuca, motivated by what she described as "an underlying faith in the American idea of freedom and fairness," could not sit by and watch such injustices. She went down to the Finck Cigar strikers' picket line to show support and paid a price for doing so.[20]

While helping the Finck Cigar strikers, Tenayuca noticed the complicity of the Catholic Church. Like her own family, Finck, she noted, was Catholic:

> That guy used the priests. I didn't have one worker tell me, I had several workers tell me that the priests, and this was Father Clem Casey and

some of the others, expressed an attitude that every union is a communist union. They backed Finck to the hilt. I was told that even in the confessional box they [workers] had been advised not to join.[21]

Tenayuca believed that the Catholic Church, like the local machine-run government, could not be relied upon to uphold and defend workers' rights. For solutions to poverty and discrimination, she turned to the Communist Party.

The Workers Alliance and the Limits of New Deal Liberalism

In 1935, Emma Tenayuca joined the Young Communist League, the youth wing of the Communist Party; she graduated into the Communist Party by 1936.[22] Led by Earl Browder, the US Communist Party of the late 1930s pursued a Popular Front strategy designed to incorporate the party into mainstream American political life. Popular Front supporters organized against fascism at home and abroad, often reminding Americans of the similarities between Franco's and Hitler's fascism in Europe and racism and ethnocentrism in the United States. They supported the Roosevelt administration, the struggle for black equality, the right of workers to organize, and a vision of a multi-ethnic nation. Like other Popular Front advocates, Tenayuca placed faith in New Deal liberalism, supporting the Roosevelt administration's efforts to reform and regulate business practices and to create an economic safety net for Americans through legislation such as the Social Security Act and the Wagner Labor Relations Act, which facilitated labor organizing.[23]

After the Finck Cigar strikes, Tenayuca stood in solidarity with garment workers who went out on strike against the Dorothy Frocks Company. By 1935 she led the Westside's unemployed council. By then, she had gained a reputation as a fiery speaker able to command the attention of large crowds. She joined the Workers Alliance of America in 1936, serving as a member of its executive committee by 1937 and as general secretary of ten Alliance chapters in San Antonio, which she set up.[24] The Workers Alliance, a national federation, was a part of the movement of the unemployed that sought to assist the jobless. The San Antonio branch included about 10,000 workers and met on Sundays. They often helped resolve relief grievances, fought for more relief, sought less degrading relief practices, stopped evictions, fought against Works Progress Administration (WPA) cuts, and struggled against the exploitation of WPA workers and deportations. Thanks to Tenayuca's efforts, Tejanos got jobs diverting the San Antonio River so that it would run through the center of town.

They also participated in the construction of a pedestrian walkway, the San Antonio River Walk, between 1939 and 1941.[25]

As a member of the San Antonio Workers Alliance, Tenayuca wrote letters to national (WPA) officials, calling for reform of the Texas Relief Commission (TRC), which administered WPA projects at the local level. As in the case with African Americans, the TRC often turned down unemployed Mexican-origin workers who applied for WPA work, assigning them to pick-and-shovel brigades or sending them to work in out-of-town fields for starvation wages and forcing them to pull their children out of school. Tenayuca believed that the TRC was operating as a cheap labor agency for Anglo farmers. She noted that many of the Mexican-origin workers denied WPA work and relegated to the fields had no experience in agricultural work and some even possessed other types of skills. Tenayuca also despaired at the slow investigative process whereby Mexican-origin workers were told to wait for the caseworker evaluating their case to visit them. Many were still waiting for the caseworker to show up at the time of Tenayuca's letters. Instead of this prolonged process, Tenayuca asked that the WPA order granting unemployed midwesterners WPA work prior to an investigation for relief status be extended to all states.[26]

Figure 5.2 Workers Alliance leader Emma Tenayuca with clenched fist in the air, speaking to a crowd outside city hall following a parade protesting scarcity of Works Progress Administration jobs, March 8, 1937. Photo Courtesy of ITC/*San Antonio-Express News*/ZUMA Press.

Tenayuca also participated in a number of street meetings, mass demonstrations, protests, and marches to pressure local authorities on behalf of Mexican Americans getting less pay than Anglos or getting the worst jobs or on behalf of laid-off WPA workers. As a result of their activism, members of the Workers Alliance were harassed and arrested. In one particular instance when they petitioned relief officials, the police destroyed their headquarters. It all started on June 29, 1937, when Emma Tenayuca and one hundred Worker's Alliance members arrived in the district WPA office. They protested the dismissal of over 1,000 workers from San Antonio's WPA rolls. To the Workers Alliance and their allies, they represented a delegation of petitioners, hoping to convince the district office to reinstate the workers or at least get the local official to take their petition seriously and send it to the federal office for consideration. However, to San Antonio Mayor C. K. Quinn, Tenayuca and her associates were "sit-down strikers" he could not tolerate. The WPA director shared the mayor's perspective and instead of hearing the Alliance petition, he summoned the police. Armed with clubs, police officers herded the men and women down five flights of stairs cursing, kicking, and punching the beleaguered group all the way to the ground floor.[27]

Later that day, the police visited the Workers Alliance headquarters and destroyed it, hacking everything to pieces with axes. They attacked a small group of people present with clubs, beating and kicking them, and ultimately driving them out. Six Alliance members were arrested including the secretary, a young Emma Tenayuca and twenty-two-year-old chapter president, Bob Williams. Police beat and choked Williams into unconsciousness. Those arrested had to make exorbitant bail and stood on trial before Judge Matthews's court with Everett Looney as defense counsel. Tenayuca was acquitted of the charge of unlawful assembly and assaulting an officer, but the charge of disturbing the peace remained. The trial for the six Alliance members was postponed.[28]

When local authorities noticed that the Workers Alliance received an outpouring of support from various organizations and individuals protesting the "un-American manner in which the San Antonio police had handled the whole matter," the press mounted a campaign to discredit the Alliance. Suddenly, the Workers Alliance found their organization under attack as a communist group, and newspaper reports were peppered with falsehoods.[29]

The Citizens' Committee for Social Justice as well as supporting organizations such as the Congregational and Federated Churches of Christ, the Women's International League for Peace and Justice, and the American Civil Liberties Union rallied around the Workers Alliance. They exhorted the public to demand the dismissal of all charges against Tenayuca and the others, full compensation for the property loss sustained by the Workers Alliance, guarantees that they would not be molested anymore, and respect for their constitutional rights. Furthermore, these sympathetic organizations reminded people about how the actions of the police posed a threat to democracy.

> These facts are (1) the right to peacefully assemble and petition has been outrageously violated, (2) peaceful citizens have been set upon and injured without provocation, (3) private premises have been violently entered without any moral and legal justification, (4) private property has been wantonly destroyed and private papers and effects confiscated. All this brutality and vandalism at the hands of the very forces brought into existence for the protection of the civil rights, private property, and the persons of citizens. But not only the liberty of these six individuals is at stake; the civil rights of every American citizen is challenged; the whole democratic procedure is brazenly attacked.[30]

At her trial, Emma Tenayuca faced a determined police chief Owen Kilday who claimed that materials confiscated at the Workers Alliance headquarters proved "my former contention that the Tenayuca woman is a paid agitator sent here to stir up trouble among the ignorant Mexican workers." Judge W. W. McCrory also condemned Tenayuca as a dangerous subversive, stating, "She belongs in jail, let her stay there. She's been raising too much hell around here anyhow. . . . She's nothing but a damned Communist and ought to be sent to Russia."[31]

The Workers Alliance worked at the local, state, national, and transnational levels to help workers in their struggle for fair labor practices. San Antonio's Workers Alliance grew to include fifteen branches with 3,000 members, making it one of the nation's strongest. As the first Mexican American woman chosen to serve on the organization's National Executive Committee, Tenayuca made history. After her release from jail, Tenayuca continued her work on behalf of workers. The pecan shellers strike of 1938 would command the attention of the Workers Alliance and provide an opportunity for Emma Tenayuca to play yet another leadership role.[32]

The Pecan Shellers Strike

During the 1930s, Texas controlled about 40 percent of the nation's pecan production. San Antonio stood at the center of this industry; half of the Texas pecan crop was grown within a 250-mile radius of the city. Southern Pecan Shelling Company owner Julius Seligman initiated a contracting system whereby he provided contractors with whole pecans on credit for about $.10 a pound and then bought the processed nuts back for $.30 to $.36 per pound. The contractors furnished the building, electricity, and water needed to process the pecans, and they dealt with labor management issues. It was common to find one hundred pickers sitting around a long table in a space of only twenty-five feet by forty feet, working under poor light. Because there was no ventilation, the brown dust from the pecans hung heavy in the air, leading many to draw a connection between the polluted air and the high rate of tuberculosis among pecan-shelling families. Workers received pitiful wages in this female-dominated industry. The average annual family income of shellers was $192, with a weekly family average of $1.00 to $4.00. Because pecan shelling was a seasonal business, workers often supplemented their incomes with migratory fieldwork.[33]

Mexican Americans found it difficult to derive benefits from federal programs designed to help workers. Local officials' prejudices predisposed them to distribute relief unevenly, and additionally, some New Deal programs disadvantaged particular ethnic groups concentrated in certain industries. The Agricultural Adjustment Administration (AAA) designated the pecan shelling industry as an agricultural enterprise, which meant industry leaders did not have to comply with government codes that mandated higher pay for nonfarm work.[34]

Ironically, it was not these abysmal conditions or federal government neglect that led to the creation of the first pecan shellers' union in 1933. According to Tenayuca, Julius Seligman hired Magdaleno Rodríguez to organize the Pecan Shelling Workers' Union because he was afraid that smaller operators might undercut him by paying workers less than he could. "He admitted to taking money from Seligman," Tenayuca declared when asked about Rodríguez's association with Seligman. Some believed that Rodríguez was also connected to Chief of Police Owen Kilday's political machine. By 1937, Rodríguez no longer led the union, which had virtually disappeared. Remnants of the union reorganized as the Texas Pecan Shelling Workers' Union, and the Communist Party brought in Albert Gonsen, a Chicano from New Mexico, to lead it. That same year the United Cannery and Agricultural Packing and Allied Workers of America (UCAPAWA), a CIO union, offered the San Antonio pecan shellers a temporary charter. The understanding was that the union would expand to include other groups working with agricultural workers. One such group was the Workers Alliance, led by Emma Tenayuca.[35]

On January 31, 1938, the Southern Pecan Shelling Company's contractors announced a pay cut from six to seven cents per pound to five to six cents per pound. Wages for pecan crackers were cut from fifty to forty cents per one hundred pounds. About 12,000 workers spontaneously walked out. The Gonsen faction of the CIO Pecan Shellers' Union stayed away, but UCAPAWA supported the strikers. Tenayuca emerged as a leader of the strikers. The strike lasted three months; over 1,000 picketers were arrested and subjected to tear gas. The police and fire departments were drafted for "riot duty," and both Mayor C. K. Quinn and Police Chief Kilday refused to acknowledge the strike.[36] Kilday, in particular, used the local media to red-bait Tenayuca and the strikers. The *San Antonio Light* reported:

> Mrs. [Emma Tenayuca] Brooks . . . was taken into custody at another
> West side factory. Chief Kilday said he ordered her arrested because he
> did not intend to let any Reds mix up in the strike.[37]

The *San Antonio Light* reported, "Kilday took the position that actually there was no strike. . . . The police chief, in a prepared statement, declared that the entire strike was a Communist movement and that it was without standing with the Committee for Industrial Organization." Red-baiting became the favored tactic of those who sought to silence demands for social and economic justice.[38]

The gross mistreatment of the strikers attracted national attention, and Texas governor James V. Allred ordered a committee of the Industrial Commission of Texas chaired by Assistant State Attorney Everett Looney to investigate violations of civil liberties. On February 14, 1938, Looney called a public meeting in San Antonio. The San Antonio Ministerial Association testified there that pecan shellers received a mere $2.50 per week. Several ministers, as well as some journalists, reported that the strikers "had behaved peacefully, although the police had taken their picket signs away from them." Looney also heard from strikers who told of arrests and beatings at the hands of police officers. Ultimately, the commission hearings determined that Kilday's police department had overstepped its authority. Unfortunately for the strikers, the commission could not enforce its own ruling, and a local judge failed to grant an injunction against the police that would have permitted picketing.[39]

Violations of civil liberties by the police occurred in an environment and time marked by strong anti-communist and anti-unionist sentiment and race-based stratification.[40] City officials, as well as representatives from the Catholic Church, attacked the strike, characterizing it as communist-inspired and therefore illegitimate. Mayor Quinn and Police Chief Kilday, leaders of the city's political machine, and Anglo males unaccustomed to seeing a Mexican American woman in a leadership role, no doubt found Tenayuca's fiery speeches to huge enthusiastic crowds threatening to their own influence and control over the masses. While Tenayuca became the target of much of this vitriol because she was a communist, a labor leader, and the wife of a former Communist Party gubernatorial candidate, her gender and ethno-racial background made her the perfect scapegoat. The attacks against Tenayuca came from the labor movement as well. Rebecca Taylor, president of the San Antonio International Ladies' Garment Workers' Union (ILGWU), refused to help the strikers because Tenayuca was one of the leaders. Taylor, who did not have any rapport with Mexican workers, drove around with police, pointing out which union activists might be communists.

Soon UCAPAWA made it clear that in order to maintain their support, Emma Tenayuca needed to step down as strike leader. Even after she did so, Tenayuca continued to put out circulars and organize pickets.[41]

This turn of events was not surprising in light of the CIO's, and more generally the Left's, position on communists within their ranks during the 1930s. Union leaders were willing and often eager to receive assistance from communists as long as they kept their political and ideological identities hidden. By 1938, Emma Tenayuca's reputation as a communist made her not only the target of reactionaries but also a potential liability for the Left, which hoped to achieve revolutionary changes in American society by attempting to mainstream its radical programs. Removing Tenayuca from a visible leadership role seemed the safer route for the union.[42]

UCAPAWA president Donald Henderson, himself a member of the Communist Party, took charge of the strike, with advice from CIO organizer Luisa Moreno. Henderson, Moreno, and George Lambert, the UCAPAWA representative in San Antonio, negotiated the strike settlement. This turn of events bothered Tenayuca because the national labor leaders failed to promote local grassroots leadership. Over thirty years later, Tenayuca, examining the factors that had prevented the organization of Mexican workers, wrote that one was the "inability of out-of-state union organizers to recognize the particular needs of Mexican workers especially with [*sic*] in relation to building leadership." Nevertheless, in 1938, the CIO did manage to secure the initial wage of seven to eight cents per pound of pecans for shellers, which increased to twenty-five cents an hour when Congress passed the Fair Labor Standards Act that same year. The settlement came about after the governor persuaded Julius Seligmann to negotiate and the union to arbitrate. Soon after, however, the pecan-shelling industry turned to mechanization, resulting in the loss of as many as 10,000 jobs. As an array of war-related industries opened up, few people missed the pecan-shelling business that had been looked upon as the employment of last resort. The significance of the pecan shellers' strike lies less in the short-lived pay increase and more in the political galvanization of workers and a community.[43]

"The Mexican Question in the Southwest"

For Emma Tenayuca to challenge the system drew the attention and hostility of many San Antonians unaccustomed to seeing a young Mexican American woman command such a high-profile position and engage in radical politics. Indeed, she drew attention for daring to inhabit public spaces and speak out against the power structure responsible for the plight of the people she defended. Ultimately, her communist affiliation provided opponents their greatest ammunition against her. How threatening were her political beliefs? An examination of "The Mexican Question in the Southwest," a political essay she co-authored with Homer Brooks, offers insights regarding Tenayuca's politics. In this essay published in the *Communist* on March 1939, Tenayuca and Brooks argued that the Mexican people in the Southwest were not a nation since their economic and political interests were far too entangled with interests of Anglo-Americans in the region to merit designation as a separate nation. Because the Mexican people in the Southwest did not constitute a territorial and economic community, the proper course for them was unification with the rest of the nation. Unfortunately, according to Tenayuca and Brooks, the American bour-geoisie had hindered national unification by treating Mexicans as a conquered people. The authors then analyzed the condition of Mexicans, comparing their fate to that of blacks in the South and explaining that the treatment accorded Mexicans was also "a carryover to the United States of Wall Street's imperialistic exploitation of Latin America."[44] These analyses seem remarkably similar to the analysis of the Mexican condition offered by Ricardo Flores Magón a generation or two earlier.[45]

The rest of the essay presented a program for social change similar to that proposed by the Congress of Spanish-Speaking Peoples in 1939 at its founding national convention in Los Angeles. That movement for "Mexican unification," as the authors characterized it, was based on struggles against economic dis-crimination, educational and cultural inequality, and social oppression. The congress also demanded that the citizenship rights of US-born Mexicans be respected and the citizenship process for non-US-born Mexicans be facilitated. Tenayuca and Brooks took special care to clarify their positions regarding citi-zenship rights:

> The majority of Mexicans are American-born. The problem is, there-fore, one of enforcing their citizenship right. This means demanding that all legal and extra-legal restrictions to the free exercise of the ballot be removed. These include residence qualifications, difficult for semi-migratory workers to meet; and in Texas, the elimination of the poll tax.[46]

Two radical positions supported by Tenayuca and Brooks as well as the congress included support for the undocumented and a call to unify with other oppressed groups, namely African Americans. The logic for supporting non-documented workers was that Mexican workers, regardless of citizenship, had earned a place in American society through their economic contributions toward the devel-opment of the Southwest. To that end, the authors of the essay critiqued the original LULAC position on the undocumented, which basically ignored and

marginalized those who could not claim US citizenship, dismissing them as lia-
bilities to LULAC's pro-integration agenda, although the organization had since
changed its stance.[47] Ultimately, Tenayuca and Brooks wanted the foreign born
to acquire citizenship rights and status, declaring:

> Those who are foreign born must join with all of the immigrant groups
> in the United States to secure the democratization of the federal
> regulations pertaining to length of time, cost, and language conditions
> required for citizenship; the aim being to simplify the process whereby
> all who intend to remain permanent residents of the United States—
> and this includes nearly all of the Mexicans—and who express a desire
> for naturalization, can become citizens.[48]

In the final section of "The Mexican Question" essay—"The Significance of the
Mexican Rights Movement"—Tenayuca and Brooks pointed out that the rise
of a Mexican people's movement was crucial to European Americans in the
Southwest, for wherever there was a large concentration of Mexican people,
wages were lower for the entire community. According to the authors, "The
status of the Mexican people in those areas has, further, tended to make them
easy prey to corrupt and reactionary political machines—a consequence that
affects the vital interests of the Anglo-American population in the Southwest."
Thus, progressive Anglo-American leaders such as Maury Maverick in Texas
and Culbert Olson in California demonstrated support for the Mexican rights
movement. Brooks and Tenayuca also tied the plight of African Americans in
the South to that of Mexicans in the Southwest. Their Marxist approach to the
question of Mexican labor exploitation allowed them to understand how poverty
cut across ethno-cultural and national lines, allowing them to see the benefits of
an alliance among Mexicans, African Americans, and progressive middle-class
and working-class whites.[49]

The second element of their argument revolved around the Good Neighbor
policy. In order for it to ring true in Latin America, this US policy needed to
begin at home with the fair and just treatment of Mexicans.[50] With World War
II impending, Tenayuca and Brooks felt the United States needed to treat all
Mexicans better, lest Nazi propaganda turn Mexicans away from an anti-fascist
path. They cited the menacing example of *Novedades*, a fascist publication in
Mexico City, which called attention to the plight of Mexicans in the Southwest,
claiming that their fate was much worse than the fate of Jews in Germany.
The magazine called for Mexicans to struggle "against the 'Jewish-dominated
capitalists' of the United States, who 'hold the Mexican population of the
Southwest in bondage.'" According to Tenayuca and Brooks, the best means of
combating this fascist fifth column in Mexico was to push the Mexican rights

movement forward and to recognize "the historical rights of the Mexican people in the Southwest."[51]

In a sense, what Tenayuca and Brooks proposed in their essay aligned with the Popular Front agenda of the 1930s. Oppressed groups in the United States, with the support of their progressive white allies, needed to unite both to claim their human and civil rights and to struggle against fascist influences targeting their communities in an effort to disrupt US-Latin American ties. LULAC, similar to African Americans with their Double V campaign calling for a victory for democracy at home and abroad, would later use this transnationalist strategy.

Nowhere in their essay did Tenayuca and Brooks advocate violent revolution between Mexicans and Anglos or between the bourgeoisie and the proletariat. They also did not advocate the establishment of a totalitarian state or adherence to a Soviet "party line." These were the sorts of things their enemies assumed simply because they belonged to the Communist Party. In fact, they called for the unity of all Americans as one nation and simply demanded the social justice implied in fundamentally American political precepts. Their message championed the fulfillment of democratic ideals, hardly a radical idea in a nation boasting of being the world's premier democracy. However, in 1930s America, it was radical to demand justice for Mexicans. Thus, the considerable harassment suffered by Emma Tenayuca cannot be understood as simply a matter of a labor organizer fighting against class-based inequities. The people Tenayuca fought for represented a racialized caste as much hated for their race as for their poverty.

The San Antonio Riot and Exile

Despite the fact that her political beliefs did not represent the grave threat that her opponents portrayed in the media, Emma Tenayuca paid a heavy price for her high profile as a labor leader and her Communist Party affiliation. Tenayuca was the chairperson of the Texas State Committee of the Communist Party from 1938 to 1941, when her husband, Homer Brooks, served as the president. Tenayuca's political activities eventually led to her self-exile from San Antonio.[52]

In 1939, a riot erupted at the Municipal Auditorium after people found out that San Antonio mayor Maury Maverick, a strong advocate of civil liberties and former New Deal congressman, had allowed Communist Party members to meet there. The American Legion knew in advance about the Communist Party's request for permission to use the auditorium. Outrage erupted when the mayor's office granted the party the permit. Maury Maverick Jr, a *San Antonio Express-News* columnist and the mayor's son, recalled, "The organizations attacking him [his father] included the Catholic Church, the Ku Klux Klan, the Elks, the Breakfast Club, all veterans' organizations, and the Texas Pioneers." According to Claude Stanush, a reporter at the scene of the riot, the American Legion and other organizations demanded that Mayor Maverick rescind this permit, but he refused on the grounds that everyone had a right to freedom of speech.[53]

On August 25, 1939, the day of the controversial meeting, a crowd 5,000 strong gathered outside the auditorium. Inside the building, Tenayuca, Homer Brooks, and Elizabeth Benson attempted to start a meeting with 150 party supporters in the audience. The mayor ordered police officers and firemen to create a barrier between the crowd and the auditorium in anticipation of trouble. The crowd grew tense when Catholic priest M. A. Valenta and American Legion leader Clem Smith did their part to stir the unstable throng. Suddenly, violence erupted when the crowd heard Communist Party members singing the "Star-Spangled Banner." Reporters and photographers reacted with horror as the crowd began throwing rocks and bricks at the building, breaking windows, and injuring people, including police officers, as they charged forward.

While all of this occurred outside the building, police officers guided those inside to safety using a tunnel that extended from the auditorium to the San Antonio River nearby. The mob eventually broke through the police barrier and charged the auditorium. Finding it empty, they unleashed their anger on the auditorium itself, slashing curtains and seats with knives. Newspapers estimated the damage done by the mob at $3,000 to $5,000. After disrupting the communist meeting, about 3,500 people held an "Americanism" meeting in the main room of the auditorium, where they denounced the mayor and the Communist Party. The rest of the mob, with Klan members among them, next moved to the mayor's home. Fortunately, police had hidden the mayor and his family. Maury Maverick Jr. recalled the event, writing, "On the night of the riot, the police hid my parents and me for fear that we would be murdered. The next morning a police escort took us home. Throughout the day, people would drive by shouting insults." That frightful night ended at city hall where the frustrated mob burned the mayor in effigy.[54]

That night cost Maury Maverick his political career. He ran for reelection as mayor but was defeated. In a newspaper interview years later, Tenayuca was asked if she had any regrets about her activist career. She said she had only one. She regretted that the progressive Maverick's political career ended the night of the riot. She also pointed out that she had not been in favor of holding the Communist Party meeting at the auditorium, but that her husband had insisted. "I didn't want to hold the meeting, but I wasn't listened to," Tenayuca was quoted as saying in a 1990 *San Antonio Express-News* article. In a 1986 article, she expressed her misgivings about the communist gathering, stating, "It was just a very bad time to organize a communist meeting. Coming right on the heels of the non-aggression pact [Soviet-German Non-Aggression Pact reached in 1939], there was a lot of anger in this country. You could almost expect this type of reaction."[55] Presumably this was the rationale that Emma Tenayuca offered Homer Brooks when she disagreed with him that the meeting should be held at the Municipal Auditorium, a memorial to American soldiers killed in World War I. But Brooks overruled her.

For all their collaborative work, Emma and Homer had their differences, and gender might help to explain some of the tensions between them that would eventually lead to their divorce. Years later in a diary entry she wrote,

> So thorough has been the education of the male to the effect that he is the superior being in all relationships between the sexes that a condition exists where man and wife, girl and boy are continuously being made miserable. It is a situation where the slightest aggressiveness on the part of the female will result in seriously deflating the ego of the male. Nay, even worse, in causing frustration, remorsefulness and misery. The very best sex relationship[s] are being constantly thrown into confusion, where impotency reigns for a few days, silence for numerous days, followed eventually by peace [which] can only be maintained by pretended submissiveness.

She went on to say she was sorry she could not provide examples, though one can assume that she spoke from personal experiences as well as observations. Below this statement, she penned another telling statement. "Relations between the sexes depend in many case[s] upon the strength, and human endurance of the female who must always flatter, console and bolster up the ego of the male."[56]

Mayor Maverick was not the only one whose public career ended that day. Besides receiving death threats, Tenayuca was also blacklisted in San Antonio, forcing her to move to Houston in 1940, where she worked various office jobs. In order to secure employment, she assumed a new identity as Emma B. Giraud. During the 1940s and 1950s, under the pressures of the second Red Scare, hundreds of communists assumed new identities and moved to different cities, some leaving activism altogether even as others continued their political work in their new communities.[57]

For the next ten years, Tenayuca faced numerous challenges. She and Brooks divorced in 1941. That same year she contracted tuberculosis and was unable to participate in Communist Party activities for several months. Although she remained the branch organizer of the Harrisburg District in Houston, she was not reelected chair of the Texas State Committee of the Communist Party. After recuperating in 1942, Tenayuca resumed her party work, traveling from Houston to San Antonio every other weekend to help organize a Communist Party branch in her hometown. By this time, the Federal Bureau of Investigation (FBI) had established an elaborate information-gathering network around Tenayuca and her associates. Her FBI file dates back to 1939, and it is evident that agents infiltrated Communist Party meetings, acquiring information about Tenayuca from her employers, school registrars, and classmates, and through interference with the US mail; eavesdropping from the apartment next door to hers; and making general observations. Tenayuca's file also indicates the rather sporadic nature of her 1940s Communist Party involvement during this period, when she held various jobs and attended the University of Houston and Sinclair Business School in Houston. These time commitments, plus illness, made it difficult for her to take on a bigger role in the party. Nevertheless, the FBI considered Emma Tenayuca a potential threat to the interests of the United States, and as early as July 1941, it placed her under consideration for custodial detention in the event of a national emergency.[58]

During World War II, Emma Tenayuca lived as a private citizen, albeit one who was often spied on by FBI agents. With a keen eye, she observed her own world and the world at large and recorded her thoughts, questions, desires, frustrations, and insights in a diary. Among the many things she wrote about, she continued to examine the connections between the Good Neighbor policy, hemispheric unity, and civil rights. On June 9, 1942, she recorded one of many racist incidents she must have been following in the newspapers. This particular one appeared in the *Houston Chronicle*. A Latin American father and son had filed a suit in district court to compel a café owner to serve them soft drinks "based on Article 4596 of the revised civil statutes of Texas known as the doctrine of Innkeepers and regulating the operation of public places." They requested $10,000 from the café owner because he had refused them service and humiliated them in front of patrons. Mexican consul Luis L. Duplan in Houston had advised the father and son to file suit. The father had recently filed his first papers for citizenship, and his son was born in the United States and had filled out his selective service forms. According to Consul Duplan, the object of the suit was to protest discrimination and to "emphasize the necessity for carrying out President Roosevelt's Good Neighbor policy, and to bring about better understanding among American nations." Tenayuca expressed agreement with Duplan's reasoning, particularly since so many Mexican-origin young men were fighting to save democracy abroad, but also because she recognized that unity must be maintained in order for the war effort to succeed. As she put it,

> The Mexican Consul correctly raises the question of hemispheric solidarity emphasizing the necessity for carrying out President Roosevelt's Good Neighbor policy, and to bring about better understanding among American nations. These are issues that all Americans should raise. Every American should be made to realize that without the aid of Latin

American countries, without complete national unity, and this means
2,000,000 living in the U.S., the war can't be won.

Despite her full support of the leadership displayed by the Mexican consulate
and the courage of the victims to take their case to court, Tenayuca seemed disturbed by these piecemeal measures. She lamented the lack of a mass labor or
Communist Party movement to address the "demands of the Mexican people."[59]

Tenayuca not only raised the issue that disunity might lead to a fascist victory
simply to promote the human and civil rights agenda of the Mexican consulate,
LULAC, and other Mexican-origin groups. She was also motivated by another
powerful potential reality. She understood that if Hitler and the rest of the Axis
powers won, any real chance at first-class citizenship for Mexicans would be
lost forever. As she saw it, in a fascist-dominated world, Mexicans would fare
far worse than Anglo-Americans. This explains her fervor in fighting fascism,
whether through the Communist Party, her labor work, or an ill-fated attempt to
join the Women's Army Auxiliary Corps (WAACs) during the war.[60]

In 1942, in an effort to contribute to the US war against fascism, she applied to
the WAACs. In Tenayuca's mind, there was no incompatibility between communism and the struggle of democracy against fascism. Still, she might have feared
that her communist affiliation would be used against her because on the application, she denied any current involvement with Communist Party politics. She
was provisionally accepted but later rejected with no official reason provided.
Clearly, the US government's knowledge of her past and current Communist
Party work played a role in the rejection. Years later, Tenayuca reflected on how,
given the anti-communist climate, she suspected even then that her party involvement influenced top military officials to reject her.[61]

In 1945, Emma Tenayuca moved to Los Angeles where she attended a few
party meetings. By 1946, however, she requested to be released from the party
and moved to San Francisco. According to an FBI agent who interviewed her
there on April 20, 1953, "Tenayuca stated that the main reason for her dropping
out of the CP was that she became disillusioned with CP work." Tenayuca's
disenchantment with the Communist Party had started as early as 1939. The
Soviet-German Non-Aggression Pact upset her. As she recalled, "I don't think
there was a communist in the country who wasn't puzzled." Still, she continued
to believe that the party offered the best avenue for social change. By the mid-
1940s, however, she concluded that the party had lost touch with the powerless
and decided to leave it.[62]

Tenayuca never returned to labor organizing and decided instead to continue her studies. She earned a bachelor's degree from San Francisco State
University and became a reading teacher. She returned to San Antonio in
1968, earned a master's degree from Our Lady of the Lake University, and

continued teaching until her retirement in 1982. Although she no longer organized workers, she never stopped caring about their plight. Throughout
her life she kept abreast of worker-related issues, clipping newspaper articles,
reading books, and helping young scholars interested in American labor history. Many of these scholars expressed a particular interest in her achievements
as a woman in the labor movement. Thus, even though subjected to harassment during the 1930s and 1940s because of her association with the US
Communist Party and exiled from the community she loved most, Tenayuca
eventually enjoyed the admiration of Chicano/a movement activists and subsequent generations of Chicanos/as.[63]

Tenayuca suffered from decades of blacklisting and harassment in Texas—
though she did enjoy the respect and esteem of many San Antonians toward
the end of her life, receiving tributes at the time of her death in 1999. While
she called for reform rather than revolution, Tenayuca's demands carried certain revolutionary implications, especially in conservative South Texas. For one,
Tenayuca defended the rights of Mexican-origin peoples, regardless of citizenship status. Moreover, in a nation that still defined Americanism in terms of
whiteness, a struggle for the rights of people considered "nonwhite" was radical in the 1930s. Second, Tenayuca never strayed from her working- and lower
middle-class roots. These grassroots origins played a key role in her outlook and
political practice. Tenayuca worked for *toda la gente* (all of the people), not for
la gente decente (the decent people). This attitude no doubt offended people
with middle-class sensibilities, Anglo or Mexican, who defined themselves in
contrast to gente corriente—those who failed to adhere to middle-class notions
of respectability and female domesticity. Finally, and perhaps most radically,
Emma Tenayuca broke with both Mexican and European American gender
conventions on both personal and professional levels. In her personal life, she
carried herself with great confidence, speaking her mind and living her life
without many inhibitions. The fact that she married an Anglo-American man
with strong communist ties illustrates her willingness to act unconventionally
on an intimate level. Later, as a divorcee, she once again operated outside the accepted social conventions. After her activist career ended, Tenayuca continued
to defy convention by raising a son on her own during the 1950s and 1960s. As
a public person, she organized men and women, formed coalitions across ethnic
lines, stormed the mayor's office, led a historic strike, banged on the doors of
politicians, and stirred up large crowds with inspirational speeches that earned
her the nickname La Pasionaria (the passionate one). Together these actions
comprised the radical reform politics of Emma Tenayuca, who combined a keen
awareness of disadvantage with a pragmatic use of privilege to serve as an agent
for community empowerment.

Just as the Magonistas had been influenced by modern radical writers, so too had Tenayuca read and absorbed the teachings of Marx, Engels, and others. These understandings led the Magonistas to develop more direct and poignant critiques of the modern nation-state than their gente decente counterparts produced, and it also influenced their strategies and tactics. For the Magonistas and Tenayuca, the objective was to liberate la raza from their subordinate position occasioned by racism and their subjugation within an economic transnationalist system, rather than to inculcate the lessons of respectability as part of a modern civil and human rights strategy.

Struggling against Jaime Crow

LULAC, Gente Decente Heir to a Transborder Political Legacy

On January 26, 1945, Emma Tenayuca wrote in her diary about a LULAC meeting she attended where the Spears Good Neighbor Bill was discussed. State Senator J. Franklin Spears from San Antonio sponsored this bill that, if passed, would make discrimination against Mexican Americans in public places of business a misdemeanor punishable by a $500 fine and/or thirty days of jail time.[1] Declaring racist practices unlawful and punishable by law represented a radical idea in Texas, and LULAC and other activist groups worked diligently for its passage. LULAC, according to leader Manuel C. (M. C.) Gonzáles, wrote 500 letters to the Women's Federation Clubs of Texas and 500 letters to American Legion posts to secure support and felt confident the bill would succeed. Tenayuca, who learned of LULAC's strategy at the meeting, seemed less confident about the organization's tactics and strategy. She wrote in her diary,

> But my opinion is that only a strong mass movement supported from all sections of the population can bring about provable action by the state legislature. There is an opportunity now to enlist the support of all sections of the population, Catholics, Jews, Chambers of Commerce, labor, etc. . . . The usual procedure of the LULAC may get the work done for the sake of the Mexican people, but there is no room for the small politicking of the LULAC.[2]

The bill failed. It was attacked heavily in the mainstream press, and in the end, it was not even put to a vote. Perhaps the bill's demise indicated that the kinds of changes needed in Texas would require far more than a letter-writing campaign and the goodwill of a few progressive Anglos such as Senator Spears. What many may not have known at the time was that forces were already at play to demolish Jaime Crow in Texas.[3] Mexican American organizations, bolstered by returning

World War II veterans no longer willing to be treated as second-class citizens, such as LULAC and the American GI Forum, accelerated the breakdown of prevailing racial discrimination. LULAC's letter-writing campaigns represented just one set of tactics in a broader civil rights strategy that combined the domestic agenda of civil rights with the nation's objectives of hemispheric unity for economic and geopolitical purposes.

This chapter highlights how LULAC's Americanization agenda worked in tandem with a long-standing tradition of transborder gente decente politics to shape their civil rights project. Like the Idars and Munguías, LULACkers sought to eradicate racist practices to allow economic and political empowerment. Similarly, they followed the model of respectability by striving to socially and culturally uplift la raza. For LULAC, redeeming la raza initially meant focusing on the plight of US-born Mexicans whose claims to citizenship facilitated struggles for rights within the American political and judicial systems. But even as they worked within the nation's institutions, these ethnic American leaders continued to strategically employ transnational approaches that dovetailed with the hemispheric geopolitics of the 1930s and 1940s.

LULAC advanced the job begun by the First Mexicanist Congress, but they did so on different terms. Unlike the earlier group of méxico-tejano activists who looked to Mexico as a political reference point and sought solutions that were organic to their communities, subsequent generations of activist organizations, such as LULAC, with a predominantly US-born membership influenced by American institutions and popular culture, chose to work through the American democratic system. Still, their methods reflected a transnational liberal reform tradition reminiscent of nineteenth-century ideas found in both the United States and Mexico. Moreover, like Tenayuca, the Munguías, and the Mexican consulate, LULAC took advantage of the Good Neighbor Policy and the wartime imperative for national and hemispheric unity to advance their civil rights agenda.[4]

Living on the border, many of the organization's members were bicultural and bilingual. Their identities and experiences facilitated their understanding and use of transnational politics. In South Texas, LULAC members pledged allegiance to the United States, used English as their organization's official language, and promoted LULAC as a civic and patriotic organization. These same people also spoke Spanish as readily or with greater fluency than English; observed Mexican holidays, customs, and traditions; made frequent trips to Mexico either to visit friends and family or on business; and considered Nuevo Laredo, Tamaulipas, Mexico to be Laredo's sister city, not some distant, foreign place. Yet living transnational lives did not mean they existed outside the ideological framework of the modern nation-state. Their shared culture of middle-class consciousness facilitated their integration into American society but also encouraged connections with a modernizing Mexico and not simply with "all things Mexican."

This story begins with the founding of LULAC, followed by an examination of the organization's respectability and racial politics, integral components of their efforts to integrate US-born Mexicans into American society. It looks at how LULAC women used a maternal feminist approach in their efforts to promote equity in 1930s society.

The discussion on gendered politics within LULAC is important not only for its own sake but because maternal feminism connects this middle-class Mexican American organization to previous gente decente organizational movements and initiatives. While LULAC's Americanization emphasis represented a departure from previous political strategies, maternal feminism and transnationalism tied one generation of activists to the next. The maternalist angle was also an important strategy for LULAC because the struggle this civil rights organization engaged in was a long-term one that required the commitment of future generations. Through the maternal feminist strategy of Alice Dickerson Montemayor and other women involved in Junior LULAC Councils, children and teenagers received the civic education and training they needed to keep propelling the movement forward.

Finally, this chapter locates LULAC within the geopolitical landscape of the United States and Latin America during the Great Depression and World War II. At the height of the organization's integrationist project during the war, LULAC members used the American rhetoric of racial liberalism, which blended well with their gente decente values, plus a transborder political strategy to build momentum for their civil rights project.

Respectability and Racial Politics in Gente Decente Struggles for Integration

LULAC emerged from organizations formed to promote Mexican American identity during and after World War I. In 1929, three organizations—the Order of Sons of America, the Order of the Knights of America, and the League of Latin American Citizens—merged to form the League of United Latin American Citizens.[5] Notably, all these groups avoided the use of "Mexican" or "Mexico," which whites often used in a pejorative sense. They chose to call themselves Latin Americans in connection with a European heritage. As Lulac News Associate Editor J. T. Canales wrote in reference to the "Latin race," "Our race has distinguished itself in the past by giving Europe the best there is in literature, arts, and sciences." He went on to exhort his readers to carry out these accomplishments in the United States where "our race is looked upon as an inferior race and demonstrate to the world that the Latin race can do in America what it has done in Europe."[6]

Anti-Mexican sentiment flared during the Great Depression, and the decade of the 1930s witnessed massive repatriation drives throughout the Southwest that substantially reduced the Mexican immigrant population. With those residents went a stronger sense of Mexican identity that had pervaded earlier political movements.[7] LULAC seemed poised to emerge as the leader of the next civil rights effort, the mobilization of Mexican Americans. After its founding in Corpus Christi, Texas, the League caught the imagination of thousands of US-born Mexicans who were ready for political experiments beyond their parents' Mexican nationalism and ethic of mutuality. By the 1940s, it had chapters throughout Texas and in New Mexico, Colorado, California, Arizona, and Washington, DC.[8] During this early phase, LULACkers dedicated themselves to civil rights volunteerist politics focused on the goals of achieving equal rights as well as political and economic integration of Mexican Americans into mainstream society. According to historian Benjamín Márquez, LULAC's leaders—conservative, middle-class, small business owners and professionals—challenged racial hierarchies but accepted and even championed bourgeois

Figure 6.1 First LULAC Convention, Corpus Christi, Texas, May 1929. Nettie Lee Benson Latin American Collection, University of Texas Libraries, University of Texas at Austin.

assumptions and the capitalist class system.[9] For LULACkers, the problem was not the American system, but the virulent racism they experienced in social, political, and economic life. They wanted greater access to the rights and privileges of US citizenship and worked to prepare themselves and their followers to take up its responsibilities.

Underlying LULAC's economic and social views were two factors: their gente decente mentality and an ideology that supported the political and economic integration of Mexican Americans into mainstream America. The 1929 LULAC Code, which contained the major principles of the Mexican American political mindset, borrowed from both Mexican and American ideological strains. On the one hand, it called for Americanization and the creation of loyal US citizens. But it also called for Mexican Americans to respect their Mexican cultural heritage, to struggle against racial discrimination directed at Mexican-origin people, and to maintain a consciousness of the "collective Mexican traditions and historical memories." The entire document, which called for the creation of a responsible, patriotic, and civic-minded citizenry, celebrated the value system of the gente decente.[10]

While the gente decente tended to be middle or upper class, working-class people were often considered gente decente if they adhered to certain principles of civility: love of country and reverence for its institutions; respect for self and others; proper comportment as befitting one's age, gender, class, and educational level; and responsibility in all endeavors, especially work. But while the working class was expected to uphold the same standard of respectability as the middle class, there was recognition among LULAC leadership that more needed to be done to uplift the masses. Examining the most serious problems faced by the Mexican American community, LULAC president Ezequiel D. Salinas of Laredo stated:

> Under the first problem, the Social problem, we are confronted with the urgent need of education and schooling for the masses of people, adults and children, also belonging to our group. A considerable number of our people exist in a state of dark illiteracy and stark ignorance. These minds must be enlightened. They must be taught SELF-DEVELOPMENT, of mind and body. Culture's doors must be opened, and they must be shown the way to those doors.[11]

Salinas also identified a civic-political problem exemplified by the vulnerability of some Mexican American voters to political machines and, just as troubling, the lack of any political participation by others who "live in fear or shyness apart and isolated from the main arteries of National life."[12] Poll taxes represented an impediment to the exercise of political rights that negatively affected working-class people. Nevertheless, Lady LULAC member Ana Velásquez exhorted Mexican Americans to pay them so they could vote for "those who are unbiased or unprejudiced towards our people, for those who will provide your child with the same educational opportunities that children of other nationalities, but American citizens all, are provided."[13] Initially, LULAC did not admit female members within the main organization, but as women sought a role, LULAC endorsed the organization of Ladies Councils in 1939. Though gender segregated, the councils did grant women equal rights within the organization and supported women in a few second-tier leadership positions.[14]

Finally, Salinas identified the deplorable economic condition of many Mexican Americans as a third, interrelated problem.

> An improved social condition, improved through education and self-development, will inevitably result in an improved economic condition, if the advancement of one is used for the advancement of the other; and thus the person, if he uses both of these improvements to best advantage, will find himself carving a prominent niche in the political pyramid of government, having a voice in the general welfare, and becoming a factor in determining the guiding forces of our civic political destinies.[15]

The ideals expressed by these LULACkers mirrored those espoused by a previous generation of gente decente activists in Mexico and Texas, with the only difference being that Mexican Americans were now more politically oriented toward the United States than Mexico.

Gente decente principles were also embedded throughout the LULAC Code. The call to Americanize reminded Mexican Americans about their duty to foster a love of country. Their willingness to work within the system reminded them to revere their country's institutions. Finally, LULACkers were reminded to oppose any "radical and violent demonstration that may tend to create conflicts and disturb the peace and tranquility of our country."[16] Like the gente decente in Mexico who opposed socialist-inspired strikes, Mexican Americans in LULAC opposed socialist- or communist-inspired unions that criticized or threatened the American system. For this reason, when the Laredo Union of the radical Workers Alliance asked Laredo LULAC in May 1938 for assistance in demanding the release of three men who were arrested for "rioting" at the Texas Relief Commission, LULAC refused to cooperate.[17] It did, however, support moderate unions willing to work within the system.

It was for US-born Mexicans that early LULAC sought to create a better America based on tolerance and cultural pluralism. LULAC members had more privileges than their parents' generation and closer links to the United States through birth and socialization in schools, the army, and mass media. These privileges allowed them greater power to negotiate and make demands on the dominant culture than previous generations of transborder activists. They used the rhetoric of patriotism to proclaim for Mexican Americans a space within the American body politic. The fact that early LULAC excluded Mexican immigrants reflected their keen understanding of the level of nativism in US society at the time, the limits of their power as a US-born ethnic group still seen as "foreign" by mainstream society, and their unwillingness to identify with undocumented immigrants.

LULACkers sought to create a world in which Mexican Americans could exist as loyal American citizens with rights and responsibilities even as they held on to their cultural heritage, a vision LULAC founder Alonso S. Perales advocated:

> We, conscious Mexican Americans, under all circumstances, consider ourselves as American as the most American person there is, and we challenge anyone to prove us otherwise. We are not trying to deny our race. On the contrary, we are proud to have Mexican blood running through our veins. And our purpose is not to ask, much less beg, Anglo Saxons to allow us to mingle socially with them. What we long for is the respect of our unalienable rights and privileges.[18]

In this particular instance, Perales used the term "Mexican blood" to emphasize the cultural distinctions between Mexicans and Anglo Americans. But a separate cultural heritage, he believed, did not disqualify Mexican Americans from the benefits of American citizenship.

In 1936, however, Mexican-origin people living in the United States knew all too well that "race" referred to biological differences and a social hierarchy. In fact, for many Anglo-Americans, terms such as "American" and "US citizen" were code words for "white or Caucasian person." As a result, some LULAC members attempted to negotiate the slippery slope of claiming "whiteness." Mexican-origin people, they argued, were "white" and therefore entitled to the same rights and privileges guaranteed to Anglo-Americans. Some LULACkers claimed whiteness as descendants of Spanish Europeans. Other LULACkers acknowledged that Mexicans were a "mixed race," proudly owning both the Spanish and Indian heritages while still claiming whiteness.[19]

Rather than seeing in them brothers and sisters of the "white race," however, most Anglo-Americans saw the large mass of poor and uneducated Mexican immigrants as a threat to their society and culture. Their racist attitudes informed the political strategy of acculturated, middle-class Mexican Americans.[20] For Mexican Americans, becoming Spanish American or Latin American allowed them to distance themselves from the dark-skinned peasants arriving in large numbers from war-torn Mexican villages and the countryside. Also, LULAC fought against efforts to label Mexican Americans "colored" because they did not want to experience the de jure segregation suffered by black Americans at the time. Jim Crow laws for "colored" people meant job discrimination, school segregation, political disfranchisement, restrictive housing covenants, and social stigma—discriminatory practices experienced by most Mexicans in the United States.[21] Besides the obvious political disadvantages of being labeled "colored," some Mexican Americans were also influenced by the racist ideas of the conservative Mexican elite class, which glorified European (white) culture, particularly the French. To their way of thinking, the white race—gente decente Mexicans among them—possessed superior racial and cultural characteristics to the black race. Thus, while some radical Mexican American activists, such as Emma Tenayuca, called for a coalition of blacks and Mexican Americans, conservative LULAC activists considered such a strategy to be political suicide.[22]

Regardless of how Mexicans in the United States thought of themselves, Anglo Americans grouped them indiscriminately as "nonwhites." In Wharton, Texas, for example, LULAC protested the practice of designating Mexicans as "colored" in poll tax receipts. On a grander scale, in 1936, LULAC began a campaign to have the federal government change categorizations of Mexicans in US census birth and death records from "colored" to "white." The campaign was motivated by the 1930 Census Bureau classification of Mexican-origin people as a race, "Mexican," instead of "white." Previously, Mexicans had been defined as "white" in these documents, and the new labels insulted Mexican American activists and mobilized them to form a strong lobby. In a letter to Vergil D. Reed, acting director of the Department of Commerce, Robert Meza, LULAC's corresponding secretary, requested that the term "Mexican" be eliminated from the forthcoming census because in so classifying Mexicans as a distinct "Mexican race," it implied they were not members of the white race when "in truth and fact we are not only a part and parcel but the sum and substance of the White race."[23] Yet, from the perspective of Edward J. Noble, the undersecretary of commerce, it was necessary to designate Mexicans in their own category.

> Mexicans should be enumerated separately rather than counted with the White population because they are different in significant respects. Both their birth rates and their death rates are far higher than those of White residents of the same area. Public health programs, both State and Federal, are therefore handicapped if they cannot have separate data

for Mexicans. From sociological, cultural, and economic standpoints, also, the Mexicans are different from the other racial groups.[24]

Many LULACkers felt that such labels amounted to taking a step backward in the process of integrating Mexican-origin people into American society. LULAC leader E. D. Salinas expressed his sentiments on the matter in the *LULAC News*:

> There are hundreds of thousands of good American citizens of Mexican origin within the borders of the United States. We are trying to become worthy, true and loyal citizens of our country. This is the first Aim and Purpose of LULAC. . . . Internally, we are trying to make our members and friends feel that they ARE AMERICANS. And externally, through personal contact, addresses, the press etc. we are trying to make those of other racial groups feel that we ALL ARE AMERICANS. But how can we accomplish this work, when the Bureau of the Census lays down the edict that we are "Mexicans"?[25]

Salinas, like many LULAC members, had deep roots in both Mexico and Texas. He was bilingual and bicultural and, as a resident of a prominent border city, he had ample transnational connections. Although these connections with Mexico doubtlessly enriched his personal and professional life, on a political front, Salinas understood that to be labeled "Mexican" by American institutions amounted to the further impoverishment, and not enrichment, of Mexican Americans.[26]

To add to their burden, LULACkers also had to contend with the new Social Security Board that had asked employers to enroll Mexicans as "nonwhite." If the plan was to demand their rights as citizens in a society where citizenship was intimately tied to whiteness, LULAC needed to attack all labels—"colored," "Mexican," or "nonwhite"—that excluded them from the inner sanctum of whiteness where society's privileges resided. LULAC's crusade was not against the institutional racial caste system but against attempts to lump them in with African Americans and the so-called yellow races, where Asians and Native Americans were placed.[27] By 1940, LULAC's effort had succeeded, and Mexican-origin people were again enumerated as "white" in the 1940 US census.[28]

Throughout the postwar period, LULAC used the courts, as well as boycotts, protests, and lobbying strategies, to eradicate discrimination against and segregation of Mexican Americans across the Southwest. In 1946, with LULAC's full support, Mexican Americans in California won an important school desegregation battle in the case of *Mendez v. Westminster*. The Federal District Court and the Ninth Circuit Court of Appeals both ruled that Mexican American school children could not be segregated on the basis of language, which was the thinly veiled racist justification used by school officials to keep Mexican American children out of the far superior schools reserved for Anglo-American children. The next year, LULAC and the American GI Forum, a Mexican American veteran's civil rights organization, won an important school desegregation case in *Delgado v. Bastrop* in Bastrop, Texas. A US District Court ruled in favor of desegregation by September 1949; however, the court allowed for separate first grade classrooms for language-deficient or non-English-speaking students. The *Delgado v Bastrop* case undermined the segregation of Mexican American schoolchildren. These cases were significant precursors to *Brown v. Board of Education of Topeka, Kansas* (1954). By 1957, the *Hernández v. Driscoll Consolidated ISD* case finally resulted in the cessation of de jure segregation and segregation based on pedagogical arguments in Texas public schools.[29]

Another landmark case in Mexican American history highlighted the "slippery slope" nature of claims to whiteness. Indeed, for Mexican Americans, the privilege of whiteness was a double-edged sword, as the struggle against discrimination in jury selection proved. In 1951, LULAC lawyer Gus García, assisted by lawyer John J. Herrera, defended Pete Hernández, who was charged with murdering another Mexican American in Jackson County. García took this opportunity to challenge the long-standing system of denying Mexican-origin people the right to be judged by a body of their peers. Mexican Americans were not allowed to serve on jury commissions, grand juries, and petit juries in Texas, which García and Herrera argued was a violation of the equal protection of the law clause of the Fourteenth Amendment by the State of Texas. When civil rights lawyers lost the case, they filed an appeal with the Texas Court of Criminal Appeals. This court rejected their request for a new trial, stating that the Fourteenth Amendment recognized only two classes in its equal protection clause: whites and blacks. Since Mexicans were considered white and the jury at the Hernández case had been composed of white people, the Fourteenth Amendment clause had not been violated and was therefore inapplicable in this case.

García, Herrera, and Carlos Cadena, a lawyer who assisted them at the appeals level, took this case to the US Supreme Court, where they argued that in fact, Mexican Americans in Texas were not treated as whites but as a special group that was subject to discrimination. On May 3, 1954, the Supreme Court overturned the Texas Court of Appeals. Led by Chief Justice Earl Warren, the Court ruled that Hernández had been denied his right to a fair trial because there were no Mexican Americans on the jury. Further, the Court rejected the "two classes" theory, stating that the Fourteenth Amendment applied to all groups, not just whites and blacks.[30]

The Hernández case represented a turning point for LULAC. Already the Mexican American organization had begun to move away from a political strategy based on claims to whiteness toward an understanding of Mexican Americans as a racialized minority group engaged in a long struggle for first-class citizenship alongside blacks and other racialized groups.[31]

Alice Dickerson Montemayor: Operating within LULAC's Gendered World

The politics of race was often at the center of LULAC's public battles, but gender politics informed the internal workings of the organization. As early as the 1930s, LULAC had grappled with the question of what role women could or should play in a Mexican American civil rights organization, and how women's political activism could be reconciled with the patriarchal ethos of the organization writ large. It was thought that female members were married and had joined the group to support their husbands' activism, a position historian Cynthia Orozco has countered.[32] Alice Dickerson Montemayor is one example of an active participant who joined independently. Her husband was a Mexican national and could not join LULAC.

Alice Montemayor joined LULAC in 1936 at the invitation of Esther N. Machuca, LULAC Ladies Organizer General from El Paso. She co-chartered Laredo's Ladies LULAC Council No. 15, serving as secretary in 1936–1937 and president in 1938–1939. Her articulate and often witty reports of her council's activities for *LULAC News* earned her national attention within the organization. In 1937, she was selected to represent her council at LULAC's annual convention in Houston, where her peers elected her second vice president general, making her the first woman elected to a national post. Montemayor continued along a pioneering path, becoming the first woman associate editor of *LULAC News* and in 1939 director general of Junior LULAC. [33] The life and work of Montemayor illustrate how Mexican American women successfully used the rhetoric of maternalism to inform the transborder political culture. Expressions of this evolving consciousness met with limited support in an organization still defined by a marked gendered hierarchy, but that did not stop Montemayor.

Alice Dickerson, known as Alicia to her family and friends, was born in Laredo, Texas, on August 6, 1902, to an Irish father, John Randolph Dickerson, and a Mexican mother, Manuela Barrera. Her father, a native of New Orleans, moved to San Antonio to work as a railroad engineer for the International and Great Northern Railway Company and participated in the extension of the railroad from Austin to San Antonio and finally to Laredo. Alicia's mother, a descendant of one of Laredo's original settler families, worked as a seamstress before her marriage.[34]

Alicia grew up proud of her mixed heritage, embracing her Irish and Mexican backgrounds alike. She identified with ethnic Mexican culture and grew up in a bilingual household. Her perfect command of the English language privileged her at a time when the Mexican immigrant population of South Texas struggled against a language barrier. Her brown skin color announced to the world that she was raza.[35]

Alicia's father provided a middle-class life for his family. She attended Colegio de Guadalupe (Guadalupe Elementary School, later called Ursuline Academy), a private Catholic school. At a time when few Mexican American youth attended high school, she graduated from Laredo High School, having distinguished herself in athletics, the drama club, the debate team, the glee club, the Nike Literary Club, the science club, the library club, and the *Live Wire*, the student newspaper. Through these groups Alicia developed her leadership qualities.[36]

When Alicia's father died two days before her high school graduation, she had to forgo plans to attend Southwest Teachers College in San Marcos and instead get a job so she could support her mother. Her father's death was not the only obstacle she faced. Her mother discouraged her interests in acting by telling her that actresses were not gente decente.[37]

Alicia worked several respectable jobs, including a short stint at a dry goods store and a clerkship at Western Union, where she was eventually placed in charge of the messenger boys. While working at Western Union, she met Francisco Montemayor, a bookkeeper for Banco Longoria, across the border in Nuevo Laredo. They married in 1927 and had a son, Francisco Jr. After staying at home for three years with her son, Señora Montemayor returned to work at Western Union and later took a supervisory position at Kress Restaurant. In 1933, she began a career in social work and soon qualified for a position as a caseworker for the Department of Public Welfare. When she was sent to Cotulla in La Salle County, she experienced daily racial discrimination for the first time. The Anglo-American county judge refused to give her the key to her county courthouse office, white clients refused to provide her with their financial information, and she had to hire a bodyguard for protection. Through sheer determination, Montemayor desegregated the county courthouse and enrolled 400–500 Mexican Americans on the welfare rolls. As effective as she was in social work, Montemayor wanted to try other ventures. In 1936, she opened Monty's Fashion Shop. When it failed, Montemayor soon found employment heading the business office of the fashion department of the Montgomery Ward store in Laredo.[38]

Montemayor exercised significant control over both her professional and personal life. Although she was unable to attend college until much later in life, that did not stop her from cultivating friendships with college-educated people she respected. In matters of the heart, she displayed an independent streak. She married Francisco Montemayor willingly but warned the groom's mother that if her son ever disrespected her, the marriage would end. Fortunately, it was a happy and long-lasting union. Her jobs were all feminized positions, but she chose to continue to work after marriage at a time when middle-class propriety still required a male breadwinner and a female homemaker. It was this spirit and her desire to contribute that motivated Montemayor to join LULAC in its struggle to eradicate discrimination and help improve the lives of Mexican Americans.

Montemayor joined LULAC when her son was of school age. Once a member of the organization, she gravitated to activities where she could involve him, principally the Junior LULACs. Youth chapters, or Junior LULAC Councils, were started in San Antonio in 1937. Montemayor did much to promote the idea, organizing the second Junior LULAC Council in Laredo by March of the same year. Unlike the adult councils, Junior LULACs were not gender segregated. One of the most active councils, the Junior LULACs of Laredo had a full set of officers, among them Montemayor's son, and most of the members were children of LULAC members.[39]

The primary goal of the Junior LULACs, as understood by Montemayor, was to train young people to take on leadership roles and to become "good Americans." This aligned with past LULAC president M. C. González's statement that the formation of Junior Lulacs was "a foundation stone on which we are

Figure 6.2 Alice Dickerson Montemayor and Junior Lulac members, circa late 1930s or 1940s. Nettie Lee Benson Latin American Collection, University of Texas Libraries, University of Texas at Austin.

building character and assuring lasting devotion to our country's service."[40] Montemayor's work with the Junior LULACs entailed teaching them how to become skilled debaters, informed citizens, independent critical thinkers, and public servants. Hand in hand with teaching children to formulate their own informed opinion was the matter of teaching young people how to read and write critically. She called for far more than general literacy. She wanted the young to read with purpose and to write intelligently. She also gave civics and acting lessons.[41] As their sponsor, she supervised the elections of the Junior members and supported them in all of their activities, such as fundraisers, social events, and participation in the larger organization, such as a LULAC banquet held in honor of President General Filemón Martínez.[42]

In a series of articles for the *LULAC News*, Montemayor exhorted members of the senior councils to organize their children ages eight to eighteen into Junior LULAC Councils. Having seen members exercise undue influence on other members during LULAC elections and probably aware of the systemic voter fraud rampant in South Texas, Montemayor wanted youngsters to learn to vote based on their own convictions and not to satisfy their friends. In fact, she warned against mixing friendship with the business of the council for it invariably led to broken relationships when friends disagreed on issues.[43]

She also wanted young people to develop compassion for their respective communities and to that end she called for adults to encourage their children to devote some time to public service. After all, as she often remarked, "A Junior Council is the training center for tomorrow's LULACker." Training young minds now, Montemayor contended, would result in a stronger and larger LULAC in the future. On a broader level, these youngsters would grow up to be assets to their community and country.[44]

Finally, Montemayor's addresses to the general membership emphasized gender equity. The Laredo Junior LULAC Council consisted of both boys and girls, and Montemayor encouraged all Junior Councils to follow this example.

> When organizing a JUNIOR COUNCIL we should make it a mixed group, that is, boys and girls, so that they learn to depend on each other for their LULAC work, to love each other as LULACers should, to work hand in hand and cooperate with each other HARMONIOUSLY and having been trained in this manner, by the time they are ready to join the senior Councils they will abandon the egotism and petty jealousies so common today among our Ladies' and Men's Councils.[45]

By having a mixed Junior group, she hoped to teach the next generation how to transcend sexist ideas. To the extent that some girls were elected to office within the Junior Council and the boys who wrote for *LULAC News* expressed contentment with their mixed gender arrangement, it appears that Montemayor succeeded in her gender parity socialization efforts.[46] She understood that the dominant patriarchal structure within LULAC could not be dismantled overnight, so she invested a significant amount of time and energy into training the next generation.

Montemayor also succeeded in getting the men's council to pay attention to the civic education of youth. Some members of the Laredo men's council No. 12 attended select Junior Council functions and at times served as guest speakers.[47] In 1943, however, LULACker George Garza of Laredo reorganized the Junior Council, shifting the focus from preteens to teenagers, because he hoped to do away with the "babysitting" element. In other places, the Junior Councils continued to be sponsored by Ladies LULAC Councils and the men's councils focused on Boy Scout troops.[48]

Although Montemayor's work with the Junior LULACs fit within a maternalist framework, her assertive leadership style threatened some men. In 1937–1938, President General Ramón L. Longoria and First Vice President Chávez both fell gravely ill, and as the next officer in line, she came close to becoming the organization's first woman president general. Some officers and members were threatened by the possibility of a female president, however, and Montemayor strongly believed that pressure from these constituencies kept the ailing superior officers from resigning. Several of these men criticized her for being independent and domineering in her ideas and convictions. She was not the demure wife of a LULAC member. She had joined Ladies LULAC for the same reasons that men joined—to struggle against racism and to promote Mexican Americanism—and she had her own agenda: to encourage the proliferation of Ladies and Junior LULAC Councils throughout the state and beyond. Her ideas and approach to civic work were popular among some sectors of LULAC and hated in others.[49]

Beyond her willingness to pioneer LULAC youth programs, her eagerness to serve as an officer, and her assertive leadership style, Montemayor displayed a feminist consciousness in a series of *LULAC News* articles and many pieces of correspondence to her and from friends and associates, among them her strongest defender, El Paso resident Juan (J. C.) Machuca, director of publicity and manager of *LULAC News*. For example, she addressed sexism within the organization and encouraged women to participate. But Montemayor had some conflicts with other members of the Laredo's Ladies LULAC Council No. 15 who sided with her male detractors.[50]

Ultimately, Montemayor's decision to follow a maternal feminist approach by focusing much of her time and energy on the development of the Junior LULACs illustrates the paradox experienced by gente decente women in politics. On the one hand, she adhered to LULAC's ideals of mothers as cultural transmitters and civics teachers. On the other hand, she criticized the sexism within the organization and used the maternalist strategy to subvert the organization's gender dynamics by training children and young men and women to create the more gender equitable civil society she envisioned.

The Local-Global Nexus: Are We Good Neighbors?

Besides the strategies of cultural redemption, Americanization, and maternal feminism that some members of LULAC employed, a transborder strategy also found appeal within the organization. Pan-Americanism, the US-Latin American "Good Neighbor" policy, and World War II presented some opportunities for civil rights advancements at a historical moment marked by the nation's geopolitical interests in maintaining friendly relationships with nations south of the border.

American efforts to maintain a close relationship with Latin American countries date back to the early nineteenth century with the development of the Monroe Doctrine, which was designed to stave off European interference in the affairs of the Americas. In its more recent uses, Pan-Americanism represented a call to unity and better relationships among the nations of the Americas. For example, in 1916, the Pan-American Round Table of San Antonio formed to pursue two objectives: "To promote mutual knowledge, understanding and friendship among the people of the Western Hemisphere; and to foster all movements leading to a higher civilization, especially those affecting the women and children of the Pan American countries."[51]

The Round Table consisted of San Antonio middle- to upper-class European American and Mexican-origin women, but both women and men throughout the country were involved in efforts to foster inter-cultural learning across the Americas. In an article published in 1938, future LULAC president and University of Texas professor George I. Sánchez argued that Pan-Americanism gave "promise to a new era—of mutual understanding and of international co-operation." He went on to praise the United States for its efforts.

> It is a matter of considerable gratification to many of us that the United States, for one, has placed great emphasis upon the premise that international cooperation must be grounded upon understanding and mutual respect.[52]

LULAC supported the efforts of Mexican American senator and LULAC member Dennis Chávez from New Mexico to refocus the nation's attention from war in Europe to the economic development of the western hemisphere. In a

1940 article, Senator Chávez outlined all the work that needed to be done for the United States to rebuild its relationship with Latin America. He reminded readers that a US imperialistic policy in the Caribbean, exemplified by the Spanish American War, acquisition of the Panama Canal, the landing of Marines in Haiti, Santo Domingo, and Nicaragua, and other forms of hostility, inspired sister republics to feel a sense distrust, suspicion, and even hatred toward what they viewed as "the colossus of the north." Chávez noted that the United States had intervened some thirty times in Latin America and fears of Yankee imperialism preoccupied the Latin American mind.[53]

Senator Chávez pointed out that even as the racial doctrines of totalitarian nations in Europe were decried in the United States, Americans had an ethnocentric view of Latin Americans. The American sense of superiority manifested in various ways, among these the nefarious Hollywood stereotype of Latin Americans as inferior. Furthermore, he challenged the United States to develop a more equitable economic policy toward Latin America. Chávez's call to action involved the procurement of strategic raw materials, such as tin and rubber, from Latin America to replace those at that time derived from Europe and Asia, and he noted that trade and commerce must be made with a view to raising the standard of living in Latin America rather than economic exploitation.[54]

Senator Dennis Chávez remained hopeful that the inter-cultural cooperation he witnessed in New Mexico would be adopted by the United States "in its consideration of the Latin Americans. They must be treated as equals." In Chávez's New Mexico, that meant mutual respect, tolerance, and understanding. In terms of concrete programming, he hoped for "the development of close cultural ties, the facilitation of travel and intercourse, and lastly, the erection of a powerful economic hegemony."[55]

Domestically, the United States had a vested interest in fostering unity among the diverse populations within its borders through the philosophy of racial liberalism. Understanding the volatility created by racism during time of war, American cultural leaders promoted educational programs to discredit racialist ideologies. They also encouraged the use of judicial and legislative measures as well as an expanded federal government role to deal with inequalities within society. By attacking the biological assumptions of the American social hierarchy, the proponents of racial liberalism hoped to solve the race problem and unify the nation under a cultural pluralist ethos best exemplified by the wartime rallying cry, "Americans All."[56]

Published in 1948 by LULAC leader Alonso Perales, the book *Are We Good Neighbors?* used the rhetoric of racial liberalism and represented the strategy of transborder politics at its best. A collection of essays by an ethnically diverse group of civic-minded leaders, it touched upon four themes: racial discrimination in the United States against Mexicans, Mexican Americans, and Hispanics in general; Pan-Americanism; the Good Neighbor Policy; and the World War II goal of unity among the nations of the western hemisphere. In a sense, the text was an indictment of the United States for failing to be a good neighbor every time racial and cultural discrimination was practiced against people in Latin America or Americans of Latin American descent.[57]

Perales reminded Americans about the commitment to democracy at home that they needed to champion. The title summoned a past marked by President Franklin Roosevelt's Good Neighbor foreign policy, with the goals of respecting Latin American nations' right to self-determination and unifying the western hemisphere. It also called to mind the United States' future as the leader of the free world, a beacon to all who yearned for democracy. Of course, the United States still had a long way to go in terms of establishing true first-class citizenship for all of its citizens, but the forces were in play that would lead to the *Brown* decision in 1954, the eradication of Jim Crow in the South, and the civil rights legislation of the 1960s. Perales sensed this and so set about penning a manifesto holding the United States accountable for its inability to live up to its political ideals, the ideals for which many lost their lives during the war, among them many Mexican Americans. This manifesto also reminded the United States that the whole world would be watching it and that as in the past, Latin America would not look kindly upon a bad neighbor who violated the rights of its own citizens, people still linked linguistically and culturally to Latin America.

Several of the essays in *Are We Good Neighbors?* brought this message home. Archbishop Robert E. Lucey's 1943 essay, for example, asked,

> Can we make the western hemisphere the bulwark of liberty and law while we maim and mangle Mexican youth in the streets of our cities? Can we condemn our Latin Americans to starvation wages, bad housing and tuberculosis and then expect them to be strong, robust soldiers of Uncle Sam? Can we tell our Spanish-speaking soldiers that dishonorable discharge from the army will deprive them of civil rights when they never had any civil rights? In a word, can we, the greatest nation on earth, assume the moral leadership of the world when race riots and murder, political crimes and economic injustices disgrace the very name of America?[58]

Clearly disturbed by the Zoot Suit Riots in Los Angeles and other forms of racial discrimination, Archbishop Lucey went on to repudiate racist stereotypes of Mexican-origin people and discussed the commonalities binding the English- and Spanish-speaking, among these the Catholic faith.[59]

Carlos Castañeda, history professor at the University of Texas at Austin and LULAC member, wrote an essay, "The Second Rate Citizen and Democracy," that got to the heart of the unequal relationship between the Anglos and Mexicans. While progressive Anglos such as Lucey stressed the commonalities, certain sectors of the Anglo community benefited from stressing differences between the two groups. As Castañeda put it,

> Why the insistence on a practice (racial discrimination) that is un-democratic, un-American, and un-christian? . . . economic exploitation. A second rate citizen, member of a group admittedly inferior, cannot render services equal in value to those of the superior group. Consequently, his remuneration and his opportunities for advancement in employment are limited. As long as the community brands him inferior by the treatment accorded him, the employer can continue to exploit him with a clear conscience.[60]

Castañeda then explained why the group he represented chose to call itself Spanish or Latin American. The term "Mexican" had come to mean "nonwhite" and therefore inferior and exploitable. Castañeda took issue with the increasingly used term "white Mexican" because its implication was that there were nonwhite Mexicans who could be mistreated. He reminded his readers that such acts of discrimination defied good neighborliness and put the United States on par with Germany. As he characterized it,

> Cooperation between the peoples of the Americas cannot be developed under such conditions. Democracy becomes a travesty if a single citizen is denied equal rights. . . . If we admit the damning theory of racial superiority implied in such a condition, we are no better than the Nazis.

The essay ended with a plea for truth-telling and radical cures for radical ailments. It was time, Castañeda argued, to make the pledge to the flag a reality: "one nation indivisible, with liberty and justice for all."[61]

Progressive Anglo- and Mexican American activists were not the only ones putting pressure on Jim (Jaime) Crow directed at Mexicans. World War II created labor shortages in agriculture. In 1942 the United States responded by initiating a bilateral agreement with Mexico, a guest worker program commonly known as the Bracero Program. This was nothing new for the transborder Mexican labor force; as historian Neil Foley writes, it had been "aggressively recruited in the 1920s, repatriated in the 1930s," and was now being "imported as contract laborers in the 1940s." In 1943, Texas growers sought to take advantage of this program and requested braceros. The Mexican government, aware of the virulent racism that defined Anglo treatment of Mexicans in Texas, refused to cooperate until the state guaranteed fair treatment and an end to segregation and racism against Mexicans and people of Mexican-origin in Texas. The governor of Texas, Coke Stevenson, a friend of the state's economic interests, responded by supporting the 1943 Caucasian Race-Equal Privileges Resolution, which promised that no Caucasian would be discriminated against. The implication was that Mexicans would be included under the rubric "Caucasian" though this was never explicitly written into the resolution. Furthermore, the governor, having been advised by Tom Sutherland of the State Department's Office of Inter-American Affairs, established the Good Neighbor Commission of Texas (GNC) to promote better understanding between Texas whites and "Caucasian Mexicans." With all of this talk of giving Mexicans their rights as white people, the Mexican government relented and allowed braceros to travel to work in Texas. The Bracero Program continued until 1964.[62]

Historian Thomas A. Guglielmo has added an interesting dimension to this story of transnational politics, arguing that LULAC was heavily involved in the drafting of the Caucasian Race-Equal Privileges resolution. This, of course, complicates the conventional wisdom about the Mexican American generation that they were solely preoccupied with things "American." In fact, as Guglielmo points out, the Mexican American civil rights effort to end race-based discrimination against people of Mexican descent in Texas was fully supported by Mexico, whose embassy and newspapers put pressure on the United States to resolve the unjust situation in Texas. Mexico's ultimate bargaining chip during this World War II period was the Bracero Program, for the country desperately needed workers from its southern neighbor. It was due to this realization that Texas Governor Coke Stevenson took actions to appease Mexico.[63]

Unfortunately, neither the resolution nor the GNC did much to change conditions for Mexican-origin people in Texas. The resolution, while written by LULAC leader M. C. Gonzales and championed by another LULAC principal, Alonso Perales, and many others, was mocked by the opposition. Furthermore, the GNC, while led by a few progressive Anglos, never had the power to execute programs and policies that might have led to effective change. It merely investigated and recommended to local communities possible solutions, but ultimately, it was up to the locals to fix things as they saw fit, if at all. During the war, the GNC seemed to be making progress in terms of educating Anglo-Americans about the necessity to treat Mexican immigrants and Mexican Americans fairly, but after the war, the common cause faded. In addition, the illegal entry of thousands of Mexican workers removed the leverage the Bracero Program had given the Mexican government. In 1945 when the Spears Bill was presented for consideration, the GNC failed to lobby for it, in part because legislating equality went against the commission's basic philosophy of educating Anglos and going after their hearts and minds rather than their anger, which, they believed, would surely be provoked through government-imposed civil rights.[64]

In time, even the Texas GNC's investigative powers were seriously curtailed. During the governorship of Allan Shivers, a conservative politician who married into a landed family heavily involved in south Texas agribusiness, the commission produced studies on the exploitation of Mexican labor by south Texas farmers. As one of those farmers, Shivers felt embarrassed and pressured GNC Executive Director Pauline Kibbe to resign in September 1947. Shivers then made the commission a permanent state agency under new director Tom Sutherland. Now under the close watch of Shivers, Sutherland avoided Mexican labor issues but still covered discriminatory practices and lobbied against school segregation.

When in 1949 the Texas community of Three Rivers refused to bury the body of a fallen Mexican American soldier named Félix Longoria, the GNC joined Dr. Hector García and the American GI Forum in bringing national attention to this case of blatant discrimination. A Texas state legislative committee whitewashed the affair, but Senator Lyndon Baines Johnson arranged for Longoria to be buried at Arlington National Cemetery. Once again, embarrassed by the actions of the GNC, Governor Shivers decided to dissolve the GNC's investigative powers. He also had other motivations besides the Longoria case. Shivers worried about a potential Truman administration inquiry into migratory labor scandals. The last thing he wanted was for the GNC to furnish the federal government with incriminating information about Texas agribusiness. In 1951, the governor weakened the GNC by splitting it in two and turning it into a public relations entity. Now the GNC focused on the international aspects of Latin Americans in Texas such as "the crossing of Mexicans." The other element of the GNC became involved in forming a network of local councils, which fell under the jurisdiction of the Human Relations Council. Gone were the weekly reports tracking discriminatory practices and the civil rights activities of the American GI Forum. In time, the privately funded Human Relations Council disappeared when funds dried up.[65]

Alonso Perales, as well as progressive Anglos, such as businessman Jack Danciger, believed that because the Good Neighbor Commission was created without the benefit of the Spears Anti-Discrimination Bill, it was bound to fail. An organization without any real power to carry out its mandate of improving race relations in Texas represented a waste of taxpayer dollars.[66] While the GNC might have been wasteful in the sense that tax dollars spent on it did not translate into immediate first-class citizenship for Mexican Americans, the great visibility it enjoyed, its investigative powers before Shivers destroyed them, and the fact that it was created as a concession to Mexico reveal the pressure that Jaime Crow was under during and after World War II. White supremacy was already cracking, and the mere existence of a Good Neighbor Commission in a southern state that developed under the shadow of the Alamo signaled the beginning of the end for anti-Mexican segregation in Texas.

LULAC, its peer organizations, and their allies did much to advance the goals of First Mexicanist Congress leaders, who could not achieve these due to the limitations of their era. The LULAC generation would inherit the task of dismantling a Jaime Crow social, political, and economic structure that kept Mexican-origin people down. The expansion of the federal government, the shift from an agricultural to an industrial economy, and their political strategies of cultural redemption, Americanization, maternalism, and transnationalism allowed these activists to carve out a realistic plan toward reaching the goal of first-class citizenship.

Since 1930, LULAC has been at the forefront of the struggle for rights using a variety of tactics to desegregate facilities and expand opportunities, everything from class action lawsuits, to putting pressure on federal agencies, to protests, to partnerships with key government leaders such as Lyndon B. Johnson, to the creation of other civil rights organizations such as the Mexican American Legal Defense Education Fund (MALDEF).[67]

Furthermore, the maternal feminist strategies of Alice Dickerson Montemayor and other LULAC women engaged in the civic education of the young ensured that the struggle would continue long after her generation was gone. This is significant because even though activists such as Montemayor, Perales, and others did much to move the LULAC agenda forward, the story of Mexican American civil rights gained momentum but did not end after World War II. For the Mexican-origin GIs returning from battlefields in Europe and Asia where they had risked their lives to defend democracy, nothing but democracy at home would do as their just reward for so great a sacrifice. World War II also showed the men and women who struggled on the home front some alternatives to the life of ceaseless underpaid fieldwork they had known. Many of them took advantage of higher-paid war-related jobs in the cities and some even traveled out of state in search of those opportunities. Awakened to their own power as American citizens, fortified by their transnational bonds with a Latin America that expressed indignation every time it received reports of racial discrimination in Texas against its own, and pledged to educate and bring about for their children that which their First Mexican Congress political forebears had worked to achieve for them, LULAC members set off on their search for America, not the America of their past as second-class citizens, but the America of their future as proud United States citizens of Mexican descent.

LULAC is an example of the transborder political culture born of disadvantage and struggle, yet strengthened by the privileges enjoyed by transborder activists. Early LULAC members were US-born or naturalized and so in addition to demanding human rights, they could call for first-class citizenship rights. They were US educated and intimately familiar with American institutions, politics, cultural norms, and the English language. Since many had served honorably in the armed forces, they could generate special attention as proven citizen warriors. Finally, they lived during a period of great possibility as the United States experienced its emergence as a global superpower. Building on a long-standing legacy of resistance and protest, the members of LULAC took their marginalities, combined them with their considerable privileges, and crafted the modern Mexican American civil rights struggle that complemented rather than opposed transborder activism. They negotiated for power at the local, state, and national levels; teamed up with Mexico when it advanced their civil rights agenda; and turned political agency into many concrete examples of community empowerment.

In sum, their use of American nationalism and transborder politics were but two sides of the same coin. Whether they used one or the other or both, their political calculations served the same purpose: to advance the gente decente struggle for rights by encouraging the adoption of middle-class values that would earn Mexican-origin people respectability and by destroying the racial construction of Mexicans as an inferior race that bound them to a subordinate status. For many, the world they bade farewell to at the end of their lives showed signs of marked improvement from the world that had greeted their birth. They could rightly claim some credit for their role in redeeming la raza.

Conclusion

"La Idea Mueve" (The Idea Moves Us)

Why Cultural Redemption Matters

In reference to capitalism's indelible mark upon human relations, historian Joyce Applyby concluded that race had served defenders of slavery by providing them with an excuse to hold men and and women in bondage. Wherever opportunity presented itself, enterprising men emerged with capital, but the matter of labor always presented challenges. Full expression of their economic freedom to exploit the land and its resources required "the mobilization of Asians, Africans, Arabs, or Native Americans—people of color" living in the places holding buried treasures and other not so hidden resources. African slavery, in particular, Appleby contends, necessitated rationalizations to soothe the guilty conscience.[1] But slavery was hardly new in the grand scheme of world history, so why the preoccupation with justifications? Part of it might have been the perpetual and devastating nature of modern slavery, but just as compelling was the giant contradiction that enslavement posed in an age awash with political discourses of freedom and human rights.

For defenders of slavery to justify the inhumane treatment of Africans during the Age of Englightenment, their humanity needed to be ideologically striped away. Scientific racism served that purpose. Racist theories also kept other groups in subordinate positions. Mexicans with mestizo, mulatto, and Indian genealogies experienced racialization in the United States. That is, modern science fixated upon physical traits to cast certain groups as biologically and socially inferior. Justifications for their ill treatment were needed when the assumed "master race" professed a belief in the "rights of man" and admired the words of Thomas Jefferson that "all men are created equal." Simply put, Americans, proud of their liberal political heritage and their democratic institutions needed to see oppressed groups as somehow unworthy, substandard, or even sub-human to reconcile their political beliefs with the nation's less than egalitarian realities. It is for this reason that the politics of redemption practiced by Mexican immigrant and Mexican American activists merits attention.

If racism highlighted the paradoxical nature of modernity, the quest to redeem la raza underscored the complex reality of gente decente activists to various extents, committed as they were to modernity's promise of progress but unwilling to sacrifice Mexican-origin people upon its altar. At the center of their efforts lay a strong belief in the potential for human perfectibility and progress. This represented the key tenet of the Enlightenment, a sweeping intellectual movement with significant political implications. The transborder activists discussed in this book belonged to that larger family of reformers that as inheritors of the Enlightenment embraced the moving idea that human potential, once liberated, was boundless.

By using their educational and class-based privileges to present themselves as the educated, upwardly mobile, and sophisticated Mexicans they were and encouraging others to follow their lead, they bravely challenged all the rationales that white supremacists used to justify inequalities in the United States. Arguably, this stance reinforced a modernist ethos of respectability with problematic gendered class biases for, in a sense, they were asking la raza to enter white America through the prism of bourgeoisie culture. What was being challenged and what was being reinforced? This strategy, laden with race, class, and gender implications, was designed to instill a sense of ethnic pride and unity among Mexican-origin people as well as to show Anglo-Americans just what a valuable and honorable people Mexicans were and how therefore discrimination against them was an unjustified, immoral act.

Not blind to the many challenges facing Mexican-origin people, these activists nevertheless optimistically believed in and worked for a better world where people of Mexican descent would enjoy human and civil rights. To that end, they critiqued both Mexico's Porfirian dictatorship and the United States' Jaime Crowism as violations of the social and political equality promised by modernity. They understood that the price of modernization had been borne by certain groups, such as Mexicans who, in the United States, had been made into a proletariat class through political disenfranchisement, economic dislocation, legal and extralegal land dispossession, racialization, and segregation.

Over the long term, this strategy of cultural redemption proved effective. The League of United Latin American Citizens and other civil rights organizations succeeded in seriously disrupting and in some cases dismantling Jaime Crow structures. Even the Mexican American claims to whiteness, when they occurred, backhandedly sabotaged the rigid black-white racial framework upon which the herronvolk democracy sustained itself. Precisely because Mexican-origin people could not fit neatly into a "white" or "black" category, their struggle for rights could potentially unravel the entire ideological apparatus upon which unequal economic and political relations depended. All it took was for Mexicans to prove that they could measure up to the standards of modernity and thereby reclaim their humanity and demand their natural rights.

For Mexican-origin people, this organized rights project started with the Primer Congreso Mexicanista (1911), but the movement would not gain momentum until World War II and the postwar period when certain historical forces aided the struggle. Nevertheless, important foundational ideas and political practices prepared the way for LULAC. The League as well as its predecessors emerged from a transborder political culture informed by modernist ideas and concepts, such as liberalism, mutualism, Freemasonry, maternal feminism, anti-clericalism, anti-racism, and nationalisms: Mexican and American, respectively.

Liberalism served as the political bedrock upon which the grand project of liberty and progress could be built. But the racism that animated the herronvolk democracy, creating a white America, represented the most serious threat to Mexican American freedom. Treated like a racialized caste, most Mexican-origin people in the United States lived below the poverty line and faced a de facto segregation system that made a mockery of the Declaration of Independence; the Treaty of Guadalupe-Hidalgo's promise to grant US citizenship to Mexicans in conquered lands; and the Fourteenth Amendment's citizenship, due process, and equal protection clauses.

Activists made it their priority to challenge this world with a strong anti-racialist agenda, and they also sought to unite and uplift Mexican-origin people, preparing them for the first-class citizenship they struggled to achieve. Mutualism encouraged this sense of community, the crafting of an all-encompassing identity as la raza. But for all the power of Mexican nationalism's magnetic pull, fissures surfaced as secular and Protestant Freemasons battled Catholic clergy and Magonistas, and class divisions informed the political choices of activists. Women, too, left their mark on the transborder political culture. Maternal feminism stretched the domestic sphere right into the political maelstrom and created spaces for women in the modern nation-state, whether in Mexico or in the United States. On a broader level, their brothers joined them in the search for belonging.

A space in the United States is precisely what LULAC sought, for theirs was a search for the America of equal rights and opportunities, not the Jaime Crow society where they had to "know their place." LULAC's American nationalism has been interpreted as a point of departure from Mexican nationalism, a "selling out" strategy from the perspective of the organization's harshest critics. Setting binary thinking aside, however, reveals the intricate nature of identity and agency. LULAC's American allegiance existed within the broader continuum of cultural redemption as did gente decente Mexican nationalism. Ultimately, both nationalisms rotated on the same pivot point. The turning point for

Mexican-origin people, argued transborder activists, would be their transformation into modern men and women committed to the nation-state. To redeem la raza was to modernize them, to make them attack proof, and to use their redemption as a weapon against an abusive system that thrived on stereotypes and caricatures of its victims. But the struggle had never been confined to the one nation, for both the United States and Mexico experienced modernization, redefinations of social relations, economic dislocations, and the development of a culture of capitalism.

The culture of capitalism brought good things to many but also framed the wretched lives of the masses of Earth's disinherited. Middle-class cultural redeemers never mounted a sustained campaign against that culture of capitalism because they hoped reforms would suffice. They also believed in capitalism's great potential to effect change, to transform, to drive the car of progress. In this way, the gente decente reformers shared with American progressives a similar vision that democracy and capitalism could be made to work together by saving the masses through movements for rights, safety nets, and an engaged body politic that both challenged the system to be more responsive to the people and called upon ordinary men and women to embrace and live up to the modern ideal.

The alternative to this gente decente reform reminds us that la raza never was a unified entity but rather an imagined community, requiring constant calls for unity through the cultivation of ethnic pride and nationalism. Thus, even though the activists in this study shared nationalist and transnationalist frames of reference, hybrid identities, and transborder life experiences, divergent strategies reveal that Mexican-origin people were far from being politically monolithic. Indeed, Ricardo Flores Magón, Mexico's early revolutionary herald, could not have been further apart the ideological spectrum from his gente decente contemporaries. Unlike them, he heavily and consistently critiqued the culture of capitalism and sought its destruction. The Magonista vision made no allowances for capitalism's inequities and saw in this system nothing but the misery of the majority as the high price paid for the fabulous fortunes of the few. For his efforts, Flores Magón paid dearly with his life, as did several of his followers.

In south Texas, Mexicans represented the many and Anglos the few, and yet the latter controlled most of the region's resources, and Mexicans had systematically lost power since the mid-nineteenth century. In this setting, the alternative vision manifested in the form of the Plan de San Diego, a manifesto declaring independence from Anglo dominion and issuing a call to arms to recapture lost lands. Complex and controversial, the plan counted on both méxico-tejanos and Mexicans, including Carrancistas who used this incident to influence US-Mexico relations. Some Anglo lives were lost; many Mexicans, most of them unconnected to the plan, perished; and property damage skyrocketed with each seditionist raid. In the end, the Planistas failed to achieve their goals, except for Carranza, who garnered United States recognition for his government, and things went back to "normal"—except that Anglos hated and distrusted Mexicans even more than before.

The "Mexican Problem" paradigm that relegated Mexican-origin people to the lowest rungs in society found many advocates during this early part of the twentieth century. Episodes such as the Plan de San Diego added fuel to the already robust fire because they could be used to smear all Mexicans as degenerate, violent, conniving, and quintessentially dishonorable *bandidos* (bandits). By the time young Emma Tenayuca began her labor organizing in the 1930s, the Anglos' negative perspectives and attitudes toward Mexicans had become so commonplace as to fall into the unassailable realm of common sense. Thus, exploiting thousands of Mexican-origin women in pecan shelling, cigar-making, and garment manufacturing sweatshops hardly raised an eyebrow within the confines of mainstream society, and neither did exploiting both Mexican men and women in the fields.

Gente decente knew about Tenayuca's work and shared her concern for the working poor as well as her understanding of the links between racism and poverty. By the same token, she knew about them. Tenayuca had been a member of LULAC and was familiar with political strategies aimed at gaining respectability. However, she quickly became disillusioned with these approaches when she realized that regardless of personal efforts, racist Anglos remained just as unwelcoming to the refined Mexicans as they had been to the coarse ones. Instead, she found hope in the Communist Party, which paid attention to the concerns of people of color at a time when other organizations ignored them. But for this alliance and for her militant trade unionism, she paid a price. As in the Plan de San Diego case, deviance from acceptable parameters of political activity in the modern nation-state illicited repression of the harshest kind. Unlike Flores Magón, Tenayuca kept her life, but it became a life marked by red-baiting, blacklisting, FBI survillenace, and many years in exile from her beloved community in San Antonio.

As individuals and as organized bodies, the gente decente achieved some of their goals without the dire consequences faced by those with alternative visions. It is altogether too easy to conclude from these outcomes that cultural redemption offered the better option or that the alternative vision represented the noblest choice. In reality, the two visions for change informed each other and set the stage for latter-day activists. Despite all of the accomplishments of the early twentieth-century transborder activists, much work remained, and the Chicana/o movement of the 1960s and 1970s addressed not only white America's racism but also issued a strong critique of the gente decente politics. Like the Black

Power movement, Chicano and Chicana activists sought to reclaim a sense of cultural autonomy and create political empowerment by challenging racial, gender, and class conventions that middle-class gatekeepers of all backgrounds used, to various extents, to determine political and economic access in society. By confronting the gendered class politics of respectability that had governed the activist lives of their middle-class Mexican and Mexican American predecessors, they strove to disrupt a modernist liberal capitalist model that had failed to create an equitable society and had justified itself through the power of ideology and culture.

Even so, for all of their critiques of previous activists, Chicanos and Chicanas built their movement on what had come before. They were the inheritors of both gente decente reformers and alternative vision militants. In fact, Chicanismos' focus on cultural self-defense directly connected them to the First Mexicanist Congress. Cultural self-defense also linked them to LULAC because the League's efforts to dismantle Jaime Crow, the institutional manifestation of the "Mexican Problem" paradigm, was a much needed stepping stone toward Chicanismos' ultimate quest for liberation and self-determination.

The eradication of racism and discrimination as well as the amelioration of poverty represented the shared goals of those promoting a gente decente vision and those opting for an alternative vision. Ideology and strategy are where they parted ways. The gente decente believed that the more egalitarian strains of the modernist project could be employed to reform its most exploitative elements. In this endeavor, respectability emerged as their strategy of choice because their priority was to deny white supremacists excuses for mistreating Mexicans, and in so doing, they would claim the higher moral ground.

For the alternative vision advocates, capitalism, modernity's economic arm, offered little of redemptive value. Because capitalism turned labor into a commodity whose cost needed to be minimized to enhance profits, the potential to exploit purveyors of labor remained ever present. This happened even in professesed democratic societies because social constructs like race and gender could always be employed to cast workers as somehow deserving of their debased economic condition. Activists who acknowledged this proposition and could not see a way around it opted for strategies of solidarity and militancy.

The legacies of the Chicana/o movement reflect their own debts to previous generations of transborder activists. Chicanismo, like gente decente advocacy, has created access for communities where none or little existed before. And like the alternative vision advocates, Chicanismo has raised critiques, awareness, and consciousness about all the work needed and accomplished as well as the work that remains. To say that one activist approach is better than the other misses the point that the struggle for rights required both because each offered something of redeeming value.

Reflection

Despite the best efforts of gente decente transborder activists, the familiar "Mexican problem" paradigm they blamed for the suffering of the Mexican people in the United States has survived their cultural redemption strategy. Such a strategy, which is less likely to get an activist persecuted or jailed than radical activity, ultimately reinforces as much as it challenges the ideas and culture of modernity. In their struggle for rights, these activists saw more of the promise than the price of modernity. These were not the Mexicans who spent their entire lifetimes working in the fields, only to be followed into those fields by their children. These were the Mexicans who possessed more education than average, who built small businesses, who became professionals, and who planned for a better life for their children in American society. Using the language of material and cultural uplift, they set out on a quest to redeem la raza.

If the "Mexican problem" remains, was cultural redemption a failure? Ultimately, the strategy made possible a movement for civil rights in the historical context of the early twentieth century. This work, together with the more militant strategies of the Magonistas, Emma Tenayuca, and others, created a society in which the "No Mexicans or Dogs Allowed" signs have come down. Still, it has left plenty of work for activists who continue to reside in the world of two flags entwined.

NOTES

Introduction

1. Carolina Munguía to the Governor of Querétaro, 26 March 1939, Rómulo Munguía Papers, Benson Latin American Collections, University of Texas Libraries, University of Texas, Austin. Hereafter cited as Munguía Papers.
2. Minutes of the Círculo Cultural "Isabel, la Católica," 12 June 1938, Munguía Papers, hereafter cited as CCIC Minutes.
3. Carolina Munguía to the governor of Querétaro, 26 March 1939 and CCIC Minutes, San Antonio, 22 January 1939, 21 July 1938, 31 July 1938, 21 August 1938, 4 September 1938, 22 November 1938, 5 February 1939, 19 February 1939, Munguía Papers.
4. "Reglamentos del Círculo Cultural 'Isabel la Católica,'" 12 June 1938, Munguía Papers.
5. On ethnic Mexican women's activism within a framework of modernization, see González, "Jovita Idar," Hernández, *Working Women into the Borderlands*, and Lomas, "Transborder Discourse"; on American women's activism, see Scott, "Most Invisible of All"; Ginzberg, *Women and the Work of Benevolence*; Scott, *Natural Allies*. For a discussion of the concept of a distinctive female morality, see Pascoe, *Relations of Rescue*, and Giddings, *When and Where I Enter*.
6. On the economic transformation of the west, see White, *It's Your Misfortune and None of My Own*.
7. Mitter, "Modernity," and Eddy U, "Modernization theory," in *The Palgrave Dictionary of Transnational History*, pp. 720–723 and pp. 723–725; *Oxford Dictionary of Sociology*, s.vv. "modernity" and "modernization theory," 421–423. For examinations of the impact of economic modernization upon ethnic Mexicans in borderlands communities, see Perales, *Smeltertown*; Cadava, *Standing on Common Ground*; Hernández, *Working Women into the Borderlands*; and Mora-Torres, *The Making of the Mexican Border*.
8. For more information about the conceptualization of ethnic Mexicans as the "Mexican Problem" or social pariahs, see De León, *They Called Them Greasers*; Montejano, *Anglos and Mexicans*; and Orozco, *No Mexicans, Women, or Dogs Allowed*.
9. On modernization forces and proletarianization of Mexicans in south Texas, see Zamora, *The World of the Mexican Worker*, 10.
10. Yans-McLaughlin, *Immigration Reconsidered*, 162–163.
11. Ibid.; Hart, *Empire and Revolution*, 168–169.
12. Historian Albert Camarillo describes a process of *barrioization* that occurred to ethnic Mexicans in Santa Barbara whereby the loss of land, economic shifts, racism, and political disenfranchisement created a devastating new reality for them. In this reality, many lived in segregated barrios or neighborhoods. Camarillo, *Chicanos in a Changing Society*, 53–54. Similar processes developed across the Southwest.

13. On competing national identities in France and Spain, see Sahlins, *Boundaries*. For an interesting look at the US-Mexico border in comparison to other border areas, see *Walls of Shame*, Aljazeera English, https://www.youtube.com/results?q=Walls+of+Shame.+Al+Jazeera+English (accessed November 5, 2010).

14. Historian David Montejano applies the term "Jim Crow" not just to the African American racialist experience but also to the experiences of Mexican-origin people in Texas. As part of the American South, Texas instituted "separate but equal" laws and structures meant to separate whites and blacks, ultimately keeping African Americans in subordinate economic, political, and social positions. While not specifically targeting them juridically, in actual political and social practice, Mexicans in Texas lived in a world that, as in the case of African Americans, treated them as second-class citizens, segregating them and even excluding them altogether from the public square, schools, and places of accommodation. Montejano, *Anglos and Mexicans*, 262–263. I concur with Montejano that African Americans and Mexican Americans shared similar experiences of racialization and marginality, but instead of Jim Crow, I prefer to use Jaime Crow, a term used by historian Albert Camarillo to acknowledge variances in their histories. Camarillo, "Navigating Segregated Life in America's Racial Borderlands, 1900–1950." On racial scripts, see Molina, *How Race is Made in America*.

15. Questions of continuity and change are often at the center of historical inquiry. In Chicana/o history, Mario T. García has argued that Mexican-origin people in the United States underwent complex generational shifts from Mexican to American identities and nationalisms. Other historians have complicated the linear assimilation model and presented the transnational nature of the Mexican experience in the United States and its cultural complexity. Vicki Ruíz, for example, presents the intriguing concept of cultural coalescence, which explains the discerning selection of cultural elements to be adopted, rejected, but mainly negotiated by Mexican-origin people in the United States. García, *Mexican Americans*, and Ruíz, *From Out of the Shadows*.

16. On the development of an ethnic Mexican middle class, see García, *Rise of the Mexican American Middle Class*, and Vallejo, *Barrios to Burbs*.

17. For a discussion of native-born Tejano class distinctions, see Peña, *The Texas-Mexican Conjunto*, 173–179. Peña argues that conjunto music reflected a working-class cultural expression characterized by the retention of "elements of an ethnic, folk society" and in response and opposition to the upwardly mobile and assimilated Mexican American middle class of the post–World War II period. Warner and Hunt, *The Social Life of a Modern Community*, 174.

18. In a strict Marxist interpretation, the working class exists within a binary class structure of proletariats and bourgeoisie and acts in the world according to its relation to production. Peña posits that once enough Tejanos held occupations with "a different structural relationship to the process of production," ethnic solidarity became more challenging to sustain and class antagonisms surfaced. The upwardly mobile found the American political and economic systems attractive and ideologically identified with mainstream society. Despite all this, the ethnic factor remained to serve as "a stumbling block to full (structural) assimilation." Peña, *The Texas-Mexican Conjunto*, 174–175.

19. French, *A Peaceful and Working People*, 4.

20. Orozco, *No Mexicans, Women, or Dogs Allowed*.

21. The primary function of the middle class in capitalist society is more ideological than economic. Whereas capitalist elites exercise economic hegemony, the middle class is what Peña calls a "politicocultural hegemon" that legitimizes "the dominant bourgeois class 'way of life.'" Peña, *The Texas-Mexican Conjunto*, 177–178.

22. Raúl Ramos, *Beyond the Alamo*, 23, and Torget, *Seeds of Empire*, 45–96.

23. On resistance movements, their suppression, and Anglo-Mexican relations, see Thompson, *Cortina: Defending the Mexican Name in Texas*; Graham, *Kings of Texas*; Rosenbaum, *Mexicano Resistance*; and Johnson, *Revolution in Texas*.

24. Many scholars have written about the Plan de San Diego. The most extensive treatment to date is Benjamin Heber Johnson, *Revolution in Texas*. Other important works that address the Plan de San Diego include Gómez-Quiñones, *Roots of Chicano Politics*; Anders, *Boss Rule in South Texas*; Orozco, *No Mexicans, Women, or Dogs Allowed*; Young, *Catarino Garza's Revolution*; and Zamora, *The World of the Mexican Worker*.

25. Several scholars have examined the multiplicity of reasons inspiring ethnic Mexicans to organize in Texas, among these, Johnson, *Revolution in Texas*; Orozco, *No Mexicans, Women, or Dogs Allowed*; and Emilio Zamora, *The World of the Mexican Worker in Texas*.

26. Johnson, *Revolution in Texas*, 36; Young, "Deconstucting 'La Raza,'" 230.

27. On Progressivism, see McGerr, *A Fierce Discontent*; Rodgers, "In Search of Progressivism"; Hofstadter, *The Age of Reform*; Kolko, *The Triumph of Conservatism*; Wiebe, *The Search for Order*; Painter, *Standing at Armageddon*; Cooper, *Pivotal Decades*; Sanders, *Roots of Reform*; and Dawley, *Struggles for Justice*. For discussions on social constructions of race and class and their impact on ethnic Mexican people, see Montejano, *Anglos and Mexicans*; Menchaca, *Recovering History, Constructing Race*; Martínez, *Genealogical Fictions*; and Katzew and Deans-Smith, *Race and Classification*.

Chapter 1

1. The reference to the "Jewish Race" is an interesting one because the writer saw a connection between the Jewish diaspora and the Mexican one. First, many Mexicans living in the far northern reaches of the newly formed Mexican nation had to or chose to move south after the Anglo-American invasion and conquest, and now, Mexicans in Mexico migrated back to their former homelands in search of economic opportunities. "Barbarismos," *La Crónica*, 12 November 1910, p. 1.

2. "Barbarismos," *La Crónica*, 12 November 1910; Limón, "El Primer Congreso Mexicanista de 1911," 88. Less than five months after Antonio Rodríguez's gruesome murder, fourteen-year-old Antonio Gómez, accused of killing a German American, found himself in a similar predicament. After Gómez's arrest in Thorndale, Texas, a mob kidnapped him, beat him to death, and dragged his body around town behind a buggy. As in the Rodríguez case, the lynching party escaped punishment. For *La Crónica*, the fact that the Mexican consul could do nothing in this matter further aggravated the situation. "Cobarde Infame e Inhumano Lynchamiento de un Jovencito Mexicano en Thorndale, Milam Co., Texas," *La Crónica*, 16 November 1911, p. 2; "Valiente Cobardía de los Linchadores de Thorndale, Texas, Los Estados Unidos y Mexico Nada Pueden Hacer Para El Castigo de los Criminales—Represalias Unica Solución Posible," *La Crónica*, 13 July 1911, p. 1.

3. "Valiente Cobardía de los Linchadores," p. 1; Limón, "El Primer Congreso Mexicanista de 1911," 88.

4. "Barbarismos," *La Crónica*, 12 November 1910, p. 1. La Crónica revealed that it had received a telegram written in French from Mexico City that stated that medical students had organized an anti-American demonstration for the people; however, it denied US news media reports of violence against Americans in Mexico.

5. "Barbarismos," *La Crónica*, 12 November 1910, p. 1; Limón, "El Primer Congreso Mexicanista de 1911," 88.

6. Primer Congreso Mexicanista, Verificado en Laredo, Texas, EEUU de A. Los Dias 14 al 22 de Septiembre de 1911. Circular que se mandó á varios prominentes méxico-tejanos para los fines que en ella se indican, Tipografía de N. Idar (1912), 2–3. Indicating the strong connection between the First Mexican Congress and fraternal orders, the author of the circular emphasized the fact that the Orden Caballeros de Honor (Order of the Knights of Honor) and the Masonic lodge "Benito Juárez" planned to hold their own conferences in Laredo during the same period. This guaranteed the strong representation of fraternal orders at the Mexican Congress.

7. Vicki Ruíz, *From Out of the Shadows*, 49–50. These new cultural forms fit the definition of what Homi Bhabha calls hybridity. That is, they possess elements of both the neo-colonizer and the neo-colonized; see Wilson, *History in Crisis?* 146–147. Thus, in terms of the transborder political culture, while middle-class méxico-tejanos promoted an agenda influenced by liberal capitalist ideas, that agenda focused on curtailing the system's abuses.

8. This aligns with assessments found in the work of both Elliot Young and David Montejano.

9. While some sections of this study explore the working-class consciousness of Tejano communities, particularly Chapter 2 that analyzes Magonismo in Texas, and Chapter 5, examining the life and work of Emma Tenayuca, much of this study focuses on an examination of the developing middle-class consciousness of some transborder activists.

10. On Laredo's social complexity, see Young, "Deconstructing La Raza," 235–237.
11. On social uplift strategies within the African American community, see Hine, "We Specialize in the Wholly Impossible," 70–93; White, "The Cost of Club Work and the Price of Black Feminism"; and Lebsock, *The Free Women of Petersburg.*
12. Historian Evelyn Brooks Higginbotham speaks of the "politics of respectability" in reference to the work of the Women's Convention of the Black Baptist Church during the Progressive Era. This concept denoted the promotion of certain values such as temperance, purity, good hygiene, thrift, and politeness. But the politics of respectability was more than a guide for personal behavior. It also served as a reform strategy known as "uplift politics." Respectability encouraged middle-class African Americans to uplift other African Americans as they climbed economically and socially. It also centered on disproving pseudo-scientific racist theories that abounded during that era. African American women of the middle class came to symbolize the politics of respectability, particularly when they entered the public forums they came to inhabit through volunteerism. For more on the politics of respectability, see Higginbotham, *Righteous Discontent.*
13. Young. "Deconstructing La Raza," 232; Johnson, *Revolution in Texas*, 70. This chapter benefits from Daniel T. Rodgers's argument that US Progressivism represented a set of languages rather than a clearly defined group. He identifies these languages as anti-monopolism, social bonds and the social nature of human beings, and social efficiency. Rodgers, "In Search of Progressivism," 123. While there were similarities between Anglo American progressives and méxico-tejano reformers, the central role of race made the méxico-tejano experience more akin to the African American experience during this period. But geography and history differentiated the histories of African American and Mexican American reform, for the méxico-tejano's was a transborder political culture.
14. The term "search for order" comes from the title of historian Robert Wiebe's book, *The Search for Order.*
15. A few examples of studies that illustrate how activist women issued gender-based critiques within anti-racist movements include Pérez, "A La Mujer" and *The Decolonial Imaginary*, and Orozco, "Alice Dickerson Montemayor."
16. Justo Sierra, secretary of education under Mexican president Benito Juárez is credited for introducing Positivism in Mexico during the mid-nineteenth century. As a student of the French philosopher Auguste Comte, Sierra believed that through scientific inquiry, methods, and knowledge, societies could advance and progress. During the Porfiriato (starting in the 1880s), positivism became the premier philosophy driving the Díaz regime, which was controlled by a group of European-educated, elderly men who called themselves the *científicos* (the scientists). Their understanding of society combined both positivist and Social Darwinian ideas that were reflected in racist policies designed to promote *criollo* (white) leadership and Indian subordination. Meyer and Sherman, *The Course of Mexican History*, 440.
17. For a discussion of pre-industrial America, focusing on American women and gender, see Ulrich, *Good Wives*. A general survey of the history of women that provides a good discussion of how nineteenth- and early twentieth-century social, cultural, and economic trends affected women is Evans, *Born for Liberty*. Works on the development of the middle-class family illustrate the social and cultural transformations taking shape in nineteenth-century America. See, for example, Blumin, *The Emergence of the Middle Class*, and Ryan, *Cradle of the Middle Class*. On the powerful corporate elite as well as the growing influence of the middle class on American culture, see Trachtenberg, *The Incorporation of America.*
18. Cuéllar, "Laredo, TX," Handbook of Texas Online; Hinojosa, *A Borderlands Town in Transition*, 4–7, Appendix, Table 1. Nuevo Santander lay in the modern Mexican state of Tamaulipas and southern Texas.
19. Cuéllar, "Laredo, TX," Handbook of Texas Online.
20. Hinojosa, *A Borderlands Town in Transition*; Adams, *Conflict & Commerce on the Rio Grande*; Cuéllar, "Laredo, TX," Handbook of Texas Online; Young, "Deconstructing La Raza."
21. Cuéllar, "Laredo, TX," Handbook of Texas Online; Young, "Deconstructing La Raza," 230.

22. Young, "Deconstructing La Raza, 232; Aquilino (Ike) and Guadalupe Idar interview.
23. Zamora, *The World of the Mexican Worker in Texas*, 61; Young, "Deconstructing La Raza," 232.
24. San Miguel, *Let All of Them Take Heed*, 55.
25. Limón, "El Primer Congreso Mexicanista de 1911," 88. Idar argued that school segregation occurred in the following counties: Val Verde, Hays, González, Atascosa, Medina, Frío, La Salle, Dimmit, McMullen, Uvalde, and Wilson as well as the towns of Pearsal, Devine, Kingsville, Asherton, Kyle, and Del Rio. *La Crónica* articles focusing on school segregation included "Los Niños Mexicanos en Texas," 26 November 1910, p. 3; "La Exclusión de los Niños Mexicanos en la Mayor Parte de las Escuelas Oficiales de Texas es Positiva," 17 December 1910, p. 1; "Tanto los Niños Mexicanos como los Mexico-Americanos son excluidos de las Escuelas Oficiales—¿ya se Olvidaron los Tratados de Guadalupe?" 24 December 1910, p. 1; "La Exclusión en el Condado de Guadalupe," and "Los Mexicanos de San Angelo Demandan a Los Sindicos de las Escuelas Públicas," 31 December 1910, p. 1; "La Exclusión de los Niños Mexicanos de la Escuelas Americanas En Algunas Partes de Texas," 26 January 1911," p. 3; "La Exclusión en las Escuelas de los Condados de Frio, Bee, Hays, Bastrop, Comal, Caldwell, Blanco, etc.etc.," 9 February 1911, p. 1.
26. Zamora, *The World of the Mexican Worker in Texas*; Calderón, "Unión, Paz y Trabajo"; Zamora, "Mutualist and Mexicanist Expressions of a Political Culture in Texas"; Acosta, "IDAR, NICASIO," in Handbook of Texas Online.
27. Zamora, "Mutualist and Mexicanist Expressions of a Political Culture in Texas," 83–84.
28. Eduardo Idar learned the newspaper trade from his father. Between 1911 and 1914, he worked for the *San Benito Light, Brownsville Herald*, and *La Crónica*. Eduardo also opened a print shop and a bookstore. In 1926 he published another newspaper, *Las Noticias*. During the 1940s he worked for *La Prensa*, a popular San Antonio Spanish-language newspaper. Orozco, "IDAR, Eduardo," Handbook of Texas Online. Besides writing for *La Crónica* and *Evolución*, Jovita Idar's journalism career also included writing for *El Progreso*, another Laredo Spanish-language newspaper, and editing articles for *El Heraldo Christiano*, a Spanish-language organ of the Methodist Church in San Antonio. "Jovita Idar," Texas Women's Biographical vertical files, hereafter cited as Jovita Idar vertical files.
29. Aquilino and Guadalupe Idar interview, and Ed Idar Jr. interview; letter, V. Carranza to Sra. Leonor Villegas de Magnón, 23 October 1916; Letter, CN Idar to Doña Leonor V de Magnón, 16 October 1916; Letter, Venustiano Carranza to Sra. Leonor Villegas de Magnón, 19 August 1916, all in Villegas de Magnón papers.
30. Aquilino and Guadalupe Idar interview.
31. Orozco, "IDAR, CLEMENTE NICASIO," Handbook of Texas Online.
32. De López, interview; Eduardo Idar Jr., interview; Aquilino and Guadalupe Idar interview.
33. Letter, Clemente N. Idar to Sr. Don Álvaro Obregón, 13 June 1921, "Friedrich Katz Archive," University of Chicago, file B-1; Archivo General de la Nación, Mexico City; Clemente N. Idar Papers, Box 2, Folder 2, Benson Latin American Collection, University of Texas, Austin. Scholars Gilbert G. González and Raúl A. Fernández have examined the integration of Mexicans within US capitalism, arguing that US investments in Mexico have reconfigured that society in ways that have led to the migration of millions of Mexicans to the United States where they have served as a backbone to the economic development of the Southwest and increasingly other areas. González and Fernández, *A Century of Chicano History*, 34–43. The American South is one of those areas where ethnic Mexicans have been economically integrated. For analysis on workers in this region, see Weise, *Corazón de Dixie*, and Guerrero, *Nuevo South*. On ethnic Mexicans in the Midwest, see Fernández, *Brown in the Windy City*; Innis-Jiménez, *Steel Barrio*; and Vargas, *Proletarians of the North*.
34. Letter, Clemente N. Idar to Sr. Don Álvaro Obregón, 13 June 1921, Clemente N. Idar Papers.
35. Zamora, *The World of the Mexican Worker in Texas*, 162–196. Samuel Gompers also supported the idea of organizing workers in Mexico. In 1924, although elderly and in failing health, he attended the inauguration of Mexican president Plutarco Calles. Calles sought to use the state to mediate class interests. Gompers also attended the Congress of the Pan-American Federation

of Labor. While there, he collapsed and was rushed to a San Antonio, Texas, hospital where he died on 13 December 1924. "Samuel Gompers: 1850–1924," Illinois Labor History Society, www.kentlaw.edu/ilhs/gompers/html. According to Clemente Idar's son, Gompers died in Idar's arms. Orozco, "IDAR, CLEMENTE NICASIO," Handbook of Texas Online.

36. Orozco, "The Origins of the League of United Latin American Citizens (LULAC)."
37. De López interview.
38. Aquilino and Guadalupe Idar interview.
39. Eduardo and Guadalupe Idar Jr. interview.
40. De López interview.
41. Aquilino and Guadalupe Idar interview; Meyer and Sherman, *The Course of Mexican History*, 531–533.
42. Aquilino and Guadalupe Idar interview.
43. Ibid.
44. "*El Estudiante*," *La Crónica*, 19 October 1911, p. 1. Students and teachers made use of *El Estudiante* for pedagogical purposes. One Anglo American teacher from Laredo, Mrs. O. P. Reid, even wrote an article explaining how she used the magazine as part of her bilingual lesson plan. "Como Aprenden los Niños Mexicanos el Inglés," *La Crónica*, 26 October 1911, p. 4.
45. Eduardo Idar Jr., interview; de López interview.
46. "The Militants: Idar Early Feminist," *San Antonio Light*, 3 May 1981.
47. Ibid. Telephone interview transcript, Jovita Idar vertical files.
48. Eduardo Idar Jr. interview; de López interview.
49. "La Mejor Educación," *El Heraldo Cristiano*, San Antonio, Texas, Octubre de 1940 found in Jovita Idar vertical files.
50. Eduardo Idar Jr. interview. Nicasio and Jovita Idar had thirteen children. Three of them died in early childhood. de López, interview. The ages of the living Idar children as recorded in the 1910 US Census were as follows: Clemente, 26; Jovita, 24; Eduardo, 22; Elvira, 18; Federico, 16; José, 14; Moises, 9; Juvencio, 7; Lola, 6; Aquilino, 5. Lola did not live past childhood. Nicasio's age was recorded as 55 and his wife Jovita's age was recorded as 43. At the time, the entire family lived at 1106 Hidalgo St. US Bureau of the Census, 1910.
51. Aquilino and Guadalupe Idar interview.
52. Aquilino and Guadalupe Idar interview; Acosta, "IDAR, NICASIO," Handbook of Texas Online.
53. "Excitativa Del Gran Concilio de La Orden Caballeros de Honor a La Raza Mexicana," *La Crónica* (Laredo), 17 December 1910, pp. 2–3.
54. Ibid.
55. Ibid.
56. Ibid.
57. Ibid.
58. The author acknowledged that the task at hand presented a formidable challenge but called for perseverance. If children with parents found it difficult to attend school, the education of orphans seemed even more elusive, but that is where the Knights of Honor would step in. These policies represented an educational fund for the children of deceased members and some financial security for the widows. Ibid.
59. Acosta, "Congreso Mexicanista," Handbook of Texas Online.
60. Limón, "El Primer Congreso Mexicanista de 1911," 91–92.
61. Orozco, "The Origins of LULAC, xi."
62. "A La Mujer Mexicana de Ambos Laredo," *La Crónica*, 14 September 1911.
63. De López, interview; Eduardo Idar Jr. interview.
64. Limón, "El Primer Congreso Mexicanista de 1911," 93–94.
65. "Congreso Mexicanista," *Primer Congreso Mexicanista, Verificado en Laredo, Texas, EEUU de A. Los Dias 14 al 22 de Septiembre de 1911. Discursos y Conferencias Por La Raza y Para La Raza. Tipografía de N. Idar* (1912), 5–6, hereafter referred to as *Primer Congreso Mexicanista*.
66. Limón. "El Primer Congreso Mexicanista de 1911," 94.
67. "Discurso pronunciado por Sr. Severo E. Peña, *Primer Congreso Mexicanista*, 32.

68. For an analysis of the Mexican government's colonization efforts, see Hernández, *Mexican American Colonization during the Nineteenth Century.*
69. Gutiérrez, "Migration, Emergent Ethnicity, and the 'Third Space,'" 481–517.
70. "Discurso pronunciado por Sr. Severo E. Peña," *Primer Congreso Mexicanista,* 33.
71. For an analysis of American lynch mob violence directed at Mexicans, see Carrigan and Webb, *Forgotten Dead.*
72. "Discurso pronunciado por "Un Mexicano," *Primer Congreso Mexicanista,*14.
73. Ibid.
74. Montejano, *Anglos and Mexicans,* 36–37.
75. *Leslie's Weekly Illustrated,* 24 March 1910, 282, and Official Souvenir Program, 17th Annual Birthday Celebration of Washington, Laredo, Texas, 12 to 23 February 1916, Washington's Birthday Celebration files, Historical Collection, Laredo Public Library, Laredo, Texas.
76. "Discurso pronunciado por Francisco J. Fernández," *Primer Congreso Mexicanista,* 23.
77. Ibid.
78. At the core of gente decente human and civil rights efforts stood the idea that challenging stereotypes of ethnic Mexicans destroyed the ideological and cultural underpinnings of racist social and institutional structures.
79. "Discurso pronunciado por Gregorio E. González," *Primer Congreso Mexicanista,* 8.
80. "Discurso pronunciado por Profesor Simón G. Domínguez," *Primer Congreso Mexicanista,* 18.
81. "Constitution de la Gran Liga Mexicanista de Beneficencia y Protection," *Primer Congreso Mexicanista,* 39.
82. "Introduction of Primer Congreso Mexicanista Program," *Primer Congreso Mexicanista,* 1.
83. "Discurso pronunciado por Francisco J. Fernández," *Primer Congreso Mexicanista,* 23.
84. "Discurso pronunciado por su autor Soledad de la Peña," *Primer Congreso Mexicanista,* 24–25.
85. Ibid.
86. Kerber, *Women of the Republic.*
87. "Discurso pronunciado por su autor Soledad de la Peña," *Primer Congreso Mexicanista,* 24–25; Zamora, "Mutualist and Mexicanist Expressions of a Political Culture in Texas," 90.
88. "Leona Vicario y Rafaela López," *La Crónica,* 19 October 1911, p. 2.
89. In *The Decolonial Imaginary,* historian Emma Pérez examines Mexicana and Tejana consciousness, referring to it as third space feminism. On Mexican feminism, see Macías, *Against All Odds.* On Marianismo and the "cult of true womanhood," see, respectively, Arrom, *The Women of Mexico City,* and Welter, "The Cult of True Womanhood, 1820–1860. On American women's culture and feminism, see Cott, *The Bonds of True Womanhood* and *The Grounding of Modern Feminism.*
90. "Adelanto de los Mexicanos," *La Crónica,* 21 September 1911, p. 4.
91. Ibid.
92. "Discurso pronunciado por su autor Profesor Simón G. Domínguez," *Primer Congreso Mexicanista,* 18–21.
93. "Discurso pronunciado por su autor Srta. Hortencia Moncayo," *Primer Congreso Mexicanista,* 26.
94. "Felicitación á la Srta. Hortencia Moncayo," *Primer Congreso Mexicanista,* 27.
95. "Discurso pronunciado por su autor Soledad Flores de la Peña," *Primer Congreso Mexicanista,* 24–25.
96. "Discurso pronunciado por su autor Srta. Hortencia Moncayo," *Primer Congreso Mexicanista,* 15.
97. Pérez, *The Decolonial Imaginary,* 31–54.
98. On benevolence, see Ginzburg, *Women and the Work of Benevolence,* and Scott, *Natural Allies.*
99. "La Liga Femenil Mexicanista," *La Crónica,* 7 December 1911, p. 4.
100. Ibid.
101. Ibid.
102. The Azteca neighborhood is the oldest residential neighborhood in Laredo, a community founded in 1755. About 141 of the 263 buildings in the Azteca neighborhood are eligible to be in the National Register of Historic Places. Neighborhood residents organized the Azteca Economic Development and Preservation Corporation to revitalize and preserve their community. Marjorie Coppock, Richard Alaniz, Adriana Craddock, Claudia García,

and Sandra P. Thompson, "Changing Cultural Patterns in the Border Community of Laredo, Texas in the Early 1900's," Texas A&M International University (TAMIU) Paper presented at the Southwestern Sociological Association Meeting, San Antonio, Texas, 31 March 1994, pp. 4–5. Copy held at the Webb County Heritage Foundation (WCHF), Laredo, Texas. Hereafter, I will provide the interview information and cite the paper as follows: TAMIU Paper, page, WCHF.

103. Elena Medellín de Ramírez (b. 1915 in Laredo), interviewed by Adriana Craddock, Spring 1993, TAMIU Paper, pp. 10–11, WCHF.

104. Reynaldo García Sr. (b. in 1909 in Lampazos, Nuevo Leon, Mexico—family moved to Laredo in 1916), interviewed by Sandra P. Thompson, Spring 1993. TAMIU Paper, pp. 12–13 and 19, WCHF.

105. "Sesión Literaria," *La Crónica*, 2 November 1911, p. 1.

106. "La Liga Femenil Mexicanista," *La Crónica*, 7 December 1911, p. 4

107. Young, "Deconstructing La Raza," 243–244. In Laredo, the gente decente category could and often did encompass Europeans and Anglo Americans. Among the upper class, inter-marriage between European immigrants as well as Anglo Americans and Spanish Mexicans became so commonplace that members of this class often claimed a mixed heritage. Luis Bruni's brother and sister, for example, both married into families able to trace their roots to Spanish land grantees. Furthermore, many European immigrants and Anglo Americans in Laredo tended to adopt the Spanish language and at times even Catholicism for social and economic reasons.

108. "La Cuestión de hoy y de mañana," *El Demócrata Fronterizo*, 29 October 1904, p. 4. Young also quotes selectively from this article. Young, "Deconstructing La Raza," 248.

109. "La Aurora de la Gran Revolución Social," *El Demócrata Fronterizo*, 5 November 1904, p. 1.

110. Young, "Deconstructing La Raza," 240.

111. Simón Domínguez to Nicasio Idar, 1 April 1909, Domínguez Papers, Dolph Briscoe Center for American History, University of Texas, Austin.

112. French, *A Peaceful and Working People*. On US history of employer-worker control, see Paul Johnson, *A Shopkeeper's Millennium*, and Boyer, *Urban Masses and Moral Order in America*.

113. Young, "Deconstructing La Raza" and Clawson, *Constructing Brotherhood*, 244–245.

114. Zamora, *The World of the Mexican Worker in Texas*, 117–118.

115. "Socialismo, capital, y trabajo," *El Demócrata Fronterizo*, 3 April 1909.

116. "Disparates Sociales: La verdad de las cosas," *El Demócrata Fronterizo*, 9 December 1906, 1.

117. "La Mujer: en la Familia, en la Sociedad, en la Patria," *El Demócrata Fronterizo*, 6 January 1906.

118. "Peligros del individualismo femenil," *El Demócrata Fronterizo*, 29 April 1911.

119. Ibid.

120. "Churches, Lodges, and Societies of Laredo, Texas," *General Directory of the City of Laredo, 1911*, Webb County Heritage Foundation.

121. "Sara Estela Ramírez," Texas Women's Biographical vertical files, hereafter cited as Sara Estela Ramírez vertical files. Texas Woman's University; Zamora, *The World of the Mexican Worker in Texas*, 144.

122. There is a photo of Adela Bruni with other Cruz Blanca women volunteers such as Leonor Villegas de Magnón, Chente Farías, Paz Martínez, Margarita de la Garza, Tina Merriweather, María Juárez, and Blasita Flores. They are posing in front of the pro-revolutionary news-paper *El Progreso*. Judging from their surnames, these women belonged to some of Laredo's elite families. De Magnón, *The Rebel*, pictures section.

123. This calls to mind elements of Benedict Anderson's analysis of the "imagined community." Anderson, *Imagined Communities*.

124. David J. Weber, *Foreigners in Their Native Land*. It needs to be stressed that the creation of a particular sociocultural construction does not occur in a vacuum. That is, a "Mexican race" develops concurrently with an "Anglo race" and the two inform each other as they emerge in opposition to each other. The same might be said about the genders male and female, the sexualities of hetero and homo, and the bourgeois and proletariat classes. As historian Mary Ann Clawson puts it, "social categories" have "interactional bases." Besides being relational, social constructions are intersectional. That is, in lived experience, "people simultaneously act out the dynamics of class and gender." I would add race and ethnicity to the list. I would

also add that the process is dynamic, meaning that while social constructions are often naturalized, they can also be contested, renegotiated, dismantled, and redefined. Clawson, *Constructing Brotherhood*, 244–245.

125. This study concurs with Elliot G. Young who views la raza as an effort to promote cultural and political unity in the face of increasing anti-Mexican sentiment in Texas. Young, "Deconstructing La Raza," 234–235.

126. Feminist anthropologists Sylvia Yanagisako and Carol Delaney studied the process through which gender inequality became naturalized. Origin myths, they argued, have served as the path to the naturalization of masculine power, connecting ontological questions about who we are and where we come from to local power structures. As this study has shown, méxico-tejanos also connected their lived experience to a set of origin stories. Thus, Yanagisako and Delaney's insights are useful in understanding how social constructions in general can become naturalized. Yanagisako and Delaney, *Naturalizing Power*.

127. Saldívar-Hull, *Feminism on the Border*, 59–63.

Chapter 2

1. This quote is taken from a manifesto delivered by Partido Liberal Mexicanista (Mexican Liberal Party) leaders in Los Angeles, California, on 23 September 1911 and appearing in an issue of the PLM newspaper *Regeneración* that same day.

2. There are numerous works on Ricardo Flores Magón and the Magonistas. Some by US-based historians are Gómez-Quiñones, *Sembradores*; Pérez, "A La Mujer: A Critique of the Partido Liberal Mexicano's Gender Ideology on Women," in *Between Borders*, pp. 459–482; Zamora, "Sara Estela Ramírez: Una rosa roja en el movimiento"; Zamora, "Sara Estela Ramírez: A Note on Research in Progress"; Raat, *Revoltosos*; Rocha, "The Tejano Revolt of 1915"; MacLachlan, *Anarchism and the Mexican Revolution*; and Albro, *Always a Rebel*. Other works that cover the Magónistas, though not exclusively, include Cockcroft, *Intellectual Precursors of the Mexican Revolution*; Katz, *The Secret War in Mexico*; Ruíz, *Labor and the Ambivalent Revolutionaries*; and Hart, *Anarchism and the Mexican Working Class*. There are many works on this topic written from a Mexican perspective, such as Blanquel, *Ricardo Flores Magón*, and Valadés, *El Joven Ricardo Flores Magón*. There are numerous compilations of the works of Ricardo Flores Magón; some offer commentary, such as Muñoz, *Ricardo Flores Magón*; Carbó, trans., *Ricardo Flores Magón*; and Magón, *Frente Al Enemigo*.

3. http://www.cityoflaredo.com/Cemetery/pdf/masons.pdf

4. "Una Excitativa al Primer Congreso Mexicanista de Texas," *La Crónica*, 2 February 1911, and "Prepotentes Trabajos de Unificación," *La Crónica*, 16 March 1911.

5. Emiliano Zapata was a mestizo insurgent who led a revolutionary faction focused in the southern state of Moreles during the Mexican Revolution. The Zapatistas struggled for tierra y libertad, land reform and liberty, in a state dominated by large sugar haciendas. The agrarian rebels declared allegiance to Francisco Madero who reached a settlement with Díaz involving the aged dictator's removal from office. Madero would soon come to power, but during the interim presidency that preceded Madero's election, the social revolution endured serious setbacks. Interim president Francisco León de la Barra, a Porfirista, reinitiated hostilities between the army and the Zapatistas who by then had begun to redistribute the land in Moreles. Once president, Madero failed to bring peace between the agrarian insurgents and the reactionary Porfiristas who refused to give up their power and privileges. When it became clear that Madero defended the large hacienda system as a vehicle for Mexico's modernization and would thus be opposed to the far-reaching land reforms *Zapatismo* called for, Emiliano Zapata withdrew his support for Madero. After Madero demanded that Zapata's army surrender, Zapata announced his Plan de Ayala on 28 November 1911. Calling the hacendados, caciques, and científicos usurpers, the plan demanded the return of land and resources to the people. Zapatismo spread in central and southern Mexican states. The Madero administration tried but failed to subdue this movement. Victoriano Huerta, one of Madero's intellectual assassins and his successor to the presidency, also sought to subdue Zapatismo to no avail. Zapata, Pancho Villa, and Venustiano Carranza fought to bring down the dictatorship of Huerta, but in time, Villa

and Zapata allied against the forces of Carranza. Once in power, Carranza's administration put a bounty on Zapata. In 1919, through the trickery of a general pretending to be switching sides from the army to the Zapatista cause, Zapata was led into a trap and killed, his body riddled with bullets. Zapatismo lost its momentum soon after, but its influence in southern Mexico continues to the present day. Keen, *A History of Latin America*, 264–277.

6. Meyer and Sherman, *The Course of Mexican History*, 511.
7. Enrique Flores Magón to Emma Goldman, 1 June 1916, reel 9; 16 August 1916 and 11 May 1917, reel 10; 6 September 1924, reel 13; Ricardo Flores Magón to Emma Goldman, 13 March 1911 and 22 April 1911, reel 5. Correspondence (M-Q), Emma Goldman Papers, Microfilm, Berkeley Library, University of California.
8. A few works that deal with the influences of *Magónismo* on méxico-tejanos include Gómez-Quiñones, *Sembradores*; Rocha, "The Tejano Revolt of 1915"; Sandos, *Rebellion in the Borderlands*; Harris and Sadler, "The Plan of San Diego and the Mexican War Crisis of 1916: A Re-Examination"; and Hager, "The Plan de San Diego." On PLM member Sara Estela Ramírez, see Zamora, "Sara Estela Ramírez: A Note on Research in Progress"; Zamora, "Sara Estela Ramírez: Una rosa roja en el movimiento."
9. Meyer and Sherman. *The Course of Mexican History*, 385–401, 414.
10. Hale, *The Transformation of Liberalism in Late Nineteenth-Century Mexico*, 2–20.
11. Hernández Chávez, *Mexico: A Brief History*, 187.
12. Ibid., 188–199.
13. Katz, "The Liberal Republic and the Porfiriato, 1867–1910," 69–71, 85–86.
14. Meyer and Sherman, *The Course of Mexican History*, 439–451; Brenner, *The Wind That Swept Mexico*, 17.
15. Katz, "The Liberal Republic and the Porfiriato, 1867–1910," 74–78; Robert Freeman Smith, "The Díaz Era"; Hernández-Chávez, *Mexico*, 175.
16. Hernández-Chávez, *Mexico*, 172–175.
17. Ibid., 177–186.
18. Hernández-Chávez, *Mexico*, 171; Brenner, *The Wind That Swept Mexico*, 107–292.
19. Meyer and Sherman, *The Course of Mexican History*, 488–491, 460–464.
20. Cockcroft, *Intellectual Precursors of the Mexican Revolution*, 4.
21. Gómez-Quiñones, *Sembradores*, 13–17; Cockcroft, *Intellectual Precursors of the Mexican Revolution*, 5, 27, 86.
22. González and Fernández, *A Century of Chicano History*, 79–80.
23. Cockcroft, *Intellectual Precursors of the Mexican Revolution*, 91–93.
24. Ibid.
25. Cockcroft, *Intellectual Precursors of the Mexican Revolution*, 95–97; Vazquez Leos, *Liberalismo y Masoneria en San Luis*, 107–109.
26. Cockcroft, *Intellectual Precursors of the Mexican Revolution*, 99–100.
27. Ibid.,101–102.
28. Sara Estela Ramírez's letters to Ricardo Flores Magón were published in Hernández Tovar, "Sara Estela Ramírez." This quote can be found in a letter dated 20 May 1901, 115–116. Translations by Inés Hernández Tover. Sections of these letters have been lost forever due to wear and tear and Hernández Tovar uses (. . .) to indicate such gaps. The original letters are housed in Archivo General, Secretario de Relaciones Exteriores, Asunto Ricardo Flores Magón, in Mexico City.
29. Acosta, "Sara Estela Ramírez, Handbook of Texas Online; Zamora, "Mutualist and Mexicanist Expressions of a Political Culture," 96; Zamora, "Sara Estela Ramírez: A Note on Research in Progress"; Zamora, "Sara Estela Ramírez: Una rosa roja en el movimiento."
30. Acosta, "Sara Estela Ramírez," Handbook of Texas Online; Zamora, "Mutualist and Mexicanist Expressions of a Political Culture," 96–97.
31. Hernández Tovar, "Sara Estela Ramírez" (letter dated 25 September 1903), 120.
32. Hernández Tovar, "Sara Estela Ramírez" (letter dated 8 December 1903), 134.
33. Hernández Tovar, "Sara Estela Ramírez" (letter dated 12 December 1903) , 136.
34. Ibid., 137.

35. Cockcroft, *Intellectual Precursors of the Mexican Revolution*, 117; Gómez-Quiñones, *Sembradores*, 23.
36. Cockcroft, *Intellectual Precursors of the Mexican Revolution*, 118–119.
37. Hernández Tovar, "Sara Estela Ramírez" (letter dated 9 March 1904), 141.
38. Ibid.
39. *La Crónica*, 3 September 1910, 3.
40. Cano Ruíz B., *Ricardo Flores Magón*, 29–39; Langham, "Border Trials," 14–25; Bufe and Verter, *Dreams of Freedom*, 344.
41. "El cuento de mi abuelo y El partido regenerador ó Magonista," *El Democrata Fronterizo*, 19 October 1907, 1.
42. "Timo Socialista," *La Crónica*, 15 June 1911, 2.
43. "Adquiera Usted Terreno!! Gran Opportunidad," *La Crónica*, 26 October 1911, 4.
44. Cockcroft, *Intellectual Precursors of the Mexican Revolution*, 127.
45. *La Crónica*, "México Bárbaro," 15 January 1910, pp. 1 and 4.
46. Essay, 13 February 1931, B1, F8, Federico Idar and Idar Family Papers, 1879–1938, Benson Latin American Collection, Austin, Texas.
47. Harland-Jacobs, "Hands across the Sea," pp. 237–253.
48. Scholar Inés Hernández Tovar has suggested that the strong anti-clerical bent of *La Crónica* might have been due to the influence of the revolutionary precursor movement, especially since Sara Estela Ramírez, a Magónista sympathizer, collaborated with this newspaper on a regular basis. Hernández Tovar, "Sara Estela Ramírez."
49. Historian Benjamin Johnson refers to middle-class méxico-tejano activists as "Tejano Progressives." Although the name is useful, given the similarities to reformers of the US Progressive era, their more fundamental political heritage is Mexican liberalism. Of course, US progressivism and Mexican liberalism can claim roots in the Enlightenment, thus their commonalities. Johnson, "Sedition and Citizenship in South Texas."
50. Vazquez Leos, "De Dónde Venimos, Quiénes Somos, Hacia Dónde Vamos," in his *Liberalismo y masoneria en San Luis*, pp. 1–6; Rich and De Los Reyes, "Secret Societies and Political Realities in Mexico"; Rich and De Los Reyes, "Freemasonry's Educational Role."
51. Rich and De Los Reyes, "Secret Societies and Political Realities in Mexico," 4–5; Sears, "The White Trail of Freemen and Freemasons."
52. "La Separación de la Iglesia y el Estado," *La Crónica*, 15 January 1910, p. 2.
53. Ibid.
54. "Fanatismo y Analfabetismo," *La Crónica*, 17 December 1910, p. 3.
55. Ibid.
56. "Conflicto Entre La Razón y La Superstición," *La Crónica*, 19 February 1910, p. 2.
57. "El Progreso y El Retroceso," *La Crónica*, 5 March 1910, p. 3.
58. "Contestación a la "Revista Católica," *La Crónica*, 22 January 1910, p. 1.
59. Mankiller et al., "Liberalism," and "Republicanism," 344, 514–515.
60. "Contestación a la "Revista Católica," *La Crónica*, 22 January 1910, p. 1.
61. "Luchas—Capitulo III," *La Crónica*, 22 January 1910.
62. "Luchas—Capitulo II," *La Crónica*, 1 January 1910, p. 2, and "Confesion Auricular," *La Crónica*, 15 January 1910, p. 2.
63. "Vulgariza *La Revista Catolica*," *La Crónica*, 12 February 1910.
64. "Carta De Una Cristiana," *La Crónica*, 5 February 1910, p. 1.
65. Gómez-Quiñones, *Sembradores*, 6–8. Ricardo Flores Magón and other PLM members were also influenced by the works of Peter Kropotkin, Francisco Ferrer Guardia, Karl Marx, and Frederick Engels. Pérez, "A La Mujer," 464.
66. Gómez-Quiñones, *Sembradores*, 6–8, 27, 47.
67. Zamora. *The World of the Mexican Worker in Texas*, 160–161.
68. Young, "Deconstructing La Raza," 248–254.
69. Ricardo Flores Magón to Señores Crescencio y Francisco Villarreal Márquez, Laredo, Texas, 8 October 1905, Zertuche Muñoz, comp. *Ricardo Flores Magón.*
70. Ricardo Flores Magón to Señores Crescencio y Francisco Villarreal Márquez, Laredo, Texas, 5 December 1905, Zertuche Muñoz, comp. *Ricardo Flores Magón.*

71. Profesor Librado Rivera and Antonio L. Villarreal to Señor Don José María Valenzuela of *El Porvenir*, in González Ramírez, *Epistolario y Textos de Ricardo Flores Magón*, 58. My translation.

72. "Bases Para la Unificación del Partido Liberal Mexicano," *Regeneración*, 30 September 1905, reprinted in Zertuche Muñoz, *Ricardo Flores Magón*, 80.

73. "Manifesto A Todos Los Trabajadores Del Mundo," *Regeneración*, 8 April 1911, reprinted in Zertuche Muñoz, *Ricardo Flores Magón*, 112–113.

74. Ibid., 114.

75. "La Repercusión de un linchamiento," *Regeneración*, 12 November 1910, in Bartra, *Regeneración, 1900–1918*, 252–253.

76. Ibid., 253.

77. Ibid., 254.

78. Kanellos et al., "La Intervención y los presos de Tejas," in *En otra voz*, 468.

79. Ibid., 469.

80. Ibid.

81. Whiteness Studies provide excellent insights into how race has been culturally constructed and made to overshadow the type of class solidarity dreamed of by the PLM. On how the "white" working class benefited from ideologies of racial superiority, see Roediger, *The Wages of Whiteness*, and Ignatiev, *How the Irish Became White*.

82. Neil Foley, *The White Scourge*, 64–91, 107–114.

83. French, *A Peaceful and Working People*.

84. Bartra, et al., "A La Mujer," in *Regeneración, 1900–1918*, 235. I used the translation found in "A La Mujer," Ricardo Flores Magón Collected Works, http://dwardmac.pitzer.edu/anarchist_archives/bright/magon/works/regen/mujer.html (accessed 6 February 2011).

85. Bartra, et al., "A La Mujer," in *Regeneración, 1900–1918*, 235.

86. Pérez, "A La Mujer," 459–461. The translation is Emma Pérez's from the original Spanish-language article "La Mujer," *Regeneración*, 6 November 1910.

87. Bartra, et al., "A La Mujer," in *Regeneración, 1900–1918*, 235.

88. Pérez, "A La Mujer," 459.

89. Pérez, "A La Mujer," 466.

90. Ibid., 468.

91. Ibid., 466. The reference to Josefa Fierro is from an interview of civil rights leader Josefina Fierro conducted by Albert Camarillo at Stanford University, 15 March 1995.

92. "El Partido Anti-reeleccionista," 15 December 1910. Quote appears in Lomas, "Transborder Discourse," 70.

93. Pilcher, *The Human Tradition in Mexico*, 109. The quote is originally from the autobiographical notes written by Juana Belén Gutiérrez de Mendoza in 1913. These were collected in Mendieta Alatorre, *Juana Belén Gutiérrez*, 16–18.

94. Lau Jaiven, "La Participación de las Mujeres en la Revolución Mexicana," 5.

95. Pilcher, *The Human Tradition in Mexico*, 108.

96. Ibid., 110, and Lau Jaiven, "La Participación de las Mujeres en la Revolución Mexicana," 5–6.

97. Lau Jaiven, "La Participación de las Mujeres en la Revolución Mexicana," 6.

98. Pilcher, *The Human Tradition in Mexico*, 110–111 and 115, *Regeneración*, September 24, 1910.

99. Lomas, "Transborder Discourse," 61–62.

100. Pérez, *The Decolonial Imaginary*, 73.

Chapter 3

1. De Magnón, *The Rebel*, 85–86.

2. De Magnón, *The Rebel*, 85–90, and "Appendix I: "Chronology of Events Surrounding the Mexican Revolution," 238; Lindheim, "Leonor Villegas de Magnón and the Mexican Revolution," 11–12.

3. No full-length study of Leonor Villegas de Magnón and the White Cross has been written. Scholar Clara Lomas has edited Villegas de Magnón's memoirs and these, along with an introductory chapter by Lomas, have been published. Other published sources on Villegas

de Magnón include encyclopedic entries and an essay by Bessie Lindheim. There are also a few brief references to Villegas de Magnón in a couple of books that discuss the Nuevo Laredo battles. This chapter relies on these sources and articles written by Villegas de Magnón for *La Cronica*, an extensive oral history interview with one of her sons conducted by Jorge González and located at the Webb County Heritage Foundation, and an oral history interview of one of her former students. Lindheim, "Leonor Villegas de Magnón and the Mexican Revolution;" Wilkinson, *Laredo and the Rio Grande Frontier*; Garza, "On the Edge of a Storm"; Palomo Acosta and Winegarten, *Las Tejanas*; Winegarten, *Texas Women*.

4. Evans, *Born for Liberty*.
5. Historian of Mexico Ramón E. Ruíz reinterprets the Mexican Revolution as a struggle for bourgeois reform, which in the end overshadowed the popular uprisings emanating from the masses. Ruíz, *The Great Rebellion*, 406–420.
6. De Magnón, *The Rebel*, 7.
7. It is interesting to note that although Leonor Villegas de Magnón was educated by Catholic nuns throughout her childhood and adolescence, her son Joe Magnón studied at the Holding (Methodist) Institute in Laredo. A similar situation existed in the Idar family where some of the members of the family were Catholic, others Protestant, still others might not have been religious at all. In the case of Joe Magnón, it is not clear whether he was a practicing Catholic or Methodist, just that he boarded at the Holding Institute Monday through Friday during his primary school years. Joaquín Alfredo (Joe) Magnón, interview by Jorge González, 1 June 1978, Webb County Heritage Foundation, Laredo, Texas. Hereafter referred to as Magnón interview.
8. Magnón interview; Holloway, "Independent Club," Handbook of Texas Online, de Magnón, *The Rebel*, 56–71; Lindheim, "Leonor Villegas de Magnón and the Mexican Revolution," 9; "Exhibit—'The Three R's: Leonor Villegas de Magnón, WCHF, 1998," Vertical Files, Webb County Heritage Foundation, hereafter cited as LVM's Vertical File, WCHF.
9. De Magnón, *The Rebel*, 70–75; Lindheim, "Leonor Villegas de Magnón and the Mexican Revolution," 10.
10. De Magnón, *The Rebel*, 75–78. Quote on page 75; Lindheim, "Leonor Villegas de Magnón and the Mexican Revolution," 10.
11. Keen, *A History of Latin America*, 78–79.
12. "Evolución Mexicana" (Mexican Evolution) by Leonor Villegas de Magnón, *La Crónica*, Tomo III, 7 September 1911.
13. Ibid.
14. Ibid.
15. Between 1910 and 1920, 890,371 Mexicans either immigrated legally to the United States or came in as temporary workers. This does not take into account the large numbers of people who crossed over as refugees and undocumented workers. The revolution accelerated widespread poverty, hunger, and violence, forcing many displaced Mexican workers to migrate north. In border areas, communities evacuated in response to impending battles or during these conflicts. Such was the case in Nuevo Laredo on several occasions where hundreds, perhaps thousands, of Nuevo Laredenses fled to Laredo, Texas. Lorey, *The U.S.-Mexican Border in the Twentieth Century*, 70; Garza, "On the Edge of a Storm, 27.
16. De Magnón, *The Rebel*, 80.
17. De Magnón, *The Rebel*, 82; Hall and Coerver, *Revolution on the Border*, 18–21.
18. "The American Consul at Nuevo Laredo (Alonzo B. Garrett) to the Secretary of State," 18 November 1911; 19 November 1911, and "The American Consul at Ciudad Porfirio Díaz (Luther T. Ellsworth) to the Secretary of State," 19 November 1911, United States Department of State/Papers relating to the foreign relations of the United States (Issue 1911), 522–523.
19. Garza, "On the Edge of a Storm," 23–26; Harris and Sadler, *The Border and the Revolution*, 27–50.
20. "The Mexican Ambassador to the Secretary of State," 15 November 1910; "The Acting Secretary of State to the Mexican Ambassador," 22 August 1911; United States Department of State/Papers relating to the foreign relations of the United States (Issues 1910 and 1911), 366, 513. These are but two of several letters in US State Department records addressing the

issue of violated neutrality laws. These particular letters focus on Ricardo Flores Magón; Gómez-Quiñones, *Sembradores*; Gómez-Quiñones, *Roots of Chicano Politics, 1600–1940*.

21. Vázquez and Meyer, *The United States and Mexico*, 103–105.
22. Knight, *The Mexican Revolution*, vol. 1, 485–486.
23. Knight, *The Mexican Revolution*, vol. 1, 487–489; Vázquez and Meyer, *The United States and Mexico*, 106–110. Vázquez and Meyer argue that Ambassador Henry Lane Wilson supported the coup d'état and did nothing to save Francisco Madero's life, even though he could have influenced this outcome. Despite the ambassador's efforts to have the United States recognize the Huerta regime and even though Europe issued recognition, the United States withheld this important asset from the Mexican dictator. President William Howard Taft decided to leave the matter up to incoming president Woodrow Wilson, and the new president felt that Huerta was a usurper who had come to power through immoral means. Ambassador Wilson, as Huerta's moral accomplice, was recalled to Washington, never to return to his former post in Mexico.
24. "Nuevo Laredo Joins Revolt," *Washington Post*, 16 February 1913; "The Secretary of State to the Secretary of the Treasury," 17 February 1913, United States Department of State/Papers relating to the foreign relations of the United States (Issue 1913), 719; Garza, "On the Edge of a Storm,"27.
25. De Magnón, *The Rebel*, 84.
26. De Magnón, *The Rebel*, 82–84; Knight, *The Mexican Revolution*, vol. 2, 104–105.
27. Hall and Coerver, *Revolution on the Border*, 137.
28. Ayala, "Negotiating Race Relations through Activism," 96–128.
29. The history of Mexican women in the revolution, serving as camp followers, soldiers, nurses, spies, entertainers, political writers, and propagandists has received some attention by both American and Mexican scholars. Salas, *Soldaderas in the Mexican Military*; Lau y Ramos, *Mujeres y la Revolución; Las Mujeres en la Revolución Mexicana*; Aceves, *La Mujer en la Historia de México*.
30. Gómez-Quiñones, *Sembradores*; Zamora, "Sara Estela Ramírez: A Note on Research in Progress"; Zamora, "Sara Estela Ramírez: Una Rosa Roja en el movimiento"; Hall and Coerver, *Revolution on the Border*, 17.
31. "She Dies in Battle," *Washington Post*, 18 March 1913.
32. De Magnón, *The Rebel*, 91–92, 250, 254.
33. Ibid., 92–95.
34. Exhibit—"The Three R's: Leonor Villegas de Magnón, WCHF, 1998," LVM's Vertical Files, WCHF; de Magnón, *The Rebel*, 95.
35. María del Carmen Guardiola Offer, interviewed by author on 10 August 2000, Laredo, Texas, hereafter referred to as Guardiola Offer interview.
36. "María Concepción Villarreal, Leonor Villegas de Magnón, Jovita Idar: Recalling Women of Achievement," *Laredo Times* article found in "María Villarreal," Vertical Files, The Woman's Collection, Texas Woman's University, Denton, hereafter cited as LVM's Vertical File, TWU.
37. There were also reports of barbaric acts committed by Federal soldiers against captured and wounded rebels. In one case, a wounded rebel soldier was tied to the tail of a wild horse and dragged across the plain. Other Carrancista soldiers were hung from telegraph poles. "Nuevo Laredo Attacked; 300 Left Dead on Field," *Washington Post*, 2 January 1914.
38. "Refugees Need Food: Rebels Withdraw at Laredo," *Washington Post*, 4 January 1914.
39. During this period, many Mexican families also sent their children to study in Laredo's Holding Institute, a Methodist-run boarding school. Generally speaking, according to Joe Magnón, there were "no requisitos" (requirements) impeding people from crossing the border in those days. Magnón interview.
40. De Magnón, *The Rebel*, 96–97.
41. Ibid., 98–101.
42. An analysis of Laredo's 1910 census records reveals thirty-three of the eighty-one individuals. Various possibilities account for the absence of forty-seven names. For one, not all members and affiliates of the White Cross were from Laredo. Some members resided across the river in Nuevo Laredo or in small communities either upriver or downriver from Laredo on both sides of the border. Second, some of the people who participated in the activities of the White

Cross after its founding in 1913 were not living in the Laredo area or even near it in 1910. In fact, they were part of the diaspora ignited by the Mexican Revolution. It was a diaspora that forced Mexicans in the interior as well as the border area to migrate north and cross over to the American side. Finally, some members who lived in the Laredo area in 1910 were left out of the census rolls through simple oversight or human error. US Bureau of the Census, *Thirteenth Census of the United States, 1910: Population.*

43. Ibid., Appendix II: Bio-Bibliography of Historical Characters," 263–265; "Notas sobre la Cruz Blanca Local." "Recalling Women of Achievement," *Laredo Morning Times,* and "Sra. Leonor V. Magnón, " 'La Rebelde,' " LVM's Vertical File, TWU.

44. I use the following terms to describe White Cross participants: "members" to refer to rank and file, "supporters" for material/financial benefactors, and "doctors." The term "White Cross participants" or "affiliates" refers to all thirty-three persons who fall under the umbrella of people associated with the White Cross in some capacity.

45. Photographs found in de Magnón, *The Rebel.*

46. Guardiola Offer interview.

47. Belfiglio, "BRUNI, ANTONIO MATEO," Handbook of Texas Online, Uploaded on 12 June 2010. Published by the Texas State Historical Association. United States Census, 1910.

48. Leonor Villegas de Magón to Venustiano Carranza, 22 May 1914, Box 2, Folder 11, Clemente N. Idar Papers, 1875–1938, Benson Latin American Collection, University of Texas, Austin.

49. Ibid.

50. This matters because as David Weber argued in *The Mexican Frontier,* historically the people of the borderlands were seen as peripheral and therefore marginalized by the leadership in both the American and Mexican nation-states. Prior to the rise of these nation-states, fronterizos had often been ignored by the Spanish colonial system. Weber, *The Mexican Frontier.*

51. De Magnón, *The Rebel.*

52. "Fleeing into Texas," *Washington Post,* 2 January 1914; "Refugees Need Food," *Washington Post,* 4 January 1914; "Villa the Master," *Washington Post,* 12 January 1914; "Noted Rebel Bandit Chieftain Conquerer of Northern Mexico," *Washington Post,* 12 January 1914; "Will Hold Refugees," *Washington Post,* 13 January 1914.

53. Lindheim, "Leonor Villegas de Magnón and the Mexican Revolution," 12–14; de Magnón, *The Rebel,* 96–105.

54. De Magnón, *The Rebel,* 102–103; Magnón interview.

55. De Magnón, *The Rebel,* 103.

56. Wilkinson, *Laredo and the Rio Grande Frontier,* 388–389; Otto Weffing was a close friend of Joaquín Villegas, Leonor Villegas de Magnón's father. De Magnón, *The Rebel,* 107.

57. Magnón, *The Rebel,* 105.

58. Ibid., 105–106.

59. Lindheim, "Leonor Villegas de Magnón and the Mexican Revolution," 16–18.

60. On 24 April 1914, right before evacuating the city, federal soldiers set fire to many buildings in Nuevo Laredo and even fired upon the American border patrol. "BULLETIN: Federals Fire across Border from Nuevo Laredo Killing Four Americans—Town Now Burning," *Wichita Daily Times,* 24 April 1914; Lindheim, "Leonor Villegas de Magnón and the Mexican Revolution," 18.

61. Scholar Martha Eva Rocha argues that Villegas de Magnón left Mexico City because she was not appointed as the administrator of a hospital as she had been expecting. Rocha, "The Faces of Rebellion," 22.

62. Lindheim, "Leonor Villegas de Magnón and the Mexican Revolution," 19.

63. Ibid., 19–20.

64. Ibid., 20.

65. Leonor Villegas de Magnón received A *lealtad Mayo de 1920* (Loyalty to May 1920) award from the Venustiano Carranza Association on 16 May 1941. In 1943 her humanitarian work was recognized when she received recognition from the women's Club Femenino, Protector, Cultural, Recreativo, Defensa y Amparo de la Mujer; de Magnón, *The Rebel,* 245; Rocha, "The Faces of Rebellion," 29.

66. Rocha, "The Faces of Rebellion," 15.
67. Guardiola Offer, interview.
68. Leonor Villegas de Magón to Venustiano Carranza, 22 May 1914. Rocha does mention that Villegas de Magnón had some political disagreements with her husband. Rocha, "The Faces of Rebellion," 16–17.
69. Rocha, "The Faces of Rebellion," 16–17.
70. "Adelanto de los Mexicanos," *La Crónica*, 21 September 1911, p. 4.
71. Leonor Villegas de Magnón to Venustino Carranza, undated (possibly June 1914), Box 1, Folder 17, Clemente N. Idar Papers, 1875-1938, Benson Latin American Collection, University of Texas, Austin.
72. Ibid.
73. Ibid.
74. Ibid.
75. Ibid.
76. Ibid.
77. Rocha, "The Faces of Rebellion," 22.

Chapter 4

1. Benita Kathleen Munguía, "A Man in Two Countries: The Biography of Rómulo Munguía Torres (1885–1975), MA Thesis, Yale University, 1975, Bx 17, F2, Rómulo Munguía Papers, Benson Latin American Collection, University of Texas Libraries, the University of Texas at Austin, hereafter referred to as the Munguía Papers.
2. Elvira Cisneros, interviewed by author, 19 November 1995, San Antonio, Texas, hereafter referred to as the Cisneros interview, 19 November 1995.
3. B. K. Munguía, "A Man in Two Countries," Munguía Papers; Orozco, "MUNGUÍA TORRES, JOSÉ RÓMULO," Handbook of Texas Online.
4. B. K. Munguía, "A Man in Two Countries," 4–5, Munguía Papers.
5. Ibid., 8–9.
6. Julia Tuñón Pablos argues that nineteenth-century—and to a lesser but still significant extent twentieth-century—Mexicans considered women's proper place to be the home. Women's assumed moral and spiritual superiority seemed proof enough that they were the "natural" guardians of reproduction. Whether raising soldiers, workers, or entrepreneurs, the idea that women were "adorned muses of the home" remained axiomatic even as some began to file into factories. Tuñón Pablos, *Women in Mexico*, 47–48. A similar pattern is evident in US history as noted in surveys of women's history, such as Evans, *Born for Liberty*.
7. Vaughan, "Women, Class, and Education in Mexico, 1880–1928," 64.
8. "Presentation," in "Homenaje a las Fundadoras," Munguía Papers.
9. The working classes often lived in crowded neighborhoods where daily interaction with neighbors was inevitable. Furthermore, street life and neighborhood interactions formed a part of the human mechanism of survival and resistance. Vaughan, "Women, Class, and Education in Mexico," 78. The Mexican middle class's critique of working-class street life resembles that of their American counterparts. Christine Stansell describes how nineteenth-century middle-class reformers, imbued with the ideology of domesticity, viewed working-class street life as "evidence of parental neglect, family disintegration, and a pervasive urban social pathology." Stansell, "Women, Children, and the Uses of the Streets," 134.
10. Vaughan, "Women, Class, and Education in Mexico," 64–66.
11. Ibid.
12. Meyer and Sherman, *The Course of Mexican History*, 457.
13. Vaughan, "Women, Class, and Education in Mexico," 66.
14. Vaughan, "Women, Class, and Education in Mexico," 66; Tuñón Pablos suggests that the Mexican women's role during the nineteenth century revolved around religious observances

and the country's traditions. Women were the conservers of the dominant ideology. Tuñón Pablos, *Women in Mexico*, 90.

15. The Porfiriato encouraged education for women, not as a challenge to traditional gender roles but as an acknowledgment that the modern state required a more educated citizenry, both male and female. As was the case during La Reforma (Juárez administration—1860s), educated women were considered a prerequisite for the evolution of the modern Mexican family. Vaughan, "Women, Class, and Education in Mexico," 66–67; Ignacio Ramírez defended education for women using an argument similar to the American concept of the "Republican Mother." Ramírez stated, "Nature has deemed that women be not only mothers, but teachers." For a discussion of this concept, see Kerber, "The Republican Mother," in Kerber and DeHart, *Women's America: Refocusing the Past*, 89–95. Tuñón Pablos argues that educated women were needed to teach their children about the system which they tacitly endorsed. From infancy, children were to be molded to fit the needs of the nation. Tuñón Pablos, *Women in Mexico*, 112–113

16. Cisneros interview, 19 November 1995.

17. Vaughan, "Women, Class, and Education in Mexico," 67–68; Christopher Lasch described the concept of family as a haven in a heartless world, as "an ideological support and justification in the conception of domestic life as an emotional refuge in a cold and competitive society." Lasch, *Haven in a Heartless World*, 6. According to Barbara Welter, nineteenth-century Anglo-American women were also conceived as guardians of society's moral fabric. Welter describes the society's conception of the "ideal" woman in terms of the concept of True Womanhood. The true woman was supposed to be pious, pure, submissive, and domestic. Thus, who better than women to safeguard the last bastion of all that was good in the world? Welter, "The Cult of True Womanhood," 233.

18. Vaughan, "Women, Class, and Education in Mexico," 68; Cisneros interview, 19 November 1995.

19. Orozco, "MUNGUÍA, CAROLINA MALPICA," Handbook of Texas Online. Hereafter cited as Orozco, "MUNGUÍA, CAROLINA," Handbook of Texas Online.

20. Deborah Baldwin notes, "Teachers educated in Protestant schools had no problem finding employment in public or private schools." Baldwin, *Protestants and the Mexican Revolution*, 57.

21. B. K. Munguía, "A Man in Two Countries," 21–22, Munguía Papers.

22. "Adelante Compañeras" was reprinted in 1960 in a collection of essays he wrote about his labor organizing and revolutionary experiences in Mexico titled *Salvemos a La Raza* (Let Us Save La Raza), Munguía Papers.

23. B. K. Munguía, "A Man in Two Countries," 16–19; Rómulo Munguía, *Salvemos a La Raza*, 110–111, Munguía Papers.

24. B. K. Munguía, "A Man in Two Countries," Munguía Papers, 10–13,

25. Ibid., 14–15.

26. Rubén Munguía interview with author, San Antonio, Texas, 6 May 1994, hereafter referred to as the Munguía interview, 6 May 1994.

27. Munguía, *Salvemos a La Raza*, 45, Munguía Papers.

28. B. K. Munguía, "A Man in Two Countries," 22–26, Munguía Papers.

29. Munguía interview, 6 May 1994; Elvira Cisneros, interview with author, San Antonio, Texas, 28 April 1994, hereafter cited as the Cisneros interview, 28 April 1994; B. K. Munguía, "A Man of Two Countries," Munguía Papers, 30.

30. In San Antonio, Mexicans were employed in various unskilled and semi-skilled jobs—for example, toiling as ranch hands in places such as the King and Taft ranches; picking all kinds of crops in farms of various sizes; working in light industries such as railroad yards, military bases, garment factories, and packing plants; and working in the service and retail sector in businesses such as beauty parlors, laundries, auto repair shops, funeral homes, and cleaning shops. García, *Rise of the Mexican American Middle Class*, 18–33.

31. B. K. Munguía, "A Man in Two Countries," Munguía Papers, 43–46.

32. Ibid., 46–48.

33. Cisneros interview, 28 April 1994. It should be noted that the Munguía family did go through some very difficult moments during the Great Depression. Rómulo started his printshop business in 1934 on a shoestring budget, and in order to make ends meet, Carolina took in washing and, along with the children, shelled pecans at home for sale.
34. Cisneros interview, 28 April 1994; Richard García, *Rise of the Mexican American Middle Class*, 84.
35. Cisneros interview, 28 April 1994.
36. A San Antonio Housing Authority study showed that of 14,000 Mexican families, almost 90 percent earned less than $950 a year, and over 11 percent had annual incomes of under $250. About 50 percent of San Antonio Mexicans were involved in migratory work, which paid too little. For women, the job prospects were no more promising. In 1932, the clothing manufacturing industries offered a weekly median wage of only $5.45 to $5.50. Homebound seamstresses made between $.01 and $.12 an hour. The laundry industry generated a medium weekly wage of $6.25. The largest employer of Mexican women was the pecan shelling industry, where the weekly median wage was $2.65. In 1934, these wages fell between $.32 and $1.56 a week. Some even worked for $.16 a week. This seems especially low when contrasted to the average relief wage by the Civil Works Administration in 1933–1934, which was $10 a week. Donald Zelman, "Alazan-Apache Courts," 125.
37. Blackwelder, *Women of the Depression*, 4.
38. Zelman, "Alazan-Apache Courts," 124, 129, 130; a 1915 health survey requested by the mayor and city council and conducted by the city's board of health "along San Pedro Creek, and Aransas Pass Railway" showed that many Mexicans lived in narrow lots with numerous flimsy shanties. One or two rooms, dirt floors, poor sanitary conditions, and an insufficient water supply characterized these quarters. Additionally, some of these facilities were shared with animals. The close proximity to heaps of animal manure, inadequate toilet facilities, and stagnant water bred diarrhea, typhoid fever, and tuberculosis. Schiller, "The Fight to Clean Up San Antonio's Mexican Corral," 2.
39. Blackwelder, *Women of the Depression*, 8. Despite the Westside's high poverty rate, middle- and upper-class Mexicans often sponsored extensive social, cultural, and traditional events. Through *La Prensa*, for example, exiled members of the upper classes expressed a redemptive vision for all Mexicans regardless of socioeconomic status. Working-class Mexicans, however, could not afford upper-class ideologies. García, *Rise of the Mexican American Middle Class*, 4.
40. Ibid. Blackwelder corroborates García's argument that while the early twentieth-century immigration wave from Mexico consisted predominantly of poor peasants, it also "included a large number of educated and formerly wealthy landowners who fled Mexico during the Revolution." Blackwelder, *Women of the Depression*, 18. In other words, these *ricos* (rich ones) may have lost some or most of their wealth in the conflict, but they brought to San Antonio social capital in the form of literacy, education, skills, networks, and a mentality embued with the confidence that they could rebuild and be successful in the United States. Such was the case with Ignacio Lozano, a talented Mexican journalist and political exile to San Antonio who founded two famous Spanish-language newspapers: *La Prensa* in San Antonio (1913) and *La Opinión* in Los Angeles (1926). García would qualify Lozano's family as a "rico" family. Lozano's granddaughter might agree, as she pointed out in an interview. "My family comes from a certain economic class and we were very comfortable. We didn't have to face a lot of issues in our lives that most Chicano kids [have] who are from poorer backgrounds. We were very well off." Mónica Lozano, interview, by Shirley Biagi, Los Angeles, California, 13 December 1993, http://wpcf.org/oralhistory/loz1.html (accessed 17 September 2011).
41. These were the findings of a 1930s LULAC investigation of San Antonio public schools. Orozco, "The Origins of LULAC," 60, and San Miguel, *"Let All of Them Take Heed,"* 83.
42. García, *Rise of the Mexican American Middle Class*, 195, 199.
43. Daughter Elvira Cisneros attended Jefferson High School. At that time, the student composition at Jefferson was predominantly Anglo-American. Cisneros interview, 19 November 1995.

44. This delicate balance between cultural nationalism and adaptation has also been documented by Emma Pérez among the Mexican diasporic community in Houston whose daughters created social and cultural groups designed to help them survive racist America and at the same time promote community unity. Pérez, *The Decolonial Imaginary*, 92.
45. Orozco, "MUNGUÍA, CAROLINA," Handbook of Texas Online.
46. Ibid.
47. Minutes, Círculo Cultural "Isabel la Católica," San Antonio, 12 June 1938, Munguía Papers. All translations by author. Minutes for the Círculo Cultural "Isabel la Católica, hereafter referred to as CCIC Minutes.
48. "Reglamentos del Círculo Cultural 'Isabel la Católica,'" 12 June 1938, Munguía Papers.
49. Acosta, "CRUZ AZUL MEXICANA," Handbook of Texas Online; Ayala, "Negotiating Race Relations through Activism," 96–128.
50. Cisneros interview, 19 November 1995.
51. CCIC Minutes, San Antonio, 22 January 1939, 31 July 1938, 21 August 1938, 4 September 1938, 5 February 1939, 22 November 1938, Munguía Papers.
52. Carolina Munguía to the governor of Querétaro, Querétaro, México, 26 March 1939, Munguía Papers.
53. The implication is that working-class Mexicans in Texas were in a state of economic and cultural abandonment created by multiple forces, among these the ravages of revolution in Mexico, a legacy of severe poverty in their native land, severe poverty in their new American home, and racial discrimination. Carolina Malpica de Munguía asked Mexican officials to do their part to improve the cultural landscape of their compatriots by participating in the club's art exhibition. In Mexico, middle-class people also sought to impose their value system upon the working class. French, *A Peaceful and Working People*.
54. Carolina Munguía to the governor of San Luis Potosí, México, 1 May 1939, Munguía Papers. Other Mexican states that were sent letters were Querétaro, Sinaloa, Oaxaca, Baja California, Michoacán, Nuevo León, Colima, Puebla, Guanajuato, and Hidalgo.
55. CCIC Minutes, 7 July 1938, 31 July 1938, 21 July 1938, 4 September 1938, 18 September 1938, Munguía Papers.
56. CCIC Minutes, 21 July 1938, 19 February 1939, 5 February 1939.
57. Cisneros interview, 28 April 1994.
58. Adolfo Pesquera, "Closing the door on presses, politics," *San Antonio-Express* News, 28 July 2007, Metro Edition, p. 01A; Cisneros interview, 28 April 1994.
59. "Reglamentos del Círculo Cultural 'Isabel la Católica,'" 12 June 1938, Munguía Papers.
60. "Reglamentos del Círculo Cultural 'Isabel la Católica,'" 2 October 1938, Munguía Papers.
61. Carolina Munguía to the members of the Círculo Cultural "Isabel la Católica," San Antonio, 8 January 1938, Munguía Papers.
62. "Reglamentos del Círculo Cultural 'Isabel la Católica,'" 12 June 1938, and 2 October 1938. Carolina Munguía to the members of the Círculo Cultural, San Antonio, 8 January 1939, Munguía Papers.
63. Munguía interview, 6 May 1994.
64. Carolina Munguía to the members of the Círculo Cultural "Isabel la Católica," San Antonio, 8 January 1939, Munguía Papers.
65. Munguía interview, 6 May 1994.
66. Turner, *The Dynamic of Mexican Nationalism*, 74; Munguía interview, 6 May 1994.
67. Graham, *The Idea of Race in Latin America*, 72–102. There is no evidence that the Munguías subscribed to the pro-European Porfiriato racialist thinking, nor that they participated in the propagation of Indigenista racialist thought. Absent such evidence, it is likely that as their son stated, the Munguías used the term "la raza" as an ethnic or even nationalist identifier, but not to describe a biological "race." Given that Rómulo Munguía was a strong supporter of Pan-Americanism, he likely included other Latinos under the umbrella of la raza.
68. Crockett Elementary School is located in San Antonio's Westside neighborhood.
69. Orozco, "SPANISH-SPEAKING PTA," Handbook of Texas Online; April 1941, in "PTA Annual Bulletin/San Antonio PTA Council, 1940–41," Box 19, Folder 3, Munguía Papers, hereafter referred to as PTA Annual Bulletin, 1940–41.

70. Herman Hirsch, "A Short History," PTA Annual Bulletin, 1940–41, Munguía Papers.
71. Orozco, "SPANISH-SPEAKING PTA," Handbook of Texas Online.
72. Orozco, "MUNGUÍA, CAROLINA," Handbook of Texas Online; PTA Annual Bulletin, 1940–41, Munguía Papers. Historian David Montejano has argued that the demise of Jim Crow in Texas started in 1940 with the rise of the urban-industrial order ushered in by World War II. Mexican American political activism during the 1930s and 1940s also began to pay off as LULAC took its struggle to the courts and won. This might help explain why Carolina Malpica de Munguía was able to find so many Anglo-American allies in her struggle to improve the condition of Westside education during the late 1930s. Montejano, *Anglos and Mexicans in the Making of Texas*, 9.
73. Orozco, "SPANISH-SPEAKING PTA," Handbook of Texas Online.
74. Isabelita S. de Little to Carolina Munguía, 29 November 1941, "San Antonio Council PTA," 1938–41, Box 19, Folder 2, Munguía Papers.
75. Maureen Fitzgerald, "National Congress of Mothers," in *Reader's Companion to U.S. Women's History*, Houghton Mifflin, http://college.hmco.com/history/readerscomp/women/html/wh_025200_nationalcong.htm; "National PTA: A Brief History," http://www.pta.org/aboutpta/history/history.asp.
76. "Porque Debemos Pertenecer a la Sociedad de Padres y Maestros," ("Why we should belong to the Parent, Teacher, Association,") Box 19, Folder 2, "San Antonio Council PTA, 1938–41," Munguía Papers.
77. Ibid.
78. "The Parent-Teacher Creed," Box 19, Folder 4, PTA booklet, Munguía Papers.
79. There were a number of committees designed to look out for the well-being of the child. These committees targeted potential hazards and temptations. Examples of these committees include Alcohol and Narcotics, Juvenile Protection, Safety, and Health. Others served to promote the organization or educate the community, such as Public Relations, Education, Homemaking, Parent Education, Radio, Visual Education, Music, and Library Service. On the more cutting-edge side, the San Antonio PTA Council also pioneered programming designed to establish understanding among different ethno-racial constituencies. There is a brief reference in the March 1941 bulletin to an inter-race relation movement and its continuation as manifested "by having numbers [musical numbers?] from Phillis Wheatley and Grant Schools." Carolina Munguía's leadership and work with the Spanish-Speaking PTA is also highlighted in these bulletins. "San Antonio Council Parent-Teacher Association Bulletin," November–December 1939, p. 4, Box 19, Folder 3, Munguía Papers .
80. Ibid.
81. "San Antonio Council Parent-Teacher Association Bulletin," March, 1941, p. 3, Box 19, Folder 3, Munguía Papers.
82. Untitled essay, Box 15, Folder 4, "Speeches/articles/galley proofs/poems/radio scripts (?) "Hora Estrella," 1940–1942, 1944–1945, and undated, Munguía Papers.
83. The Comisión Honorífica Mexicana was committed to organizing the Mexican community in San Antonio for mutual protection. The members of this group were often well-respected people in the community.
84. B. K. Munguía, "A Man in Two Countries," 53; *El Pueblo*, 8 July, 7 and 14 October, 4 and 13 November, 1938. On race discrimination, see the 29 July 1938 issue, Munguía Papers.
85. B. K. Munguía, "A Man in Two Countries," 54–55, Munguía Papers .
86. Ibid., 55–57.
87. Ibid., 60–61.
88. Ibid., 62.
89. Ibid., 62–65.
90. Ibid., 65–66.
91. Ibid., 67–69.
92. Ibid., 69–70.
93. Vázquez and Meyer, *The United States and Mexico*, 163–164.
94. B. K. Munguía, "A Man in Two Countries," 71, Munguía Papers.

95. The resident branch still operates today, with its expressed goal being "to promote a better understanding between Mexico and the United States through the teaching of Spanish, English, and other topics important to both countries." UNAM website, http://www.usa.unam.edu

96. B.K. Munguía, "A Man in Two Countries," 72–74, Munguía Papers.

Chapter 5

1. Carolina Malpica de Munguía to the members of the Círculo Cultural "Isabel, la Católica," San Antonio, 8 January 1938, Munguía Papers.

2. Allan Turner, "A Night that Changed San Antonio," *Houston Chronicle*, 14 December 1986, p. 46; Vargas, "Tejana Radical," 57; Minutes, Círculo Cultural "Isabel la Católica," San Antonio, 27 August 1939, Munguía Papers.

3. Carolina Malpica de Munguía to the members of the Círculo Cultural "Isabel la Católica," San Antonio, 8 January 1939, Munguía Papers; and Jeannie Kever, "Women: Tenayuca Spent Years as a Strike Leader," *San Antonio Light*, 6 March 1988, p. J6.

4. Emma Tenayuca interview by Emilio Zamora and Oralia Cortez, 19 June 1986, Emma Tenayuca MSS 420, box 11, folder 5, The Woman's Collection, Texas Woman's University, Denton, hereafter cited as Tenayuca interview by Emilio Zamora and Oralia Cortez; Emma Tenayuca interview by Gerry Poyo, 21 February 1987, Institute of Texan Cultures Oral History Program, University of Texas at San Antonio, hereafter cited as Tenayuca interview by Gerry Poyo; Jan Jarboe Russell, "The Voice that Shook San Antonio," *Texas Observer*, 20 August 1999.

5. "Emma Tenayuca" Texas Women's Biographical vertical files, The Woman's Collection, Texas Woman's University, Denton, hereafter cited as "Tenayuca" vertical files; Tenayuca interview by Gerry Poyo.

6. Tenayuca interview by Emilio Zamora and Oralia Cortez. Some of the materials about Emma Tenayuca found at TWU form a part of the body of research notes and documents from the "Women in Texas History" exhibit. I would like to thank Texas women's historian Ruthe Winegarten, one of the organizers of that exhibit, for pointing me to these materials.

7. Tenayuca interview by Emilio Zamora and Oralia Cortez.

8. Tenayuca interview by Gerry Poyo; Geoffrey Rips, "Living History: Emma Tenayuca Tells Her Story," *Texas Observer: A Journal of Free Voices*, 28 October 1983, 8.

9. Vargas, *Labor Rights Are Civil Rights*, 119–122 and 136–137

10. Tenayuca interview by Emilio Zamora and Oralia Cortez.

11. Tenayuca interview by Emilio Zamora and Oralia Cortez; Montejano, *Anglos and Mexicans in the Making of Texas*, 232.

12. "Living History, *Texas Observer*, 9; "Emma Tenayuca, 1916–1999"; "Tenayuca," vertical files; Tenayuca interview by Emilio Zamora and Oralia Cortez; Blackwelder, *Women of the Depression*, 103–104.

13. "Miss Gonzales, Financial Secretary, Cigar Makers' Union, San A., October 7, 1936," Labor Movement in Texas Collection, F 12, Dolph Briscoe Center for American History, University of Texas, Austin. Hereafter cited as Labor Movement in Texas Collection.

14. Ibid.; "Mrs. W. H. Ernst, Concerning the Cigar Makers' Union and the Trouble with the Finck Cigar Co., October 8, 1936," Labor Movement in Texas Collection; Vargas, *Labor Rights Are Civil Rights*, 80–81.

15. "Mrs. W. H. Ernst, Concerning the Cigar Makers' Union and the Trouble with the Finck Cigar Co., October 8, 1936," Labor Movement Collection; Vargas, *Labor Rights Are Civil Rights*, 80–81.

16. Ibid.

17. Vargas, *Labor Rights Are Civil Rights*, 80–81, and Vargas, "Tejana Radical," 559.

18. Tenayuca interview by Emilio Zamora and Oralia Cortez; Tenayuca interview by Gerry Poyo; Jan Jarboe Russell, "The Voice that Shook San Antonio," *Texas Observer*, 20 August 1999.

19. Sharyll Soto Teneyuca, telephone conversation with author, May 7, 2003. The author has her permission to quote.

20. Rips, "Living History," *Texas Observer*, 9.

21. Tenayuca interview by Emilio Zamora and Oralia Cortez.

22. FBI report, 6 December 1941, Houston, Texas, Department of Justice, Federal Bureau of Investigation, Freedom of Information and Privacy Acts, Subject Emma Beatrice Tenayuca, hereafter cited as Tenayuca's FBI file. I thank Professor Albert Camarillo for bringing this important source to my attention.

23. Naison, "Remaking America," 45–70.

24. Vargas, *Crucible of Struggle*, 230.

25. "The Unemployed Movements of the 1930s," in Buhle, Buhle, and Georgakas, eds. *Encyclopedia of the American Left*, 796; Tenayuca interview by Gerry Poyo, 24, 31; Calderón and Zamora, "Manuela Solis Sager and Emma B. Tenayuca: A Tribute," in Del Castillo, *Between Borders*, 272; Rips, "Living History," *Texas Observer*, 9–10; Vargas, "Tejana Radical," 555, 558, 561–562; Vargas, *Crucible of Struggle*, 230.

26. Emma Tenayuca, Secretary of Workers Alliance in San Antonio to Mr. Harry L. Hopkins, WPA Administrator, 15 November 1937; and Emma Tenayuca, Secretary of Workers Alliance in San Antonio to Mr. Aubrey Williams, Deputy WPA Administrator, 13 January 1938 and 19 January 1938 ("General Correspondence: Friends and Associates," Tenayuca MSS. 420, Box 5, Folder. 42). Vargas, *Labor Rights Are Civil Rights*, 130–134; Vargas, *Crucible of Struggle*, 230.

27. "Gangster Police Methods Come to Texas!" Public letter signed by Cassie Jane Winfrey, secretary of the Citizens' Committee for Social Justice, Box 2E189, Folder 5, Labor Movement in Texas Collection; Vargas, *Crucible of Struggle*, 230; "Use of Axes by Police Rapped," *San Antonio Light*, 30 June 1937.

28. "Gangster Police Methods Come to Texas!" Public letter signed by Cassie Jane Winfrey, secretary of the Citizens' Committee for Social Justice, Box 2E189, Folder 5, Labor Movement in Texas Collection; "Use of Axes by Police Rapped," *San Antonio Light*, 30 June 1937.

29. "Gangster Police Methods Come to Texas!" Public letter signed by Cassie Jane Winfrey, secretary of the Citizens' Committee for Social Justice, Box 2E189, Folder 5, Labor Movement in Texas Collection.

30. Ibid.

31. Vargas, *Labor Rights Are Civil Rights*, 130–134.

32. Vargas, *Labor Rights Are Civil Rights*, 130–134, and Vargas, *Crucible of Struggle*, 230.

33. Croxdale, "The 1938 San Antonio Pecan Sheller's Strike," 24, 25. "Tenayuca" vertical files. Selden Menefee and Orin C. Cassmore, *The Pecan Shellers of San Antonio* (Washington, DC: Government Printing Office, 1940), 6, 10; Vargas, "Tejana Radical," 565.

34. Vargas, "Tejana Radical," 564.

35. Tenayuca interview by Emilio Zamora and Oralia Cortez; Croxdale, "The 1938 San Antonio Pecan Sheller's Strike," 26, 27. Menefee and Cassmore, authors of a study on the pecan shellers in San Antonio conducted by the WPA, did not make the claim that Seligman hired Rodríguez; however, their study did corroborate Tenayuca's claim that there was a close relationship between the two. The study further confirmed Tenayuca's claim that Rodríguez received financial support from Seligman because the union helped to "prevent small operators from undercutting the piecework scale paid by the larger companies" (Menefee and Cassmore, *The Pecan Shellers of San Antonio*, 16–17).

36. Menefee and Cassmore, *The Pecan Shellers of San Antonio*, 17. Others who opposed the strike included the American Chamber of Commerce, the Mexican Chamber of Commerce, LULAC, and the Catholic Church. One church official offered to help strikers on the condition that they reject CIO leadership, which some conflated with communism. Strikers decided to stick with the CIO. García, *Rise of the Mexican American Middle Class*.

37. "Pecan Plant Workers Strike," *San Antonio Light*, 31 January 1938, p. 1.

38. "Pecan Strike Heads Offer to Quit," *San Antonio Light*, 3 February 1938, pp. 1, 4. Emphasis on the communist angle came from a national source as well. In a *Time* magazine article on Emma Tenayuca and the pecan shellers' strike, the writer characterized Tenayuca as "little Emma Tenayuca, a slim, vivacious labor organizer with black eyes and a Red philosophy . . . [who] from her office at the local Workers Alliance . . . continued to pull strings with the assistance of her 'gang,' some 300 devoted followers whom she deploys with a masterly hand in picket lines or mass meeting" ("*La Pasionaria de Texas*," *Time*, 28 February 1938, 17).

39. Menefee and Cassmore, *The Pecan Shellers of San Antonio*, 18. "S.A. Strikers Tell Police Beatings," *San Antonio Light*, 15 February 1938, p. 1; Blackwelder, *Women of the Depression*, 143.

40. Blackwelder, *Women of the Depression*, 3–11.

41. Vargas, "Tejana Radical," 568–572; Homer Brooks ran unsuccessfully for governor of Texas in 1936. Naison, "Remaking America," 49.

42. Croxdale, "The 1938 San Antonio Pecan Sheller's Strike," 28. Tenayuca interview by Gerry Poyo; Rips, "Living History," 13; Allan Turner, "A night that changed San Antonio: Woman recalls riot over communism in '39," *Houston Chronicle*, 14 December 1986.

43. Emma Tenayuca to Mrs. Jiménez, 31 July 1973, part of the "Texas Women in History" exhibit documents found in the Emma Tenayuca Collection, The Women's Collection, Texas Woman's University, Denton. Croxdale, "The 1938 San Antonio Pecan Sheller's Strike," 31–32.

44. Emma Tenayuca and Homer Brooks, "The Mexican Question in the Southwest," in *The Communist*, March 1939, 262.

45. "La Repercusión de un linchamiento." *Regeneración*, 12 November 1910.

46. Tenayuca and Brooks, "The Mexican Question in the Southwest," 264.

47. Ibid., 265–266.

48. Ibid., 264.

49. Ibid., 267.

50. Meyer and Beezley, *The Oxford History of Mexico*, 520–521; Zamora, *Claiming Rights and Righting Wrongs in Texas*, 2.

51. Tenayuca and Brooks, "The Mexican Question in the Southwest," 267–268.

52. Tenayuca FBI file; Calderón and Zamora, "Manuela Solis Sager and Emma Tenayuca: A Tribute," 274.

53. Ernie Villarreal, "San Antonio Landmark Site of Riot in 1939," *Texas Public Radio Newsroom*, aired 24 August 2001. Legionnaires were outraged because the mayor had granted the communists permission to meet in a building that had been dedicated to San Antonio's fallen World War I heroes. Maury Maverick, "One San Antonio Maverick Sticks by Another," *San Antonio Express-News*, 1 August 1999, p. 3H.

54. Jeannie Kever, "Women: Tenayuca Spent Years as a Strike Leader," *San Antonio Light*, March 6, 1988, p. J6.; and Jan Jarboe, "S.A.'s Linen Needs Airing," *San Antonio Express-News*, 3 March 1985; Allan Turner, "A Night that Changed San Antonio," *Houston Chronicle*, 14 December 1986," p. 1. A number of photographs of Father M. A. Valenta and Clem Smith place them at the Municipal Auditorium on 25 August 1939. Villarreal, "San Antonio Landmark Site of Riot in 1939." Gus. T. Jones to director, Federal Bureau of Investigation, 26 August 1939, Tenayuca's FBI file. Maury Maverick, "Tenayuca's Lessons Are Worth Another Look," *San Antonio Express-News*, 26 September 1999, p. 3G. The *San Antonio Light* Collection at the Institute of Texan Cultures in San Antonio contains a black and white photograph (2223-VV) of Maury Maverick hanged in effigy at City Hall dated 25 August 1939.

55. Marina Pisano, "Labor Leader's Legacy Endures: Former Union Organizer Living a Quiet Life—Sort Of," *San Antonio Express-News*, 1 February 1990, p. 3-C; Allan Turner, "A Night that Changed San Antonio," *Houston Chronicle*, 14 December 1986, p. 46.

56. Emma Tenayuca, 22 September 1944, Diary, Box 1, Folder 2, Mss. 420, Texas Woman's University, Denton.

57. "Tenayuca, 1916–1999." R. J. Abbaticchio Jr to Director, FBI, 8 September 1941, Tenayuca's FBI file; Isserman, *If I Had a Hammer*, 7–8.

58. "Divorce Decree, 1941, from Homer Brooks, and Restoration of Her Maiden Name," Tenayuca MSS. 420, Box 7, Folder 6; SAC, San Francisco to Director, FBI, 20 April 1953, Tenayuca's FBI file; FBI report, 6 December 1941, Tenayuca's FBI file; FBI reports, 6 May 1942, and Special Agent in Charge (SAC), San Francisco to Director, FBI, 20 April 1953, Tenayuca's FBI file. Evidence for these claims can be found throughout the Emma Tenayuca FBI file, which extends from 1939 to 1953. In 1953, the FBI ended its surveillance of Tenayuca, adding only one other document to her file in 1968. This document simply recorded her new address in San Antonio, Texas, Tenayuca MSS. 420, Box 1, Folder 9; and "Emma Tenayuca, 1916–1999."

59. Emma Tenayuca, 9 June 1942, Diary, Box 1, Folder 2, Mss. 420, Texas Woman's University, Denton.

60. Emma Tenayuca, 12 June 1942, Diary, Box 1, Folder 2, Mss. 420, Texas Woman's University, Denton.

61. Robert L. Sikes, 2nd Lieut., Assistant Recruiting Officer, to Miss Emma B. Giraud, 29 December 1942; Charles D. Apple, Assistant Recruiting and Induction Officer to Miss Emma Teneyuca, 8 January 1943; Stanley Kock, Colonel, Cavalry, Recruiting and Induction Officer to Mrs. Emma Teneyuca, 29 January 1943, Tenayuca MSS. 420, Box 1, Folder 9; and "Emma Tenayuca, 1916–1999."

62. SAC, San Francisco to Director, FBI, 20 April 1953, Tenayuca's FBI file; Isserman, *If I Had a Hammer*, 3–34; and Allan Turner, "A Night that Changed San Antonio," *Houston Chronicle*, 14 December 1986, p. 46.

63. Allan Turner, "A Night that Changed San Antonio," *Houston Chronicle*, 14 December 1986," p. 46; "Emma Tenayuca, 1916–1999," Nomination form for the Texas Women's Hall of Fame, Tenayuca MSS. 420, Box 5, Folder 22. Some of the scholars who corresponded with or received assistance from Emma Tenayuca include Teresa Palomo Acosta, Irene Blea, Roberto Calderón, Martha Cotera, Julia Curry, Juan Gómez-Quiñones, Margarita Melville, Cynthia E. Orozco, Jerry Poyo, Carmen Tafolla, Zaragosa Vargas, Ruthe Winegarten, and Emilio Zamora. She also assisted high school students with their projects. Tenayuca continued to keep up with local, state, and national politics, supporting the San Antonio mayoral campaigns of Henry G. Cisneros and the Texas gubernatorial campaign of Ann Richards. For more information, see "General Correspondence: Friends and Associates," Tenayuca MSS. 420, Boxes 3–5.

Chapter 6

1. "The Spears Bill," in F. Arturo Rosales, *Testimonio: A Documentary History of the Mexican American Struggle for Civil Rights*, 192–193.

2. Emma Tenayuca, 26 January 1945, Diary, Box 1, Folder 2, Mss. 420, Texas Woman's University, Denton. Emphasis is original. Key works on LULAC include the following: Márquez, *LULAC*; Kaplowitz, *LULAC, Mexican Americans, and National Policy*; Orozco, *No Mexicans, Women, or Dogs Allowed*; Orozco, "Alice Dickerson Montemayor"; Zamora, *Claiming Rights and Righting Wrongs*; Orozco, "The Origins of the League of United Latin American Citizens (LULAC)."

3. Montejano, *Anglos and Mexicans in the Making of Texas*, 263–264.

4. Several works have addressed issues of Mexican American civil rights in relation to the Good Neighbor Policy and World War II; see Zamora, "La guerra en pro de la justicia y la democracia en Francia y Texas"; Zamora, "Fighting on Two Fronts"; Zamora, "Mexico's Wartime Intervention on Behalf of Mexicans in the United States"; Zamora, "The Failed Promise of Wartime Opportunity for Mexicans in the Texas Oil Industry"; Zamora, *Claiming Rights and Righting Wrongs in Texas*; Guglielmo, "Fighting for Caucasian Rights"; Gutiérrez, *Walls and Mirrors*.

5. Gómez-Quiñones, *Roots of Chicano Politics*, 347.

6. J. T. Canales, "Intelligent Citizenship and Civic Pride," *Lulac News* 6, no. 3 (March 1939). *Lulac News* issues found in LULAC Archives, Benson Latin American Collection, University of Texas at Austin.

7. Rosales, *Testimonio*, 157.

8. Orozco, "Alice Dickerson Montemayor," 436.

9. Márquez, *LULAC*, 10–13. Márquez thinks of LULAC activists as conservative, for while they challenged racism, they did not challenge capitalism. It is more accurate to say that early LULAC fell into a classical liberal mold than a conservative one.

10. "Aims and Purposes of the League of Latin American Citizens," *Lulac News* 5, no. 5, (August 1938); García, *Rise of the Mexican American American Middle Class*, 269–271.

11. Ezequiel D. Salinas, "The Need for Lulac," *Lulac News* 4, no. 7 (October 1937) .

12. Ibid.

13. Miss Ana Velásquez, "Pay Your Poll Tax," *Lulac News* 5, no. 8 (November 1938).

14. García, *Mexican Americans*, 38; Orozco, "LADIES LULAC," Handbook of Texas Online.

15. Ezequiel D. Salinas, "The Need for Lulac," *Lulac News* 4, no. 7 (October 1937).

16. "Aims and Purposes of the League of Latin American Citizens," *Lulac News* 5, no. 5, (August 1938); García, *Rise of the Mexican American American Middle Class*, 269.

17. "Laredo LULACs Censor 'Pressure' Voice Confidence in District Court," *LULAC News*, October 1938.

18. "Alonso S. Perales on the Ideals of Mexican Americans," taken from Alonso S. Perales, *En defensa de mi raza*, Vol. 1, 28–29, and reprinted in Rosales, *Testimonio*, 167.

19. García, *Mexican Americans*, 43–45.

20. Márquez, *LULAC*, 30.

21. Neil Foley, "Becoming Hispanic: Mexican Americans and the Faustian Pact with Whiteness," 53–66; Gómez-Quiñones, *Roots of Chicano Politics*, 368.

22. Foley, "Becoming Hispanic," 54; Tenayuca and Brooks, "The Mexican Question in the Southwest"; Márquez, *LULAC*, 31.

23. Robert Meza to Vergil D. Reed, 20 October 1939, decimal file 811.5011/105, Records of the United States Department of State, RG59 (National Archives, College Park, MD.)

24. Edward J. Noble to Mr. Secretary, September 14, 1939, decimal file 811.5011/105, Records of the United States Department of State, RG59 (National Archives, College Park, MD.)

25. E. D. Salinas, "The 1940 Census" in *LULAC News* 6, no. 11 (November 1939), Alice Dickerson Montemayor collection, Benson Latin American Library, University of Texas, Austin.

26. Ibid.

27. Márquez, *LULAC*, 32–33.

28. Rosales, *Testimonio*, 172–173.

29. Mario T. García, *Mexican Americans*, 58–61; Allsup, "Delgado v Bastrop ISD, Handbook of Texas Online.

30. García, *Mexican Americans*, 50–51.

31. Ibid., 58–61.

32. Orozco, "Alice Dickerson Montemayor," 435.

33. Orozco, "MONTEMAYOR, ALICE DICKERSON," Handbook of Texas Online.

34. Orozco, "Alice Dickerson Montemayor," 439.

35. Ibid; interview with Aurelio Montemayor, 9 October 2000, San Antonio, Texas.

36. Orozco, "Alice Dickerson Montemayor, 440; Aurelio Montemayor, interviewed by author on 9 October 2000, San Antonio, Texas, hereafter referred to as Aurelio Montemayor interview.

37. Aurelio Montemayor interview.

38. Orozco, "Alice Dickerson Montemayor," 441, Aurelio Montemayor interview.

39. Orozco, "Alice Dickerson Montemayor," 445.

40. M. C. González, "Lulac Was First in the Effort to Stem Foreign Anti-American Propaganda," *LULAC News* 5, no. 8 (November 1938) .

41. Ibid.

42. "Laredo Junior LULAC Council," *LULAC News* 5, no. 2 (March 1938); "Station L-A-R-E-D-O: The Voice of the Laredo JUNIOR LULAC COUNCIL," *LULAC News* 6, no. 4 (April 1939); "The Laredo Junior Council," *LULAC News* 5, no. 9 (December 1938); "President General and Three Laredo Councils," *LULAC News* 5, no. 9 (December 1938).

43. Mrs. F. I. Montemayor, "Let's Organize Junior Councils," *LULAC News* 5, no. 7 (October 1938).

44. "Mrs. F. I. Montemayor," "Let's Organize Junior Councils," *LULAC News* 5, no. 5 (August 1938) .

45. Ibid.

46. "The Laredo Junior Council," *LULAC News* 5, no. 9 (December 1938); Orozco, "Alice Dickerson Montemajor," 445.

47. "The Laredo Junior Council," *LULAC News* 5, no. 9 (December 1938); "Station L-A-R-E-D-O: The Voice of the Laredo JUNIOR LULAC COUNCIL," *LULAC News* 6, no. 4 (April 1939).

48. Orozco, "Alice Dickerson Montemayor, 446.

49. Orozco touches upon conflicts that Montemayor experienced with some of the male leadership in LULAC. Orozco, "Alice Dickerson Montemayor," 446–450.

50. Some articles written by Alice Dickerson Montemayor include "Women's Opportunity in Lulac," "We Need More Ladies Councils," *LULAC News*, July 1937; "Son Muy Hombres," *LULAC News* 5, no. 2 (March 1938); and "When and Then Only," *Lulac News*, March 1939. Correspondence between Alice Dickerson Montemayor and some of her friends,

among them, J. C. Machuca, also illustrate the tensions in LULAC between people such as Montemayor and Machuca who felt that some members of LULAC were being sexist and those who presumably were sexist. Mr. J. C. Machuca to Mrs. F. I. Montemayor, 7 October 1937, Alicia Dickerson Montemayor Papers, Benson Latin American Collection, University of Texas Libraries, the University of Texas at Austin.

51. Lawhn, "The Mexican Revolution and the Women," 163–164.
52. Geo. I. Sánchez, "A New Pan-Americanism," *LULAC News* 5, no. 9 (December 1938).
53. Dennis Chávez, "America Must Choose—Pan Americanism or War," *LULAC News* 7, no. 8 (September 1940).
54. Ibid.
55. Ibid.
56. Examining the history of Latinas in Los Angeles during World War II, Elizabeth Escobedo refers to the concept of racial liberalism to explain the transition from biologically based to culturally based understandings of American identity. Another component of racial liberalism was the belief that women were critical to a strong democracy. Escobedo, *From Coveralls to Zoot Suits*, 6 and 60–61. This is something that LULAC members also believed, but their ideas stemmed from gente decente gendered norms, although by the 1930s, American influences may have been at play as well. For more on racial liberalism, see Brilliant, *The Color of America Has Changed*; Horton, *Race and the Making of American Liberalism*; and Jackson, *Gunnar Myrdal and America's Conscience*.
57. Perales, *Are We Good Neighbors?* 10, 17, 22, 30, 39, 44, 45, 64, 78; Sloss-Vento, *Alonso S. Perales*,12.
58. Opening Address of Archbishop Robert E. Lucey before the Conference on Spanish-Speaking People of the Southwest, San Antonio, 20 July 1943, in Perales, *Are We Good Neighbors*, 11–12.
59. Ibid., 12–15.
60. Castañeda, "The Second-Rate Citizen and Democracy," 19.
61. Ibid., 20.
62. Neil Foley, *The White Scourge*, 205–207; Green, *The Establishment in Texas Politics*, 81.
63. Guglielmo, "Fighting for Caucasian Rights," 1–3, 8.
64. Green, *The Establishment in Texas Politics*, 253 footnote 6.
65. Green, *The Establishment in Texas Politics*, 139–141; Montejano, *Anglos and Mexicans*, 270–271.
66. Danciger, "Statement of Racial Discrimination," 28; "The Good Neighbor Commission and Commentary of Alonso S. Perales," in Sloss-Vento, *Alonso S. Perales,* 15–16.
67. This is a proud legacy prominently showcased in LULAC's website but also documented by scholars, http://www.lulac.org/about/history; Márquez, *LULAC*; Kaplowitz, *LULAC, Mexican Americans, and National Policy*; Orozco, *No Mexicans, Women, or Dogs Allowed*; Orozco; "Alice Dickerson Montemayor"; Zamora, *Claiming Rights and Righting Wrongs*; Orozco, "The Origins of the League of United Latin American Citizens (LULAC)."

Conclusion

1. Appleby, *The Relentless Revolution*, 134.

BIBLIOGRAPHY

Primary Sources

MANUSCRIPT COLLECTIONS

Archivo General de la Nación, Mexico City.

Alice Dickerson Montemayor Papers, Benson Latin American Collection, the University of Texas at Austin Libraries.

Simón E. Domínguez Letter Press, 1904-1925 letters, Dolph Briscoe Center for American History, University of Texas, Austin, Texas.

Hector P. García Papers, Mary and Jeff Bell Library, Texas A&M, Corpus Christi.

Emma Goldman Papers [microform]: A microfilm edition, Berkeley Library, University of California.

Jovita González de Mireles Manuscripts and Works, Benson Latin American Collection, the University of Texas at Austin Libraries.

Clemente N. Idar Papers, Nettie Lee Benson Latin American Library, University of Texas, Austin, Texas.

Eduardo Idar, Jr. Papers, Nettie Lee Benson Latin American Library, the University of Texas, at Austin, Texas.

Federico Idar and Idar Family Papers, Benson Latin American Collection, University of Texas, Austin, Texas.

Jovita Idar biographical file, Special Collections, Texas Woman's University.

"Friedrich Katz Archive," The University of Chicago.

Labor Movement in Texas Collection, F 12, Dolph Briscoe Center for American History, University of Texas, Austin.

League of United Latin American Citizens (LULAC) Archives, Benson Latin American Collection, University of Texas at Austin Libraries.

Munguía Family Papers, Benson Latin American Library, University of Texas at Austin Libraries.

Official Souvenir Program, 17th Annual Birthday Celebration of Washington, Laredo, Texas, February 12 to 23, 1916, Washington's Birthday Celebration files, Historical Collection, Laredo Public Library, Laredo, Texas.

Primer Congreso Mexicanista, Verificado en Laredo, Texas, EEUU de A. Los Dias 14 al 22 de Septiembre de 1911. Discursos y Conferencias Por la Raza y Para la Raza. Tipografía de N. Idar, 1912, Center for American History, University of Texas, Austin, Texas.

Emma Tenayuca Collection, Blagg-Huey Library, the Woman's Collection, Texas Woman's University, Denton, Texas.

Leonor Villegas de Magnón Papers, M.D. Anderson Library, University of Houston, Houston, Texas.

Published Primary Sources

Bartra, Armando, et al., *Regeneración, 1900–1918: La Corriente más radical de la revolución mexicana de 1910 a través de su periódico de combate.* México, D.F.: Era, 1977.

Castañeda, Carlos E. "The Second-Rate Citizen and Democracy." In *Are We Good Neighbors?*, edited by Alonso S. Perales. 1948. Reprint. New York: Arno Press, 1974.

Clark, Victor S. *Mexican Labor in the United States.* Department of Commerce and Labor Bulletin no. 78. Washington, DC: Government Printing Office, 1908. Reprinted in Carlos E. Cortes, *Mexican American Labor in the United States.* New York: Arno Press, 1974, 466–522.

Danciger, Jack. "Statement of Racial Discrimination." In *Are We Good Neighbors?*, edited by Alonso S. Perales. 1948. Reprint. New York: Arno Press, 1974.

De Magnón, Leonor Villegas. *The Rebel.* Edited by Clara Lomas. Houston: Arte Público Press, 1994.

González Ramírez, Manuel. *El Porvenir.* In *Epistolario y Textos de Ricardo Flores Magón.* Fondo de Cultura Económica, Mexico, 1964.

Kanellos, Nicolás, et al., eds. *En otra voz: Antología de la literature hispana de los Estados Unidos.* Houston: Arte Público Press, 2002.

Lindheim, Bessie. "Leonor Villegas de Magnón and the Mexican Revolution." The Story of Laredo Series, No. 16, ed. Stan Green. Laredo: Border Studies Publications, 1991.

Malloy, Joseph I. *May Catholics Be Masons?* Mahwah, NJ: Paulist Press, 1927.

Perales, Alonso S. *En defensa de mi raza.* Vol. 1. San Antonio: Artes Gráficas, 1936.

Perales, C. "Why the Border Needs the Free Zone." In *U.S.-Mexico Borderlands: Historical and Contemporary Perspectives*, edited by Oscar Martínez, 98–100. Wilmington, DE: Scholarly Resources, 1996.

Rosales, F. Arturo. *Testimonio: A Documentary History of the Mexican American Struggle for Civil Rights.* Houston: Arte Público Press, 2000.

Tenayuca, Emma, and Homer Brooks. "The Mexican Question in the Southwest." *The Communist*, March 1939.

Turner, John Kenneth. *Barbarous Mexico.* Chicago: Charles H. Kerr & Company, 1910.

Zertuche Muñoz, Fernando, comp. *Ricardo Flores Magón: El Sueño Alternativo.* México, D.F.: Fondo de Cultura Economica, 1995.

Government Documents

Menefee, Selden, and Orin C. Cassmore. *The Pecan Shellers of San Antonio.* Washington, DC: Government Printing Office, 1940.

Emma Tenayuca file, Federal Bureau of Investigation, Freedom of Information Act.

US Bureau of the Census. *Abstract of the Thirteenth Census (1910), Statistics for Texas, Containing Statistics of Population, Agriculture, Manufacturers, and Mining for the State, Counties, Cities, and Other Divisions.* Washington, DC: Government Printing Office, 1913.

US Department of State. Records Relating to Internal Affairs of Mexico, 1910–1929, Record Group 59. National Archives, College Park, Maryland.

US Department of State. Papers relating to the foreign relations of the United States. Issues 1910, 1911, 1913. National Archives, Washington, D.C.

Newspapers and Periodicals

El Defensor del Obrero
El Democrata Fronterizo
Evolucíon
La Crónica
La Voz
La Prensa
Leslie's Weekly Illustrated

Regeneración
Houston Chronicle
Laredo Daily News
Laredo Morning Times
San Antonio Express-News
San Antonio Light
Washington Post
Wichita Daily Times
Texas Observer
Times Magazine

Oral History Interviews

Cantú, Norma E. Interview by Gabriela González, 14 September 2000, San Antonio, Texas.

Cantú, Norma E. Interview by Gabriela González, 25 September 2000, San Antonio, Texas.

Cisneros, Elvira. Interview by Gabriela González, 28 April 1994, San Antonio, Texas.

Cisneros, Elvira. Interview by Gabriela González, 19 November 1995, San Antonio, Texas.

Cisneros, Elvira. Interview by Gabriela González, 1 September 2000, San Antonio, Texas.

Cisneros, Elvira. Interview by Gabriela González, 5 September 2000, San Antonio, Texas.

Cisneros, Elvira. Interview by Gabriela González, 15 September 2000, San Antonio, Texas.

De López, Jovita Fuentes. Interview by Gabriela González, 11 September 2000, San Antonio, Texas.

Idar, Eduardo Jr. Interview by Gabriela González, 31 August 2000, San Antonio, Texas.

Idar, Aquilino (Ike) and Guadalupe Idar. Interview by Dr. Jerry Poyo and Tom F. Shelton, 26 October 1984, Institute of Texan Cultures, University of Texas, San Antonio, Texas.

Lozano, Mónica. Interview by Shirley Biagi, Los Angeles, California, 13 December 1993, http://beta.wpcf.org/oralhistory/loz1.html (accessed September 17, 2011).

Magnón, Joaquín Alfredo (Joe). Interview by Jorge González, 1 June 1978, Webb County Heritage Foundation, Laredo, Texas.

Montemayor, Aurelio. Interview by Gabriela González, 9 October 2000, San Antonio, Texas.

Munguía, Rubén. Interview by Gabriela González, 6 May 1994, San Antonio, Texas.

Munguía, Rubén. Interview by Gabriela González, 30 August 2000, San Antonio, Texas.

Offer, María del Carmen Guardiola. Interview by Gabriela Gonzálaz, 10 August 2000, Laredo, Texas.

Tafolla, Carmen. Interview by Gabriela González, 5 October 2000, San Antonio, Texas.

Tenayuca, Emma. Interview by Gerry Poyo, 21 February 1987, Institute of Texan Cultures, University of Texas, San Antonio.

Tenayuca, Emma. Interview by Emilio Zamara and Oralia Cortez, 19 June 1986, The Woman's Collection, Texas Woman's University, Denton.

Marjorie Coppock, Richard Alaniz, Adriana Craddock, Claudia García, and Sandra P. Thompson. "Changing Cultural Patterns in the Border Community of Laredo, Texas in the Early 1900's," Texas A&M International University Paper presented at the Southwestern Sociological Association Meetings, San Antonio, Texas, 31 March 1994, pp. 1–20. This paper contains excerpts from oral history interviews.

Adriana Craddock interview of Elena Medellín de Ramírez (b. 1915 in Laredo), Spring 1993.

Sandra P. Thompson interview of Reynaldo García, Sr., (b. in 1909 in Lampazos, Nuevo Leon, Mexico—family moved to Laredo in 1916), Spring 1993.

Published Secondary Sources

Aceves, Ricardo Romero. *La Mujer en la Historia de México*. México, D.F.: Costa- Amic Editores, S.A., 1982.

Adams, John A. Jr. *Conflict and Commerce on the Rio Grande: Laredo, 1755–1955*. College Station: Texas A&M University Press, 2008.

Alamillo, José M. *Making Lemonade out of Lemons: Mexican American Labor and Leisure in a California Town, 1880–1960*. Urbana: University of Illinois Press, 2006.

Albro, Ward S. *Always a Rebel: Ricardo Flores Magón and the Mexican Revolution*. Fort Worth: Texas Christian University Press, 1992.

Albro, Ward S. *To Die on Your Feet: The Life, Times and Writing of Práxedis Guerrero*. Fort Worth: Texas Christian University Press, 1996.

Allsup, Carl. *The American G.I. Forum: Origins and Evolution*. University of Texas Center for Mexican American Studies Monograph, no. 6. Austin: University of Texas, 1982.

Almaguer, Tom. *Racial Fault Lines: The Historical Origins of White Supremacy in California*. University of California Press, 1994.

Almaráz, Félix D. Jr. *Knight without Armor: Carlos Eduardo Castañeda, 1896–1858*. College Station: Texas A&M University Press, 1990.

Alonzo, Armando. *Tejano Legacy: Rancheros and Settlers in South Texas, 1734–1900*. Albuquerque: University of New Mexico Press, 1998.

Anders, Evan. *Boss Rule in South Texas: The Progressive Era*. Austin: University of Texas Press, 1982.

Anderson, Benedict. *Imagined Communities: Reflections on the Origin and Spread of Nationalism*. Rev. ed. London: Verso, 1991.

Anzaldúa, Gloria. *Borderlands/La Frontera: The New Mestiza*. 2nd ed. San Francisco: Aunt Lute Books, 1987.

Appleby, Joyce. *The Relentless Revolution: A History of Capitalism*. New York: W.W. Norton, 2010.

Aranda, José F.Jr., and Silvio Torres-Saillant, eds. *Recovering the U.S. Hispanic Literary Heritage*. Vol. 4. Houston: Arte Publico Press, 2002.

Aron, Stephen. "Returning the West to the World." *OAH Magazine of History* 20, no. 2 (2006): 53–60.

Arredondo, Gabriela F. *Mexican Chicago: Race, Identity, and Nation, 1916–1939*. Urbana: University of Illinois Press, 2008.

Arreola, Daniel D. *Tejano South Texas: A Mexican American Cultural Province*. Austin: University of Texas Press, 2002.

Arrom, Silvia Marina. *The Women of Mexico City, 1790–1857*. Stanford, CA: Stanford University Press, 1985.

Baker, Nancy E., Juliana Barr, Angela Boswell, Jessica Brannon-Wranosky, Light T. Cummins, Victoria H. Cummins, Mary Ellen Curtin, et al. *Texas Women: Their Histories, Their Lives*. Edited by Elizabeth Hayes Turner, Stephanie Cole, and Rebecca Sharpless. Athens: University of Georgia Press, 2015.

Baker, Paula. "The Domestication of Politics: Women and American Political Society, 1780–1920." In *Unequal Sisters: A Multicultural Reader in U.S. Women's History*, 2nd ed., edited by Vicki L. Ruíz and Ellen Carol DuBois. New York: Routledge, 1994.

Balderrama, Francisco. *In Defense of La Raza: The Los Angeles Mexican Consulate and the Mexican Community, 1929 to 1936*. Tucson: University of Arizona Press, 1982.

Baldwin, Deborah J. *Protestants and the Mexican Revolution: Missionaries, Ministers, and Social Change*. Urbana: University of Illinois Press, 1990.

Barton, Paul. *Hispanic Methodists, Presbyterians, and Baptists in Texas*. Austin: University of Texas Press, 2006.

Bauman, Zygmunt. *Modernity and the Holocaust*. Ithaca, NY: Cornell University Press, 1989.

Behnken, Brian D., ed. *Civil Rights and Beyond: African American and Latino/a Activism in the Twentieth-Century United States*. Athens: University of Georgia Press, 2016.

Behnken, Brian D. *Fighting Their Own Battles: Mexican Americans, African Americans, and the Struggle for Civil Rights in Texas*. Chapel Hill: University of North Carolina Press, 2011.

Behout, Lee. *Mythohistorical Interventions: The Chicano Movement and Its Legacies*. Minneapolis: University of Minnesota Press, 2011.

Bender, Thomas, ed. *Rethinking American History in a Global Age*. Berkeley: University of California Press, 2002.

Bernstein, Shana. *Bridges of Reform: Interracial Civil Rights Activism in Twentieth Century Los Angeles*. New York: Oxford University Press, 2011.

Bernstein, Shana. "Interracial Activism in the Los Angeles Community Service Organization: Linking the World War II and Civil Rights Eras." *Pacific Historical Review* 80, no. 2 (2011): 231–267.

Bethell, Leslie, ed. *Mexico since Independence*. London: Cambridge University Press, 1991.

Blackwelder, Julia Kirk. *Women of the Depression: Caste and Culture in San Antonio, 1929–1939*. College Station: Texas A&M Press, 1984.

Blackwell, Maylei. *¡Chicana Power! Contested Histories of Feminism in the Chicano Movement*. Austin: University of Texas Press, 2011.

Blanquel, Eduardo. *Ricardo Flores Magón*. México, D.F.: Terra Nova, 1985.

Blanton, Carlos Kevin. *George I. Sánchez: The Long Fight for Mexican American Integration*. New Haven, CT: Yale University Press, 2014.

Blanton, Carlos Kevin. *The Strange Career of Bilingual Education in Texas, 1836–1981*. College Station: Texas A&M University, 2004.

Blumin, Stuart M. *The Emergence of the Middle Class: Social Experience in the American City, 1760–1900*. Cambridge: Cambridge University Press, 1989.

Boyer, Paul S. *Urban Masses and Moral Order in America, 1820–1920*. Cambridge, MA: Harvard University Press, 1978.

Brear, Holly Beachley. *Inherit the Alamo: Myth and Ritual at an American Shrine*. Austin: University of Texas Press, 1995.

Brenner, Anita. *The Wind That Swept Mexico: The History of the Mexican Revolution of 1910–1942*. Austin: University of Texas Press, 1971.

Brilliant, Mark. *The Color of America Has Changed: How Racial Diversity Shaped Civil Rights Reform in California, 1941–1978*. New York: Oxford University Press, 2010.

Brown, Michael E. et al., eds. *New Studies in the Politics and Culture of U.S. Communism*. New York: Monthly Review Press, 1993.

Bufe, Chaz, and Mitchell Cowen Verter, eds. *Dreams of Freedom: A Ricardo Flores Magón Reader*. Oakland, CA: AK Press, 2005.

Buff, Rachel Ida. "The Deportation Terror." *American Quarterly* 60, no. 3 (2008): 523–551.

Buhle, Mari Jo, Paul Buhle, and Dan Georgakas, eds. *Encyclopedia of the American Left*. Urbana: University of Illinois Press, 1992.

Buhle, Paul, and Dan Georgakas, eds. *The Immigrant Left in the United States*. SUNY Series in American Labor History. New York: State University of New York Press, 1996.

Burgos, Adrian, Donna Gabaccia, María Cristina García, Matthew García, Kelly Lytle Hernández, Jesse Hoffnung-Garskof, María E. Montoya, George J. Sánchez, Virginia Sánchez Korrol, and Paul Spickard. "Latino History: An Interchange on Present Realities and Future Prospects." *Journal of American History* 97, no. 2 (2010): 424–463.

Cadava, Geraldo L. "Borderlands of Modernity and Abandonment: The Lines within Ambos Nogales and the Tohono O'odham Nation." *Journal of American History* 98, no. 2 (2011): 362–383.

Cadava, Geraldo L. *Standing on Common Ground: The Making of a Sunbelt Borderland*. Cambridge, MA: Harvard University Press, 2013.

Calderón, Roberto R. *Mexican Coal Mining Labor in Texas and Coahuila, 1880–1930*. College Station: Texas A&M University Press, 2000.

Calderón, Roberto R. "Unión, Paz y Trabajo: Laredo's Mexican Mutual Aid Societies, 1890s." In *Mexican Americans in Texas History*, edited by Emilio Zamora, Cynthia Orozco, and Rodolfo Rocha, 63–81. Austin: Texas State Historical Association, 2000.

Calderón, Roberto R., and Emilio Zamora. "Manuela Solis Sager and Emma B. Tenayuca: A Tribute." In *Between Borders: Essays on Mexicana/Chicana History*, edited by Adelaida R. Del Castillo. La Mujer Latina Series. Encino, CA: Floricanto Press, 1990.

Calvert, Robert A., and Arnoldo De Leon. *The History of Texas*. Arlington Heights, IL: Harlan Davidson, 1990.

Camacho, Alicia Schmidt. *Migrant Imaginaries: Latino Cultural Politics in the U.S. Mexico Borderlands.* Nation of Newcomers, Immigrant History as American History. New York: New York University Press, 2008.

Camarillo, Albert M. *Chicanos in a Changing Society: From Mexican Pueblos to American Barrios in San Barbara and Southern California, 1848–1930.* Cambridge, MA: Harvard University Press, 1979.

Camarillo, Albert. "Looking Back on Chicano History: A Generational Perspective." *Pacific Historical Review* 82, no. 4 (November 2013): 496–504.

Camarillo, Albert. "Navigating Segregated Life in America's Racial Borderhoods, 1910s–1950s." *Journal of American History* 100, no. 3 (December 2013): 645–662.

Cano Ruíz B. *Ricardo Flores Magón: Su Vida, Su Obra.* Translated by Proudhon Carbó. México, D.F.: Editores Mexicanos Unidos, 1976.

Cantú, Norma Elia. *Canícula: Snapshots of a Girlhood en la Frontera.* Albuquerque: University of New Mexico Press, 1995.

Carnes, Mark C. *Secret Ritual and Manhood in Victorian America.* New Haven, CT: Yale University Press, 1989.

Carrigan, William D. and Clive Webb, *Forgotten Dead: Mob Violence against Mexicans in the United States, 1848–1928.* New York: Oxford University Press, 2013.

Carroll, Patrick J. *Félix Longoria's Wake: Bereavement, Racism, and the Rise of Mexican American Activism.* Austin: University of Texas Press, 2003.

Carson, James Taylor. "American Historians and Indians." *Historical Journal* 49, no. 3 (2006): 921–933.

Castañeda, Antonia I. "Engendering the History of Alta California, 1769–1848: Gender, Sexuality, and the Family." *California History* 76, no. 2/3 (1997): 230–259.

Castañeda, Antonia I. "Sexual Violence in the Politics of Conquest: Amerindian Women and the Spanish Conquest of Alta California." In *Building with Our Hands: New Directions in Chicana Studies,* edited by Adela de la Torre and Beatríz M. Pesquera, 15–33. Berkeley: University of California Press, 1993.

Castañeda, Antonia I. "Women of Colour and the Rewriting of Western History: The Discourse, Politics and Decolonization of History." *Pacific Historical Review* 61, no. 4 (1992): 501–533.

Castañeda, Antonia, Susan H. Armitage, Patricia Hart, and Karen Weatheron, eds. *Gender on the Borderlands: The Frontier Reader.* Lincoln: University of Nebraska Press, 2007.

Castañeda, Antonia I., and Luz María Gordillo. *Three Decades of Engendering History: Selected Works of Antonia I. Castañeda.* Edited by Linda Heidenreich. Denton: University of North Texas Press, 2014.

Castañeda, Antonia, Patricia Hart, Karen Weathermon, and Susan H. Armitage, eds. *Gender on the Borderlands: The Frontiers Reader.* Lincoln: University of Nebraska Press, 2007.

Castillo, Pedro, and Albert Camarillo, eds. *Furia y Muerte: Los Bandidos Mexicanos.* Aztlán Publications Monograph, no. 4. Los Angeles: Chicano Studies Center, University of California, 1973.

Chávez, Ernesto. "Chicano/a History: Its Origins, Purpose, and Future." *Pacific Historical Review* 82, no. 4 (November 2013): 505–519.

Chávez, Ernesto. *"¡Mi Raza Primero!" (My People First!) Nationalism, Identity, and Insurgency in the Chicano Movement in Los Angeles, 1966–1978.* Berkeley: University of California Press, 2002.

Chávez, John R. "Aliens in Their Native Lands: The Persistence of Internal Colonial Theory." *Journal of World History* 22, no. 4 (2011): 785–809.

Chávez, Marisela R. "Pilgrimage to the Homeland: California Chicanas and International Women's Year, Mexico City, 1975." In *Memories and Migrations: Mapping Boricua and Chicana Histories,* edited by Vicki L. Ruíz and John R. Chávez. Champaign: University of Illinois Press, 2008.

Chávez, Marisela R. "'We Have a Long, Beautiful History': Chicana Feminist Trajectories and Legacies." In *No Permanent Waves: Recasting U.S. Feminist History,* edited by Nancy A. Hewitt. New Brunswick, NJ: Rutgers University Press, 2010.

Chávez-García, Miroslava. *Negotiating Conquest: Gender and Power in California, 1770s to 1880s.* Tucson: University of Arizona Press, 2006.

Chávez-García, Miroslava. *States of Delinquency: Race and Science in the Making of California's Juvenile Justice System.* Berkeley: University of California Press, 2012.

Chávez-García, Miroslava."The Interdisciplinary Project of Chicana History: Looking Back, Moving Forward." *Pacific Historical Review* 82, no. 4 (November 2013): 193–228.

Clawson, Mary Ann. *Constructing Brotherhood: Class, Gender, and Fraternalism.* Princeton, NJ: Princeton University Press, 1989.

Cockcroft, James D. *Intellectual Precursors of the Mexican Revolution, 1900–1913.* Austin: University of Texas Press, 1968.

Coerver, Don M., and Linda B. Hall. *Tangled Destinies: Latin America and the United States.* Dialogos Series. Albuquerque: University of New Mexico Press, 1999.

Cohen, Deborah. *Braceros: Migrant Citizens and Transnational Subjects in the Postwar United States and Mexico.* Chapel Hill: University of North Carolina Press, 2011.

Cole, Stephanie, and Alison M. Parker, eds. *Beyond Black and White: Race, Ethnicity, and Gender in the U.S. South and Southwest.* College Station: Texas A&M University Press, 2003.

Cooper, John Milton Jr. *Pivotal Decades: The United States, 1900–1920.* New York: W. W. Norton, 1992.

Coronado, Raúl. *A World Not to Come: A History of Latino Writing and Print Culture.* Cambridge, MA: Harvard University Press, 2013.

Cott, Nancy F. *The Bonds of True Womanhood: "Women's Sphere" in New England, 1780–1835.* 2nd ed. New Haven, CT: Yale University Press, 1997.

Cott, Nancy F. *The Grounding of Modern Feminism.* New Haven, CT: Yale University Press, 1987.

Croxdale, Richard. "The 1938 San Antonio Pecan Sheller's Strike." In *Women in the Texas Workforce: Yesterday and Today,* edited by Richard Croxdale and Melissa Hield. Austin: People's History in Texas, 1979.

Croxdale, Richard, and Meslissa Hield, eds. *Women in the Texas Workforce: Yesterday and Today.* Austin: People's History in Texas, 1979.

Cuellár, Carlos. *Stories from the Barrio: A History of Mexican Fort Worth.* Fort Worth: Texas Christian University Press, 2004.

Davis, Allen F., and Harold D. Woodman, eds. *Conflict and Consensus in Early American History.* 8th ed. Lexington, MA: C. Heath, 1992.

Dawley, Alan. *Struggles for Justice: Social Responsibility and the Liberal State.* Rev. ed. Cambridge, MA: Belknap Press of Harvard University Press, 1993.

Deans-Smith, Susan and Ilona Katzew. "Introduction: The Alchemy of Race in Mexican America." In *Race and Classification: The Case of Mexican America,* edited by Ilona Katzew and Susan Deans-Smith. Stanford, CA: Stanford University Press, 2009.

Del Castillo, Adelaida R. *Between Borders: Essays on Mexicana/Chicana History.* La Mujer Latina Series. Encino, CA: Floricanto Press, 1990.

De la Torre, Adela, and Beatríz M. Pesquera, eds. *Building with Our Hands: New Directions in Chicana Studies.* Berkeley: University of California Press, 1993.

De León, Arnoldo. *The Tejano Community, 1836–1900.* Dallas, TX: Southern Methodist University Press, 1982.

De León, Arnoldo. *They Called Them Greasers: Anglo Attitudes toward Mexicans in Texas, 1821–1900.* Austin: University of Texas Press, 1983.

De León, Arnoldo, ed. *War along the Border: The Mexican Revolution and Tejano Communities.* University of Houston Series in Mexican American Studies, Center for Mexican American Studies. College Station: Texas A&M Press, 2012.

De León, Arnoldo. "Whither Tejano History: Origins, Development, and Status." *Southwestern Historical Quarterly* 106, no. 3 (2003): 349–364.

Delgado, Grace Peña. *Making the Chinese Mexican: Global Migration, Localism, and Exclusion in the US-Mexico Borderlands.* Stanford, CA: Stanford University Press, 2012.

Deutsch, Sarah. *No Separate Refuge: Culture, Class, and Gender on an Anglo-Hispanic Frontier in the American Southwest, 1880–1940*. New York: Oxford University Press, 1987.

Dumenil, Lynn. *Freemasonry and American Culture, 1880–1930*. Princeton, NJ: Princeton University Press, 1984.

Dussel, Enrique. *The Invention of the Americas: Eclipse of "the Other" and the Myth of Modernity*. Translated by Michael D. Barber. New York: Continuum, 1995.

Dysart, Jane. "Mexican Women in San Antonio, 1830–1860: The Assimilation Process." *Western Historical Association* 7 (October 1976): 365–377.

Engstrand, Iris H. W. "In Virtual Search of the Spanish Borderlands." *Historian* 66, no. 3 (2004): 501–508.

Escobar, Edward J. *Race, Police, and the Making of a Political Identity: Mexican Americans and the Los Angeles Police Department, 1900–1945*. Berkeley: University of California Press, 1999.

Escobedo, Elizabeth R. *From Coveralls to Zoot Suits: The Lives of Mexican American Women on the World War II Home Front*. Chapel Hill: University of North Carolina Press, 2013.

Escobedo, Elizabeth R. "The Pachuca Panic: Sexual and Cultural Battlegrounds in World War II." *Western Historical Quarterly* 38, no. 2 (Summer 2007): 133–156.

Espinosa, Gastón. "'El Azteca': Francisco Olazábal and Latino Pentecostal Charisma, Power, and Faith Healing in the Borderlands." *Journal of the American Academy of Religion* 67, no. 3 (September 1999): 597–616.

Espinosa, Gastón, and Mario T. García, eds. *Mexican American Religions: Spirituality, Activism, and Culture*. Durham, NC: Duke University Press, 2008.

Evans, Sara M. *Born for Liberty: A History of Women in America*. New York: Free Press, 1989.

Fernández, Delia. "Becoming Latino: Mexican and Puerto Rican Community Formation in Grand Rapids, Michigan, 1926–1964." *Michigan Historical Review* 39, no. 1 (Spring 2013): 71–100.

Fernández, Lilia. *Brown in the Windy City: Mexicans and Puerto Ricans in Postwar Chicago*. Chicago: University of Chicago Press, 2012.

Flores, Lori A. "A Community of Limits and the Limits of Community: MALDEF's Chicana Rights Project, Empowering the 'Typical Chicana,' and the Question of Civil Rights, 1974–1983." *Journal of American Ethnic History* 27, no. 3 (2008): 81–110.

Flores, Lori A. "An Unladylike Strike Fashionably Clothed: Mexicana and Anglo Women Garment Workers against Tex-Son, 1959–1963." *Pacific Historical Review* 78, no. 3 (August 2009): 367–402.

Flores, Lori A. *Grounds for Dreaming: Mexican Americans, Mexican Immigrants, and the California Farmworker Movement*. The Lamar Series in Western History. New Haven, CT: Yale University Press, 2016.

Flores Magón, Enrique. *Frente Al Enemigo*. México D.F.: Ediciones Antorcha, 1987.

Foley, Douglas E., Clarice Mora, Donald E. Post, and Ignacio Lozano. *From Peones to Politics: Class and Ethnicity in a South Texas Town, 1900–1987*. Center for Mexican American Studies Monograph, no. 3, rev. ed. Austin: University of Texas Press, 1988.

Foley, Neil. "Becoming Hispanic: Mexican Americans and the Faustian Pact with Whiteness." In *Reflexiones 1997: New Directions in Mexican American Studies*, edited by Neil Foley. Austin: University of Texas Press, 1998.

Foley, Neil. *Quest for Equality: The Failed Promise of Black-Brown Solidarity*. Cambridge, MA: Harvard University Press, 2010.

Foley, Neil, ed. *Reflexiones 1997: New Directions in Mexican American Studies*. Austin: University of Texas Press, 1998.

Foley, Neil. *The White Scourge: Mexicans, Blacks, and Poor Whites in Texas Cotton Culture*. Berkeley: University of California Press, 1997.

Fowler-Salamini, Heather and Mary Kay Vaughan, eds. *Women of the Mexican Countryside, 1850–1990. Creating Spaces, Shaping Transitions*. Tucson: University of Arizona Press, 1994.

Fox, Claire F. "Commentary: The Transnational Turn and the Hemispheric Return." *American Literary History* 18, no. 3 (2006): 638–647.

Fredrickson, George M. *Racism: A Short History*. Princeton, NJ: Princeton University Press, 2002.

Fredrickson, George M. *The Black Image in the White Mind: The Debate on Afro-American Character and Destiny, 1817–1914.* Middletown, CT: Wesleyan University Press, 1987. First published 1971 by Harper Row, Publishers.

Fredrickson, George M. *White Supremacy: A Comparative Study in American and South African History.* Oxford: Oxford University Press, 1981.

Freedman, Estelle B. *Maternal Justice: Miriam Van Waters and the Female Reform Tradition.* Chicago: University of Chicago Press, 1996.

Freedman, Estelle B. "Separatism Revisited: Women's Institutions, Social Reform, and the Career of Miriam Van Waters." In *U.S. History as Women's History: New Feminist Essays,* edited by Linda K. Kerber, Alice Kessler-Harris, and Kathryn Kish Sklar. Chapel Hill: University of North Carolina Press, 1995.

Fregoso, Rosa Linda. *MeXicana Encounters.* Vol. 12. American Crossroads. Berkeley: University of California Press, 2003.

French, William E. *A Peaceful and Working People: Manners, Morals, and Class Formation in Northern Mexico.* Albuquerque: University of New Mexico Press, 1996.

French, William E. "Imagining and the Cultural History of Nineteenth-Century Mexico." *Hispanic American Historical Review* 79, no. 2 (1999): 249–267.

García, Ignacio M. *Chicanismo: The Forging of a Militant Ethos among Mexican Americans.* Tucson: University of Arizona Press, 1997.

García, Ignacio M. *Hector P. García: In Relentless Pursuit of Justice.* Houston: Arte Público Press, 2003.

García, Ignacio M. *White but Not Equal: Mexican Americans, Jury Discrimination, and the Supreme Court.* Tucson: University of Arizona Press, 2009.

García, Juan R. *Mexicans in the Midwest, 1900–1932.* Tucson: University of Arizona Press, 1996.

García, Mario T. *Católicos Resistance and Affirmation in Chicano Catholic History.* Austin: University of Texas Press, 2008.

García, Mario T. *Desert Immigrants: The Mexicans of El Paso, 1880–1920.* New Haven, CT: Yale University Press, 1981.

García, Mario T. "*La Frontera*: The Border as Symbol and Reality in Mexican American Thought." *Mexican Studies/Estudios Mexicanos* 1 (Summer 1985): 195–225.

García, Mario T. *Mexican Americans: Leadership, Ideology, and Identity.* New Haven, CT: Yale University Press, 1989.

García, Mario T., with Sal Castro. *Blowout! Sal Castro and the Chicano Struggle for Educational Justice.* Chapel Hill: University of North Carolina Press, 2011.

García, Matt. *A World of Its Own: Race, Labor, and Citrus in the Making of Greater Los Angeles, 1900–1970.* Chapel Hill: University of North Carolina Press, 2002.

García, Matt. *From the Jaws of Victory: The Triumph and Tragedy of Cesar Chávez and the Farm Worker Movement.* Berkeley: University of California Press, 2014.

García, Richard A. *Rise of the Mexican American Middle Class: San Antonio, 1921–1939.* College Station: Texas A&M Press, 1991.

Garcilazo, Jeffrey M. "McCarthyism, Mexican Americans, and the Los Angeles Committee for Protection of the Foreign-Born, 1950–1954." *Western Historical Quarterly* 32, no. 3 (Fall 2001): 273–295.

Garza-Falcón, Leticia. *Gente Decente: A Borderlands Response to the Rhetoric of Dominance.* Austin: University of Texas Press, 1998.

Gellner, Ernest. *Nations and Nationalism.* Ithaca, NY: Cornell University Press, 1983.

Giddings, Paula. *When and Where I Enter: The Impact of Black Women on Race and Sex in America.* 2nd ed. New York: William Morrow Paperbacks, 1996.

Gilmore, Glenda. *Gender and Jim Crow: Women and the Politics of White Supremacy in North Carolina, 1896–1920.* Chapel Hill: University of North Carolina Press, 1996.

Ginzburg, Lori. *Women and the Work of Benevolence: Morality, Politics, and Class in the 19th Century United States.* Yale Historical Publications Series. New Haven, CT: Yale University Press, 1990.

Gómez, Laura F. *Manifest Destinies: The Making of the Mexican American Race.* New York: New York University Press, 2007.

Gómez-Quiñones, Juan. *Chicano Politics: Reality and Promise, 1940–1990.* Albuquerque: University of New Mexico Press, 1990.

Gómez-Quiñones, Juan. *Roots of Chicano Politics, 1600–1940.* Albuquerque: University of New Mexico Press, 1994.

Gómez-Quiñones, Juan. *Sembradores: Ricardo Flores Magón y El Partido Liberal Mexicano: A Eulogy and Critique.* Chicano Studies Center Publications Monograph, no. 5. Los Angeles: University of California, 1973.

González, Deena J. *Refusing the Favor: The Spanish-Mexican Women of Santa Fe, 1820–1880.* New York: Oxford University Press, 1999.

González, Deena J. "Las Tules of Image and Reality: Euro-American Attitudes and Legend Formation on a Spanish-Mexican Frontier." In *Building with Our Hands: New Directions in Chicana Studies,* edited by Adela de la Torre and Beatriz M. Pesquera, 75–90. Berkeley: University of California Press, 1993.

Gonzales, Manuel G. *Mexicanos: A History of Mexicans in the United States.* Bloomington: Indiana University Press, 1999.

Gonzales, Manuel G. *The Hispanic Elite of the Southwest.* Southwestern Studies Series, no. 86. El Paso: University of Texas at El Paso Press, 1989.

González, Gabriela. "Carolina Munguía and Emma Tenayuca: The Politics of Benevolence and Radical Reform, 1930s." In *Gender on the Borderlands: The Frontier Reader,* edited by Antonia Castañeda, Susan H. Armitage, Patricia Hart, and Karen Weatheron, 200–229. Lincoln: University of Nebraska Press, 2007.

González, Gabriela. "Jovita Idar: The Ideological Origins of a Transnational Advocate for La Raza." In *Texas Women: Their Histories, Their Lives,* edited by Elizabeth Hayes Turner, Stephanie Cole, and Rebecca Sharpless. Athens: University of Georgia Press, 2015.

González, Gilbert G. *Culture of Empire: American Writers, Mexico, and Mexican Immigrants, 1880–1930.* Austin: University of Texas Press, 2004.

González, Gilbert G. *Mexican Consuls and Labor Organizing: Imperial Politics in the American Southwest.* Austin: University of Texas Press, 1999.

González, Gilbert G. and Raúl A. Fernández. *A Century of Chicano History: Empire, Nations, and Migration.* Routledge: New York, 2003.

Gordillo, Luz María. *Mexican Women and the Other Side of Immigration: Engendering Transnational Ties.* Austin: University of Texas Press, 2011.

Gordon, Linda. *Pitied but Not Entitled: Single Mothers and the History of Welfare, 1890–1935.* New York: Free Press, 1994.

Graham, Don. *Kings of Texas: The 150-Year Saga of an American Ranching Empire.* New York: Wiley, 2004.

Graham, Richard. *The Idea of Race in Latin America, 1870–1940.* Austin: University of Texas Press, 1990.

Gray, LaGuana. *We Just Keep Running the Line: Black Southern Women and the Poultry Processing Industry.* Baton Rouge: Louisiana State University Press, 2014.

Green, George Norris. *The Establishment in Texas Politics: The Primitive Years, 1938–1957.* Norman: University of Oklahoma Press, 1979.

Green, Laurie B., John McKeirnan-González, and Martin Summers, eds. *Precarious Prescriptions: Contested Histories of Race and Health in North America.* Minneapolis: University of Minnesota Press, 2014.

Griswold del Castillo, Richard. *La Familia: Chicano Families in the Urban Southwest 1848 to the Present.* Notre Dame, IN: University of Notre Dame Press, 1984.

Gross, Ariela J. *What Blood Won't Tell: A History of Race on Trial in America.* Cambridge, MA: Harvard University Press, 2008.

Guerrero, Perla M. *Nuevo South: Latinas/os, Asians, and the Remaking of Place.* Austin: University of Texas Press, 2017.

Guglielmo, Thomas A. "Fighting for Caucasian Rights: Mexicans, Mexican Americans, and the Transnational Struggle for Civil Rights in World War II Texas. *Journal of American History* 92, no. 4 (March 2006).

Gutiérrez, David G. *Between Two Worlds: Mexican Immigrants in the United States*. Wilmington, DE: Rowman and Littlefield, 1996.

Gutiérrez, David G. "Migration, Emergent Ethnicity, and the 'Third Space': The Shifting Politics of Nationalism in Greater Mexico." *Journal of American History* (September 1999): 481–517.

Gutiérrez, David G. *Walls and Mirrors: Mexican Americans, Mexican Immigrants, and the Politics of Ethnicity*. Berkeley: University of California Press, 1995.

Gutiérrez, Ramón A. "Unraveling America's Hispanic Past: Internal Stratification and Class Boundaries." *Aztlán* 17 (Spring 1986): 79–102.

Gutiérrez, Ramón A., and Elliott Young. "Transnationalizing Borderlands History." *Western Historical Quarterly* 41, no. 1 (Spring 2010): 26–53.

Gutiérrez, Ramón, and Genaro Padilla, eds. *Recovering the U.S. Hispanic Literary Heritage*. Houston: Arte Público Press, 1993.

Haas, Lisbeth. *Conquests and Historical Identities in California, 1769–1936*. Berkeley: University of California Press, 1996.

Hager, William A. "The Plan de San Diego: Unrest on the Texas Frontier in 1915." *Arizona and the West* 5 (1963): 327–336.

Hale, Charles A. *The Transformation of Liberalism in Late Nineteenth-Century Mexico*. Princeton, NJ: Princeton University Press, 1989.

Hall, Linda B., and Don M. Coerver. *Revolution on the Border: The United States and Mexico,1910–1920*. Albuquerque: University of New Mexico Press, 1988.

Hämäläinen, Pekka, and Samuel Truett. "On Borderlands." *Journal of American History* 98, no. 2 (2011): 338–361.

Haney-López, Ian. *Racism on Trial: The Chicano Fight for Justice*. Cambridge, MA: Harvard University Press, 2004.

Haney-López, Ian. *White by Law: The Legal Construction of Race*. New York: New York University Press, 1996.

Harland-Jacobs, Jessica. "Hands across the Sea": The Masonic Network, British Imperialism, and the North Atlantic World." *Geographical Review* 899, no. 2 (April 1999): 237–253.

Harris III, Charles, and Louis Sadler. *The Border and the Revolution*. Las Cruces: New Mexico State University, 1988.

Harris, Charles III, and Louis Sadler. "The Plan of San Diego and the Mexican War Crisis of 1916: A Re-Examination." *Hispanic American Historical Review* 57 (1978): 381–408.

Hart, John Mason. *Anarchism and the Mexican Working Class, 1860–1931*. Austin: University of Texas Press, 1978.

Hart, John Mason. *Empire and Revolution: The Americans in Mexico since the Civil War*. Berkeley: University of California Press, 2002.

Hernández, José Angel. *Mexican American Colonization during the Nineteenth Century: A History of the US-Mexico Borderlands*. New York: Cambridge University Press, 2012.

Hernández, Kelly Lytle. "Borderlands and the Future History of the American West." *Western Historical Quarterly* 42, no. 3 (2011): 325–330.

Hernández, Kelly Lytle. *Migra! A History of the US Border Patrol*. Berkeley: University of California Press, 2010.

Hernández, Kelly Lytle. "The Crimes and Consequences of Illegal Immigration: A Cross-Border Examination of Operation Wetback, 1943 to 1954." *Western Historical Quarterly* 37, no. 4 (Winter 2006): 421–444.

Hernández, Soñia. *Working Women into the Borderlands*. College Station: Texas A&M University Press, 2014.

Hernández Chávez, Alicia. *Mexico: A Brief History*. Translated by Andy Klatt. Berkeley: University of California Press, 2006.

Herzog, Lawrence A. *Changing Boundaries in the Americas: New Perspectives on the U.S.-Mexican, Central American, and South American Borders*. San Diego: Center for U.S.-Mexican Studies, University of California, 1992.

Hewitt, Nancy A., ed. *No Permanent Waves: Recasting U.S. Feminist History*. New Brunswick, NJ: Rutgers University Press, 2010.

Hewitt, Nancy A. and Suzanne Lebsock, eds. *Visible Women: New Essays on American Activism*. Urbana: University of Illinois Press, 1993.

Higginbotham, Evelyn Brooks. "African American Women and the Metalanguage of Race." *Signs* 17 (Winter 1992): 251–274.

Higginbotham, Evelyn Brooks. *Righteous Discontent: The Women's Movement in the Black Baptist Church, 1880–1920*. Cambridge, MA: Harvard University Press, 1993.

Hine, Darlene Clark. "We Specialize in the Wholly Impossible: The Philanthropic Work of Black Women." In *Lady Bountiful Revisited: Women, Philanthropy, and Power*, edited by Kathleen D. McCarthy. New Brunswick, NJ: Rutgers University Press, 1990.

Hinojosa, Felipe. *Latino Mennonites: Civil Rights, Faith, and Evangelical Culture*. Baltimore, MD: Johns Hopkins University Press, 2014.

Hinojosa, Gilberto Miguel. *A Borderlands Town in Transition: Laredo, 1755–1870*. College Station: Texas A&M University Press, 1983.

Hofstadter Richard. *The Age of Reform*. New York: Vintage, 1960.

Horsman, Reginald. *Race and Manifest Destiny: The Origins of American Racial Anglo-Saxonism*. Cambridge, MA: Harvard University Press, 1981.

Horton, Carol A. *Race and the Making of American Liberalism*. New York: Oxford University Press, 2005.

Hsu, Madeline Y. *Dreaming of Gold, Dreaming of Home: Transnationalism and Migration between the United States and South China, 1882–1943*. Stanford, CA: Stanford University Press, 2000.

Hurtado, Aida. *The Color of Privilege: Three Blasphemies on Race and Feminism*. Ann Arbor: University of Michigan Press, 1996.

Ignatiev, Noel. *How the Irish Became White*. New York: Routledge, 1995.

Innis-Jiménez, Michael. *Steel Barrio: The Great Mexican Migration to South Chicago, 1915–1940*. New York: New York University Press, 2013.

Isserman, Maurice. *If I Had a Hammer: The Death of the Old Left and the Birth of the New Left*. Urbana: University of Illinois Press, 1993.

Jackson, Walter A. *Gunnar Myrdal and America's Conscience: Social Engineering and Racial Liberalism, 1938–1987*. Chapel Hill: University of North Carolina Press, 1990.

Jameson, Elizabeth, and Susan Armitage, eds. *Writing the Range: Race, Class, and Culture in the Women's West*. Norman: University of Oklahoma Press, 1997.

Johnson, Benjamin Heber, *Revolution in Texas: How a Forgotten Rebellion and Its Bloody Suppression Turned Mexicans into Americans*. The Lamar Series in Western History. New Haven, CT: Yale University Press, 2005.

Johnson, Benjamin Heber. "The Cosmic Race in Texas: Racial Fusion, White Supremacy, and Civil Rights Politics." *Journal of American History* 98, no. 2 (September 2011): 404–419.

Johnson, Paul. *A Shopkeeper's Millennium: Society and Revivals in Rochester, New York, 1815–1837*. New York: Hill & Wang, 1979.

Kaplan, Caren, Norma Alarcón, and Minoo Moallem, eds. *Between Woman and Nation: Nationalisms, Transnational Feminisms, and the State*. Durham, NC: Duke University Press, 1999.

Kaplowitz, Craig A. *LULAC, Mexican Americans, and National Policy*. Fronteras Series. College Station: Texas A&M Press, 2005.

Katz, Friedrick. "The Liberal Republic and the Porfiriato, 1867–1910." In *Mexico since Independence*, edited by Leslie Bethell, 49–124. London: Cambridge University Press, 1991.

Katz, Friedrick. *The Secret War in Mexico: Europe, the United States, and the Mexican Revolution*. Chicago: University of Chicago Press, 1981.

Katzew, Ilona, and Susan Deans-Smith, eds. *Race and Classification: The Case of Mexican America*. Stanford, CA: Stanford University Press, 2009.

Kearney, Milo, and Anthony Knopp. *Border Cuates: A History of the U.S.-Mexican Twin Cities.* Austin, TX: Eakin Press, 1995.

Keen, Benjamin. *A History of Latin America.* Boston: Houghton Mifflin, 1992.

Kerber, Linda K. "The Republican Mother." In *Women's America: Refocusing the Past,* edited by Linda K. Kerber and Jane Sherron DeHart, 4th ed., 89–95. New York: Oxford University Press, 1995.

Kerber, Linda K. *Women of the Republic: Intellect and Ideology in Revolutionary America.* Chapel Hill: University of North Carolina Press, 1980.

Linda K. Kerber and Jane Sherron DeHart, eds. *Women's America: Refocusing the Past.* 4th ed. New York: Oxford University Press, 1995.

Kerber, Linda K., Alice Kessler-Harris, and Kathryn Kish Sklar, eds. *U.S. History as Women's History: New Feminist Essays.* Chapel Hill: University of North Carolina Press, 1995.

Knight, Alan. *The Mexican Revolution: Porfirians, Liberals, and Peasants.* Cambridge: Cambridge University Press, 1986.

Knight, Alan. *The Mexican Revolution: Counter-Revolution and Reconstruction.* Vol. 2. Cambridge: Cambridge University Press, 1986.

Kolko, Gabriel. *The Triumph of Conservatism: A Reinterpretation of American History, 1900–1916.* New York: Free Press, 1963.

Koven, Seth, and Sonya Michel, eds. *Mothers of a New World: Maternalist Politics and the Origins of Welfare States.* New York: Routledge, 1993.

Kreneck, Thomas H. *Mexican American Odyssey: Félix Tijerina, Entrepreneur and Civic Leaders, 1905–1965.* College Station: Texas A&M University Press, 2001.

Krochmal, Max. *Blue Texas: The Making of a Multiracial Democratic Coalition in the Civil Rights Era.* Chapel Hill: University of North Carolina Press, 2016.

Langham, Thomas C. "Border Trials: Ricardo Flores Magón and the Mexican Liberals. *Southwestern Studies* 65 (1981): 14–25.

Las Mujeres en la Revolución Mexicana: 1884–1920. México, D.F.: Cámara de Diputados, LV Legislatura, Instituto Nacional de Estudios Históricos de la Revolución Mexicana, 1992.

Lasch, Christopher. *Haven in a Heartless World: The Family Besieged.* New York: Basic Books, 1977.

Lau, Ana, and Carmen Ramos. *Mujeres y la Revolución, 1900–1917.* México, D.F.: Instituto Nacional de Estudios Históricos de la Revolución Mexicana, 1993.

Lau Jaiven, Ana. "La Participación de las Mujeres en la Revolución Mexicana: Juana Belén Gutiérrez de Mendoza (1875–1942)." *Diálogos Revista Electrónica de Historia* 5, nos. 1–2 (April–August 2005): 5.

Lawhn, Juanita Luna., "The Mexican Revolution and the Women of *El México de Afuera,* the Pan American Round Table, and the *Cruz Azul Mexicana.*" In *War Along the Border: The Mexican Revolution and Tejano Communities,* edited by Arnoldo de León. University of Houston Series in Mexican American Studies, Center for Mexican American Studies. College Station: Texas A&M Press, 2012.

Lebsock, Suzanne. *The Free Women of Petersburg: Status and Culture in a Southern Town, 1784–1860.* New York: W. W. Norton, 1985.

Lee, Shelley Sang-Hee. *Claiming the Oriental Gateway: Prewar Seattle and Japanese America.* Philadelphia: Temple University Press, 2012.

Levario, Miguel Antonio. *Militarizing the Border: When Mexicans Became the Enemy.* College Station: Texas A&M University Press, 2012.

Leys Stepan, Nancy. "The Hour of Eugenics": Race, Gender, and Nation in Latin America.* Ithaca, NY: Cornell University Press, 1991.

Limerick, Patricia Nelson. *The Legacy of Conquest: The Unbroken Past of the American West.* New York: W. W. Norton, 1987.

Limón, José E. *American Encounters: Greater Mexico, the United States, and the Erotics of Culture.* Boston: Beacon Press, 1998.

Limón, José E. "El Primer Congreso Mexicanista de 1911: A Precursor to Contemporary Chicanismo." *Aztlán* 5, nos. 1–2 (Spring–Fall, 1974): 85–117.

Lomas, Clara. "Transborder Discourse." In *Gender on the Borderlands: The Frontier Reader*, edited by Antonia Castañeda, Susan H. Armitage, Patricia Hart, and Karen Weatheron, 200–229. Lincoln: University of Nebraska Press, 2007.

Lomnitz-Adler, Claudio. *Deep Mexico, Silent Mexico: An Anthropology of Nationalism*. Minneapolis: University of Minnesota Press, 2001.

López, Sarah Lynn. *The Remittance Landscape: Spaces of Migration in Rural Mexico and Urban USA*. Chicago: University of Chicago Press, 2014.

Lorey, David E. *The U.S.-Mexican Border in the Twentieth Century: A History of Economic and Social Transformation*. Wilmington, DE: SR Books, 1999.

Loza, Mireya. *Defiant Braceros: How Migrant Workers Fought for Racial, Sexual, and Political Freedom*. Chapel Hill: University of North Carolina Press, 2016.

Macías, Anna. *Against All Odds: The Feminist Movement in Mexico to 1940*. Westport, CT: Greenwood Press, 1982.

MacLachlan, Colin M. *Anarchism and the Mexican Revolution: The Political Trials of Ricardo Flores Magón in the United States*. Berkeley: University of California Press, 1991.

MacLachlan, Colin M., and William H. Beezley, eds. *El Gran Pueblo: A History of Greater Mexico*. Englewood Cliffs, NJ: Prentice Hall, 1994.

Mankiller, Wilma, et al., eds. "Liberalism" and "Republicanism." In *The Reader's Companion to U.S. Women's History*, 344, 514–515. Boston: Houghton Mifflin, 1999.

Mantler, Gordon Keith. *Power to the Poor: Black-Brown Coalition and the Fight for Economic Justice, 1960–1974*. Chapel Hill: University of North Carolina Press, 2013.

Mariscal, George. *Brown-Eyed Children of the Sun: Lessons from the Chicano Movement, 1965–1975*. Albuquerque: University of New Mexico Press, 2005.

Márquez, Benjamín. *LULAC: The Evolution of a Mexican American Political Organization*. Austin: University of Texas Press, 1993.

Márquez, Raquel R., and Harriett D. Romo, eds. *Transformations of La Familia on the U.S.-Mexico Border*. Notre Dame, IN: University of Notre Dame Press, 2008.

Martínez, Anne M. *Catholic Borderlands: Mapping Catholicism onto American Empire, 1905–1935*. Lincoln: University of Nebraska Press, 2014.

Martínez, María Elena. *Genealogical Fictions: Limpieza de Sangre, Religion and Gender in Colonial Mexico*. Stanford CA: Stanford University Press, 2008.

Martínez, Oscar J. *Border People: Life and Society in the U.S.-Mexico Borderlands*. Tucson: University of Arizona Press, 1994.

Martínez, Oscar J. *Troublesome Border*. Tucson: University of Arizona Press, 1988.

Martínez, Oscar J., ed. *U.S.-Mexico Borderlands: Historical and Contemporary Perspectives*. Jaguar Books on Latin America, no. 11. Wilmington, DE: Scholarly Resources, 1996.

Martínez, Richard Edward. *PADRES: The National Chicano Priest Movement*. Austin: University of Texas Press, 2005.

Martínez-Catsam, Ana Luisa. "Frontier of Dissent: El Regidor, the Regime of Porfirio Díaz, and the Transborder Community." *Southwestern Historical Quarterly* 112, no. 4 (2009): 388–408.

Martínez-Matsuda, Verónica. "'A Transformation for Migrants': Mexican Farmworkers and Federal Health Reform during the New Deal Era." In *Precarious Prescriptions*, 185–210. Contested Histories of Race and Health in North America. Minneapolis: University of Minnesota Press, 2014.

Matovina, Timothy. *Guadalupe and Her Faithful: Latino Catholics in San Antonio, from Colonial Origins to the Present*. Baltimore, MD: Johns Hopkins University Press, 2005.

Matthaei, Julie A. *An Economic History of Women in America: Women's Work, the Sexual Division of Labor, and the Development of Capitalism*. New York: Schocken Books, 1982.

McArthur, Judith N. *Creating a New Woman: The Rise of Southern Women's Progressive Culture in Texas, 1893–1918*. Urbana: University of Illinois Press, 1998.

McCarthy, Kathleen D., ed. *Lady Bountiful Revisited: Women, Philanthropy, and Power*. New Brunswick, NJ: Rutgers University Press, 1990.

McGerr, Michael. *A Fierce Discontent: The Rise and Fall of the Progressive Movement in America, 1870–1920.* New York: Oxford University Press, 2003.

McKiernan-González, John. *Fevered Measures: Public Health and Race at the Texas Mexico Border, 1848–1942.* Durham, NC: Duke University Press, 2012.

Medina, Lara. *Las Hermanas: Chicana/Latina Religious-Political Activism in the U.S. Catholic Church.* Philadelphia: Temple University Press, 2004.

Meeks, Eric V. *Border Citizens: The Making of Indians, Mexicans, and Anglos in Arizona.* Austin: University of Texas Press, 2007.

Menchaca, Martha. *Naturalizing Mexican Immigrants: A Texas History.* Austin: University of Texas Press, 2011.

Menchaca, Martha. *Recovering History, Constructing Race: The Indian, Black, and White Roots of Mexican Americans.* Joe R. and Teresa Lozano Long Series in Latin American and Latino Art and Culture. Austin: University of Texas Press, 2002.

Mendieta Alatorre, Angeles, ed. *Juana Belén Gutiérrez (1875–1942): extraordinaría precursora de la Revolución Mexicana.* Cuernavaca, Mor: Impresores de Morelos, 1983.

Mendoza, Alexander. "'For Our Own Best Interests': Nineteenth-Century Laredo Tejanos, Military Service, and the Development of American Nationalism." *Southwestern Historical Quarterly* 115, no. 2 (October 2011): 125–152.

Meyer, Michael C., and William H. Beezley, eds. *The Oxford History of Mexico.* New York: Oxford University Press, 2000.

Meyer, Michael C., and William L. Sherman. *The Course of Mexican History.* 4th ed. New York: Oxford University Press, 1991.

Milkis, Sidney M., and Jerome M. Mileur, eds. *Progressivism and the New Democracy.* Political Development of the American Nation: Studies in Politics and History. Amherst: University of Massachusetts, 1999.

Milkis, Sidney M. eds. *The New Deal and the Triumph of Liberalism.* The Political Development of the American Nation: Studies in Politics and History. Amherst: University of Massachusetts Press, 2002.

Miller, Char, and Heywood T. Sanders. *Urban Texas: Politics and Development.* Texas A&M Southwestern Studies, no. 8. College Station: Texas A&M Press, 1990.

Miller, Darlis A. "Cross-Cultural Marriages in the Southwest: The New Mexico Experience, 1846–1900." *New Mexico Historical Review* 57 (October 1982): 33559.

Miller, Nicola. *In the Shadow of the State: Intellectuals and the Quest for National Identity in Twentieth-Century Spanish America.* Critical Studies in Latin American and Iberian Cultures. London: Verso, 1999.

Mirande, Alfredo, and Evangelina Enrique. *La Chicana: The Mexican-American Woman.* Chicago: University of Chicago Press, 1979.

Mireles, Jovita González, and Eve Raleigh. *Caballero: A Historical Novel.* Edited by José E. Limón and María Cotera. College Station: Texas A&M University Press, 1996.

Mireles, Jovita González. *Dew on the Thorn.* Edited and introduced by José E. Limón. Recovering the U.S. Hispanic Literary Heritage Project Publication. Houston: Arte Público Press, 1997.

Mitchell, Stephanie, and Patience A. Schell, eds. *The Women's Revolution in Mexico, 1910–1953.* Lanham, MD: Rowman and Littlefield, 2007.

Mitter, Rana. "Modernity." In *The Palgrave Dictionary of Transnational History: From the Mid-19th Century to the Present Day,* edited by Akira Iriye and Pierre-Yves Saunier, 720–723. London: Macmillan, 2009.

Mohl, Raymond. "Latinization in the Heart of Dixie: Hispanics in Late-Twentieth Century Alabama." *Alabama Review* 87, no. 4 (2002): 243–274.

Molina, Natalia. "Examining Chicana/o History through a Relational Lens." *Pacific Historical Review* 82, no. 4 (November 2013): 520–541.

Molina, Natalia. *Fit to Be Citizens? Public Health and Race in Los Angeles, 1879–1939.* Berkeley: University of California Press, 2006.

Molina, Natalia. *How Race Is Made in America: Immigration, Citizenship, and the Historical Power of Racial Scripts.* Berkeley: University of California Press, 2013.

Molina, Natalia. "The Long Arc of Dispossession: Racial Capitalism and Contested Notions of Citizenship in the US-Mexico Borderlands in the Early Twentieth Century." *Western Historical Quarterly* 45, no. 4 (Winter 2014): 431–447.

Molina, Natalia. "The Power of Racial Scripts: What the History of Mexican Immigration to the United States Teaches Us about Relational Notions of Race." *Latino Studies* 8, no. 2 (2010): 156–175.

Monroy, Douglas. "Fence Cutters, *Sediciosos,* and First-Class Citizens: Mexican Radicalism in America." In *The Immigrant Left in the United States,* edited by Paul Buhle and Dan Georgakas. Suny Series in American Labor History. New York: State University of New York, 1996.

Monroy, Dougla. *Rebirth: Mexican Los Angeles from the Great Migration to the Great Depression.* Berkeley: University of California Press, 1999.

Montejano, David. *Anglos and Mexicans in the Making of Texas, 1836–1986.* Austin: University of Texas Press, 1987.

Montejano, David. *Quixote's Soldiers: A Local History of the Chicano Movement, 1966–1981.* Austin: University of Texas Press, 2010.

Montoya, María E. "And Now, about the Women . . ." *Western Historical Quarterly* 38, no. 3 (2007): 313–317.

Mora, Anthony P. *Border Dilemmas: Racial and National Uncertainties in New Mexico, 1848–1912.* Durham: NC: Duke University Press, 2011.

Mora, Anthony P. "Resistance and Accommodation in a Border Parish." *Western Historical Quarterly* 36, no. 3 (Autumn 2005): 301–326.

Mora, Magdalena, and Adelaida R. Del Castillo, eds. *Mexican Women in the United States: Struggles Past and Present.* Los Angeles: Chicano Studies Research Publications, University of California, 1980.

Mora-Torres, Juan. *The Making of the Mexican Border: The State, Capitalism, and Society in Nuevo León, 1848–1910.* Austin: University of Texas Press, 2001.

Naison, Mark. "Remaking America: Communists and Liberals in the Popular Front." In *New Studies in the Politics and Culture of U.S. Communism,* edited by Michael E. Brown et al., 45–70 (New York: Monthly Review Press, 1993).

Newman, Louise Michele. *White Women's Rights: The Racial Origins of Feminism in the United States.* New York: Oxford University Press, 1999.

Nieto-Phillips, John M. *The Language of Blood: The Making of Spanish-American Identity in New Mexico, 1880s–1930s.* Albuquerque: University of New Mexico Press, 2004.

Nolan-Ferrell, Catherine. *Constructing Citizenship: Transnational Workers and Revolution on the Mexico-Guatemala Border, 1880–1950.* Tucson: University of Arizona Press, 2012.

Nugent, Daniel, ed. *Rural Revolt in Mexico: U.S. Intervention and the Domain of Subaltern Politics.* American Encounters/Global Interactions. 2nd expanded ed. Durham, NC: Duke University Press, 1998.

Olivas, Michael A., ed. *"Colored Men" and "Hombres Aqui": Hernández v. Texas and the Emergence of Mexican American Lawyering.* Houston: Arte Público Press, 2006.

Olivas, Michael A., ed. *In Defense of My People: Alonso S. Perales and the Development of Mexican-American Public Intellectuals.* Houston: Arte Público Press, 2012.

O'Malley, Illene V. *The Myth of the Revolution: Hero Cults and the Institutionalization of the Mexican State, 1920–1940.* Contributions to the Study of World History, no. 1. New York: Greenwood Press, 1986.

Omi, Michael, and Howard Winant. *Racial Formation in the United States from the 1960s to the 1990s.* 2nd ed. New York: Routledge, 1994.

Ong, Aihwa. *Flexible Citizenship: The Cultural Logistics of Transnationality.* Durham, NC: Duke University Press, 1999.

Ontiveros, Randy J. *In the Spirit of a New People: The Cultural Politics of the Chicano Movement.* New York: New York University Press, 2014.

Oropeza, Lorena. *¡Raza Si! ¡Guerra No! Chicano Protest and Patriotism during the Viet Nam War Era.* Berkeley: University of California Press, 2005.

Oropeza, Lorena. "The Heart of Chicano History: Reies López Tijerina as a Memory Entrepreneur." *The Sixties* 1, no. 1 (2008): 49–67.

Orozco, Cynthia E. "Alice Dickerson Montemayor: Feminism and Mexican American Politics in the 1930s." In *Writing the Range: Race, Class, and Culture in the Women's West*, edited by Elizabeth Jameson and Susan Armitage. Norman: University of Oklahoma Press, 1997.

Orozco, Cynthia E. *No Mexicans, Women, or Dogs Allowed: The Rise of the Mexican American Civil Rights Movement.* Austin: University of Texas Press, 2009.

Orozco, Cynthia E. "Regionalism, Politics, and Gender in Southwest History: The League of United Latin American Citizens' Expansion into New Mexico from Texas, 1929–1945." *Western Historical Quarterly* 29, no. 4 (Winter 1998): 459–483.

Overmyer-Velázquez, Mark, ed. *Beyond La Frontera: The History of Mexico-U.S. Migration.* New York: Oxford University Press, 2011.

Overmyer-Velázquez. "Good Neighbors and White Mexicans: Constructing Race and Nation on the Mexico-US Border." *Journal of American Ethnic History* 33, no. 1 (Fall 2013): 5–34.

Oxford Dictionary of Sociology, edited by John Scott and Gordon Marshall. Oxford: Oxford University Press, 2005, s.vv. "modernity" and "modernization theory," 421–423.

Pagán, Eduardo Obregón. *Murder at the Sleepy Lagoon: Zoot Suits, Race, and Riot in Wartime L.A.* Chapel Hill: University of North Carolina Press, 2003.

Painter, Nell Irvin. *Standing at Armageddon: The United States, 1877–1919.* 9th ed. New York: W. W. Norton, 1989.

Painter, Nell Irvin. *The History of White People.* New York: W.W. Norton, 2010.

Palomo Acosta, Teresa, and Ruthe Winegarten, *Las Tejanas: 300 Years of History.* Jack and Doris Smothers Series in Texas History, Life and Culture, no. 10. Austin: University of Texas Press, 2003.

Paredes, Américo. *Between Two Worlds.* Houston: Arte Público Press, 1991.

Paredes, Américo. *Folklore and Culture on the Texas-Mexican Border.* Austin: University of Texas Press, 1993.

Pascoe, Peggy. *Relations of Rescue: The Search for Female Moral Authority in the American West, 1874–1939.* New York: Oxford University Press, 1990.

Patiño, Jimmy. *Raza Sí, Migra No: Chicano Movement Struggles for Immigrant Rights in San Diego.* Durham, NC: University of North Carolina Press, 2017.

Peloso, Vincent C., and Barbara A. Tenenbaum, eds. *Liberals, Politics, and Power: State Formation in Nineteenth-Century Latin America.* Athens: University of Georgia Press, 1996.

Peña, Manuel H. *The Texas-Mexican Conjunto: History of a Working-Class Music.* Mexican American Monograph, no. 9. Austin: University of Texas Press, 1985.

Perales, Alonso S. *Are We Good Neighbors?* 1948. Reprint. New York: Arno Press, 1974.

Perales, Mónica. "Fighting to Stay in Smeltertown: Lead Contamination and Environmental Justice in a Mexican American Community." *Western Historical Quarterly* 39, no. 1 (2008): 41–63.

Perales, Mónica. *Smeltertown: Making and Remembering a Southwest Border Community.* Chapel Hill: University of North Carolina Press, 2010.

Pérez, Emma. "A La Mujer: A Critique of the Partido Liberal Mexicano's Gender Ideology on Women." In *Between Borders: Essays on Mexicana/Chicana History*, edited by Adelaida R. Del Castillo, 459–482. La Mujer Latina Series. Encino, CA: Floricanto Press, 1990.

Pérez, Emma. *The Decolonial Imaginary: Writing Chicanas into History.* Theories of Representation and Difference. Bloomington: Indiana University Press, 1999.

Petit, Jeanne. "Working for God, Country, and 'Our Poor Mexicans': Catholic Women and Americanization at the San Antonio National Catholic Community House, 1919–1924." *Journal of American Ethnic History* 34, no. 3 (2015): 5–33.

Pilcher, Jeffrey, M. *The Human Tradition in Mexico.* The Human Tradition around the World Series, no. 6. Rowman and Littlefield, 2002.

Pitti, Stephen J. *The Devil in Silicon Valley: Northern California, Race, and Mexican Americans.* Princeton, NJ: Princeton University Press, 2003.

Poyo, Gerald E., and Gilberto M. Hinojosa. "Spanish Texas and Borderlands Historiography in Transition: Implications for United States History." *Journal of American History* 75, no. 2 (1988): 393–416. doi:10.2307/1887864.

Pulido, Alberto López, Barbara Driscoll de Alvarado, and Carmen Samora, eds. *Moving beyond Borders: Julian Samora and the Establishment of Latino Studies.* Urbana: University of Illinois Press, 2009.

Pulido, Laura. *Black, Brown, Yellow, and Left: Radical Activism in Los Angeles.* Berkeley: University of California Press, 2006.

Purnell, Jennie. *Popular Movements and State Formation in Revolutionary Mexico: The Agraristas and Cristeros of Michoacán.* Durham, NC: Duke University Press, 1999.

Pycior, Julie Leininger. *Democratic Renewal and the Mutual Aid Legacy of US Mexicans.* College Station: Texas A&M University Press, 2014.

Pycior, Julie Leininger. *LBJ and Mexican Americans: The Paradox of Power.* Austin: University of Texas Press, 1997.

Quezada, J. Gilberto. *Border Boss: Manuel B. Bravo and Zapata County.* The Canseco Keck History Series, no. 1. College Station: Texas A& M University Press, 1999.

Quirk, Robert E. *The Mexican Revolution and the Catholic Church, 1910–1929.* Bloomington: Indiana University Press, 1973.

Quiroz, Anthony. *Claiming Citizenship: Mexican Americans in Victoria, Texas.* College Station: Texas A&M University Press, 2005.

Raat, Dirk, ed. *Mexico: From Independence to Revolution: 1810–1910.* Lincoln: University of Nebraska Press, 1982.

Raat, W. Dirk. *Mexico and the United States: Ambivalent Vistas.* 2d. ed. The United States and the American Series. Athens: University of Georgia Press, 1996.

Raat, W. Dirk. *Revoltosos: Mexico's Rebels in the United States, 1903–1923.* College Station: Texas A&M Press, 1981.

Ramírez, Catherine S. *The Women in the Zoot Suit: Gender, Nationalism, and the Cultural Politics of Memory.* Durham, NC: Duke University Press, 2009.

Ramírez, José A. *To the Line of Fire! Mexican Texans and World War I.* College Station: Texas A&M University Press, 2009.

Ramos, Henry A. J. *The American GI Forum: In Pursuit of the Dream, 1948–1893.* Arte Publico Press, 1998.

Ramos, Raúl A. *Beyond the Alamo: Forging Mexican Ethnicity in San Antonio, 1821– 1861.* Chapel Hill: University of North Carolina Press, 2009.

Ramos, Raúl A. "Chicano/a Challenges to Nineteenth-Century History." *Pacific Historical Review* 82, no. 4 (November 2013): 566–580.

Reisler, Mark. "Always the Laborer, Never the Citizen: Anglo Perceptions of the Mexican Immigrant during the 1920s." *Pacific Historical Review* 2 (May 1976).

Reisler, Mark. *By the Sweat of Their Brow: Mexican Immigrant Labor in the United States, 1900– 1940.* Westport, CT: Greenwood Press, 1976.

Reséndez, Andrés. *Changing National Identities at the Frontier: Texas and New Mexico, 1800–1850.* New York: Cambridge University Press, 2005.

Rips, Geoffrey, "Living History: Emma Tenayuca Tells Her Story." *Texas Observer*, 28 October 1983, 7–15.

Rivas-Rodríguez, Maggie, ed. *Mexican Americans and World War II.* Austin: University of Texas Press, 2005.

Rivas-Rodríguez, Maggie, and Emilio Zamora, eds. *Beyond the Latino World War II Hero: The Social and Political Legacy of a Generation.* Austin: University of Texas Press, 2009.

Rocha, Martha Eva. "The Faces of Rebellion: From Revolutionaries to Veterans in Nationalist Mexico." In *The Women's Revolution in Mexico, 1910–1953,* edited by Stephanie Mitchell and Patience A. Schell. Lanham: Rowman and Littlefield, 2007.

Rocha, Rodolfo. "The Tejano Revolt of 1915." In *Mexican Americans in Texas History*, edited by Emilio Zamora, Cynthia Orozco, and Rodolfo Rocha. Austin: Texas State Historical Association, 2000.

Rochín, Refugio I., and Dennis N. Valdés, eds. *Voices of a New Chicana/o History*. East Lansing: Michigan State University Press, 2000.

Rodgers, Daniel T. "In Search of Progressivism." *Reviews in American History* 10, no. 4 (December 1982): 113–132.

Rodríguez, Jaime E., and Kathryn Vincent., eds. *Common Border, Uncommon Paths: Race, Culture, and National Identity in U.S.-Mexican Relations*. Wilmington, DE: SR Books, 1997.

Rodríguez, Marc Simon. "A Movement Made of 'Young Mexican Americans Seeking Change': Critical Citizenship, Migration, and the Chicano Movement in Texas and Wisconsin." *Western Historical Quarterly* 34, no. 3 (Autumn 2003): 274–299.

Rodríguez, Marc Simon. *The Tejano Diaspora: Mexican Americanism and Ethnic Politics in Texas and Wisconsin*. Chapel Hill: University of North Carolina Press, 2011.

Rodríguez, Richard T. *Next of Kin: The Family of Chicano/a Cultural Politics*. Durham, NC: Duke University Press, 2009.

Roediger, David R. *The Wages of Whiteness: Race and the Making of the American Working Class*. London: Verso, 1999.

Roediger, David R. *Working toward Whiteness: How America's Immigrants Became White*. New York: Basic Books, 2005.

Romero, Yolanda. "Trini Gámez, the Texas Farm Workers, and Mexican American Community Empowerment: Toil and Trouble on the Texas South Plains." In *Mexican Americans in Texas History*, edited by Emilio Zamora, Cynthia Orozco, and Rodolfo Rocha. Austin: Texas State Historical Association, 2000.

Romo, Ricardo. *East Los Angeles: History of a Barrio*. Austin: University of Texas Press, 1983.

Rosales, F. Arturo. ¡*Pobre Raza! Violence, Mobilization, and Justice among México Lindo Immigrants, 1900–1936*. Austin: University of Texas Press, 1999.

Rosales, F. Arturo. "Shifting Self-Perceptions and Ethnic Consciousness among Mexicans in Houston, 1908–1946." *Aztlán* 16, nos. 1&2 (1987): 71–94.

Rosales, Rodolfo. *The Illusion of Inclusion: The Untold Political Story of San Antonio*. CMAS History, Culture, and Society. Austin: University of Texas Press, 2000.

Rosales, Steven. "Fighting the Peace at Home: Mexican American Veterans and the 1944 GI Bill of Rights." *Pacific Historical Review* 80, no. 4 (November 2011): 597–627.

Rosas, Ana Elizabeth. *Abrazando el Espíritu: Bracero Families Confront the US-Mexico Border*. Berkeley: University of California Press, 2014.

Rosenbaum, Robert J. *Mexicano Resistance in the Southwest*. William P. Clements Center for Southwest Studies. Dallas: Southern Methodist University Press, 1998.

Ruíz, Ramón Eduardo. *Labor and the Ambivalent Revolutionaries, 1911–1923* Baltimore: Johns Hopkins University Press, 1976.

Ruíz, Ramón Eduardo. *On the Rim of Mexico: Encounters of the Rich and Poor*. Boulder, CO: Westview Press, 2000.

Ruíz, Ramón Eduardo. *The Great Rebellion: Mexico 1905–1924*. Revolutions in the Modern World. New York: W. W. Norton, 1980.

Ruíz, Vicki. *Cannery Women, Cannery Lives: Mexican Women, Unionization, and the California Food Processing Industry, 1930–1950*. Albuquerque: University of New Mexico Press, 1987.

Ruíz, Vicki. *From Out of the Shadows: Mexican Women in Twentieth Century America*. New York: Oxford University Press, 1998.

Ruíz, Vicki. "Morena/o, blanca/o y café con leche: Racial Constructions in Chicana/o Historiography." *Mexican Studies/Estudios Mexicanos* 20, no. 2 (Summer 2004): 343–360.

Ruíz, Vicki. "Nuestra America: Latino History as United States History." *Journal of American History* 93, no. 3 (December 2006): 655–673.

Ruíz, Vicki. "Una Mujer Sin Fronteras: Luisa Moreno and Latina Labor Activism." *Pacific Historical Review* 73, no. 1 (February 2004): 1–20.

Ruíz, Vicki L., and John R. Chávez, eds. *Memories and Migrations: Mapping Boricua and Chicana Histories*. Champaign: University of Illinois Press, 2008.

Ruíz, Vicki L., and Ellen Carol Dubois. *Unequal Sisters: A Multi-Cultural Reader in U.S. Women's History*. New York: Routledge, 1994.

Ruíz, L. Vicki, and Susan Tiano, eds. *Women on the U.S.-Mexico Border: Responses to Change*. Thematic Studies in Latin America. Boston: Allen & Unwin, 1987.

Ruíz, Vicki L., and Virginia Sánchez Korrol, eds. *Latina Legacies: Identity, Biography, and Community*. New York: Oxford University Press, 2005.

Ryan, Mary. *Cradle of the Middle Class: The Family in Oneida County, New York, 1790–1865*. Cambridge: Cambridge University Press, reprint edition, 1983.

Sahlins, Peter. *Boundaries: The Making of France and Spain in the Pyrenees*. Berkeley: University of California Press, 1991.

Said, Edward. *Orientalism*. New York: Vintage, 1979.

Salas, Elizabeth. *Soldaderas in the Mexican Military: Myth and History*. Austin: University of Texas Press, 1990.

Saldaña-Portillo, María Josefina. "'How Many Mexicans [Is] a Horse Worth?' The League of United Latin American Citizens, Desegregation Cases, and Chicano Historiography." *South Atlantic Quarterly* 107, no. 4 (Fall 2008): 809–831.

Saldívar, José David. *Border Matters: Remapping American Cultural Studies*. American Crossroads. Berkeley: University of California Press, 1997.

Saldívar-Hull, Sonia. *Feminism on the Border: Chicana Gender Politics and Literature*. Berkeley: University of California Press, 2000.

Samponaro, Frank N., and Paul J. Vanderwood. *War Scare on the Rio Grande: Robert Runyon's Photographs of the Border Conflict, 1913–1916*. The Barker Texas History Center Series. Austin: Texas State Historical Association, 1992.

Sánchez, George J. *Becoming Mexican American: Ethnicity, Culture and Identity in Chicano Los Angeles, 1900–1945*. New York: Oxford University Press, 1993.

Sánchez, George J. "Edward R. Roybal and the Politics of Multiracialism." *Southern California Quarterly* 92, no. 1 (2010): 51–73.

Sánchez-Walsh, Arlene. *Latino Pentecostal Identity: Evangelical Faith, Self, and Society*. New York: Columbia University Press, 2003.

Sanders, Elizabeth. *Roots of Reform: Farmers, Workers, and the American State, 1877–1917*. Chicago: University of Chicago Press, 1999.

Sandos, James A. *Rebellion in the Borderlands: Anarchism and the Plan de San Diego, 1904–1923*. Norman: University of Oklahoma Press, 1992.

San Miguel, Guadalupe. *Brown, Not White: School Integration and the Chicano Movement in Houston*. College Station: Texas A&M University Press, 2001.

San Miguel, Guadalupe. *Chicana/o Struggles for Education: Activism in the Community*. College Station: Texas A&M University Press, 2013.

San Miguel, Guadalupe. *"Let All of Them Take Heed:" Mexican Americans and the Campaign for Educational Equality in Texas, 1910–1981*. Austin: University of Texas, 1987.

San Miguel, Guadalupe. *Tejano Proud: Texas-Mex Music in the Twentieth Century*. College Station: Texas A&M University Press, 2002.

Scharff, Virginia. "What's Love Got to Do with It? A New Turner Thesis." *Western Historical Quarterly* 40, no. 1 (2009): 5–21.

Schiller, Diana L. "The Fight to Clean Up San Antonio's Mexican Corrals, 1930–1950," Annual Bulletin, no. 15. Briscoe Library, University of Texas Health Science Center at San Antonio (Fall 1986).

Schmidt Camacho, Alicia R. *Migrant Imaginaries: Latino Cultural Politics in the U.S Mexico Borderlands*. New York: New York University Press, 2008.

Schott, Linda K. *Reconstructing Women's Thoughts: The Women's International League for Peace and Freedom before World War II*. Stanford, CA: Stanford University Press, 1997.

Scott, Anne F. "Most Invisible of All: Black Women's Voluntary Associations." *Journal of Southern History* 56, no. 1 (February 1990): 3–22.

Scott, Anne F. *Natural Allies: Women's Associations in American History.* Urbana: University of Illinois Press, 1993.

Scott, Joan. "Gender: A Useful Category of Historical Analysis." *American Historical Review* 91, no. 5 (December 1986): 1053–1075.

Sharpless, Rebecca. *Fertile Ground, Narrow Choices: Women on Texas Cotton Farms, 1900–1940.* Chapel Hill: University of North Carolina Press, 1999.

Sklar, Kathryn Kish. "The Historical Foundations of Women's Power in the Creation of the American Welfare State, 1830–1930." In *Mothers of a New World: Maternalist Politics and the Origins of Welfare States,* edited by Seth Koven and Sonya Michel. New York: Routledge, 1993.

Sloss-Vento, Adela. *Alonso S. Perales: His Struggles for the Rights of Mexican Americans.* San Antonio, TX: Artes Graficas, 1977.

Smith, Heather A., and Owen J. Furuseth. *Latinos in the New South: Transformations of Place.* Burlington, VT: Ashgate, 2006.

Smith, Robert Freeman. "The Díaz Era: Background to the Revolution of 1910." In W. *Mexico: From Independence to Revolution,* edited by Dirk Raat. Lincoln: University of Nebraska Press, 1982.

Soto, Shirlene. *Emergence of the Modern Mexican Woman: Her Participation in Revolution and Struggle for Equality, 1910–1940.* Women in the Revolution Series. Denver: Arden Press, 1990.

St. John, Rachel. *Line in the Sand: A History of the Western U.S.-Mexico Border.* Americans in the World. Princeton, NJ: Princeton University Press, 2011.

Stansell, Christine. "Women, Children, and the Uses of the Streets: Class and Gender Conflict in New York City, 1850–1860." In *Womens' America: Refocusing the Past,* 3rd ed., edited by Linda K. Kerber and Jane Sherron De Hart. New York: Oxford University Press, 1991.

Stephen, Lynn. "Expanding the Borderlands: Recent Studies on the U.S.-Mexico Border," edited by Rodolfo F. Acuña, Wayne A. Cornelius, Jessa M. Lewis, Tony Payan, Denise A. Segura, Patricia Zavella, and Samuel Truett. *Latin American Research Review* 44, no. 1 (2009): 266–277.

Stern, Alexandra Minna. "On the Road with Chicana/o History: From Aztlán to the Alamo and Back." *Pacific Historical Review* 82, no 4 (November 2013): 581–587.

Strachwitz, Chris, and James Nicolopulos, compilers. *Lydia Mendoza: A Family Autobiography.* Houston: Arte Público Press, 1993.

Telles, Edward M., Vilma Ortiz, and Joan W. Moore. *Generations of Exclusion: Mexican-Americans, Assimilation, and Race.* New York: Russell Sage Foundation, 2009.

Tenorio-Trillo, Mauricio. *Mexico at the World's Fairs: Crafting a Modern Nation* Berkeley: University of California Press, 1996.

Thomson, Guy P. C. *Patriotism, Politics, and Popular Liberalism in Nineteenth-Century Mexico: Juan Francisco Lucas and the Puebla Sierra.* Wilmington, DE: Scholarly Resources, 1999.

Thompson, Jerry. *Laredo: A Pictorial History.* Norfolk, VA: Donning Company, 1986.

Thompson, Jerry. *Cortina: Defending the Mexican Name in Texas.* Fronteras Series. College Station: Texas A&M University Press, 2007.

Thompson, Jerry, ed. *Juan Cortina and the Texas-Mexico Frontier, 1859–1877.* Southwestern Studies, no. 99. El Paso: Texas Western Press, University of Texas at El Paso, 1994.

Tijerina, Andrés. *Tejano Empire: Life on the South Texas Ranchos.* The Clayton Wheat Williams Texas Life Series, no. 7. College Station: Texas A&M University Press, 1998.

Tinker Salas, Miguel. *In the Shadow of the Eagles: Sonora and the Transformation of the Border during the Porfiriato.* Berkeley: University of California Press, 1997.

Torget, Andrew J. *Seeds of Empire: Cotton, Slavery, and the Transformation of the Texas Borderlands, 1800–1850.* Chapel Hill: University of North Carolina Press, 2015.

Trachtenberg, Alan. *The Incorporation of America: Culture and Society in the Gilded Age.* New York: Hill & Wang, 1982.

Treviño, Roberto R. "Prensa y patria: The Spanish-language Press and the Biculturation of the Tejano Middle Class, 1920–1940." *Western Historical Quarterly* 22 (November 1991): 451–472.

Treviño, Roberto R. *The Church in the Barrio: Mexican American Ethno-Catholicism in Houston.* Chapel Hill: University of North Carolina Press, 2006.

Truett, Samuel, and Elliott Young, eds. *Continental Crossroads: Remapping U.S.- Mexico Borderlands History*. Durham, NC: Duke University Press Books, 2004.

Truett, Samuel. *Fugitive Landscapes: The Forgotten History of the U.S.-Mexico Borderlands*. New Haven, CT: Yale University Press, 2008.

Truett, Samuel. "Neighbors by Nature: Rethinking Region, Nation, and Environmental History in the U.S.-Mexico Borderlands." *Environmental History* 2, no. 2 (1997): 160–178.

Tuñón Pablos, Julia. *Women in Mexico: A Past Unveiled*. Translations from Latin American Series. Translated by Alan Hynds. Austin: University of Texas Press, 1999.

Turner, Elizabeth Hayes. *Women, Culture, and Community: Religion and Reform in Galveston, 1880–1920*. New York: Oxford University Press, 1997.

Turner, Elizabeth Hayes, Stephanie Cole, and Rebecca Sharpless, eds. *Texas Women: Their Histories, Their Lives*. Athens: University of Georgia Press, 2015.

Turner, Frederick C. *The Dynamic of Mexican Nationalism*. Chapel Hill: University of North Carolina Press, 1968.

Tsu, Cecilia M. *Garden of the World: Asian Immigrants and the Making of Agriculture in California's Santa Clara Valley*. New York: Oxford University Press, 2013.

Tutino, John, ed. *Mexico and Mexicans in the Making of the United States*. Austin: University of Texas Press, 2012.

U, Eddy, "Modernization theory," In *The Palgrave Dictionary of Transnational History: From the Mid-19th Century to the Present Day*, edited by Akira Iriye and Pierre-Yves Saunier, 723–725. London: Macmillan, 2009.

Ulrich, Laurel Thatcher. *Good Wives: Image and Reality in the Lives of Women in Northern New England, 1650–1750*. New York: Vintage, 1991.

Valadés, José C. *El Joven Ricardo Flores Magon*. México, D.F.: Extemporaneos, 1983.

Valerio-Jiménez, Omar S. *River of Hope: Forging Identity and Nation in the Rio Grande Borderlands*. Durham, NC: Duke University Press, 2013.

Vallejo, Jody Aguis. *From Barrios to Burbs: The Making of the Mexican American Middle Class*. Stanford, CA: Stanford University Press, 2013.

Vargas, Zaragosa. *Crucible of Struggle: A History of Mexican Americans from Colonial Times to the Present Era*. AAR Aids for the Study of Religion Series. New York: Oxford University Press, 2010.

Vargas, Zaragosa. *Labor Rights Are Civil Rights: Mexican American Workers in Twentieth-Century America*. Princeton, NJ: Princeton University Press, 2005.

Vargas, Zaragosa, ed. *Major Problems in Mexican American History: Documents and Essays*. Boston: Houghton Mifflin, 1999.

Vargas, Zaragosa. *Proletarians of the North: Mexican Industrial Workers in Detroit and the Midwest, 1917–1933*. Berkeley: University of California Press, 1999.

Vargas, Zaragosa. "Tejana Radical: Emma Tenayuca and the San Antonio Labor Movement during the Great Depression." *Pacific Historical Review* 66, no. 4 (November 1997): 553–580.

Vaughan, Mary Kay. *Cultural Politics in Revolution: Teachers, Peasants, and Schools in Mexico, 1930–1940*. Tucson: University of Arizona Press, 1997.

Vaughan, Mary Kay. *The State, Education, and Social Class in Mexico, 1880–1928*. DeKalb: Northern Illinois University Press, 1982.

Vaughan, Mary Kay. "Women, Class, and Education in Mexico, 1880–1928." *Latin American Perspectives* (Special issue: Women and Class Struggle) 4, nos. 1–2 (Winter–Spring, 1977): 135–152.

Vázquez, Josefina Zoraida, and Lorenzo Meyer. *The United States and Mexico*. Chicago: University of Chicago Press, 1985.

Vázquez Leos, J. Jesús Eloy. *Liberalismo y masonería en San Luis*. Rev. ed. San Luis Potosí, México: s.n., 1994.

Vélez-Ibánez, Carlos G. *Border Visions: Mexican Cultures of the Southwest United States*. Tucson: University of Arizona Press, 1997.

Bibliography 245

Vila, Pablo. *Crossing Borders: Social Categories, Metaphors, and Narrative Identities on the U.S.-Mexico Frontier.* Inter-American Series. Austin: University of Texas Press, 2000.

Villarreal, Mary Ann. *Listening to Rosita: The Business of Tejana Music and Culture, 1930–1955.* Race and Culture in the American West Series. Norman: University of Oklahoma Press, 2015.

Walsh, Casey. *Building the Borderlands: A Transnational History of Irrigated Cotton along the Mexico-Texas Border.* College Station: Texas A&M University Press, 2008.

Warner, W. Lloyd, and Paul S. Hunt. *The Social Life of a Modern Community.* New Haven, CT: Yale University Press, 1941.

Weber, David J., ed. *Foreigners in Their Native Land: Historical Roots of the Mexican Americans.* Albuquerque: University of New Mexico Press, 1973.

Weber, David J. *The Mexican Frontier, 1821–1846: The American Southwest under Mexico.* Histories of the American Frontier. Albuquerque: University of New Mexico Press, 1982.

Weber, Devra. *Dark Sweat, White Gold: California Farm Workers, Cotton, and the New Deal.* Berkeley: University of California Press, 1994.

Weber, Devra. "Oral Sources and the History of Mexican Workers in the United States." *International Labor and Working-Class History* 23 (1983): 47–50.

Weber, John. *From South Texas to the Nation: The Exploitation of Mexican Labor in the Twentieth Century.* Chapel Hill: University of North Carolina Press, 2015.

Weise, Julie M. *Corazón de Dixie: Mexicanos in the US South since 1910.* Chapel Hill: University of North Carolina Press, 2015.

Weise, Julie M. "Mexican Nationalisms, Southern Racisms: Mexicans and Mexican Americans in the US South, 1908–1939." *American Quarterly* 60, no. 3 (September 2008): 749–777.

Welter, Barbara. "The Cult of True Womanhood, 1820–1860." *American Quarterly* 18 (Summer 1966): 151–174.

Welter, Barbara. "The Cult of True Womanhood, 1820–1860." In *Conflict and Consensus in Early American History,* 8th ed., edited by Allen F. Davis and Harold D. Woodman. Lexington, MA: D. C. Heath, 1992.

White, Deborah Gray. "The Cost of Club Work, the Price of Black Feminism." In *Visible Women: New Essays on American Activism,* edited by Nancy A. Hewitt and Suzanne Lebsock, 247–269. Urbana: University of Illinois Press, 1993.

White, Richard. *"It's Your Misfortune and None of My Own": A New History of the American West.* Norman: University of Oklahoma Press, 1991.

Wiebe, Robert H. *The Search for Order, 1877–1920.* American Century Series, no. 8. New York: Hill & Wang, 1967.

Wilkinson, J. B. *Laredo and the Rio Grande Frontier.* Austin, TX: Jenkins, 1975.

Wilson, Norman J. *History in Crisis? Recent Directions in Historiography.* 2nd ed. Upper Saddle River, NJ: Pearson Prentice Hall, 2005.

Winegarten, Ruthe. *Texas Women: A Pictorial History: From Indians to Astronauts.* Austin, TX: Eakin Press, 1986.

Wood, Andrew Grant, ed. *On the Border: Society and Culture between the United States and Mexico.* Lanham, MD: Rowman and Littlefield, 2001.

Yanagisako, Sylvia, and Carol Delaney, eds. *Naturalizing Power: Essays in Feminist Cultural Analysis.* London: Routledge, 1995.

Yans-McLaughlin, Virginia, ed. *Immigration Reconsidered: History, Sociology, and Politics.* New York: Oxford University Press, 1990.

Young, Elliot G. *Catarino Garza's Revolution on the Texas-Mexico Border.* American Encounters/Global Interactions. Durham, NC: Duke University Press, 2004.

Young, Elliot G. "Deconstructing La Raza: Identifying the Gente Decente of Laredo, 1904–1911." *Southwestern Historical Quarterly* 98, no. 2 (October 1994): 227–259.

Young, Elliot G. "Red Men, Princess Pocahontas, and George Washington: Harmonizing Race Relations in Laredo at the Turn of the Century." *Western Historical Quarterly* (Spring 1998): 49–85.

Zamora, Emilio. *Claiming Rights and Righting Wrongs in Texas: Mexican Workers and Job Politics during World War II*. College Station: Texas A&M University Press, 2009.

Zamora, Emilio. "Fighting on Two Fronts: José de la Luz Saenz and the Language of the Mexican American Civil Rights Movement." In *Recovering the U.S. Hispanic Literary Heritage*, vol. 4, edited by José F. Aranda Jr. and Silvio Torres-Saillant, 214–239. Houston: Arte Publico Press, 2002.

Zamora, Emilio. "La guerra en pro de la justicia y la democracia en Francia y Texas: José de la Luz Sáenz y el lenguaje del movimiento mexicano de los derechos civiles." *ISTOR, Revista de Historia Internacional* 4, no. 13 (Summer 2003): 9–35.

Zamora, Emilio. "Mexico's Wartime Intervention on Behalf of Mexicans in the United States." In *Mexican Americans Americans and World War II*, edited by Maggie Rivas-Rodríguez. Austin: University of Texas Press, 2005.

Zamora, Emilio. "Mutualist and Mexicanist Expressions of a Political Culture." In *Mexican Americans in Texas History*, edited by Emilio Zamora, Cynthia Orozco, and Rodolfo Rocha. Austin: Texas State Historical Association, 2000.

Zamora, Emilio. "Sara Estela Ramírez: A Note on Research in Progress." *Hembra: Hermanas en Movimiento Brotando Raíces de Aztlán*. Austin: Center for Mexican American Studies, University of Texas, 1976.

Zamora, Emilio. "The Failed Promise of Wartime Opportunity for Mexicans in the Texas Oil Industry." *Southwestern Historical Quarterly* 95 (January 1992): 323–350.

Zamora, Emilio. *The World of the Mexican Worker in Texas*. College Station: Texas A&M University Press, 1993.

Zamora, Emilio. "Sara Estela Ramírez: Una rosa roja en el movimiento." In *Mexican Women in the United States: Struggles Past and Present*, edited by Magdalena Mora and Adelaida R. Del Castillo. Los Angeles: Chicano Studies Research Center, University of California, 1980.

Zamora, Emilio, Cynthia Orozco, and Rodolfo Rocha, eds. *Mexican Americans in Texas History*. Austin: Texas State Historical Association, 2000.

Zelman, Donald. "Alazan-Apache Courts: A New Deal Response to Mexican American Housing Conditions in San Antonio." *Southwestern Historical Quarterly* 87, no. 2 (1983): 122–150.

Dissertations and Theses

Ayala, Adriana. "Negotiating Race Relations Through Activism: Women Activists and Women's Organizations in San Antonio, Texas during the 1920s" (Ph.D. diss., The University of Texas, 2005).

Bueno Marianne M. "Military Formations: Mexican American Civil Rights and Community Belonging During the World War II Era." Ph.D. Dissertation, University of California, Santa Cruz, 2012.

Calderón, Roberto Ramón. "Mexican Politics in the American Era, 1846-1900: Laredo, Texas." Ph.D. dissertation, University of California, Los Angeles, 1993.

Garza, James Alex. "On the Edge of a Storm: Laredo and the Mexican Revolution, 1910-1917," M.A. Thesis, Texas A&M University International, Laredo, Texas, 1996.

González, Gabriela. "Two Flags Entwined: Transborder Activists and the Politics of Race, Ethnicity, Class, and Gender in South Texas, 1900-1950," Ph.D., Stanford University, 2005.

Hernández, José Angel. "El México Perdido, El México Olvidado, y El México de Afuera": A History of Mexican American Colonization, 1836-1892" (Ph.D. Dissertation, The University of Chicago, 2008).

Hernández Tovar, Inés. "Sara Estela Ramírez: The Early Twentieth Century Texas Mexican Poet." Ph.D. dissertation, University of Houston, 1984.

Johnson, Benjamin Heber. "Sedition and Citizenship in South Texas, 1900-1930." Ph.D. dissertation, Yale University, 2000.

Orozco, Cynthia E. "The Origins of the League of United Latin American Citizens (LULAC) and the Mexican American Civil Rights Movement in Texas with an Analysis of Women's Political Participation in a Gendered Context, 1910–1920." PhD dissertation, University of California, Los Angeles, 1992.

Pycior, Julie Leininger. "La Raza Organizes: Mexican American Life in San Antonio, 1915–1930 as Reflected in Mutualista Activities." PhD dissertation, University of Notre Dame, 1979.

Young, Elliot Gordon. "Crossing Borders: Race, Nation, Class, and Gender on the South Texas Border, 1877–1911" MA thesis, University of Texas, 1993.

Electronic Sources

Acosta, Teresa Palomo. "IDAR, NICASIO," *Handbook of Texas Online*, http://www.tshaonline. org/handbook/online/articles/fid02, accessed 4 December 2002. Published by the Texas State Historical Association.

Acosta, Teresa Palomo. "CONGRESO MEXICANISTA," *Handbook of Texas Online*, http://www. tshaonline.org/handbook/online/articles/vecyk, accessed 4 December 2002. Published by the Texas State Historical Association.

Acosta, Teresa Palomo. "CRUZ AZUL MEXICANA," *Handbook of Texas Online*, http://www. tshaonline.org/handbook/online/articles/sbc04, accessed 4 December 2002. Published by the Texas State Historical Association.

Acosta, Teresa Palomo. "Sara Estela Ramírez, *Handbook of Texas Online*, http://www.tshaonline. org/handbook/online/articles/RR/fra60.html, accessed 5 December 2002. Published by the Texas State Historical Association.

Aljazeera English. *Walls of Shame*, http://english.aljazeera.net/Services/Search/Default. aspx?P=walls%20of%20shame, accessed 5 November 2010.

Allsup, V. Carl. "Delgado v Bastrop ISD," *Handbook of Texas Online*, accessed 20 February 2016, Uploaded on 12 June 2010. Published by the Texas State Historical Association, http:// www.tshaonline.org/handbook/online/articles/jrd01.

Belfiglio, Valentine J. "BRUNI, ANTONIO MATEO," *Handbook of Texas Online*, http://www. tshaonline.org/handbook/online/articles/fbrbf, accessed 27 April 2015. Uploaded on 12 June 2010. Published by the Texas State Historical Association.

Chipman, Donald E. "SPANISH TEXAS," *Handbook of Texas Online*, http://www.tshaonline. org/handbook/online/articles/nps01, accessed 4 December 2002. Published by the Texas State Historical Association. *www.City of Laredo.com.*

Cuéllar, Carlos E. "LAREDO, TX," *Handbook of Texas Online*, http://www.tshaonline.org/ handbook/online/articles/hdl02, accessed 1 October 2011. Published by the Texas State Historical Association.

De León, Arnoldo. "Mexican Americans." *Handbook of Texas Online*, http://www.tshaonline.org/ handbook/online/articles/pqmue, accessed 4 December 2002.

Fitzgerald, Maureen. "National Congress of Mothers." In *Reader's Companion to U.S. Women's History*, Houghton Mifflin, http://college.hmco.com/history/readerscomp/women/html/ wh_025200_nationalcong.htm; "National PTA: A Brief History," http://www.pta.org/ aboutpta/history/history.asp.

Holloway, Elena. "Independent Club," *Handbook of Texas Online*, 4 December 2002, http://www. tsha.utexas.edu/handbook/online/articles/view/II/wmiqt.html.

League of United Latin American Citizens. http://www.lulac.org/about/history.

Orozco, Cynthia E. "IDAR, CLEMENTE NICASIO," *Handbook of Texas Online*, http://www. tshaonline.org/handbook/online/articles/fid04, accessed 4 December 2002. Published by the Texas State Historical Association.

Orozco, Cynthia E. "IDAR, EDUARDO," *Handbook of Texas Online*, http://www.tshaonline.org/ handbook/online/articles/fid05, accessed 4 December 2002. Published by the Texas State Historical Association.

Orozco, Cynthia E. "LADIES LULAC," *Handbook of Texas Online*, http://www.tshaonline.org/ handbook/online/articles/wel06, accessed 17 September 2011. Published by the Texas State Historical Association.

Orozco, Cynthia E. "MONTEMAYOR, ALICE DICKERSON," *Handbook of Texas Online*, http://www.tshaonline.org/handbook/online/articles/fmobl, accessed 23 February 2010. Published by the Texas State Historical Association.

Orozco, Cynthia E. "MUNGUÍA, CAROLINA MALPICA," *Handbook of Texas Online*, http://www.tshaonline.org/handbook/online/articles/fmusq, accessed 4 December 2002. Published by the Texas State Historical Association.

Orozco, Cynthia E. "MUNGUÍA TORRES, JOSÉ RÓMULO," *Handbook of Texas Online*, http://www.tshaonline.org/handbook/online/articles/fmu36, accessed 17 November 2010. Published by the Texas State Historical Association.

Orozco, Cynthia E. "SPANISH-SPEAKING PTA," *Handbook of Texas Online*, http://www.tshaonline.org/handbook/online/articles/kas03, accessed 4 December 2002. Published by the Texas State Historical Association.

Rich, Paul, and Guillermo De Los Reyes. "Freemasonry's Educational Role." *American Behavioral Scientist (ABS)* 40, no. 7 (June/July 1997), http://www.paulrich.net/publications/abs-vol.40_nr7.html.

Rich, Paul, and Guillermo De Los Reyes. "Secret Societies and Political Realities in Mexico." A version of this paper was presented at the American Political Science Association, Atlanta, 3 September 1999, http://www.paulrich.net/papers/apsa99/masons.html.

"Samuel Gompers: 1850–1924," Illinois Labor History Society, www.kentlaw.edu/ilhs/gompers/html.

Sears, Olivia E., ed. "The White Trail of Freemen and Freemasons," Stanford University, 1995, http://www.paulrich.net/publications/two_lines_spring_1995.html.

UNAM website, http://www.usa.unam.edu.

Villarreal, Ernie. "San Antonio Landmark Site of Riot in 1939," *Texas Public Radio Newsroom*, aired 24 August 2001.

Other Sources

"Churches, Lodges, and Societies of Laredo, Texas." *General Directory of the City of Laredo, 1911.* Webb County Heritage Foundation.

"Emma Tenayuca." Biographical Vertical File, Huey Library, the Woman's Collection, Texas Woman's University, Denton.

"Exhibit—The Three R's: Leonor Villegas de Magnón, WCHF, 1998." Vertical File, Webb County Heritage Foundation.

"Jovita Idar." Biographical Vertical File, Huey Library, the Woman's Collection, Texas Woman's University, Denton.

"Sara Estela Ramírez." Biographical Vertical File, Huey Library, the Woman's Collection, Texas Woman's University, Denton.

Sharyll Soto Teneyuca, telephone conversation with author, 7 May 2003. The author has her permission to quote.

"Sra. Leonor V. Magnón, "La Rebelde." Leonor Villegas de Magnón Vertical File, Huey Library, the Woman's Collection, Texas Woman University, Denton.

INDEX

CPSIA information can be obtained
at www.ICGtesting.com
Printed in the USA
BVHW032343200819
556358BV00003B/8/P